Where Are All
the Young Men
and Women of Color?

Columbia University Press
Publishers Since 1893
New York Chichester, West Sussex

Library of Congress Cataloging-in-Publication Data

Delgado, Melvin.
    Where are all the young men and women of color? capacity
enhancement practice in the criminal justice system / Melvin Delgado.
        p. cm.
    Includes bibliographical references and index.
    ISBN 0-231-12040-0 (cloth : alk. paper) – ISBN 0-231-12041-9 (pbk. :
alk. paper)
    1. Social work with criminals—United States. 2. Social work with
minorities—United States. 3. Discrimination in criminal justice
administration—United States. 4. Discrimination in juvenile justice
administration—United States. 5. Crime and race—United States. I.
Title.
    HV7428 .D45 2001
    362.84'0086'927—dc21
                                                        2001028606

To Denise, Laura, and Barbara

Contents

Preface

I customarily set aside a final chapter, or epilogue, as a means of sharing the twists and turns and joys and frustrations associated with writing a book. An author never fully comprehends the experience of writing a particular book until he or she has written the final chapter and sentence. In this case, I have decided to deviate from my usual practice and instead write a preface. This preface, as a result, is intended to raise issues and identify unexpected surprises and challenges for the reader. It will not be burdened by quotes, citations, and "scholarly" language. I will speak in the first person here, and throughout the book, as a means of communicating to the reader my thoughts and feelings.

Critics often argue that a preface, or epilogue as the case may be, is often an excuse for points not raised or poorly addressed, or is indicative of the author's inability to "let go" of the book. I do not view this preface as an attempt to cover myself before the book goes to print. I do not, in addition, have difficulty letting go of a major writing assignment. Having said this, the reader should know that I was totally unprepared for the "journey" of writing this book. That journey resulted in my finding a state of affairs that I could not possibly have anticipated. Maybe the reader, too, will get more than he or she bargained for in reading this book.

This preface seeks to prepare the reader for the more scholarly presentation that follows—replete with definitions, quotations, and extensive citations to the literature, both popular and academic. Everything stated here, unless specifically noted, is addressed in greater detail later on in this book. This preface can best be conceptualized as a road map to the book. It serves its purpose, however, in a manner that does not disguise the pain and sorrow that one experiences in the writing of a book on such a sad and tragic topic. The wasting of human life always pains me, particularly when people's potential to grow and contribute to society can never be fully realized.

When the average person in the street thinks of his or her country being at war, it invariably means that another nation is the enemy being fought. Unfortunately, this is not true. I sincerely believe that, in effect, the United States is in a perpetual state of war. It has declared war on poverty, war on drugs, and war on crime. A nation at war causes casualties and captures prisoners of war. We now have close to two million prisoners of an ongoing war that, for all intents and purposes, has focused on America's cities and communities of color. Where is the United Nations in this matter? Maybe it considers these wars to be of a civil nature, and that nations have a right to engage in civil war. Whatever the case, the American public's and the world's indignation is not present, and that disturbs me.

To take the analogy further, the United States, under the pretense of fighting the supply side of the war, is actively involved in countries such as Peru, Colombia, and Panama in an effort to stem the flow of drugs into this country. Interestingly, the United States invaded Panama under the guise of dethroning General Noriega because of his drug connections and the flow of drugs through Panama to the United States. However, the flow of drugs continues through Panama at an unprecedented pace today. Was the intervention an effort to stem the flow of drugs or a pretense to take back the Panama Canal? Although the canal has been handed back to Panama, will it remain in its hands for very long? Narcopolitics, unfortunately, is alive and well. The reader may well ask how all these events can be related. I believe they are. This nation, I believe, is really not interested in stopping the abuse of drugs and instead is more interested in waging war on its citizens of color, *men as well as women*. Simply put, the question is not "Why do people abuse drugs in the first place?" Rather, it is "Why does abuse persist?"

There are few topics that can guarantee as much discussion, debate, and disagreement as the status of social work practice. It seems as if every practitioner, educator, and researcher has strong opinions about what is right or wrong with the profession. Mind you, I don't believe anyone is arguing that there is not anything wrong with the profession. Strong opinions, incidentally, are also held by outsiders to the profession. Debates are common between micropractitioners and macropractitioners, between urban and rural practice, between B.S.W.'s and M.S.W.'s, and between the private and public sectors of practice. Disagreements about method and about the merits of quantitative versus qualitative evaluations are also common. These are just a handful of differences. I have not absented myself from these debates. The point is, there is no lack of thought and feelings on the subject of social work.

I was struck by the magnitude of the problem of correctional supervision in urban communities of color and by the almost total absence of social workers in that field. The paucity of social workers in the field of corrections is nothing short of amazing. I realize that the social control functions of prisons and community alternatives to prison may scare away all but the bravest of social workers. However, community-based programs and agencies can actively seek to address the needs of the correctionally supervised and their families; thus, social workers do not have to be directly accountable to correctional supervisors and administrators.

I do not address the impact of an aging prison population in this book, an issue that is starting to get attention at the state and national level (Elser, 1998). An aging inmate population means that the likelihood of various forms of disabilities compromising prisoners' health increases (Murray, 1998). In 1999 the state of Virginia opened the nation's first prison dedicated to housing inmates in need of assisted-living care (Aoki, 1999). Social workers are not completely absent from the fields of aging and disabilities. However, we are not "in the picture" regarding prisoners. These arenas provide us with an excellent opportunity to work in the correctional field and will continue to do so well into this century.

Nevertheless, it seems that programs specifically targeting prisoners and ex-prisoners generally are run by just one professional along with nonprofessionals or volunteers. A perusal of continuing education programs sponsored by social work schools and departments will rarely find a workshop focused on *any* aspect of work with the correctionally supervised. I did not expect workshops on various aspects of community enhancement practice. However, correctional supervision is definitely not a "high draw" workshop! I believe that the introduction of a "new" way of viewing and undertaking practice will require much effort, time, and patience. However, the question is not whether this approach sees the light of day; it is more like "When will it?"

The general absence of social workers in the field of correctional supervision made my discovery of those social workers that *are* in this field that much more gratifying. My conversations with social workers practicing in prisons left me with the impression that prison is not an easy place to practice many of the principles we hold dear to the profession. Issues related to balancing control with empowerment, particularly when that involves female social workers in prisons for men, highlight the tension between those two functions. Nevertheless, there is little question that we need to be in places such as these. I talked to one social worker who was attending graduate school in social work after many years of working in a community-based program in the Southwest. This individual stood out as a result of her commitment to the field of criminal justice and her belief in offenders having strengths. The major task she faced, however, was getting them to believe in themselves and their capacities. That goal was not simple to achieve; nevertheless, it needed to be addressed in practice.

The statistics do not really tell the story about how the nation has steadily and systematically gone about incarcerating a group of young men and women, and has done so with minimal public debate. Incarceration is not a phenomenon that occurs to just one member of a family: instances of both parents being incarcerated are not unusual; nor is it unusual to find a parent and child serving concurrent time. In essence, it is rare to find a family of color that does not have an immediate or distant relative under some form of correctional supervision. In cases where both parents are incarcerated, grandparents (most likely grandmothers) are thrust into parenting roles at a point in their lives when their own well-being is threatened due to poor health and or economic conditions. There is widespread recognition that there is something fundamentally wrong when a country imprisons so many of its citizens, particularly during a time of unprecedented prosperity.

The United States has surpassed the former Soviet Union and South Africa in having the highest percentage of residents in prison. Further, there seems to be no letup in sight concerning the building and staffing of prisons, with its tremendous financial and psychological costs to taxpayers. Unfortunately, the public debate on the subject centers on how to make prisons even harsher, with current efforts afoot in several states to remove television sets, exercise equipment, libraries, and other "soft" privileges. Interestingly, the effort to do away with these recreational outlets is strongly opposed by prison guard unions, who fear increased hostilities from prisoners.

Nevertheless, in the process of writing this book, I came across numerous organizations and community programs that have been established to help prisoners and their families. Many of the more formal efforts were undertaken with minimal financial support. Volunteers have often been the major staff component of these programs. Further, the degree of willingness to help me with this book was both heartwarming and impressive. I was pleasantly surprised to find staff who work with offenders to be so open and eager to share their stories with me. Quite frankly, I expected a certain degree of suspicion and anger toward someone from a university writing a book on the subject. However, only rarely did I hit the proverbial brick wall in my quest to write this book. There was almost a "hunger" to share with the world the needs of offenders and to emphasize their potential contributions to society if given the opportunity to do so. This openness bodes well for potential collaborative relationships between programs.

There was a common sense of urgency for any effort that would spotlight national attention on the problem of incarceration and other forms of correctional supervision. Many of the organizations that assisted me did not have a lot of funds to photocopy and mail material pertaining to their work. In some instances I provided postage envelopes or sent stamps to help defray the costs of the materials. There were even instances where my offers to help defray the costs of postage, photocopying, and so on were turned down even though the organization providing the materials was not well funded.

Many of the formal efforts initiated by coalitions and grassroots organizations are funded with minimal money. Some of the organizations refuse to turn to established funding sources because of their fears that the funder will seek to exert undue control over the work being undertaken, particularly when it involves controversial subjects. Others, in turn, have great difficulty getting funding sources to support the work they are doing. Their frustration is further compounded by the need to attempt highly creative and innovative approaches that can be classified as "unconventional." The work of these organizations is valuable, innovative, and much needed, and more efforts such as these are in order.

I found that there is a certain stigma to funding the work of organizations targeting the correctionally supervised. It seems as if many funders, private as well as government, put up significant barriers to these organizations and often make unnecessary demands of them, effectively limiting their potential to make a lasting contribution to society. An undue emphasis on gathering data on who utilizes services, for example, makes efforts intrusive in nature, particularly for a population group that is distrustful, and rightly so, of how the information is going to be used. Thus, any effort to seriously work with and study the correctionally supervised, regardless of gender and ethnicity, must take into account the barriers associated with working with clients who are labeled "convicts" or "ex-cons." This reality will necessitate a certain degree of flexibility in the business-as-usual approach that often characterizes human services today.

The need for the mainstream media to focus on the consequences of imprisonment for offenders, their families, and communities raises serious questions for me concerning the influential role the media play in shaping stories. Such stories have, unfortunately, served to further stigmatize the correctionally supervised and their families. The media have a responsibility to report on all aspects of correctional supervision, instead of focusing on high-publicity crimes or launching programs that focus on catching criminals. Personally, I think it would be great if one of the major networks developed a television program on white-collar crime; unfortunately, there is no demand for such programming. Consequently, social programs that serve the correctionally supervised must be vigilant to counteract news media events focused on further stigmatizing the correctionally supervised. Undue energy and resources are often diverted from their own programming to writing letters to newspapers and advocating in this realm.

A number of critics of current media foci contend that crime stories take on added significance on television news programs because most local news coverage focuses on government-related stories generated by elected officials and the like. Since government generally closes down at five o'clock, the only local government that stays open after that hour is the police. Thus, police-related stories are "fresh" for the late-night news. These stories seem ready-made for television because they often provide graphic details, do not require extensive research, and often feature officials responsible for disseminating information to the press. Consequently, although the argument that media coverage of violence encourages violence may be debatable, the media's influence on the public's attitude toward crime may hold more promise for research.

There is no mistaking that the U.S. prison industry is a multibillion-dollar business. Lobbyists for unions and those who build and maintain prisons are alive and functioning at both the state and federal levels. It seems that the next twenty years will find a majority of the nation either in prison or working in a prison-related job. The United States, as a result, has replaced pre-Mandela South Africa as the country with the highest incarceration rate of people with African heritage. The nation builds institutions and then systematically goes about filling them in order to substantiate their huge budgets. It is estimated that more than 50 percent of U.S. prisons have been built in the last twenty years or so. These prisons, in turn, can be considered as having a life span of fifty years (Mauer, 1999; Parenti, 1999). It does not take a rocket scientist to realize what this means for the future. Can society easily decide to close down institutions and put hundreds of thousands of people out of work, particularly in distressed areas of the country? I do not think so. We as a nation are no longer in an "arms race"; however, we have replaced that race with an "incarceration race."

The increasing number of women, particularly of color, who have been incarcerated over the past ten years or so represents a disturbing trend. Their incarceration, as I discuss in the book, has a most profound impact on families and communities. Further, greater numbers of women on death row and, in general, the increased severity of women's penalties when compared with those of men signal that this group has become a potential "feeder" for the prison system. Failure of the correctional system to "redesign" prisons to take into account gender-related factors raises serious questions about what is meant by "cruel and unusual" punishment. Women, as a result, suffer greater punishment than their male counterparts. The increased number of youths who are waived to adult court, too, will dramatically change the composition of prison populations. The failure of the prison system to alter itself will increase the likelihood that punishment rather than rehabilitation continues its prevailing influence over prisoners.

I, nevertheless, am struck by the nation's silence, particularly that of its elected leaders, about a disturbing trend that seems as if it has no end in sight; a trend that has taken a prodigious toll on the nation's economic and social resources, has placed the world's foremost democracy on stage and made it vulnerable to being called "hypocritical," and has made it the world's leader in imprisoning people of color. The development of an index comparable to that of "leading economic indicators" is in order. Maybe it can be called "leading incarceration indicators" and used to measure the country's progress toward liberating an entire group of people, allowing us to compare our progress with that of other nations in the world. The average citizen needs a context against which to compare what is going on in the United States pertaining to prisons. A global context, for example, would show that this country and Russia now compete for the highest rates of incarceration in the world.

I suppose some readers would like to see more sharing of personal stories of success in this book. Personal stories of success are always inspirational and seem to lend "meaning" to the work we do. I, for one, never get tired of hearing such stories. However, I was torn between providing more such stories and at the same time grounding capacity enhancement practice with the correctionally supervised in a theoretical foundation and drawing broader implications for practice. I have elected to follow the latter course at the expense of more personal stories. In a way, though, I have attempted a compromise in section 3, "Reflections from the Field," where I include a personal story of success in the case studies whenever possible.

My hope is that someone out there becomes sufficiently motivated to write a book that focuses specifically on clinical and programmatic examples—almost like a casebook that can be used in class and to which theoretical material can be applied. Providing balance in a book of the sort that you are now reading is never an easy task. Nevertheless, a continuing trend toward incarceration will create a crisis in this country and a search for a workable alternative that involves not only prevention but also greater use of community alternatives and an emphasis on rehabilitation.

Critics, and the reader for that matter, may be of the opinion that too much attention has been paid to "criminals" and not enough to their victims in this book. I do not, for example, address the recent emphasis on restorative justice programs that bring offenders, their victims, and members of the community together to revisit the consequences of a crime. Restorative justice programs are worthy of a book unto themselves, and the topic is clearly beyond the scope of this one. The last ten years have witnessed greater attention paid to the needs of victims, and social workers often play influential roles in these types of services and programs (Wilson, 2000). A book specifically focused on capacity enhancement and victim-related services is warranted, but I sincerely believe that had I addressed both offenders and victims in this book, I would not have been able to pursue in depth either of these two important subjects.

Nevertheless, I certainly do not want to minimize the pain and suffering that victims, particularly in cases where physical harm resulted from the crime, have experienced. Financial losses and psychological pain are also associated with nonviolent crimes, such as forgery, larceny, and the like. I remember very vividly the participants in a conference devoted to cultural perspectives on helping victims in their recovery process. I listened to the stories of parents whose children had been murdered and the questions they raised about the final moments of their child's life and about whether their child had been raped before being murdered. I am the father of two daughters, and my heart broke as I listened to these parents share their pain. Consequently, this book is not intended as an "apologist" perspective on offenders.

There is a tremendous need for the creation of community-wide coalitions to address the needs of the correctionally supervised and their families. The magnitude of the incarceration rates in certain communities warrants concerted, systematic, and purposeful initiatives to help communities address this social problem. Much attention is often given to developing coalitions to deter crime within communities. Few readers, I am sure, have not heard about neighborhood watch efforts initiated in communities to prevent crime. However, systematic efforts to address the postincarceration experiences of former prisoners and families living in these same communities are often missing.

These community-wide coalitions must actively seek to achieve broad involvement from the public and private sectors. These initiatives, in turn, must involve nontraditional settings such as houses of worship and other community-based organizations that actively address the needs of ex-offenders and their families. The coalitions also can play an active role in advocating for increased funding of community programs and services targeting ex-offenders. Having said this, I realize that such coalitions will face incredible barriers. The stigma associated with the correctionally supervised makes it difficult for even the bravest among us to put forth such a concept as a coalition. Nevertheless, identifying and addressing these barriers is imperative if progress regarding criminal justice is to be made at the community level in the foreseeable future.

It was gratifying to find so many organizations at the national and local levels addressing issues related to incarceration. They are too numerous to mention here; however, their thrust toward socioeconomic justice themes speaks well to a cadre of people who realize the importance of this subject. In many ways, they realize that the future of our country ultimately rests with our abilities not to violate human rights and the need to provide viable, cost-effective alternatives to prison. These organizations, unfortunately, have not received the national attention they deserve and, as a result, have not been properly thanked for the important work they do.

I am also pleased by the wide range of efforts at the national and state levels to curtail gun accessibility ("Officials Ban Gun Shows," 1999). I realize that most gun owners are not criminals and do not seek to use firearms in harmful ways (Verhovek, 1999). However, stricter laws concerning ownership of guns cannot but help minimize their misuse. No law can prevent or guarantee that a gun will not be used to commit a crime. By curtailing access, in combination with making guns with safety mechanisms, it is hoped that an accidental use of a gun will not kill or hurt someone. Are these ideas controversial? Yes! It seems like anything that threatens "individual freedom" is controversial. However, increased use of litigation, as in the case of the tobacco industry, will go a long way toward increasing accountability in the weapons industry.

It would be irresponsible for me to put forth the strategy of capacity enhancement without noting the need for evaluative studies of such efforts. The relatively fresh approach characterized by capacity enhancement has not withstood the attention associated with stringent program evaluation. However, as with any new shift in paradigms and the programs based on these efforts, evaluation is only possible in the most rudimentary fashion. It is only after the concept of capacity enhancement has been tried in many different types of settings, with many different types of people and situations, that a meta-evaluation can transpire.

Having said this, I realize that any effort at evaluating capacity enhancement with the correctionally supervised will require innovative and highly participatory approaches and techniques. It will definitely not be business as usual in evaluation design and implementation and in analysis of evaluation results. This is both exciting and anxiety provoking for evaluators and nonevaluators alike. The development of these evaluation methods will require active participation and collaboration between practitioners, consumers, and academics. Such a partnership holds much promise for work in this area, particularly with undervalued groups.

Recent federal statistics on crime, with some notable exceptions, show that rates in all categories of crime have fallen dramatically, including statistics regarding youth-related criminal offenses. It remains to be seen, however, whether this dramatic decrease will result in a shift in national and state policies concerning incarceration. I predict, unfortunately, that this will not be the case, and that the need for prison cells will reach record numbers in the next few years. In essence, crime statistics do not have a relationship with incarceration and other forms of correctional supervision. There is something wrong with that statement.

However, if viewed from the perspective that this country needs to punish people of color, male and female, young and old alike, then there is no reason to believe that incarceration rates will decrease anytime soon. I believe it will take a concerted national and international effort to force the country to shift its policies. In essence, incarceration is serving multiple purposes in this society under the guise of public safety.

The nature of the subject matter and the extent of imprisonment's effect in urban communities of color proved extremely troubling at times to write about. Interviews with former prisoners, their families, and providers brought to light the issues and challenges prisoners face during and after their release. Some of the stories were very, very sad. There were numerous instances where families were never the same again or were broken apart after a parent or, in some cases, both parents were imprisoned. Instances of women being imprisoned because of their involvement with significant others who were in the drug trade raised issues of fairness, particularly when their sentences were far harsher than those of males convicted for the same crimes.

Nevertheless, there were also happy and joyous moments when I would interview someone who had overcome astronomical odds to make it in this society. These uplifting stories further reinforce the need for a shift in paradigms to one that makes use of capacity enhancement. The potential of the human spirit to circumvent or overcome hardships should not be underestimated. The will to succeed is alive and well and waiting to be brought forth in countless numbers of people under correctional supervision, just as it is waiting to be fostered in the homeless and other undervalued groups in this society.

I hope that the reader has had the patience to stay with me these last few pages and is willing to entertain the "words of wisdom" being imparted in this preface. Although I have finished this book, I do not have the satisfaction of having completed the project. This is because of the nature of the problem—namely, the systematic incarceration of people of color in such alarming rates that if it continues until 2020, more than two-thirds of African American and one-quarter of Latino males ages 18 to 34 will be in prison. America's communities, cities, and states cannot survive this rate of incarceration without paying a heavy price economically and morally. The impact, as noted throughout this book, is not felt just by those who face imprisonment. Their family members, particularly the children of incarcerated parents, will bear witness to the consequences well into the twenty-first century.

The trend toward incarceration is not one that can be easily reversed because of the damage already caused to individuals, families, and communities. If the nation were to close down all its prisons tomorrow, and not imprison another person, a generation of men and women will have essentially been "left out of the loop" as the country marches into the twenty-first century. Getting back into the loop will necessitate a prodigious amount of time, energy, resources, and healing before these "former" members of society can take their rightful place. However, before such a shift can occur, we must acknowledge that we have failed in our experiment to reduce crime and substance abuse in this country and that a tremendous injustice has been perpetrated in the process. This acknowledgment, I believe, is essential before the country can move forward in shifting paradigms regarding substance abuse and incarceration of young men and women of color. Dyer (2000), however, sounds an ominous note when arguing that the new "prison-industrial complex" has made the United States' war on crime very profitable in certain circles. Thus, the public's fear of crime serves as a powerful backdrop for the increased reliance on prisons, even though crime rates have declined considerably over the past five years.

The profession of social work, as a result, cannot afford to sit on the sideline and allow this condition to continue to develop without actively lobbying and organizing against it at the national and state levels. Mind you, this is not to say that some state chapters have not done this or have not established committees specifically focused on working with the correctionally supervised. Rather, influencing the nation to shift funding priorities, repeal mandatory sentencing laws, increase in-prison treatment options, and fund defense intervention services cannot be done at the local level and requires a major national effort, an effort that necessitates social work's developing collaborative partnerships with other professions and communities.

However, this does not translate into a major national movement on the part of the profession. Putting aside the moral issues associated with this trend, the economic consequences will prove devastating to the profession. Social workers employed in other systems will quickly see their budgets cut to pay for the increased costs of incarceration. Thus, the very survival of the profession is at stake in this equation, not to mention that of other helping professions. Social work has a long and rich tradition of not shying away from aligning itself with the marginalized of society.

However, much has happened since the birth of the profession to cause it to shift away from its traditional mission, and serious questions can be raised about our willingness, or ability, to embrace issues of oppression in American society. Some critics would argue that such a political move will seriously jeopardize the advancements the profession has made to "professionalize" itself in the eyes of the world. This move, as a result, may undermine past and current efforts at obtaining third-party reimbursements for services.

In 1969 President Johnson created a commission to investigate the strife and violence that had engulfed the United States. The subsequent report included a number of predications of what would happen to the country should it neglect its most impoverished urban citizens—urban residents trapped in "places of terror" and suburbanites residing in "fortified cells." The Milton S. Eisenhower Foundation, which grew out of the commission created by President Johnson, issued a report in 1999 looking at the thirty years since the initial report. Elliott Currie, one of the few remaining staff members from the original study, notes that in the thirty years since the report was issued few gains can be found:

> "I would not really have dreamed in 1969 that violent crime would get so much worse in the '80s and early '90s and that we have made so few gains. . . . By some measure, I'd have to say we've gone backwards. I think we made a lot of wrong choices." Those wrong choices, foundation members said, have included a national preoccupation with hard-line policies—building prisons, waging the war on drugs, creating "zero tolerance" policies on crime. The get tough approach has come at the expense of longer-term solutions. . . . "Prisons have become our nation's substitute for effective policies on crime, drugs, mental illness, housing, poverty and employment of the hardest to employ." (Lichtblau, 1999, p. 3)

Acknowledgments

It would be irresponsible for an author to write a book and not acknowledge the countless number of people who played a role in bringing the project to fruition. At Boston University School of Social Work several individuals stand out for acknowledgment. Ben Cook, research assistant, Suzanne Logan, administrative assistant, and Dean Wilma Peebles Wilkins. Dean Wilkins's support throughout the project facilitated my completing this book in a timely manner! Special thanks go to Paul Vozzo, research assistant. Paul was involved through all phases of the book starting with the prospectus and ending with the name index. He solved problems and supported me during the difficult times associated with writing a book on this subject.

In the field, a number of people provided assistance in the form of getting program literature and being willing to be interviewed. These individuals are, in alphabetical order, Karen Chapple, Nusrat Choudhury, Linda Maxwell, Jose Quintanar, Fred Smith, Dr. Earl Strimple, Steve Stuerer, Dr. Alice Tracy, Susan Warner, and Vicki Zubovic.

This project was partly supported by a National Institute on Drug Abuse grant (5 R24 DA 12203). The opinions expressed herein are those of the author and do not necessarily reflect the opinions or official policy of the National Institute on Drug Abuse or any part of the U.S. Department of Health and Human Services.

Where Are All
the Young Men
and Women of Color?

1

Setting the Stage

This section's primary goal is to provide the reader with a context in which to better understand why the topic of correctional supervision (prison, probation, and parole) is important for social work practice. The section comprises four chapters. The first, "Setting the Context," introduces the reader to the general subject. Chapter 2, "Incarceration Profiles and Trends," provides a detailed picture of who is under correctional supervision and affected by current trends. This picture, although distressing, highlights why the subject is important for the social work profession to address in education and practice. "Substance Abuse and Incarceration," the third chapter, examines drug-related legislation and its dramatic impact on incarceration, particularly among groups of color. Finally, chapter 4, "The Impact of Correctional Supervision: A Multifaceted Perspective," focuses on identifying the key needs and issues resulting from correctional supervision. Special attention will be paid to the impact it has on families and informal community institutions.

1

Setting the Context

The goal of a "good" introductory chapter is to provide the reader with a brief glimpse into the topic the book is addressing, serving to contextualize the subject matter to be discussed. An author must be capable of conveying to the reader the enthusiasm experienced in writing the book. Failure to achieve this goal may well result in a reader not sensing the importance and joy a book wishes to transmit. An introductory chapter, as a result, fulfills many important goals!

The United States has witnessed a revolutionary change in how best to address the subject of crime. The increased reliance on prisons has slowly, but quite profoundly, changed society in ways that only now are being fully understood by a small percentage of the nation. The majority of Americans are "clueless" regarding the price, both financial and social, exacted by the ever-expanding prison-industrial complex. Exploring this issue, and what has happened to those unfortunate enough not to possess the financial resources to avoid prison, requires a book-length study.

Crime Rates and the Nation

Much attention has been paid to the propitious drop in the nation's crime rates, and more specifically, the murder rate. The overall crime rate in the

United States dropped considerably in the second half of the 1990s, 7 percent in 1998, and that reduction is particularly evident in most of the nation's largest cities (Butterfield, 1999b, 2000a). Much debate has resulted concerning the reasons for this dramatic and steady drop in crime rates (Sasson, 1995). It is often ascribed to (1) a robust economy, providing jobs for those who have historically been imprisoned; (2) community policing; and (3) tougher sentencing laws that have targeted the repeat offender.

An increased rate of incarceration is considered one of the key factors behind this drop, although a number of notable criminologists disagree. Incarceration is one of the major consequences for youth and young adults arrested for committing violent crimes such as murder, rape, robbery, and aggravated assault (Butterfield, 1999b). Between the mid-1980s and 1995 the number of young adults (18 to 24 years) in jail doubled from 178,000 in 1986 to 359,000 in 1995, with the Justice Department estimating that the number arrested from this age group will double by the year 2010 (Sum et al., 1997).

The number of people currently in prison is close to two million, or almost 1 out of every 150 people in this country. It has been estimated that an American born in 1999 has a 1 in 20 chance of living some part of his or her life in a correctional facility. For an African American that probability increases to 1 in 4 (Egan, 1999a, 1999b). In essence, the United States leads all democracies in the number of its citizens that are incarcerated. Not surprisingly, arrests rates, as do homicide rates, fall disproportionately on African American and Latino youth and young adults. African Americans and Latinos are disproportionately incarcerated in federal penal institutions. In 1993, for example, African Americans constituted 33.8 percent of all federal inmates (Free, 1998).

The wide acceptance of the importance of culturally competent services has inspired a much needed search for innovative approaches to interventions serving those under correctional supervision. The search for innovative intervention strategies has been necessitated by past reliance on models of service delivery that were racist, biased, deficit driven, and not culturally based. Social work, as a result, has moved toward, and in some cases has played a leading role in, incorporating culturally competent concepts into practice and education. Capacity enhancement practice, in turn, has slowly entered the dialogue concerning the best way of operationalizing cultural competence with individuals, groups, communities, and institutions. The criminal justice system is one example of how this perspective can bring about a shift in thinking about service delivery.

Social Work and the Criminal Justice System

Social work played a prominent role in prison reform in the early days of the profession. The nineteenth-century reformer Dorothea Dix advocated for better prison conditions for women inmates (Lightner, 1999; Trattner, 1994). Unfortunately, the institution that had its inception in the eighteenth century has not become obsolete in the twenty-first: "While the new century brings with it promises of horizon-expanding technology, it is ironic that the institution of the prison, an invention of the eighteenth century, is not only still with us but expanding at a rapid rate. Those in the field of criminal justice who seek to develop creative approaches to involving communities in crime prevention must now compete with proposals to reinstate chain gangs and other relics of a time we had thought had past" (Mauer, 1999, p. xiii). Thus, the conditions that led the profession of social work to become involved in prison reform in the nineteenth century challenge it to do so again in the twenty-first.

The profession essentially has limited itself to a select number of areas of practice. It has, with some exceptions, focused on educating social workers to practice various forms of clinical intervention, most of which are focused on mental health. Most students in graduate-level education programs have selected this form of practice as their primary method, and this has not changed dramatically over the past few decades. This is not to say that clinical intervention focused on mental health cannot be practiced with the correctionally supervised. As is noted in chapter 2, prisons can easily be reconceptualized as "mental hospitals" based on the percentage of mentally ill inmates currently in those institutions.

The subject of incarceration (in prisons and jails) and postincarceration experiences has not received the attention it deserves from the social work profession, particularly in regard to statistics related to incarceration in communities of color in the United States: "Surprisingly, little has been done by the profession to integrate social work and the law, perhaps because of the tendency of social workers to view themselves as general practitioners primarily engaged in health and mental health counseling" (Lynch and Mitchell, 1995, p. 11). The impact of incarceration on urban communities of color is quite striking. For example, arrest history has been found to be related to problems entering the labor market (Busway, 1998). Thus, any community with a high rate of incarceration will find it difficult to achieve economic sustainability. This book is in response to the paucity of systematic and comprehensive examinations of how communities, particularly those of color, in the United States have been affected by the incarceration of young and adult men and women and of what social work can do to address this social problem.

According to Roberts and Brownell (1999), other helping professions (e.g., psychology, psychiatry, and nursing) have made an effort over the past few years to specialize in criminal justice. Social workers (at least members of the National Association of Social Workers [NASW]) with a primary practice area, unfortunately, are not highly represented in the criminal justice field (Gibelman and Schervish, 1997). In 1995, social workers with a B.S.W. degree accounted for 2.5 percent of all NASW members working in the criminal justice field; those with M.S.W. degrees accounted for 1.1 percent; and staff with a doctorate in social work accounted for a similar 1.1 percent (Gibelman and Schervish, 1997).

Why should social workers need to know more about populations under correctional supervision (prison, parole, and probation)? The answer depends on the nature of the social work that either is hoped to be practiced, as in the case of students, or is currently being practiced, as in the case of the practitioner (May and Vass, 1996; Roberts, 1998; Wormer and Roberts, 1999). Social workers with no interest in urban-based practice, for example, will have little use for this book. Social workers based in urban areas and unwilling to leave their offices, too, will have little use for this book. However, social workers who have a desire to view themselves as community social workers and who have an interest in new forms of practice with challenging population groups should have great use for this book.

Reeser (1996) sums up quite well the challenge for social work in the next century:

> Social workers need to be able to operate under a variety of conditions in complex practice environments using a variety of responses. The mission needed for the next century is that social workers should work with individuals, groups, and communities, especially those on the margins of society, to alleviate and prevent pain, deprivation, and inequality. . . . Social workers need to work both sides of the road. The profession needs to prepare students to carry out this mission and to develop appropriate job opportunities. (pp. 251–52)

The twenty-first century, as a result, will present the profession of social work with many challenges, including the need to expand its vision of practice frontiers in order to carry out its mission of working with undervalued groups and to open up opportunities for employment for social workers entering the field. Work focused on those under correctional supervision can provide a tremendous employment opportunity in the twenty-first century. However, such work is not without its critics.

I am aware of the great demands social work students and practicing social workers face every day. It is rare for a social worker to pick up a professional journal or book and not be told, sometimes quite boldly, that what he or she is practicing needs to be expanded or discarded all together. The general public still sees us as either those who "take away people's children," "do gooders," or "misguided souls." It seems that we are always being asked to do more with less. Thus, the reader may ask what else must he or she incorporate into his or her practice in order to be "culturally competent." Practice, however, is dynamic; changes are not only inevitable, but to be welcomed. Context influences how we conceptualize and carry out our practices. Thus, new forms of knowledge and perspectives are introduced, new population groups emerge, and changes in the funding of services, for example, necessitate changes in practice. The introduction of managed care is such an example. This form of funding has had a dramatic impact on how services are structured and funded. Social work education, in turn, has had to change to better prepare students for time-limited practice.

What makes social work a profession that I can proudly be a part of? Simply, social work is the only profession that has so openly, boldly, and historically embraced principles and practices for addressing people and communities that are marginalized and oppressed in U.S. society. There are many non–social workers, not to mention significant others and relatives of social workers, who have an arduous time trying to understand that! I entered social work in the early 1970s because it offered the greatest promise of reaching people who were undervalued in our society. My desire to work with undervalued groups in urban settings could best be accomplished by being a social worker. Thus, the choice of social work as a career was relatively easy for me to make. A life without a purpose, after all, is a life with little meaning.

I have found meaning working with the homeless, substance abusers, the poor, people of color, and so on. Prisoners and former prisoners very often fall into these and other categories. These and other groups have essentially been "written off" by U.S. society. It is estimated that more than 1.5 million children, most of whom are either African American or Latino, have had or will have at least one parent in prison during their lifetimes (Seymour, 1998). The profession of social work, as a result, is in a favorable position to make a difference in a community's life. This book represents an effort to better assist the profession in reaching out to urban communities and people under court supervision, at a time when there is great need for a generation of men and women, particularly those of low income and of color, to reenter society and their communities as productive members. Further, by utilizing a capacity enhancement perspective, social work can build upon community assets in the development of initiatives and intervention strategies.

The social work profession is at a unique juncture concerning prisoners and former prisoners and their needs (Johnson, Selber, and Lauderdale, 1998; Roberts, 1998; Sheridan, 1996). Social workers practicing in urban communities of color have seen a disproportionate share of men and women return from prison ill prepared to reenter society, let alone make successful contributions to their families, community, and nation. The competencies (strengths) of such individuals are largely ignored by policymakers, providers, and their organizations.

The ability to simply survive in prison, in my opinion, can be considered an "ego strength" and should never be underestimated by practitioners. How many of us could hope to survive in subhuman conditions for several weeks or months, not to mention years? Survival, in this case, refers to actual physical survival as well as one's psychological and social well-being. There are many critics of the prison system who would argue that the state of mind necessary to survive in prison falls apart upon release, making "survival" in the outside world frightening and an ever-greater challenge than survival within an institution.

Thus, it is almost as if former prisoners have no competencies to help them readjust to society or to allow them to become contributing members of families and communities. Further, the communities such individuals belong to are also perceived as being without assets, limiting the potential of interventions that actively seek to collaborate with indigenous institutions (Delgado, 1999). In essence, the thinking is that the correctionally supervised, their families, and communities are without strengths and can best be conceptualized as deficit driven! According to this line of thought, any hope of their advancement in this society must depend upon the goodwill and generosity of government and private funding sources.

Why an Urban Focus?

It is hard to imagine that I could have found a publisher for this book ten years ago. However, much has transpired in this country and in the profession of social work in the intervening years to warrant a book on this subject. The nation's rates of incarceration and the profile of those incarcerated have made the country stop and take notice. The economic, moral, and social costs of incarceration have raised serious concerns about what kind of country the United States will be in the twenty-first century. Cities have experienced the burden of incarceration more than suburban and rural areas because of their disproportionate number of people of color.

Hairston (1998b) summed up quite well why the subject of correctional supervision is a national problem and one most profoundly felt by urban communities of color in the United States:

> A look at the size and makeup of the correctional population provides one indicator of the nature and magnitude of the criminal justice problem. At mid year 1995, more than 1.5 million adults were confined in prisons and jails. The majority of persons were poor and a substantial number, in some states as many as 60 percent, were African Americans. Most were young and parents of dependent children and many were convicted on drug charges. Most new admissions to the system during the year were of nonviolent, economic-related crimes. More than five million adults were under correctional supervision with some groups affected more negatively than others. One out of every three African Americans between the ages of 20 and 24 was under some form of correctional supervision, up from one out of every four only five years earlier. (p. ix)

There are more African American males in prison than in college.

I am well aware of the importance of writing a book with broad appeal. The broader the potential audience, the greater the possibility of selling more books. However, a book focused on urban practice, regardless of the population served by social workers, is not without its merits. There are surprisingly few books that target urban practice in the field of social work, even though the majority of social workers work within cities of various sizes in all geographical regions of the country. The nature of social work practice necessitates that it be contextualized. A book focused on rural social work practice will read very differently than one focused on social work in cities. Universal concepts such as empowerment, for example, will be operationalized differently in the different context.

In this case, my endeavor to contextualize incarceration and postincarceration, for example, necessitates that this book provide in-depth details about the origin and extent of the problem, examples of social service programs, and an understanding about the nature of the subject at hand. Crime rates and victimization rates in cities are generally higher than those in rural areas or in the suburbs (Johnson, 1998). Thus, the more specific the setting and context, the greater the applicability of the book for practice. Cities, particularly large ones, have become more and more "of color" in the last two decades, and as a result of immigration and high birth rates, they have an increasingly higher concentration of poor people. Communities of color will continue to grow in numerical representation in the next century (Pear, 1999).

This trend, when combined with the importance of social work in urban areas, lends the subject of the correctionally supervised sufficient importance to warrant a book focused on urban areas. That is not to say that rural and suburban areas of the country do not have people who are incarcerated or that those areas do not face challenges following the release of such people from prison. However, how rural and suburban communities and social workers in those communities address such challenges will be dramatically different from how such challenges are met with in Chicago or New York City, for example. That ecological difference, as a result, needs to be taken into account when an intervention is conceptualized and carried out by practitioners (Delgado, 1999).

Over the past century social work has grown from being primarily an urban-based profession, as epitomized through the work of the settlement house and charity organization movement, to include suburban and rural practice settings. This period of growth has also witnessed the introduction and adoption of many different methods of practice in a countless number of settings, involving many different population groups. The period has also witnessed the introduction of practice-based evaluation as a means of providing funders and practitioners with the necessary tools to evaluate the success of intervention. In essence, the changes society has experienced have also shaped the profession of social work. Although this book takes an urban focus, its lessons can hopefully find relevance in suburban and rural areas, with the necessary modifications.

Finally, in all fairness, I have always been fascinated by cities and the issues confronting them. My experiences being born and raised in the South Bronx, New York, served to socialize me to urban issues. Those experiences also served to prepare me to better identify and tap indigenous resources, such as in the case of nontraditional settings (Delgado, 1999). Consequently, my history with cities has continued to this very day.

A Capacity Enhancement Perspective

The reader may wonder why and how I will apply a capacity enhancement perspective to the subject of the correctionally supervised (Saleebey, 1992). The reader, too, may be wary of yet another "innovative" approach in human services. Cunningham's (1998) sharing of an experience underscores the danger of accepting innovative approaches without seriously questioning them: "At a workshop several years ago a respected colleague with over 40 years of practice in the field of juvenile justice confided to the rest of the participants that among the benefits of becoming a senior citizen was knowing what 'new' approaches were worth getting excited about and which were simply old ideas being rediscovered by a new generation" (p. 295). Although I do not have forty years of practical experience in the field, that does not invalidate the excitement of a new approach—in this case, capacity enhancement—to addressing the needs of the correctionally supervised.

Most of the literature, professional and popular, has been deficit driven and has served to identify many of the problems associated with prison and postprison life. However, I could find few references—and those were mostly in the popular press—regarding some of the outstanding work being undertaken by prisoners who are helping fellow prisoners and who have taken on productive roles during postprison life. I have encountered numerous staff members with prison backgrounds working in community-based programs. These individuals bring with them a wealth of experience and have served as excellent role models for youth and young adults. Family, friends, houses of worship, and other indigenous institutions, too, play influential support roles in the community. Thus, a capacity enhancement perspective has been practiced by indigenous institutions without much support or recognition from social workers and other human services providers.

Capacity enhancement can be defined as the systematic use of indigenous assets in the construction and implementation of intervention strategies. Those strategies, in turn, actively seek the involvement of those they target to play instrumental roles, roles that, incidentally, serve to enhance competencies in the process (Delgado, 2000a; Poole, 1997). Capacity enhancement initiatives can be successful only if they take a cultural competence perspective and actively seek to have services take into account the cultural context of the population being targeted (Delgado, 2000b). Culture, in this instance, refers not only to beliefs, values, and customs but also to ecological context—namely, an urban community with limited access to needed formal resources.

A capacity enhancement perspective is very important to provide a "balanced" view of such a population and to identify areas, services, and programs with which social workers can collaborate in service to the community. Although McQuaide and Ehrenreich's comments (1998) are directed at women, men, too, have strengths that often go unnoticed and untapped:

> It is easy to construct an image of prison inmates as helpless, their lives completely controlled by the rules and staff of an all-embracing, total institution. . . . People retain the ability to act despite what may seem like overwhelming powerlessness; they both act and are acted on. As women tell their stories, they narrate how they have survived and created arenas for choice. Strengths, resilience, and coping mechanisms are identified as women's attempts to transcend the loss of freedom, and the actual or potential emotional and physical brutality of prison, are recounted. (p. 239)

The introduction of strengths and assets is critical in creating interventions targeting women and men with prison backgrounds.

This book examines the productive and important roles individuals in prison and who have left prison can play; it also identifies programs that systematically build upon institutional and community assets. For example, it is estimated that more than 90 percent of prisoners cannot read at a functional level (Bratt, 1998). Their inability to read seriously hampers such individuals' adjustment to their community upon release and severely limits their chances at gainful employment. Reading Academy, a program at the Maryland Correctional Institute–Jessup, uses twenty-one inmates as tutors to work with other inmates (adults reading at or below a third-grade level). This program has been credited with reducing recidivism as a result of education (Bratt, 1998). (See the detailed case study in chapter 9.) Experimental Gallery, a program that targets juvenile offenders in Washington's juvenile rehabilitation system using the arts as the primary intervention method, has successfully reduced the recidivism rate from the state average of 80 percent to 50 percent. (See chapter 10 for a detailed case study.) This program teaches youth painting, sculpture, creative writing, and video production (Rook, 1998). The Experimental Gallery in Seattle takes a strengths approach toward youth inmates; it seeks to provide avenues for expressing themselves that are not conflict driven, and it can help prepare them for release into society. These two examples typify programs that will be examined and highlighted in this book. There are numerous examples of programs in and out of prisons in which a capacity enhancement perspective has been used to reach inmates and former inmates. Unfortunately, many of those programs do not involve social workers, although social workers can make significant contributions to such programs given an opportunity to do so.

A capacity enhancement perspective is needed in order to better identify and mobilize the potential of inmates, former inmates, and others to contribute to their community and society. A capacity enhancement perspective, in turn, also serves to help practitioners place the issues, problems, and challenges within a context that emphasizes using indigenous resources as a means of better serving communities, particularly those communities that do not have ready access to formal resources such as those in human services organizations.

Book Goals

A book specifically devoted to urban community social work practice in the criminal justice field must, by its very nature, be practice centered and never lose sight of the social worker in the field. In essence, it must ask what social workers need to know in order to be more effective and more humane in their practice. Although simple questions, the answers invariably are quite profound and arrived at only through an arduous process. This book, as a result, is directed toward urban community social work practice, and the book's goals reflect that orientation.

The subject of crime and violence is very much integrated into the national fabric, with virtually every member of society, regardless of race, ethnicity, and economic status, viewing it as a major social problem (Sheley and Wright, 1995). In 1998 a national survey found that Americans considered crime and violence the greatest problem (cited by 30.2 percent) facing the United States today (Horatio Alger Association, 1998–1999).

Crime, particularly that associated with violence and personal injury, has captured national attention, resulting in an increased demand for stiffer prison sentences, the building of more prisons, and reduced possibilities for probation and parole. This general fear related to violence, however, is misguided at best and highly influenced by sensationalism and, some would rightfully argue, sexist, racist, and classist sentiments. Nevertheless, incarceration of young men and women from low-income backgrounds and of color is a major social issue in this country and will continue to be so well into the twenty-first century.

What do I mean by *young* men and women? Generally speaking, I have no specific age in mind, although if pressed to come up with an age range, it would be adolescent (13 years or older) to young adulthood (mid-20s). The term *young* ought to symbolize a period in life when an individual is healthy, has his or her entire future ahead of him or her, and is about to commence seeking to fulfill his or her dreams. A tragic event occurring during this developmental period, and imprisonment qualifies as such an event, is of epic proportion.

This book addresses five key questions that have direct implications for the profession of social work: (1) What are the trends associated with and characteristics of men and women who are incarcerated, and what are the challenges they face inside prison and once they are released into society? (2) To what extent are community-based organizations (formal and informal) coping with the return of former prisoners? (3) What challenges face social workers in addressing the needs of former prisoners? (4) How are capacity enhancement principles and strategies used to reach and serve population groups with prison experience? and (5) How can professional social work education better support practitioners in their quest to provide services based on capacity enhancement concepts and principles at both the community and institutional level? This book, however, does not directly address the question of how capacity enhancement can be used to help victims of crime. Although that is an important subject, and one that affects most social workers in the course of their daily activities, it is beyond the scope of this book. In fact, the subject is of sufficient importance to warrant a book unto itself.

Although the questions above involve both men and women, most of the book will be devoted to the experiences of men, since their numbers are more significant in the correctionally supervised population. Nevertheless, every effort is also made to address women, since their numbers in the incarcerated population have steadily increased this decade and by all indications will continue to do so in the foreseeable future (Gilbert, 1999). I also seek answers to a multitude of questions pertaining to how stakeholders, residents, and community organizations (formal and informal) view residents with histories of incarceration. The reader will develop an in-depth understanding of the influence of correctional supervision on urban communities, and he or she will be better able to develop interventions that are capacity enhancement based and culture specific. Any book devoted to prisoners and former prisoners must seek to prepare social workers for examining the topic from a multifaceted perspective. A community's responses to the incarceration of its members will vary according to context. Rural communities, for example, may approach the subject very differently than urban communities may. Thus, this book seeks to help ground the social worker in the realities of the urban setting.

Conclusion

I hope that the reader has developed a better appreciation for what this book is about by reading the preface and this chapter. What each reader gets out of this book, however, will greatly depend on his or her professional goals and commitments. Some will approach this book as an intellectual exercise and learn more about a world that is foreign to them. Others will undertake this journey with great fear and trepidation because the topic is near and dear to them. For yet others, it will highlight the importance of doing community social work.

I have attempted to be quite explicit about my vision for the profession and why work with prisoners and former prisoners typifies how we as social workers can be more responsive to marginalized urban communities. In addition, the application of a capacity enhancement perspective to this endeavor fits well with the thrust many social work scholars are taking toward practice in the next century. Any book devoted to "redirecting" the profession of social work will not be without its critics, and rightly so. However, I believe that it is rare that an open debate does not ultimately result in a "better" outcome.

The preface and this chapter have sought to lay the groundwork for that type of discussion, or debate, if you wish. I realize that no book attempting to predict the future, and this book is no exception, is without limitations. However, the spirit in which this argument is put forth, particularly when rationales for the argument are explicit, cannot but help to move the profession forward into the twenty-first century.

The next century is full of opportunities, challenges, and rewards for practice. Major forces will be operative in this country and throughout the world. The days of an event occurring somewhere in the world that does not have an impact on this country are long gone. The "globalization" of the world's social and economic resources has resulted in an interlocking network where nations no longer can exist in isolation from each other. Political upheaval in one country, for example, can manifest itself in the migration of uprooted peoples to other countries. These countries, however, do not necessarily have to border each other.

It is hoped that the book lives up to the lofty goals outlined in this chapter. The reader, in any event, has a clear sense of the "journey" he or she is about to undertake, the methods that will be used in setting the context, and the limitations of the book. I hope that the journey is not only informative but also relatively "pain free" for the reader. This journey, however, will ultimately result in better, more empowering, and capacity-enhancing interventions with the correctionally supervised and the communities in which they live.

There are many critics of social work both within and without the profession. I count myself as one. Specht and Courtney (1994), for example, have argued that the future of social work must be very much tied to its community roots and focus on more than individuals:

> Professionals who claim to do social work should not be secular priests in the church of individual repair. They should be working to build communities. They should not ask, "Does it feel good for *you*?" They should ask, "Is it good for the *community*?" We must not concentrate our resources on helping individuals increase their self-esteem and realize their potential. We must use our resources to help groups in the community to build a community-based system of social care that leads to the creation of healthy communities. That is how we can help make people healthy. (p. 175)

As already noted, the twenty-first century will bring incredible challenges to the profession in its quest to reenter the urban communities that it historically, at its origins, served. Former prisoners can continue to live in urban communities without even a glance from social workers, for example. However, urban community social work–led initiatives can stand as a testament to the profession's willingness to venture into new and exciting arenas of practice—arenas that, if properly embraced, can rejuvenate the profession and provide a badly needed beacon to help guide us through the storms we will encounter in the next century. Cities, after all, will continue to play important roles in the twenty-first century.

2

Incarceration Profiles and Trends

The impact of the correctional system on urban communities, particularly communities of low income and of color, is significant and cannot fully be appreciated without examining statistics related to the criminal justice system. These statistics serve to quantify the problem, and they paint a picture that at times is very difficult to imagine, let alone comprehend. This chapter introduces the reader to data, most of which have been gathered by federal and state governments, highlighting distinct patterns and trends concerning who is under correctional supervision in this country.

Statistics on "social problems" such as those related to criminal justice must always be contextualized for fear that they will paint a picture that serves only the purpose that the gathers of those statistics wish to convey, particularly in cases involving various forms of government:

> Official statistics, we are continually reminded, have to be treated with extreme caution. It is often the case, however, that many of those who issue such warnings subsequently proceed to employ the data, as if it were unproblematic. The dilemma is that there is a need to use official statistics because they provide an important source of information, but it is difficult to scrutinize every figure and to assess every table and graph critically. The reality is

that we have to develop a critical orientation to the data that makes us continuously aware of its limitations and at the same time allows us to interpret and decode its meaning. This is no easy task. Interpreting the official statistics on crime and punishment is a precarious business and even experienced criminologists fall victim to its many traps. (Matthews, 1999, p. 81)

"Official" crime and punishment statistics, for example, rarely reflect quality of life and the experiences of those who are imprisoned. Further, they rarely seek to identify the strengths of those convicted of a crime as a means of generating information that can be systemically used in planning rehabilitation efforts. Official statistics generally provide a broad picture without offering necessary details regarding the person who is being punished. Thus, they tell only part of the story, and some would argue quite persuasively, a very biased story.

This chapter does use "official" statistics. However, every effort has been made to broaden the range of sources of data. A variety of sources is used as a means of creating a picture that is quite distressing yet important to face. I have been careful not to overload the reader with a multitude of data and tables. However, some exposure is unavoidable in order to capture the significance of trends related to the criminal justice system. Periodically, interpretations of statistics are offered to contextualize the numbers and to note what they mean for those who are being punished, their families, and their communities. Since this book specifically focuses on men and women of color, an effort is made to highlight that group, particularly in comparison with white non-Latinos. This chapter, therefore, examines data primarily from a gender and ethnic/racial perspective, with a special focus on African Americans and Latinos, the two groups most highly represented in prisons. Examination of ethnic/racial factors, unfortunately, may prove arduous at times because of data-gathering systems placing Latinos into either "white" or "black" categories. Nevertheless, every effort will be made to separate out Latinos where possible.

Oppression and Communities of Color

To effectively address the needs of the correctionally supervised without at the same time examining the forces at work increasing incarceration rates would be foolhardy. After all, how can an intervention be attempted out of context? In essence, a willingness to "entertain" the operation of oppressive forces such as classism, racism, sexism, ablism, and homophobia is not out of the mainstream of discourse in most social work education programs. How much attention is paid to these forces in the field, on the other hand, will vary considerably from setting to setting. Thus, this perspective adds a dimension to correctional supervision that is generally missing from most public debates on the subject.

This section has been added to the chapter in order to specifically highlight the issues of oppression related to the nation's effort to address the "crime problem." Issues of oppression can be found in almost any social problem; however, they take on added significance when one is examining imprisonment. The reader will find this perspective at work throughout the book, and particularly in chapter 3, "Substance Abuse and Incarceration." Nevertheless, the subject is of sufficient importance to warrant its own section, as well as to be integrated throughout the book.

An examination of statistics related to correctional supervision reveals distinct patterns and trends concerning who is incarcerated in U.S. prisons or on probation or parole. Data related to a variety of correctional dimensions show why work with this population group will grow in importance for the profession of social work in the twenty-first century, particularly involving communities of color, and most notably African American and Latino communities. The disparity in the administration of social justice cannot help but raise disturbing questions about the role of the criminal justice system in the United States and the systematic targeting of under-valued groups for imprisonment. This perspective has been raised by a number of scholars.

Feld (1998), for example, looked at the subject of criminal justice from a juvenile court perspective and argued that the increased number of youth of color entering the system has changed the focus of the court from one that is rehabilitation driven to one that is punishment driven. This shift has resulted in the issuing of more severe penalties for youth offenders and an increased number of youth waived to adult court. Singer (1996), in turn, coined the phrase "recriminalization of delinquency" to explain how waivers to criminal court have set back the juvenile justice system. Elikann (1999) has coined the term "demonization" to refer to this phenomenon.

Bartollas and Miller (1994) have stated the issue from a social justice viewpoint: "The juvenile justice system has too long been a disposal unit for the children of the poor. The lack of social justice for poor and minority groups is a grave indictment of our society. At the same time that the heavy-handed ministrations of the state have harshly processed the poor, the justice system has worked very hard at saving the 'saved'—the middle-class youths who have committed minor offenses. These juveniles are usually the ones diverted from the system, placed on probation, and retained in community-based corrections" (p. 395). Consequently, issues of classism and racism at the very least serve to introduce reasons why a disproportionate number of people of color are in the criminal justice system in this country. The introduction of racism and classism forces, unfortunately, is just that, an introduction. The lucky ones will leave the system and never return. Most will have many more "contacts" with this system.

Looking at oppression and imprisonment from a different viewpoint, namely, in regard to children, it is estimated that currently 1.96 million children have a parent or close relative in jail or prison on any given day in the United States, and 5 million more have parents who have been incarcerated and currently are on probation or parole (Butterfield, 1999a).

This impact, however, is most acutely felt by children of color: "The impact on children can fall most heavily on blacks in poor city neighborhoods, where a disproportionate number of people go to prison, contributing to a concentration of fatherless families" (Butterfield, 1999a, p. A18). Children of color, in turn, have a higher likelihood when compared with white, non-Latino children of having a major significant figure in their lives missing for some period of time. If it is their mother and they are very young, the absence occurs during a major developmental period in their lives.

There are probably very few families and communities of color in U.S. cities that have not been affected directly, through imprisonment of a family member, by the criminal justice system. An increased rate of imprisonment, as is noted later in this chapter, will have a profound and lasting impact on the nation's cities and the major institutions supporting them such as schools. Christianson (1998) raises a series of provocative questions concerning this country's proclivity to incarcerate:

> What explains the paradox of a country that prides itself as being the citadel of individual liberty, yet imprisons more persons per capita than any other nation in the world with the possible exception of Russia? Why does a country founded on equality imprison mostly people of color, showing a rate of incarceration of blacks that is more than eight times that of whites? How is it that the United States, which epitomizes and sanctifies democracy, continues to build and maintain a huge and growing complex of totalitarian institutions in its midst? (pp. ix–x)

The answers to the questions raised by Christianson strike at the heart of the argument that imprisonment is being used as a deliberate and systematic method of social control fueled by racist, classist, and most recently, sexist sentiments and agendas. Approximately 1.5 million African American men out of a total of 10.4 million have lost their right to vote as the result of a felony conviction (Thomas, 1997). I am hard pressed to come up with an alternative explanation when the data, as addressed in this chapter, are so convincingly clear. The increased use of prisoners as forced labor further supports this premise (Parenti, 1996, 1999).

The "militarization" of the war on drugs and crime at all levels of government has created a siege mentality in many low-income urban communities of color and raised questions about the role of government as an occupying force. In 1997 for example, the National Guard averaged 1,300 counterdrug operations per day, involving more than 4,000 troops on duty (Munger, 1997). Police departments as well, through their paramilitary units (currently 89 percent have such units), are active in drug-curtailment operations. Their involvement is primarily through serving drug-related search warrants, and these types of warrants invariably consist of no-knock entries into homes (Kraska and Kappeler, 1997). Finally, the hiring of a retired general as the "drug czar" to head the Office of National Drug Control Policy seems fitting when one considers the role of the military in interdiction and drug-arrests initiatives. (See chapter 3 for a more detailed look at interdiction as a strategy.)

The term *prisoner of war* has increasingly been used to refer to inmates of color who have been the prime target of the nation's "war on drugs" and "war on crime." The term, however, was used in this sense as early as the 1960s. Consider the following from Eldrige Cleaver's (1960) widely read book *Soul on Ice:*

> Malcolm X had a special meaning for black convicts. A former prisoner himself, he had risen from the lowest depths to great heights. For this reason he was a symbol of hope, a model for thousands of black convicts who found themselves trapped in the vicious PPP cycle; prison-parole-prison. . . . One thing that judges, policemen, and administrators of prisons seem never to have understood, and for which they certainly do not make any allowances, is that Negro convicts, basically, rather than see themselves as criminals and perpetrators of misdeeds, look upon themselves as prisoners of war, the victims of a vicious, dog-eat-dog system that is so heinous as to cancel out their own malefactions: in the jungle there is no right or wrong. (p. 64)

Thus, the currency of the term *prisoner of war* serves to politicize this nation's policies of incarceration and forced labor.

The prison-related experiences of inmates raise a number of issues, and one cannot help but draw parallels with the African American slave experience. Although some critics argue that drawing similarities between prison inmates and slaves is far fetched, I, and I am sure many other social work scholars and practitioners of color, for example, beg to differ. Conditions in U.S. prisons are getting harsher, more punitive, and repressive, with implications reaching far into an inmate's family and community (Haberman, 2000).

Citizens losing the right to vote, for example, has profound implications for a community. As of 1998, forty-six states and the District of Columbia prohibited inmates from voting while serving a felony sentence. The exceptions were Maine, Massachusetts, Utah, and Vermont (Sengupta, 2000b). A total of thirty-two states prohibit felons from voting upon their parole, and twenty-nine of those states exclude felony probationers as well. Ten states disenfranchise all ex-offenders upon completion of their sentence. One point four million, or 13 percent, of all African American men are disenfranchised. Their rate of disenfranchisement is seven times that of the national average. The Sentencing Project (1998a) estimates that if present incarceration trends continue, 30 percent of the next generation of African American men can expect to lose their right to vote sometime in their lives. In select states that disenfranchise ex-offenders the percentage may reach a high of 40.

The trend toward having prisoners pay a greater and greater share of their "upkeep," and in some cases the total cost of their trials, is evident in this country (Parenti, 1996, p. 26). Kenneth Stewart Sr.'s son Kenny is on Virginia's death row and owes the state $57,756.20 for the cost of his jury trial—not his defense, but his whole trial. In Virginia, a jury trial is still a right, but one that losing defendants must literally pay for. "Last week I sent $50 up to Kenny's account and there wasn't six cents left in it after the authorities took their share," Stewart says. These charges when combined with the increased costs of health services—for example, removing an abscessed tooth costs $50—puts a tremendous burden on a family's budget. In Stewart's case, Stewart Sr. sends $200 a month to his son's account. This sum represents 25 percent of the father's monthly income from his social security check and part-time employment.

It is estimated that at least twenty-one states require at least some inmates to pay some portion of their room and board. Michigan, for example, requires inmates to pay $40 per day during their imprisonment (Prisoners Reimbursement Act). Nevada requires that inmates upon conviction disclose all of their personal assets and be willing to pay a portion of the costs of incarceration. In Pennsylvania (Berks County Prison), inmates now pay $10 per day, or 25 percent of the costs of incarceration. Prisoners who are employed while in prison often work for below minimum wage and are charged a percentage of their wages to help defray the costs of imprisonment.

Nevertheless, distressing as the costs of paying for incarceration may be, copayments for medical care bring a new, and even more disturbing, dimension to the prison experience:

> These small (but, for prisoners, nonetheless expensive) fees are usually introduced with the stated aim of "deterring frivolous health complaints." In October 1995, Allen County, Kentucky, started charging $10 for a doctor's visit. Not surprisingly, the average number of monthly doctor visits plunged from 1,125 to 225. . . . a similar program in Mobile, Alabama, showed a 50 percent reduction in inmate visits to the clinic. . . . The same story emerges throughout the nation, from the San Diego County jail to numerous state prison systems. Florida claims $3 a visit; Oklahoma $2, plus $2 per prescription; California $5 (soon to be boosted to $10), plus up to $200 for dentures and over $60 for eye glasses; Nevada $4, with the costs of medication and prosthetics running much higher. (Parenti, 1996, p. 28)

A number of partnerships between prisons and private industries have been established in the last decade (Lewis, 1999). Proponents argue that prison-based employment prevents idleness and reduces recidivism by providing inmates with marketable skills upon their release. It is estimated that in 1998 federal inmates in the nation's ninety-four federal prisons generated $540 million of items such as furniture, clothing, and electronic components, among others, which were sold to federal agencies (Lewis,

1999). Inmates earn from 23 cents to $1.15 per hour as part of this prison-work program. Critics argue that these enterprises have worked toward benefiting state governments and companies, at the expense of prisoners:

> Many states, most notably California . . . operate private prison-labor programs . . . and set their own rules for how firms can use prison labor. California, Nevada, Oregon, and Washington lead the nation in leasing prison labor to private firms, as states are moving toward a partnership with private industry. . . . In Arizona, the press reports that even the 109 residents of death row are now pulling their own weight on a prison run vegetable farm. One of the positive side effects of employing the condemned—as far as the governor's press secretary is concerned—is that the inmates will be too busy to file "frivolous lawsuits in attempts to circumvent their death sentences." (Parenti, 1996, p. 29)

The "cheap" labor available to work in some of these industries lends credence to the comparisons with slavery (Leonhardt, 2000).

Last, and to add insult to injury, states are increasingly making considerable sums of money charging commissions on collect telephone calls made by prisoners to their relatives. New York, for example, made between $20 and $21 million from collect calls from prisoners in 1998; Illinois made between $12 and $16 million; California made $15 million (Sullivan, 1999). Telephone calls very often represent the only viable way for prisoners to maintain contact with their families. However, states are able to charge commissions that often can be cast as exploitive.

These and other efforts—not to mention the slow erosion of rights—to further punish prisoners raise the specter of a slavery system that bears many parallels with the one "officially" abolished as the result of the American Civil War. The ethnic/racial composition of prisons is increasingly becoming browner and drawing from poor and low-income communities. Thus, the leap between the slavery system abolished in the nineteenth century and the one that has replaced it in the late twentieth and early twenty-first centuries is not great. The reader, in all fairness, must arrive at his or her own interpretation of the data and material presented in this chapter. At the very least, he or she must consider imprisonment as a serious social problem that has significantly affected one sector of society. Other readers, in turn, will be much more indignant concerning the role of prisons in this society and the continued impact they will have on the nation's cities in the next century. Their interpretation may well be similar to mine.

However, along with Parenti (1999), I cannot imagine that the current state of affairs regarding imprisonment would be the same if imprisonment necessitated putting white, middle-class individuals into dangerous and unhealthy prison cells: "It is hard to imagine that this compliancy would exist if the more than a million and a half prisoners were the sons and daughters of the white middle-class. However, as the image of the criminal as an urban black male has hardened into public consciousness, so too, has support for punitive approaches to social problems been enhanced. . . . In a changed economy with less demand for the labor of many unskilled workers, imprisonment begins to be seen as an appropriate, if unfortunate, outcome" (p. 12).

Profiles and Trends Among the Correctionally Supervised

A good deal of the data reported in this chapter originated from federal sources, most notably the Department of Justice's Bureau of Justice Statistics. As a result, the biases inherent in having a federal agency gathering data are present here. However, every effort has been made to present data from nongovernmental sources as well. I am aware, however, that funding sources gather data on what they consider to be important. What they may consider important may not be shared by the community. Consequently, the more sources of information, the greater the likelihood of a more balanced picture.

The field of criminal justice has struggled with interpreting data regarding the correctionally supervised because of methodological and data-gathering limitations. Issues related to selective enforcement, for example, single out people of color and their communities in the intensity of policing. Particular types of crime—for example, those related to substance abuse—will have a higher likelihood of being detected in those communities when compared with primarily white and middle-class communities.

With regard to another aspect of data gathering and interpreting, the reduction in crime may have been influenced by falsification of statistics because of political pressures to show reductions:

> Even as politicians and police commissioners were touting the reduction of crime statistics, particularly in major cities, accusations of falsifying statistics forced the resignation or demotion of high-ranking police officers in New York, Philadelphia, Atlanta, and Boca Raton (FL). . . . In Boca Raton a police captain's systematic downgrading of property crime made the city's felony rate in 1997 appear more than 10.5% lower than it really was. And because of underreporting of crimes and unjustified downgrading of felonies to misdemeanors by its police department, Philadelphia had to withdraw its crime numbers from the FBI's national compilation. Philadelphia Police Commissioner John F. Timoney vowed to eliminate this problem saying, "If we are going to get this right and reduce crime, we have to start with accurate statistics." (*Collier's Year Book*, 1999, p. 205)

There is little question that crime-related statistics are often used to promote law enforcement and help to substantiate crime-related budgets across the United States (Butterfield, 1997).

Crime-related statistics can also be influenced by improper arrests. In New York City, there has been a dramatic increase in what are referred to as "flawed arrests" in the last few years, which have resulted from police raids in search of criminals: "Though crime in the city has ebbed to historic lows, the New York City police arrested more people than ever last year. The inevitable result, courthouse lawyers and some former prosecutors say, is a surge in the number of flawed arrests. More and more of those arrested . . . were jailed and released without ever having been formally charged with a crime. Last year [1998], prosecutors tossed out 18,000 of the 345,000 arrests made in the city even before a judge reviewed the charges, more than double the number of four years before" (Fessenden and Rohde, 1999, p. 15). The majority of those flawed arrests took place in low-income communities of color, which are often the focus of overpolicing. Many of those arrested spend anywhere from a few hours to overnight in jail before being released when prosecutors reject the charges made against them. These arrests cause a great deal of anger and anguish in the communities and reflect overzealous police enforcement at the expense of individual rights.

Incarceration Rates and Trends

Zimring and Hawkins (1991), who foretold the trend toward increased imprisonment in the United States during the 1990s, note that there are three key questions that must be asked about a society's use of criminal law: (1) What is the general justification of the use of imprisonment as a criminal sanction? (2) What is the justification for using imprisonment in particular cases? and (3) What is the scale of the use of prisons as a penal method? The addition of the following question adds an important dimension to Zimring and Hawkins's questions: Why is the profile of the typical inmate African American or Latino? These four questions combined bring the issue of incarceration in this society to a head (Mauer, 1999).

In 1998, the prison population grew at a record-breaking pace and numbered almost 1.8 million, an increase of close to 60,000 inmates from the year before, a 4.9 percent increase, or 650 inmates per 100,000 (Bureau of Justice Statistics, 1999c). During 1998 an additional 108,746 juveniles were incarcerated in public or private juvenile facilities (Office of National Drug Control Policy [ONDCP], 1998). The vast majority (1,185,000) of those imprisoned in 1998 can be considered as nonviolent offenders (Irwin, Schiraldi, and Ziedenberg, 1999).

At the start of 1990 the incarceration rate in the United States was 292 per 100,000 residents. By the end of 1998 it had increased to 461 per 100,000 (Bureau of Justice Statistics, 1999c). The regions of the South (from 316 to 520) and the West (from 277 to 417) showed the greatest increases in this period (Bureau of Justice Statistics, 1999c). Between 1997 and 1998, Mississippi (16.7 percent), North Dakota (14.8 percent), Wisconsin (13.4), Vermont (12.3 percent), and Oregon (11.6 percent) led the nation in percentage increases (Bureau of Justice Statistics, 1999c). Longer sentences and increased parole revocations have been cited as the most common reasons for this increase.

As already noted, the prison population has expanded steadily over the past twenty-five years: "On a given day in 1992, 372 whites and Hispanics were incarcerated for each 100,000 in the overall population, while the rate for blacks was 2,678 per 100,000. Blacks, 13 percent of the U.S. population, represented 45 percent of those arrested for violent felonies and roughly half of those held in state and federal prisons. On a typical day in 1994 nearly one-third of black men aged 20–29 were either incarcerated, on parole or on bail awaiting trial" (Loury, 1996, p. 23). The United States currently has the world's largest penal system, and it is expected to continue to increase well into the next century (Egan, 1999a). The number of inmates per 100,000 U.S. residents increased from 263 in 1990 to 390 in 1995 (*Census of State and Federal Correctional Facilities,* 1996). By 1996 approximately 8.3 percent of African American men aged 25 to 29 years old were inmates compared with 0.8 percent for white, non-Latino men. The vast majority of the crimes committed involved other people of color (Bureau of Justice Statistics, 1994, 1998b)

The major question is at what point does the world's largest penal system hit a plateau? Regardless of how much crime rates drop, the United States will still have to add the equivalent of a new 1,000-bed jail or prison every week—for perhaps another decade (Egan, 1999a). The National Rifle Association (1997) has publicly stated that the nation needs at least 250,000 new prison cells to adequately punish offenders. One estimate (Gilliard and Beck, 1998) notes that if present trends continue the prison population will reach 2.1 million by the year 2002. Ironically, the number of deaths resulting from gunshot decreased to 32,436 in 1997, the latest year for which statistics are available, from a high of 39,595 in 1993 (Johnston, 1999).

In 1996, according to the Bureau of Justice, there were 5.5 million adults in the United States under correctional supervision, of which 1.6 million (29.8 percent) were in prison or jail and 3.9 million (70.2 percent) on probation or parole (Bureau of Justice Statistics, 1999e). Along with an increase in incarceration, there has been a corresponding increase in the incidence of death in prisons related to violence or AIDS, and this has resulted in an increased use of hospice care in prisons (Maull, 1998). In 1996, 907 inmates in state prisons died from AIDS, accounting for 29 percent of all deaths in state prisons (Altman, 1999). The prevalence of AIDS in prisons is 500 percent greater than that found in the general population of the United States. In 1997 there were an estimated 8,500 inmates with AIDS and approximately 35,000 to 47,000 with HIV (Altman, 1999). However, only a relatively small percentage of prisons—only 10 percent of state and federal prisons and 5 percent of city and county jails—offered comprehensive HIV prevention programs. In 1996 those released from prisons and jails accounted for approximately 17 percent of the total of Americans with AIDS that year (Altman, 1999).

The prison population has increased more than 400 percent since 1990 (Butterfield, 1998). Another perspective on this trend is that every year enough people are imprisoned to fill Yankee Stadium and then some. Most of the new offenders have violated drug laws—60 percent of all inmates in federal prison and 22 percent in state and local jails, for a total of 400,000 (Egan, 1999a). African Americans (48 percent), Latinos (14 percent), Native Americans (1 percent), and Asian/Pacific Islanders (1 percent) accounted for almost two-thirds (64 percent) of all inmates in the nation's federal and state prisons in 1995.

In one Florida city (Jacksonville) in 1995, for example, African American youths represented 85 percent of all those jailed on a given day, yet they accounted for only 11 percent of Jacksonville's total population. The alarm regarding the imprisonment of African American males is not new to society or to social work (Towney, 1981). Gibbs (1988) has highlighted the endangered status of young African American men, with incarceration being one indicator of this precarious state. In Baltimore more than 50 percent of those under court supervision are African American (Currie, 1998). In Washington, D.C., too, almost half (24,377 out of 48,856) of all African American men aged 18 to 35 were under correctional supervision—5,081 were in jail or halfway houses, 6,965 were on probation, and 4,427 were on parole (Thompson, 1997). To make matters worse, 4,427 were on bond awaiting trail and 4,516 had warrants out for their arrest. The 1997 figure represents an increase from 42 percent five years earlier (Thompson, 1997). In 1992 in Baltimore over 56 percent of African American men aged 18 to 35 were under correctional supervision (Donziger, 1996).

The number of individuals on parole, like the number incarcerated, has increased since 1996, and it exceeds four million for the first time in history. In the United States, a total of 704,964 people were on parole at the end of 1998, an increase from 694,787 in 1997 (Bureau of Justice Statistics, 1999e; Schmid, 1999). Those on probation, in turn, increased from approximately 3.3 million to 3.4 million in the same period. The overall increase in numbers is due to a decrease in the nation's prison release rate, which decreased from 37 per 100 prisoners to 31 in 1997, with the average time served increasing from twenty-two months to twenty-seven months in 1997 (Schmid, 1999).

A racial breakdown of those on probation and parole reveals a very high percentage of people of color. In 1998 African Americans accounted for more than a third (775,600) of all those on probation and more than half (281,000) of those on parole (Bureau of Justice Statistics, 1999c). Latinos, in turn, who may be of any race, represented 16 percent (287,100) of those on probation and 21 percent (108,300) of parolees. Latinos between 1980 and 1993 constituted the fastest growing group of color in prisons. Their numbers increased from 7.7 percent to 14.3 percent, with their rate of imprisonment tripling from 163 to 529 prison inmates per 100,000 (Donziger, 1996). In 1998, African Americans (44 percent) and Latinos (21 percent) made up 65 percent of the parolee population. In contrast, in 1990, although the percentage also totaled 65 percent, African Americans accounted for 47 percent and Latinos 18 percent (Schmid, 1999). Turning to probation, African Americans (35 percent) and Latinos (15 percent) accounted for 50 percent of all those in this form of correctional supervision.

Brownell's (1998) analysis of the profile of women in prison paints a picture that is remarkably similar in many regards to that of men in prison:

> Most women prisoners and detainees are from uneducated, urban, poor sections of the population. They are disproportionately women of color: African American women comprise 46 percent of women prisoners and 43 percent of women in jail. . . . This is compared with white women, who comprise 40 percent of women in prison and 38 percent of women in jail. Hispanic women comprise 12 percent of women in prison and 16 percent of women in jail. Because African Americans comprise under 13 percent of the overall population in the United States, their overrepresentation in prisons and jails is startling. (p. 328)

In 1998 women accounted for 7.9 percent (125,700) of those imprisoned and 18.8 percent (733,700) of those on probation or parole (Bureau of Justice Statistics, 1999e). The United States has seen a dramatic increase in the numbers of women incarcerated (McQuaide and Ehrenreich, 1998; Wilson, Quinn, Beville, and Anderson, 1998). Similar observations have been made in other countries such as Japan (Johnson, 1996). However, the incarceration rate for women in U.S. prisons and jails is almost ten times greater than that in western European countries. The combined female population of all these countries is similar to that of the United States (Amnesty International, 1999).

The number of women inmates has increased steadily and even surpassed the rates for their male counterparts over the last ten years (Stodghill and Anderson, 1999). Women are clearly the fastest growing and least violent segment of the incarcerated population with 85.1 percent being sentenced for nonviolent offenses (Irwin, 1999). Their numbers increased by 6.5 percent during 1998 compared with a 4.7 percent increase for men (Bureau of Justice Statistics, 1999c).

In 1970 there were only 5,635 women in federal and state prisons. However, by the end of 1996 that number had grown to 74,730 (Bureau of Justice Statistics, 1997a). Their numbers have increased by 182 percent per annum, compared with a rate of growth of 158 percent for male inmates during the same period (Bureau of Justice Statistics, 1999c). A review of the time period between 1980 and 1993 will reveal a greater growth rate of 313 percent compared with 182 percent for men. Women, since the inception of mandatory sentencing in 1986, and covering the period up to 1996, have been sentenced to state prison for drug crimes at a tenfold rate from approximately 2,370 to 23,700 per year (Amnesty International, 1999). This is widely considered the primary reason for the increase in incarceration of women in this country.

In 1998 more than one-third of all female prisoners were held in the three largest jurisdictions—California (11,694), Texas (10,343), and the federal system (9,186). That same year, Washington, D.C., was the only jurisdiction in the United States to report a decrease in the number of female prisoners since 1990, averaging a 2.9 percent annual decrease during that period. (Bureau of Justice Statistics, 1999c). North Dakota reported the highest average annual increase of female inmates during the 1990 to 1998 period with an annual average increase of 16.7 percent. It is important to note that this figure is relatively small and translates into an increase from 20 prisoners in 1990 to 67 prisoners in 1998. This statistic pales in comparison with California (where the number of female prisoners increased from 6,502 to 11,694) and Texas (from 2,196 to 10,343).

Incarcerated women present different needs from those of men, as is noted in greater detail in chapter 4. Greater than 75 percent of incarcerated women are mothers, most of whom have two or more children (Morton, 1995). These women, in turn, have a higher likelihood of having been abused physically or sexually at some point in their lifetime (Latour, 1999; Sheridan, 1996). Forty-four percent of all women inmates in federal prisons and 40 percent of all those in state prisons have reported being abused (Women's Prison Association, 1995).

African American women prisoners have not received the attention they deserve even though their percentage of the prison population is greater than their male counterparts. Binkley-Jackson, Carter, and Rolison's (1993) research, in one of the few published studies specifically comparing African American women prisoners with their white counterparts, reporting on African American women in a maximum security prison in Oklahoma, found that they differed from white female prisoners in five critical dimensions: (1) family structure (more likely to be unmarried, have more children, siblings, and give birth at an earlier age); (2) age at first arrest and incarceration (younger); (3) drug use before incarceration (greater use of crack cocaine); (4) exposure to physical and emotional abuse (less); and (5) self-esteem (higher).

An examination of juvenile crime rates will show that the 1980s and early 1990s witnessed a dramatic increase in crime, particularly violence related (Egan, 1999b). That increase, as a result, served to create an atmosphere that was more punishment related than treatment related for the juvenile offender (Zimring, 1998). The nation's crime rate, however, has decreased dramatically over the last five years. Rates of violent crime between 1993 and 1998 fell 7 percent to 37 per 1,000 Americans aged 12 years or older from 50 per 1,000 ("Violent Crime Falls 7 Percent," 1999).

Nevertheless, the nation still responds as if juvenile rates had not changed from that of the earlier period, during which adolescent homicide rates increased significantly—154 percent between 1985 and 1991 (Butterfield, 1997). The same period witnessed a corresponding increase in homicide arrest rates for adolescents—127 percent. The 1980s witnessed a significant increase (60 percent) in juvenile arrests for murder and manslaughter; they increased an additional 45 percent between 1990 and 1993 (Chaiken, 1998). Nationally, youth perpetrated 137,000 more violent crimes in 1994 than in 1985 and were responsible for 26 percent of the growth in violent crime over that period of time. More specifically, they accounted for 50 percent of the increase in robberies, 48 percent of the increase in rapes, and 35 percent of the increase in murders (Office of Juvenile Justice and Delinquency Prevention, 1996).

Recidivism, as a result, is also considered to be a problem (Archwamety and Katsiyannis, 1998; Wilson, Quinn, Beville, and Anderson, 1998). Among women, for example, age at first offense and first commitment, previous gang affiliation, basic educational deficits, location of residence, and length of sentence all play influential roles in determining the probability of reentering prison. Needless to say, the subject of how best to reintegrate former prisoners into society has received considerable attention (Terrell, 1998).

The number of cases handled by courts with juvenile jurisdiction has increased over the past ten years, with the courts handling 1.7 million delinquency cases in 1995, a 7 percent increase from 1994. Between 1986 and 1995, the number of cases increased 45 percent (Sickmund et al., 1998). It is estimated by the Department of Justice that because of an increase in the number of adolescents in the general population between 1992 and 2010, juvenile violent crime rates will double during that period (Synder and Sickmund, 1995). However, there are those who argue that this will not occur (Males, 1999; Steinberg, 1999). Although the arrest rate for youth who have committed violent crimes decreased by 12 percent between 1994 and 1996, it still remained very high at 464.7 arrests for every 100,000 youths between 10 and 17 years old (National Collaboration for Youth, 1998). Crimes committed by juveniles of color invariably were committed against other youth of color (Department of the Treasury and Department of Justice, 1999).

Analysis of the racial and ethnic characteristics of youth who are arrested for felonies and tried as adults will highlight differences between youth of color and white non-Latinos (Lewin, 2000). In a Los Angeles study, approximately 12 percent of the almost 24,000 youths arrested for felonies in 1996 were white non-Latino, while 56 percent were Latino, 25 percent African American, and 6 percent were Asian. However, of the 561 cases that were waived to adult court, only 5 percent were white non-Latino, while 59 percent were Latino, followed by 30 percent African American and 6 percent Asian (Lewin, 2000).

Society's response to youth who commit crime has been to incarcerate them. The case of Willie Bosket, who at the age of 15 killed two subway riders in New York City, played an instrumental role in the nation's shift toward trying juveniles as adults (Butterfield, 1995). Bosket had a long history of encounters with the criminal justice system prior to his conviction for murder. However, because of his age, he was given a maximum sentence of five years in a state juvenile facility. Public outrage over the leniency of the sentence resulted in the New York state legislature passing a law whereby juveniles as young as 13 could be tried for murder as adults. The "Willie Bosket law" was widely credited with similar efforts in other states.

The U.S. Bureau of Prisons handled 239 juveniles in 1998, an increase from 111 in 1990. These prisons, it is important to note, were built for an adult population.

Incarceration may entail having youths in out-of-state institutions, which severely limits visiting by family because of cost and geographic accessibility (Kresnak, 1998). It is estimated that 80 percent of juveniles will reoffend (Rook, 1998). Between 1988 and 1992 the number of juveniles waived to criminal courts increased by 68 percent from 7,000 to 11,700 (Synder and Sickmund, 1995; U.S. General Accounting Office, 1995). Forty-four states have adopted new juvenile justice laws since 1992 that specifically allow children to be tried as adults, with Michigan adopting what many experts consider one of the toughest in the nation (Bradsher, 1999).

There are those in the criminal justice system who are critics of the tendency to incarcerate juveniles in adult prisons. The case of Nathaniel Abraham, convicted of murder at 11 years old, the nation's youngest individual ever charged and convicted as an adult of murder, highlights an alternative approach. Judge Eugene Arthur Moore (Michigan) sentenced Abraham to serve time in a juvenile facility until the age of 21 and then to be released: "The judge called for changes in the 3-year-old state law that makes it possible for children of any age to be tried as adults in Michigan. He called the law fundamentally flawed and suggested that the state return to its practice before 1997 of reserving such trials and sentences for children who are at least 14 when they commit crimes. 'The Legislature has responded to juvenile criminal activity not by helping to prevent and rehabilitate, but rather by treating juveniles more like adults,' Judge Moore said. 'The real solution is to prevent an adult criminal population ever coming into existence' " (Bradsher, 2000, p. A1).

Crimes committed by girls, however, represent a dimension often overlooked in the professional literature and by the public media. Violent crimes committed by girls, too, have increased since 1987. According to FBI statistics, crimes committed by girls under the age of 18 increased by 118 percent (6,418 incidents to 13,995); aggravated assaults (124 percent) and robberies (117 percent) also witnessed significant increases (Ford, 1998). This trend toward greater participation by girls in criminal activity, including violence, is expected to continue in the future. A greater awareness on the part of authorities concerning girls' criminal behavior will undoubtedly result in an increase in their incarceration rate.

Prison Construction and Overcrowding

The prodigious increase in prison construction has not eliminated prison overcrowding in state prisons (Sullivan, 2000). A number of prominent criminologists have argued that crime rates are not related to, or a product of, incarceration rates (Christianson, 1998). As already noted, the nation's crime rates have decreased dramatically over the past few years, yet incarceration rates have continued to rise. The increased rates of incarceration and other forms of correctional supervision have taken an alarming situation to an extreme state in the last decade.

Prison construction in this country can be looked at from a variety of perspectives. However, measuring construction using time provides a glimpse of a system that is out of control. It is estimated that every twenty seconds someone is imprisoned on a drug offense, and every week of the year a new prison is constructed (Egan, 1999c). Prison overcrowding is the leading reason for state facilities to be operated under a court order—that is, an order restricting the number of people who can be imprisoned. In both 1990 and 1995, 323 and 378 state facilities, respectively, or 27 percent in both years, were under court order for overcrowding (Bureau of Justice Statistics, 1999a). In 1995, there were 113 federal prisons under court order for similar reasons (Bureau of Justice Statistics, 1999b).

Approximately 67 percent of the increase in the prison population is considered to be the result of increased sentencing time (Bureau of Justice Statistics, 1999f; Sentencing Project, 1998b). The number of offenders committed to federal prison for life has also increased dramatically during the last eleven years, with 36 having had that designation in 1986 and 314 being so designated in 1997 (Bureau of Justice Statistics, 1999f).

The national increase in prison population has been greatest in states such as California and Texas because of their overall population. California has experienced a 700 percent increase in its prison population in the last twenty years (Currie, 1998). The case example of California serves to highlight how the number of available prison cells cannot keep up with the rate of imprisonment: "In 1989, officials in northern California opened a 1,000 bed maximum-security prison at Pelican Bay. A 1,200 bed wing was added soon thereafter, bringing the capacity of the nation's largest state prison system to almost 50,000 inmates. There was one slight problem: By the end of 1989, the California state prison system already had 87,000 people in custody, with 250 being added every week" (Benjamin and Miller, 1991, p. 76).

Since 1989, the California state prison system has continued to increase in size, with the most recent estimate putting the number of prisoners at 161,904 (Bureau of Justice Statistics, 1999c). The states of California (91,807, or 422 per 100,000) and Texas (103,000, or 823 per 100,000) had the highest number of parolees in 1996 (Bureau of Justice Statistics, 1999e). In 1997 these two states also led the nation in the number of individuals on probation with Texas (429,329, or 3095 per 100,000) in front followed by California (286,526, or 1,306 per 100,000) (Bureau of Justice Statistics, 1999e). No state in the country has escaped the trend toward greater imprisonment.

Lifetime Chances of Incarceration

Lifetime chances of imprisonment differ according to racial/ethnic and gender factors. Men (9 percent) unquestionably have a higher lifetime chance of incarceration when compared with women (1.1 percent) in this country. African Americans (16.2 percent) and Latinos (9.4 percent) are more likely than non-Latino whites (2.5 percent) to be sent to prison (Bureau of Justice Statistics, 1999c). Based on current rates of first incarceration, an estimated 28 percent of all African American males will enter either state or federal prisons during their lifetime, compared with 16.9 percent of Latino males and 4.4 percent of white, non-Latino males (Bureau of Justice Statistics, 1999c). The likelihood of a man being incarcerated sometime during his lifetime is 5.1 percent (one out of every twenty persons). However, as is to be expected, the chances vary according to ethnic/racial and gender factors, with African Americans having a one in four likelihood (Egan, 1999a).

The National Criminal Justice Commission (Donziger, 1996) estimated that if rates of incarceration of African Americans and Latinos continued at the same pace as in the 1980–1993 period, approximately 66 percent (4.5 million) of all African American males ages 18 to 34 and approximately 25 percent (2.4 million) of all Latino males would be in prison by the year 2020, for a total of 6.9 million. This trend is obviously based on a number of factors remaining constant. However, it provides a vivid picture of what incarceration means for males and low-income communities of color.

When African Americans and white non-Latinos are sentenced for drug offenses, the former are more likely to get a harsher sentence. It is estimated that 54 percent of African Americans convicted of drug offenses get sentenced to prison compared with 34 percent of white non-Latinos convicted for the same offenses. Forty-four percent of African Americans get prison sentences for possession compared with 29 percent of white non-Latinos, while 60 percent of African Americans get sentenced to prisons for trafficking compared with 37 percent of white non-Latinos for the same crime (Bureau of Justice Statistics, 1996).

Death Row

Although the subject of death row is beyond the scope of this book, and deserving of a book itself, it is not possible to complete this chapter without making note of it. Those who advocate the death penalty do so based on the assumption that it will deter future crimes. Critics say that the death penalty is morally offensive and discriminates against those who are of color. The death penalty is used in ninety-four countries and territories, including the United States, whereas a total of fifty-seven countries have abolished all uses of capital punishment (Doan, 1997). Fifteen countries have abolished its use except in the cases of military crimes or crimes committed in wartime.

A number of national organizations, such as the American Society of Criminology (ASC) and the American Bar Association (ABA), have passed resolutions addressing how the death penalty discriminates against people of color. The ASC passed the following resolution at its 1987 conference in Montreal: "Be it resolved that because social science research has demonstrated the death penalty to be racist in application and social science research has found no consistent evidence of crime deterrence through execution, the ASC publicly condemns this form of punishment and urges its members to use their professional skills in legislatures and the courts to seek a speedy abolition of this form of punishment." Since 1976, eighty-two convicts sentenced to be executed have been exonerated, or a ratio of one freed for every seven put to death, raising questions about the possibility of the innocent being put to death (Lovinger, 1999).

The ABA passed a resolution on February 3, 1997, which stated as follows: "Resolved, That the American Bar Association calls upon each jurisdiction that imposes capital punishment not to carry out the death penalty until the jurisdiction implements policies and procedures that are consistent with the following longstanding American Bar Association policies intended to (1) ensure that death penalty cases are administered fairly and impartially, in accordance with due process, and (2) minimize the risk that innocent persons may be executed." Recently, George Ryan, the Republican governor of Illinois, instituted a moratorium, the first in the nation, on executions in his state. Although Governor Ryan is not philosophically against the death penalty, he has raised serious questions about a process that has convicted innocent people and placed them on death row in his state (Johnson, 2000). Governor Ryan noted that since 1977 thirteen men have been sentenced to death for crimes they did not commit. Illinois, however, is not unique in facing the issues associated with wrongful conviction and execution of innocent people (Rimer, 2000).

Probably no situation is more striking concerning racial/ethnic disparities than who is placed on death row and executed. The annual number of executions, like the number of inmates on death row, increased substantially in 1997 when seventy-four inmates were put to death, the most since 1955 (*Collier's Year Book*, 1998).

In 1997 California led the nation in the number of prisoners on death row with 486, followed by Texas (438), Florida (370), Pennsylvania (214), and Ohio (177). That year, Texas led the nation in executions carried out with 37, followed by Virginia (9), Missouri (6), Arkansas (4), and Alabama (3) (Bureau of Justice Statistics, 1998d). At the end of 1997, a total of 3,335 prisoners were on death row in thirty-four states and the federal system, an increase of 3 percent from 1996 (Bureau of Justice Statistics, 1998d). The average age at time of arrest for an inmate sentenced to death was 28 years, with a range from 18 (African American man) to 82 (white, non-Latino male).

During the 1980s and 1990s approximately half of all the inmates on death row at any given time were African American (O'Shea, 1993). A racial/ethnic breakdown of the 74 men who were executed in 1997 shows that white non-Latinos accounted for 41, followed by African Americans with 26, Latinos with 5, and Native Americans and Asians with 1 each. Inmates of color accounted for 33 out of the 74, or 44.6 percent (Bureau of Justice Statistics, 1998d). Women, in turn, had a higher likelihood than did men of being given a death sentence on their first offense (Schittroth, 1991). In 1999 285 people were sentenced to death in the nation's courts, up from 268 the year before, and 96 were executed ("Average Stay," 1999). The number executed is the highest since 105 were executed in 1951. The average convict executed in 1998 spent ninety fewer days on death row than those who were executed in 1997 ("Average Stay," 1999). There are efforts on the way to make the process of death more efficient by limiting death row appeals, with the state of Texas leading the way in this arena (Yardley, 2000).

The profile of who is on death row in any state with a death penalty is very similar—African American or Latino male, low-income, and limited formal educational achievement. As of December 31, 1997, African Americans (1,406) accounted for 42.6 percent of all those on death row, an increase from 27.5 percent in 1987. In 1997, Latino inmates on death row numbered 283, or 9.2 percent of all inmates with a known ethnicity (Bureau of Justice Statistics, 1998d). More than 75 percent (226 out of 283) of all Latinos on death row were incarcerated in four states—Texas (88), California (79), Florida (41), and Arizona (18) (Bureau of Justice Statistics, 1998d).

The number of women on death row has increased dramatically over the years (O'Shea, 1993). Currently, the United States has the largest number of women on death row in its history. California also led the nation in the number of women on death row with eight, followed closely by Texas (seven), Florida (six), and Pennsylvania (four). Women of color were also overrepresented on death row. African American women accounted for 42.2 percent, and Latinas (who could be counted as either white or black) accounted for 9.2 percent (Bureau of Justice Statistics, 1998d).

The subject of racial discrimination regarding death row has historically been recognized: "Some of the most blatant racial discrimination in the area of sentencing takes place in the application of the death penalty. The most comprehensive study of the death penalty found that killers of whites were eleven times more likely to be condemned to death than killers of African-Americans" (Donziger, 1996, p.115).

Historically, men of color have been overrepresented on death row, comprising 50 percent of the total of 5,416 persons sentenced to death from 1977 to 1997. This period also witnessed an overrepresentation of people of color who were executed—191 out of 432 men and women, or 44.2 percent (Bureau of Justice Statistics, 1998d).

It may surprise the reader to find that death row is not restricted to adults. The execution of juveniles in this country has been traced back to

1642 (Thomas Graunger, Plymouth County, Massachusetts). In over 350 years there have been 357 juveniles executed (Streib, 1999). The United States executed 10 juveniles during the 1990s, half of whom were in the state of Texas (Grossfield, 1999a, 1999b). Currently 70 juveniles are awaiting execution, and at least twenty-five states allow for execution of juveniles aged 16 to 17. The United States is currently in violation of at least three international treaties (the United Nations Convention on the Rights of the Child; the International Covenant on Civil and Political Rights; and the American Convention on Human Rights) by executing juveniles. The official position of the United States is that it has not ratified two of these treaties and it is exempt from the third.

The president of the American Bar Association notes:

> While the American Bar Association believes that young people who commit violent crimes should be appropriately punished, it has long opposed imposition of the death penalty on any person for an offense committed while they were under the age of 18. Recognizing the paired trends of a growing reliance on capital punishment generally and a willingness to prosecute juveniles, the ABA in 1983 cited a looming specter of juvenile executions, but could find no rational justification for killing juvenile offenders. . . . With no deterrent benefit, the only other possible rationale to execute those who killed when they were juveniles is to satisfy our need for vengeance. . . . It reflects more upon us as a society than it does on the offender that we would seek legal vengeance through execution for the crimes of a child. (Paul, 1999, p. 1)

Economic Costs of Incarceration

Estimates of costs incurred by taxpayers for prisons from 1980 to 1996 are $31 billion a year, or an 800 percent increase from 1975 (Elikann, 1996). One estimate showed that 94 percent of violent-crime-fighting funds is spent on punishment, with the remaining 6 percent on prevention (Elikann, 1996). Construction of new prisons between 1980 and 1993 resulted in increased federal spending for correctional programs (in 1998 dollars) 521 percent (Currie, 1998). New York ($272 million) led the nation in the amount of dollars allocated for prison construction in 1996, followed by Texas ($149 million), Ohio ($141 million), Florida ($124 million), and California with $112 million (Bureau of Justice Statistic, 1999d).

The number of correctional institutions, both confinement and community-based, increased from 1,287 to 1,500 between 1990 and 1995, or almost 17 percent (Census of State and Federal Correctional Facilities, 1996). The costs per bed can be considerably higher than the figures presented here because states usually borrow funds to pay for the construction of prisons, raising costs from $54,000 per bed to well over $100,000 (Donziger, 1996).

Federal facilities experienced the greatest increase in construction (56 percent) during this period when their number increased from 80 to 125. State facilities, in turn, increased by 14 percent from 1,207 to 1,375 during the same period. In 1993, state correctional costs exceeded $19 billion, an increase of 243 percent from 1982 (ONDCP, 1998). The tremendous growth in prison population coupled with a corresponding increase in costs of constructing and maintaining prisons has resulted in states seeking economically viable routes toward prison construction and operation. Private prisons, otherwise known as "prisons for profit," have emerged in many states (Schichor, 1995). Prisons for profit are not uniquely a U.S. phenomenon. This form of management has also found acceptance in other countries, most notably Australia, France, and the United Kingdom (Cavise, 1998).

Christianson (1998) notes the tremendous impact privatization has had and is projected to have in future years: "Privatization was one of the stimuli affecting the changes in prison labor. From 1985 to 1995, there was a 500 percent increase in private prisons; 18 companies had rehabilitated 93 private prisons, creating space for some 51,000 prisoners. By 1996 at least 30 states had legalized the contracting out of prison labor to private companies. From 1995 to 2005, the number of prison beds under private management was expected to increase from 60,000 to more than 350,000" (p. 291).

The economic costs of incarceration, including the building of new prisons, have had a staggering impact on many states across the nation. The financial costs of prison construction and operation can vary based on a variety of factors such as labor, land, construction materials, and type of prison (maximum, medium, and minimum security). Construction of prisons accounted for only 6 percent of expenditures ($1.3 billion) during 1996, with salaries and wages taking the major share of costs with 49 percent (Bureau of Justice Statistics, 1999d). Fiscal year expenditures for states and Washington, D.C., for building, staffing, and maintaining facilities accounted for $22 billion (Bureau of Justice Statistics, 1999d).

According to the National Center on Addiction and Substance Abuse (CASA) at Columbia University, the year 2000 will, if current trends continue, see daily costs reach $100 million per day in money spent to incarcerate persons with serious drug and alcohol problems (CASA, 1998). One estimate in the late 1980s (1987) put the price for building one cell at $50,000 to $75,000 (Byrne, Lurigio, and Petersilia, 1992). Another 1988 estimate by the federal government noted that the average construction cost per bed in a maximum security state prison was $71,000, with a medium security prison bed costing $53,000, and a minimum security bed costing $30,000 (Bureau of Justice Statistics, 1988). A county bed cost an estimated $43,000, with costs of some state prison beds reaching $110,000 in 1987 (Castle, 1991).

Corrections is labor intensive with anywhere from 60 to 80 percent of total operating costs being labor related (Bureau of Justice Statistics, 1999d; Schichor, 1995). It is estimated that it costs taxpayers $20,000 a year to feed and house a new inmate, not including the cost of building new prisons and jails (Egan, 1999c). The costs of incarcerating inmates in maximum security prisons is also calculated at $20,000 per year. There are fifty-seven maximum security prisons in the United States (forty-two states), holding 1 percent of the nation's state and federal prisoners (Brooke, 1999). The costs of building these high security prisons is considerably above the national average for prisons, as is to be expected. The Florence, Colorado, prison, for example, cost taxpayers $60 million to build and costs an average of $50,000 annually per inmate to maintain (Brooke, 1999). If corrections, judicial, and legal costs are combined they total $39,201 per inmate. If police costs are added to that amount, incarceration winds up costing $71,465 per inmate per year (Bureau of Justice Statistics, 1997b).

It is costing states approximately $30 billion annually to maintain prison systems, almost double what it cost ten years ago. California, for example, constructed twenty-one new institutions in the last fifteen years and currently spends approximately $2 billion on construction and $4 billion a year in running the state system (Egan, 1999c; Elikann, 1996). However, California built only one new university in that time period (Ambrosio and Schiraldi, 1997). In 1979, California allocated 3 percent of its budget for prisons and 18 percent for higher education. In 1994, the allotment for prisons had increased to 8 percent and for higher education had decreased to 8 percent (Donziger, 1996). California, unfortunately, is not alone. Between 1979 and 1990, state expenditures nationally increased 325 percent for prison maintenance and 612 percent for prison construction (Donziger, 1996).

Comparing the number of four-year public colleges and the number of state prisons provides an interesting perspective—Texas has ninety-six prisons and forty public four-year colleges; Florida has ninety-four prisons and nine public four-year colleges; California has eighty-seven prisons and thirty-one public four-year colleges; and New York has sixty-nine prisons and forty-two public four-year colleges (CASA, 1998).

The shifting of taxpayer dollars away from education and human services has not been restricted to states like California. Jefferson County, Colorado, home to Columbine High School, illustrates the possible consequences of such actions:

> The diversion of revenues has been devastating on the county level as well. Jefferson County, Colorado, has been diverting millions of dollars out of its general fund and into an 800-bed expansion to its jail complex since 1998. While more tax dollars are going toward corrections, the county is being forced to cut its education budget by as much as $12 million for the 1999–2000 school session. Following the 1999 Columbine school shooting that took place in Jefferson County, angry residents questioned authorities as to why students who showed obvious signs of mental dysfunction were not getting the counseling and health care

they needed. Officials explained that there wasn't enough money in the budget for counselors and that the Jefferson County school system couldn't afford to get saddled with psychiatric bills if it recommended treatment. (Dyer, 2000, p. 258)

State prison expenditures increased from $12 billion in 1990 to $22 billion in 1996 (83 percent increase), an average of 11 percent per year during that period (Bureau of Justice Statistics, 1999d). That cost translated into $103 dollars (in constant 1996 dollars) per U.S. resident, up from $53 in 1985 (Bureau of Justice Statistics, 1999d). Federal expenditures during that time period increased 311.5 percent (Donziger, 1996). Federal prison expenditures, too, grew during the 1990 to 1996 period, increasing from $946 million in 1990 to $2.5 billion in 1996, an average increase of 17 percent per year (Bureau of Justice Statistics, 1999d).

The rate of cost per resident in the states increased an average of 7.3 percent between 1985 and 1996, a rate more than double the 3.6 percent average rise in spending for state public education (Bureau of Justice Statistics, 1999d). These costs compared closely with those for health expenditures ($123 billion). Nevertheless, pro-correction critics would argue that these costs constitute a small percentage of the overall education budget of $994 billion (Bureau of Justice Statistics, 1999d).

Prisons are making a concerted effort to offset costs by having prisoners pick up a portion of the costs of their incarceration, as noted earlier in this chapter (Lewis, 1999; Parenti, 1999). However, the success of these efforts has not impressed critics. Some critics argue that such efforts can best be thought of as "forced" prison labor that happens to be "cheap" and plentiful in an age of scarce workers. Others, like Parenti (1999), view the function of prison labor as providing an "illusion" to the general public: "In purely financial terms, attempts to make prisons self-sufficient will, and do, fail. Prisoners are drawn from the poorest sectors of the population and even if they are gouged for every penny in prison and hounded for all of their post-release lives by the debts of incarceration, they will never cough up enough money to pay for the overpriced, high-tech island of concrete in which they are kept. The main effect of squeezing funds from prisoners is to justify the gargantuan costs of America's gulag, which grows larger every day" (p. 29).

Between 1990 (91,317) and 1995 (115,592) those incarcerated increased 27 percent nationally (Willing, 1997). Many states have passed tough sentences for youth convicted of violent crimes (Rook and Alexander, 1999; Willing, 1997). The cost of incarceration of youth is playing a more prominent role in local government expenditures. For example, in 1992 the average cost for an incarcerated youth was $33,000 (Kellogg Foundation, 1996). Johnson, Selber, and Lauderdale (1998) summed up quite well the onus of costs on states and the need to find alternative, less costly, and at the same time more humane ways of punishing offenders: "In the last decade, the overburdened criminal justice system has slowly begun to realize that incarceration serves to relieve public concerns about safety. The fiscal burdens of incarceration demand that state officials seek other less costly and more effective preventive responses" (p. 612).

The "correctional-industrial complex" is a term that is increasingly being used by critics of current imprisonment policies. Parenti (1999) calls this prison buildup "a small scale form of Keynesian, public-works-style stimulus." In some communities, the building of prisons is both welcomed and feared by residents, Vermont being a case in point (Browne, 1999; "Where Prison Plans Cast a Pall," 1999). Nevertheless, the economic rewards prisons offer small towns and cities far outweigh the drawbacks:

> Little town and big prison: it is a marriage that has been replicated scores of times in recent years. From Bowling Green, Missouri, to rural Florida, economically battered towns are rolling over for new prisons. Nationally the tab for building penitentiaries averaged about $17 billion annually over the last decade; in 1996 alone contractors broke ground on twenty-six federal and ninety-six state prisons. . . . one report has more than 523,000 full-time employees working in American corrections—more than in any Fortune 500 company except General Motors. In the American countryside punishment is such a big industry that, according to the National Criminal Justice Commission, 5 percent of the growth in rural population between 1980 and 1990 was accounted for by prisoners, captured in cities and exiled to the new carceral arcadia. (Parenti, 1999, p. 213)

Prisons offer potential jobs for residents as well as contracts for food and other supplies. This is particularly welcomed in distressed communities that have experienced an exodus or closing of factories, leaving many residents either under- or unemployed. It is estimated that more than 600,000 prison and jail guards, administrators, service workers, and others have their livelihoods directly tied to prisons, and this group, through unions, makes a powerful lobby for the industry (Mauer, 1999). However, the presence of a prison in a community is not without its critics, particularly those who are concerned about having criminals so close to their homes and fear the impact these institutions will have on property values. Elikann (1996) notes that there is tremendous political gain to be had in a district getting a prison: "In fact, prisons have become such a lucrative job-creating enterprise for communities that politicians now fight hard to bring them into their localities. This prompted one state legislator, whose desk was swamped with requests from various politicians to bring prisons into their locale, to say that prisons have become 'the juiciest pork in the barrel' " (p. 104). The construction of prisons, however, has not resulted in a dramatic decrease in drug use or an increase in the number of jobs for staff of color. Drug use among prisoners is widely understood to be a common phenomenon (Albanese, 1999). The majority of staff in federal prisons are white non-Latinos (66.4 percent), whereas African Americans (20 percent), Latinos (10.2 percent), Asians (1.8 percent), and Native Americans (1.5 percent) account for almost one-third (Bureau of Justice Statistics, 1999b).

Conclusion

The answer regarding where the young men and women of color have gone is partially revealed by the statistics in this chapter. It is clear that every year the number of young people of color in the correctional system grows, whether they are in prison or on probation or parole. Those imprisoned are most likely housed out of the city and in the countryside, far away from their families and communities. Recent efforts at further eroding the rights of the accused (repeal of the *Miranda* decision as an example) does not bode well for undervalued groups in this country (Forero, 1999).

The social work profession must decide if it wishes to play a pivotal role in a system that has historically not attracted social workers. That does not mean that social workers must, in order to work with the correctionally supervised, be directly employed by the correctional system. There are few social service agencies where the correctionally supervised are not part of the system in a variety of ways. Thus, there are opportunities to work with this group in a much more direct manner than social workers have in the past. For example, virtually any kind of work with substance abusers cannot be accomplished without also working with the criminal justice system. The two systems cannot be separated.

Nevertheless, the statistics noted here raise important questions for both the profession and the nation. To what extent can the nation "afford" to have an increasingly large percentage of its population in prison or on probation or parole? How long can the nation turn the other way when presented with the racial disparities within the justice system? At what point will taxpayers, at the federal and state levels, say "enough is enough?" Also, how can communities from which the correctionally supervised come continue to witness a greater and greater share of their own systematically eliminated from being productive members? How will their children adjust in a society where being a single parent can be widely considered a critical "high-risk" factor? In essence, the data are not ambiguous regarding the state of affairs in urban communities of color in the United States.

The enormous costs associated with the criminal justice system were examined from only one perspective in this chapter—prisons. However, the costs of adding judges, prosecutors, probation workers, juries, etc., not to mention building additional courthouses, are not to be dismissed— because of the need to increase taxes. Unfortunately, an increase in taxes is rarely an option at the national, state, and local levels. Consequently, the costs of the criminal justice system very often come at the expense of education, recreation, and social service programs!

This trade-off must be viewed from a zero-sum perspective. Namely, every new prison bed constructed will cost the nation some form of service at the other end—maybe a teacher, an after-school program, sports activities at the town or city level, new computers for a school, or a health aide for someone with disabilities. An understanding of these trade-offs will go a long way toward helping the decisions regarding increased incarceration to be more fairly debated in the nation's corridors of power. The economic costs are staggering, as noted in this chapter. However, the social costs are immeasurable for American society. Social work can play an important role in disseminating this information.

According to the Milton S. Eisenhower Foundation's thirty-year update of the 1969 National Violence Commission report, the nation has adopted a policy toward crime that is and will continue to be doomed to fail:

> There is a new "triumphalism" about crime that is misleading. The triumphalism exaggerates the role of tough sentencing and "zero tolerance" policing and underestimates the role of explanations that may be more important, like the economic boom and the related waning of the crack epidemic. Prisons have become our nation's substitute for effective policies on crime, drugs, mental illness, housing, poverty and employment of the hardest to employ. In a reasonable culture we would not say we had won the war against disease just because we had moved a lot of sick people from their homes to hospital wards. And in a reasonable culture we would not say we have won the war against crime just because we have moved a lot of criminals from the community into prison cells. (Eisenhower Foundation, 1999, pp. iv–v)

3

Substance Abuse and Incarceration

The interrelationship among substance abuse, crime, and incarceration, for both women and men, is undeniable, as noted in the previous chapter. The impact of substance abuse and the nation's response to it clearly is a major generator of the statistics presented in chapter 2. Substance abuse, as a result, warrants closer examination in this book. The subject, however, is complex and controversial, making a "rational" approach to its understanding arduous, if not impossible. The subject of alcohol and other drug abuse is one that has touched virtually every family in this country—some, obviously, more than others. I seriously doubt that any social worker in the profession has not been touched quite closely by this problem.

Increases in incarceration rates in the United States come at a time when there is widespread recognition that crime rates have decreased dramatically. Few areas of the country, and particularly the cities, have not been affected by the decrease in crime rate. However, that decrease has not resulted in a corresponding decrease in rates of incarceration and other forms of correctional supervision. Thus, this enigma needs to be addressed in order to better understand the consequences of incarceration, particularly for people of low income and of color.

According to the Office of National Drug Control Policy (1999), more than 1.5 million people were arrested for drug law violations in 1997, the highest number in the nation's history. More Americans were in prison in 1997 than on active military duty. The dramatic increase in incarceration rates for adult males and females and juveniles is the result of various factors, some of which overlap. However, there is general agreement that drug-related factors have played important roles in the increased rates.

According to the Bureau of Justice (1999i), in 1997, 83 percent of state prisoners and 73 percent of federal prisoners reported they had used drugs at some point in their lives. The same year, 57 percent of state prisoners and 45 percent of federal prisoners said they had used drugs in the month prior to their offense, an increase from 50 percent and 32 percent in a 1991 study (Bureau of Justice Statistics, 1999i). In essence, drugs are a key factor in any effort to better understand crime in the United States.

It is estimated that more than 11,000 deaths annually are due to illicit drug use (Lille-Blanton, 1998). The National Center on Addiction and Substance Abuse (CASA) estimated that of the $38 billion in correctional expenditures in 1996, $30 billion, or 78.9 percent, was spent imprisoning those who had a history of drug and/or alcohol abuse, were using at the time of their crime, were convicted of drug and/or alcohol violations, or perpetrated their crime to obtain money to buy drugs (CASA, 1998). Approximately $27 billion annually is spent at the state and federal levels to fight substance abuse, and it costs society more than $67 billion in costs associated with health care and drug addiction prevention and treatment programs, drug-related crime, and lost wages as a result of lower worker productivity or deaths (Lille-Blanton, 1998). In essence, drugs cost the nation a considerable sum of money in a variety of ways, with criminal justice being a key element. This chapter, as a result, introduces the reader to the relationship between drugs, crime, and incarceration. In addition, particular attention is paid to the extent to which the problem of substance abuse has been addressed in the prison system, since it plays such a prominent role in people being imprisoned to begin with.

The Impact of Substance Abuse on One American City

Substance abuse, like any other social problem, can best be understood, and for that matter, "felt," at the local level. Substance abuse is not restricted to any one geographical setting in this country. However, it has had a particularly severe impact on the nation's cities. In U.S. cities there are an estimated 4,000 African Americans and 2,000 Latinos who were paralyzed in violent incidents between 1987 and 1994, during the peak of the crack epidemic, with New York City witnessing more than its equal share of the casualties (Rohde, 2000). Columbia University's Center for Addiction and Substance Abuse has taken a unique approach toward examining the impact of addiction and substance abuse by focusing on New York City and exploring the multifaceted aspects of this problem (CASA, 1996; the reader is referred to this report for a more detailed examination of the material presented in this section.) CASA's approach focuses on the problem of drugs at the local level and in so doing identifies the social, economic, and political implications of the problem.

It is virtually impossible to accurately place a dollar value on the impact of substance abuse on a city's economy. However, it is possible to calculate the sum within certain spheres. In 1994, substance abuse cost New York City more than $20 billion ($5.1 billion in health care; $4.9 billion in lost productivity; $4.1 billion in criminal justice; $3.5 billion in public and private social services; $1.6 billion in increased insurance, security, and workers' compensation costs; and $835 million in property taxes). Crime-related statistics indicate that drugs resulted in law enforcement devoting $1.8 billion, or 75 percent of its budget, to addressing this problem. Interestingly, only 3.7 percent ($375 million) of the $20 billion specifically went to treat the abuser, and $80 million went to prevent the problem. The $20 billion in 1994 represented 9 percent of the $225 billion gross city product, or a sum greater than the budgets of forty out of fifty states. In essence, substance abuse from an economic perspective can be considered significant. Lost earnings as the result of incarceration due to alcohol- and drug-related crimes (26,800 out of 43,900) cost the city $520 million.

In many ways, it is both easier and more arduous to assess the social impact of substance abuse on the life of a city. Nevertheless, a social perspective on substance abuse presents a very disturbing picture, as is to be expected, putting aside the social consequences of imprisonment. In 1993, 20 percent of all newborns in New York City (27,000 out of 134,000) were exposed to legal or illegal drugs prior to their birth as a result of mothers' use of alcohol, tobacco, and other drugs. Drug- and alcohol-related placements in foster care during 1994 accounted for 77 percent of the overall budget. In 1993, 13,400 (20.6 percent) recorded deaths were the result of alcohol-, drug- or tobacco-related conditions. Among the 1-to-14-year age group, 73 (17 percent) out of 432 deaths were the result of long-term effects of maternal prenatal substance abuse or accidents and homicides involving drugs and alcohol. In 1994, driving while under the influence of alcohol and drugs accounted for close to 50 percent (240 deaths) of car-related deaths and 35 percent of motorcyclists' deaths (170). Twenty-six percent of all pedestrians killed during that year had also been drinking or using drugs, or both.

Substance abuse is estimated to account for 65 percent of all those residing in the city's homeless shelters. Visits to emergency rooms involving alcohol and drugs accounted for 25 percent (800,000) of all visits. In 1994, 1,700 children under the age of 16 years were arrested for drug dealing and possession. It was estimated that there were 490,000 drug abusers in the city, with only 40,000 state-funded treatment slots available. It was also estimated that there were 540,000 alcoholics and problem drinkers, but only 54,000 treatment admissions to sites receiving public funds.

In summary, the CASA study does a commendable job of highlighting the multifaceted nature of substance abuse and its influence on the life of a city and its residents: "The CASA study documents the daily impact of substance abuse on children and families; crime and violence; health and health care; neighborhood life from parks to housing; and the economy, business and taxes. . . . It is filled with numbers, but it cannot quantify the personal tragedy substance abuse and addiction imposes on thousands of New Yorkers or the sinister threat it poses to every child and family" (CASA, 1996, p. 10). Clearly, the impact of substance abuse and addiction reaches into every community and age, racial, ethnic, gender, and income group in a city. However, it has a particularly devastating impact on low-income communities of color, particularly those that are African American and Latino.

The Nation's War on Drugs and Crime

The United States has historically attempted a variety of strategies to deal with substance abuse. The nation's effort to stem the use of drugs through incarceration has had its share of critics because of its failure to reduce substance abuse in this country and its consequences for communities of color. The White House has acknowledged the disproportionate number of men and women of color in the nation's federal, state, and local correctional institutions and has issued a directive to all federal law enforcement agencies to gather data and better define the scope of the problem (Office of the Press Secretary, 1999).

The nation's drug war is an excellent, if sad, example of how periods of intense public concern with particular types of crime can have a profound and lasting impact on government at the national and state levels (Zimring, 1998). In 1996, the vast majority (approximately 71 percent) of wiretaps undertaken at the federal and state level focused on drug enforcement (Maguire and Pastore, 1997). New York City has recently experienced an upturn in its murder rate, and this is the result, according to one noted criminologist, of the continued relationship between drugs and crime: "New York City succeeded in reducing murder . . . by targeting young men who were involved in drug sales, and carried guns as a tool of the trade. But as drug sales waned and moved indoors . . . it has become harder for the police to match those sharp declines" (Flynn, 1999b, p. 29).

As noted in chapter 2, the subject of incarceration of people of color has been cast as a national effort at controlling communities of color through the use of prison, other forms of correctional supervision, and methadone maintenance. Although crack appealed to a narrow range of people, and it essentially "ran its course" in a period of a few years, it nevertheless left its impact on the nation's cities, law enforcement, and criminal justice system (Egan, 1999c). Its impact can best be seen in the rate of imprisonment and prison construction.

The metaphor of "war on drugs" is common in national campaigns for the presidency and is easily embedded in the nation's psyche (Heath, 1998). However, as Reverend Jesse Jackson once stated—"The nation should not declare war on its own citizens." The war on drugs, however,

takes on added meaning if rephrased as a "war on race." Thus, the decla-
ration of war serves to heighten awareness of a national issue, mobilizes
significant national resources to bear on this problem, and signals a political will to win the war at all costs, since a nation does not enter into war
without serious thought concerning the consequences. It is the latter commitment that can prove very troubling, since winning at all costs does not
necessarily mean reducing drug use or drug-related crime, but it does mean
taking a significant number of prisoners of war.

Benjamin and Miller (1991), in the early 1990s, argued that the war
on drugs would only succeed in increasing criminal justice budgets and
imprisoning "non-violent" and "victimless moral" offenders. Such an
approach, needless to say, would not have a significant impact on substance abuse! Currie (1998) states that the increasing use of prisons as
"America's social agency" of first resort for coping with the deepening
problems of society will have disastrous consequences for the country.
Curtis (1992) goes on to argue that antidrug policies have shifted the role
of the federal government from investing in youth and people to con-
taining and punishing them, with incarceration being one of the consequences. Such an approach takes a tremendous amount of resources
from other areas and instead invests them in controlling significantly
larger and larger groups of people, particularly those that are poor and of
color.

Davis (1999) notes that the war on drugs has served to distract the
nation from looking at other major national problems: "Importantly, from
the critical ecology perspective the most destructive aspect of a war is that
the metaphors of war distract us from the realities of class, race and power;
of poverty and disadvantage; of third world poor communities in the
midst of first world prosperity; and of social exclusion and isolation of
young people, minorities, poor families, and other vulnerable populations" (p. 180). The shifting of focus away from social problems such as
the widening gap between rich and poor, homelessness, and inadequate
public education also allows the nation to refuse to acknowledge how all
of these problems are closely interrelated. In addition, it seriously under-
estimates the social and economic costs of these social problems because
they are often treated as if they existed separately from each other. A holistic perspective rather than a narrow viewpoint highlights the challenge
the country faces as we enter the twenty-first century.

Critics of the nation's drug policies are not necessarily restricted to
those that can be labeled "liberals," "radicals," or "academics." The governor of New Mexico, Gary E. Johnson (a Republican), has openly questioned the nation's policies on drugs and incarceration: "He contends that
the costly campaign against drugs has left courts and prisons overwhelmed
with people arrested for possessing only small amounts of drugs. . . . 'We
are spending incredible amounts of our resources on incarceration, law
enforcement, and courts,' he said. 'As an extension of everything I have
done in office, I made a cost-benefit analysis and this one really stinks' "
(Janofsky, 1999, p. 16). Milton Friedman (1998), in turn, has raised con-

cerns about who is imprisoned and has argued about the disproportionate number of imprisoned African Americans: "Can any policy, however high-minded, be moral if it leads to widespread corruption, imprisons so many, has so racist an effect, destroys our inner cities, wreaks havoc on misguided and vulnerable individuals, and brings death and destruction to foreign countries?" (p. 211).

These and other critics of the nation's efforts at addressing substance abuse consistently point out that current policies, particularly those focused on incarceration, are ineffective, seriously undermine the nation's constitution, and are very costly economically and socially. When incarceration is the preferred route to address the nation's drug problems, particularly when it disproportionately affects cities, people of color who are poor, and other low-income groups, it needs to be seriously questioned on moral and economic grounds. Prevention, rehabilitation, and treatment have been relegated to the background in the nation's debate on how best to address crime and substance abuse, raising important questions that need to be answered in the twenty-first century. An emphasis on punishment rather than rehabilitation will have long-term consequences as the nation's prisoners are released back into society at the conclusion of their sentences. Being thrust back into communities without rehabilitation will, in all likelihood, result in reimprisonment, and it will continue a vicious cycle of prison-probation-prison.

Punishment Versus Rehabilitation and Treatment

There are basically two approaches to solving, or addressing, the nation's drug problem. One focuses on punishment, and the other stresses rehabilitation and prevention. Needless to say, severe punishment, rather than rehabilitation and treatment, characterizes the thrust of recent policy decisions concerning the best way of addressing drug addiction and drug-related crime; the result has been more severe punishment and lengthier prison sentences. This statement applies to both juveniles and adults and men as well as women (Gelman and Pollack, 1997). However, it takes on added significance in the case of juveniles if they also happen to be of color, low income, and from urban backgrounds.

Although substance abuse–related causes accounted for a majority of those imprisoned in the United States in the past decade, there are other factors at work. Some are imprisoned (pretrial detention) because they are not able to obtain bail money (Finder, 1999). Such people are detained arbitrarily, not on their willingness to return, but because they lack sufficient funds. Poor and working-class defendants often lack sufficient funds to make bail and as a result can be incarcerated for a year or more before their fate is determined by the court—innocent or guilty. Harris (1995) writes: "I know of a woman with eight children who spent three weeks on Rikers Island, the huge jail compound in New York City, because she couldn't raise $75 for bail. A local charitable group finally heard about her and bailed her out. It costs $56,000 per year to keep a prisoner on Rikers Island, so it cost the city of New York over $3,000 to hold this woman because she didn't have $75. In the meantime, she didn't know what had happened to her eight children, and they didn't know what had happened to her" (p. vii).

A Connecticut study of 150,000 criminal cases found that African American and Latino men paid on average double the bail of white non-Latinos for the same offense, with the disparity increasing to four times in drug cases. Latinas paid on average 197 percent higher than white non-Latinas (Donziger, 1996). Another study in Florida found results similar to those in Connecticut with unemployed African American defendants awaiting trial on "public order" offenses being 300 percent more likely of being kept in prison than white non-Latinos arrested on similar charges (Donziger, 1996).

Although the numbers are still small, the trend is evident. It has been estimated that anywhere from 10 to 25 percent of inmates suffer from some form of mental illness (Gelman and Pollack, 1997). Currie (1998) and Kupers (1999), among others, argue that jails and prisons have become de facto alternatives to current mental health systems throughout the nation. It is estimated that there are more mentally ill in the nation's prisons and jails (200,000) than in state hospitals (61,700). With 3,000 mentally ill inmates, Rikers Island in New York City is considered New York's largest psychiatric facility (Winerip, 1999). A recent class-action lawsuit in New York City charges that the city and its medical provider were releasing inmates who were undergoing mental health treatment without proper provision for follow-up care in the community (Bernstein, 1999a). The lawsuit argues that the city is engaging in "cruel and unusual punishment" by not providing referrals and the means for obtaining medication for those inmates under treatment. A recent estimate by the U.S. Department of Justice put the number of emotionally disturbed inmates at 283,800, or 16 percent of the total prison and jail population (Butterfield, 1999c).

Source Control and Interdiction

The topic of interdiction generally does not receive a great deal of public scrutiny even though it plays a central role in this nation's efforts to curtail drug abuse and the country, as a result, spends billions of dollars on the strategy. Ninety-three percent of the federal government's drug control budget goes for programs concerning source control, interdiction, and law enforcement (Rydell and Everingham, 1994). Interdiction needs to be examined from a multifaceted perspective to better understand it. Bewley-Taylor (1999) argues that the end of the Cold War has thrust drug trafficking into a key role in influencing foreign policy in this country: "The end of the Cold War brought many new challenges for American diplomacy. The familiar contours of superpower confronting gave way to a plurality of diverse and complex transnational concerns. While a wide range of interests vie for predominance, the past decade has seen the illicit drugs trade stake its claim as a significant focus of American foreign policy" (p. 1).

First of all, illegal drug activities generate more than $400 billion (8 percent) in trade around the world (Associated Press, 1997). Interdiction efforts at curtailing production of drugs have generally focused on destroying production of coca (Wren, 1996). In Colombia, officials seized a record 57 metric tons of coca products in 1998, yet that did not result in a net reduction in the processing of cocaine or the exportation of it to the United States (General Accounting Office, 1999). Two years of extensive herbicide spraying did not result in a net reduction of coca cultivation either. In fact, there was a 50 percent increase (General Accounting Office, 1999; Golden, 1999).

Colombia surpassed Peru and Bolivia in 1998 to become the world's largest coca-producing nation, in spite of the United States spending more than $625 million in counternarcotics operations in the country between 1990 and 1998 (General Accounting Office, 1999). New methods such as creating "black cocaine" have emerged in an effort to stop government seizures. Black cocaine hinders detection because it has no smell and does not react when subjected to the usual chemical tests (General Accounting Office, 1999). Drug suppliers simply overproduce for their markets, expecting a percentage of the drugs to be lost due to government seizures of various kinds (Rydell and Everingham, 1994). Sharpe and Bertram (1997) note that a significant increase in efficiency in intercepting cocaine would not seriously affect the price of cocaine in the United States: "If US interdiction programs were to seize 50 percent of all cocaine shipped from Colombia—an impossibly high figure—this would add less than 3 percent to the retail price of cocaine in this country. And even the smuggling costs—from Colombia to the mainland United States—account for less than 5 percent of the retail price" (p. E2).

Interdiction efforts are estimated to intercept 10 to 15 percent of the heroin and 30 percent of the cocaine entering the United States (Associated Press, 1997). Further, it is estimated that at least a 75 percent reduction in drug trafficking would be necessary in order to make a sufficient impact to reduce supply. It will require either $34 million to be spent on drug treatment or $783 million (twenty times that of treatment) to be spent on interdiction to seriously reduce cocaine consumption in the United States, for example (Rydell and Everingham, 1994).

Substance Abuse–Related Offenses

As already indicated, substance abuse–related offenses are the prime factors for the increase in incarceration rates, and have been so for an extended period (Harlow, 1991). There is very little dispute concerning the close association between violence and substance abuse, particularly the use of crack. As a result of that relationship, it becomes artificial to treat the two social problems (drugs and crime) separately. It is important to pause and systematically examine the type of crime that usually results in incarceration. The relationship between drugs and crime can occur in a variety of ways such as possession, manufacture, distribution, stealing to obtain money to purchase drugs, and violence toward rival distributors (ONDCP, 1998). Later in this chapter, I focus specifically on who is abusing drugs. However, examination of drug-related crime reveals important and distinctive patterns regarding ethnicity/race and gender.

State-based estimates of inmates in need of substance abuse treatment have found that anywhere from 70 to 85 percent are in need of some form of treatment (Bureau of Justice Statistics, 1999i; Donnelly, 2000a; Lipton, 1995). However, only 13 percent received any kind of drug treatment in 1996 (ONDCP, 1998). Approximately 10 to 20 percent of inmates in federal prisons participated in drug treatment programs even though inmates in need of treatment accounted for approximately 60 percent of the prison population in 1997 (ONDCP, 1998).

National Legislation

Efforts at the national and state levels to address the social problems related to substance abuse have resulted in the passage of various types of legislation addressing those who use drugs. Public fears pertaining to the nation's drug problem, helped by the media, have played an instrumental role in supply-versus-demand–related policies (Egan, 1999b; Sasson, 1995). The second half of the 1980s witnessed the widespread use of crack cocaine and heightened the strong relationship between drugs and crime, particularly random acts of violence, gang activities, and shootings, in the public's mind (Lipton, 1995). "Get tough" policies have resulted in stricter sentencing and legislative mandates that severely punish criminals who are repeat offenders, regardless of the nature of their crimes. Gelman and Pollack (1997) attribute the public's and officials' "get tough" response to the impact crack cocaine had on the public's image of drugs: "The shift in attitude toward crime is partly a function of the shift in the types and manner of crimes being committed. Since the mid-1980s, there has been a rise in the use of crack cocaine and an attendant increase in crime. . . . The increase in crime triggered an intensified debate between those advocating for more prisons and those emphasizing more treatment availability" (p. 66).

A recent federal report noted that 59 percent of all male and 68 percent of all female inmates in federal prisons were there as a result of a drug offense (Bureau of Justice Statistics, 1998). During 1995–1996, the federal prison population grew by more than 5 percent (87,996 to 92,672), with the greatest growth attributed to drug offenders (2,604 out of 4,676), or 55.7 percent of the total increase (Bureau of Justice Statistics, 1998c). Rosenthal (1998) argues that the vast majority of women in prison, regardless of crime conviction, have some form of serious drug problem, with estimates ranging from 60 to 80 percent.

The percentage of sentenced prisoners who were drug offenders has increased dramatically over the last three decades: 1970, 16.3 percent; 1975, 26.7 percent; 1980, 24.9 percent; 1985, 34.3 percent; 1990, 52.3 percent; 1995, 60.6 percent (Bureau of Justice Statistics, 1999b). In sheer numbers, an estimated 227,400 inmates were in state prisons in 1998 because of drug offenses (Bureau of Justice Statistics, 1999c). Between 1990 and 1997, women serving time for drug offenses nearly doubled, while the number of males incarcerated for drug offenses increased by 48 percent (Bureau of Justice Statistics, 1999c).

Drug courts seek to divert nonviolent substance abusers from prison and place them into intensive court-supervised treatment. Drug courts, for example, provide a viable alternative to prison for pregnant substance abusers. Nevertheless, drug courts, although increasing in popularity, have not managed to stem the number of incarcerations of both men and women in the nation's prisons.

Mandatory Minimum Sentencing

Mandatory sentencing can take various forms (CASA, 1998): it can (1) mandate that certain types of crimes require prison sentences, (2) require that a minimum amount of a sentence be served before parole is a possibility, and (3) necessitate that a "determinate" sentence be served without the offender being eligible for release or probation. The latter type of mandatory sentence will be served regardless of whether an inmate enters treatment, if warranted, or makes any effort to prepare himself or herself for life in society.

Rossi and Berk (1997), in their analysis of sentencing guidelines written by the U.S. Sentencing Commission for the federal courts, reveal that the commission was able to match prescribed punishments closely to public consensus on most crimes with one notable exception. The guidelines were much more severe regarding drug trafficking. An analysis by the federal government of factors that affect sentencing determinations under the federal sentencing guidelines found that race plays the most profound role in sentencing for drug trafficking when compared with sentencing for other criminal offenses (Bureau of Justice Statistics, 1993).

Critics of mandatory minimum sentences also have argued that these types of sentences have not reduced sentencing discrepancy but have instead transferred this power from judges to prosecutors (Caulkins, Rydell, Schwabe, and Chies, 1997). Prosecutors have the discretion of deciding on the charges to be brought in court, negotiating reductions in charges, and accepting a plea bargain. If someone is brought up on charges of drug trafficking who is a low-level offender and cannot provide information that would be helpful to prosecutors seeking high-level drug dealers (information that could be traded for a lighter or suspended sentence), he or she may very well serve time in prison. The Rand Corporation (Caulkins et al., 1997) concluded that extending sentences to mandatory minimum lengths would reduce cocaine consumption less than would a million dollars allocated to the pre-mandatory-minimum mix of arrests, prosecution, and sentencing. However, neither would reduce cocaine use or cocaine-related crime as much as the same sum of money spent on heavy cocaine users.

Drugs combined with mandatory sentencing have not only served to increase the number of persons entering prison but also lengthened their sentence, further increasing the inmate population (Bureau of Justice Statistics, 1999f; Cloud, 1999; Stodghill, 1999; Sentencing Project, 1998b). Sentencing time for drug offenses more than doubled between 1986 and 1997, increasing from an average of 20.4 months to 42.5 months served (Bureau of Justice Statistics, 1999f). Political motivations are widely acknowledged to be the prime reasons behind passage of legislation on minimum sentencing (Elikann, 1996).

Congress's passage of the Violent Crime Control and Law Enforcement Act of 1994 has put pressure on the criminal justice system to increase sentences and has led to mandated minimum sentences (Bureau of Justice Statistics, 1999b). The Crime Act provides states with economic incentives to build or expand correctional facilities. However, in order to obtain these funds, states are required to have individuals convicted of a "Part 1" violent crime serve not less than 85 percent of the prison sentence. Needless to say, states have increased the rate of incarceration: "As a result of truth-in-sentencing practices, the State prison population is expected to increase through the incarceration of more offenders for longer periods of time. . . . On average, between 1990 and 1997 the prison population grew by 7% annually. . . . Drug offenders comprised 19% of the growth" (Bureau of Justice Statistics, 1999b, pp. 3–4).

Mandatory minimum sentences for nonviolent drug crimes, for example, have resulted in situations where someone convicted of a drug crime can receive a sentence much more severe than someone convicted of sexual abuse (Cloud, 1999; Ranalli, 1999; Staples, 1999). Discrepancies do exist within the type of drug used, however. Mandatory minimum sentences for use of crack cocaine are currently one hundred times more severe than those for use of powdered cocaine, and that has a great impact on youth of color who have a higher likelihood of using crack cocaine (Cloud, 1999).

The racial disparity in sentencing between those convicted of possessing cocaine (5 grams) and those possessing crack cocaine (5 grams) is considerable: "This . . . law is problematic for two reasons: First, since crack is more prevalent in black, inner-city neighborhoods, the law has fostered a perception of racial injustice in our criminal justice system. In fact, 90 percent of those convicted on crack cocaine are African-American. Second, harsher penalties for crack possession over powder have resulted in long incarceration levels for low-level crack dealers instead of a greater focus on the apprehension of middle and large scale movers of powder cocaine" (ONDCP, 1999, p. 68).

Before the passage of mandatory minimum sentences for crack

cocaine in 1986, the average federal drug offense sentence for African Americans was 11 percent longer than that of their white, non-Latino counterparts. However, four years later, following implementation of minimum sentencing, the average federal drug-related sentence had increased to 49 percent longer for African Americans than for white non-Latinos (Meierhoefer, 1992).

It is estimated that 55 percent of all federal drug defendants are what are considered "low-level" offenders ("mules" or street sellers), with 11 percent being classified as high-level crack dealers. Further, only 5.5 percent of federal crack defendants are considered high-level crack dealers (U.S. Sentencing Commission, 1995). Low-level crack dealers and first-time offenders sentenced for trafficking in crack cocaine receive an average sentence of ten years and six months, which compares with an average sentence of twelve years and nine months for someone convicted of murder or manslaughter (U.S. Sentencing Commission, 1995). Crack cocaine is the only drug for which the first offense of possession (5 grams or more) can result in a five-year federal mandatory minimum sentence (U.S. Sentencing Commission, 1995). Possession of a similar amount of cocaine, on the other hand, is a misdemeanor and punishable by a maximum of one year in prison. Haney and Zimbardo (1998) reflect on the consequences of harsher sentencing guidelines: "A disproportionate number of young Black and Hispanic men are likely to be imprisoned for life under scenarios in which they are guilty of little more than a history of untreated addiction and several prior drug-related offenses" (p. 718).

Gender-related disparities have surfaced and are a focus of concern among critics of mandatory sentencing (Robertson, 1997; Rigert, 1997a, 1997b). As noted in other sections of this book, women, particularly those of color, have borne a disproportionate burden in the sentencing process when drugs were involved. The percentage of women of color imprisoned due to drug convictions varies from state to state. In New York 91 percent of women of color who are sentenced to prison are incarcerated as a result of drugs, yet they represent 32 percent of the state's population. In California 54 percent of incarcerated women of color are there for drug offenses, yet they represent 38 percent of the state's population. In Minnesota, the respective numbers are 27 percent compared with 5 percent (Mauer, Potler, and Wolf, 1999).

District attorneys very often look for ways of obtaining information that will lead to "significant" arrests and prosecutions. Women, because of their relationships with a significant other, may get involved in the drug business. However, upon arrest they are expected to provide information on their significant others and other important drug dealers. If they refuse to cooperate with prosecutors, or they simply do not have access to valuable information on drug dealers, then they cannot plea-bargain for lighter sentences.

The case of Phillippi and Pebbles in Minnesota highlights the disparity in sentencing:

Jan Phillippi—mother of two, onetime office manager and sometime cleaning woman in St. Paul—saw a chance to make $1,000
a trip carrying packages from a high-living lawyer she had met
in a bar, according to her trial testimony. The packages contained
cocaine, and she was caught in a government trap. She also had
been buying cocaine on her own. St. Paul lawyer Larry Pebbles
was the leader of a $25 million cocaine ring. The longtime drug
dealer drove Rolls-Royces, traveled the world and distributed
cocaine in five states, using female couriers to avoid detection.
But one of them—a mother of two—turned on him and brought
about his arrest. The difference between Phillippi and Pebbles is
that she would not cooperate with the government and thus
received a 10-year sentence. She recently was released after serving almost nine years. Pebbles, on the other hand, quickly agreed
to help the government. For four years, while living in county
jails, he was available for government duty. He testified in a Ken-
tucky case, assisted in gathering wiretap evidence and testified
against one of his own major distributors, a stockbroker. His
cooperation won favor from federal prosecutors and enabled him
to escape a mandatory minimum sentence. (Rigert, 1997a, p. 11)

Ironically, men are often in a more strategic position and are more inclined
to offer information of value to prosecutors, and they obtain a lighter
sentence as a result of charges being reduced. The impact of imprisoning
women, as is noted in chapter 4, "The Impact of Correctional Supervision:
A Multifaceted Perspective," is far greater because very often they are also
mothers.

Forfeitures of Property

Forfeitures of property have been used in the last decade as a strategy to
punish drug dealers and to send a message to those seeking financial gains
from drug-related business. The popular media have been quick to televise
stories of forfeitures involving mansions, sports cars, boats, airplanes, and
other property. This property is then auctioned to the general public. These
stories, in turn, have served to inform the public that drug dealers, in this
case high-level ones, will not be able to keep the items purchased through
illegal businesses involving drugs.

In 1994 federal forfeitures totaled almost $730 million (Heilbroner,
1994). Forfeiture can be legally used even when there is insufficient evidence to make a criminal case. This law, as a result, has dramatically
changed the function of law enforcement because government, to further
finance drug-curtailment operations, can use the money generated from
the sale of property seized. Abuses, however, are inevitable when budgets,
and careers, are dependent on how much money can be generated by
forfeitures (Blumenson and Wilson, 1998). One study found that during

a ten-month period, 80 percent of the people who had property forfeited were never charged with a crime (Schneider and Flaherty, 1991).

Juveniles Waived to Adult Correctional System

As already noted in chapter 2, there is a trend in the correctional system to treat juveniles as adults (waivers): "Data, when partitioned by race and offense, lends support to the contention . . . that we are currently operating under a 'get-tough' philosophy regarding delinquent behavior by minority youth. In fact, when it comes to minority youth who are charged with drug offenses, we are headed rapidly toward treating them as adult criminals" (McNeece, 1997, p. 35). In examining 1990 data on dispositions for 17-year-old males charged with drug offenses, youth of color were more than three times more likely (78.6 percent versus 21.4 percent) than white, non-Latino youth to be waived to adult courts (McNeece, 1997).

There has been an increase in legislation at the state level making it easier for youth to be tried as adults. Between 1992 and 1995, forty-eight states passed legislation facilitating this process, with an estimated 200,000 youth prosecuted in adult courts per year (Elikann, 1999). Some of the legislative changes have lowered the age of a child to be tried and sentenced in an adult court. Elikann's (1999) examination of this factor noted that six states (Illinois, Mississippi, New Hampshire, New York, North Carolina, and Wyoming) have a minimum age of 13 before a child can be tried in an adult court. In three states (Colorado, Missouri, and Montana), the age limit is 12. Three states (Indiana, South Dakota, and Vermont) allow a child as young as 10 years old to be tried in adult court. In twenty states, there is no minimum age limit for exclusion from adult court. Youth of color had a higher likelihood (1.9 percent versus 1.2 for white, non-Latino youth) of being waived to adult court, and African American youth were more likely to have been waived for drug offenses.

Alcohol-Related Crime

The role of alcohol in crime has generally escaped public scrutiny, even though its impact can be considered significant (Shine and Mauer, 1993). Some critics of current policies argue that alcohol and drinking while driving is primarily associated with white males, raising serious questions of race and class (Shine and Mauer, 1993). Alcohol, for example, is more closely associated with crimes of violence committed by inmates. Alcohol is more likely to be associated with murder, assault, rape, and abuse (spouse and child) than any other illicit drug. Two-thirds of victims who were assaulted by a significant other (spouse, former spouse, boy- or girlfriend) reported alcohol to have been a factor (Bureau of Justice Statistics, 1998e). In fact, almost three million violent crimes occur each year where a victim perceives the offender to have been drinking at the time of the assault (Bureau of Justice Statistics, 1999e).

The subject of drunken driving, or driving under the influence, has received national attention in this country. Organizations such as Mothers Against Drunk Driving (MADD) and Students Against Destructive Decisions (SADD) have been very effective advocates at the state level making sure that sentencing related to drunken driving is taken seriously by the local courts. In 1996 there were 17,126 alcohol-related traffic deaths, which accounted for almost 41 percent of all traffic fatalities during that year, a 29 percent (24,000 deaths) reduction from that of ten years earlier (Bureau of Justice Statistics, 1998e). Nevertheless, the number of alcohol-related fatalities in 1996 is still considerable. Underage drinking, for example, results in costs of more than $8 billion annually and is considered the largest youth drug problem, killing 6.5 times more young people than all other illicit drugs combined (MADD, 1999).

Correctional supervision involvement as a result of drunken driving offenses has increased dramatically over the past decade from 270,000 cases in 1986 to 513,000 in 1997 (Molotsky, 1999). Incarceration related to drunken driving offenses generally falls to local jails, with the sentencing reflecting the "low" severity of the crime. State prisons, in turn, have received an increased number of prisoners due to crimes resulting from driving while under the influence. In 1997 convictions resulted in 454,500 on probation, 41,100 imprisoned in local jails, and 17,000 incarcerated in state prisons (Yost, 1999). Although the rate of arrests fell from 1,124 per 100,000 licensed drivers in 1986 to 809 in 1997, the consequences of those arrests have resulted in a greater likelihood of imprisonment or probation (Bureau of Justice Statistics, 1999f; Molotsky, 1999). For every 1,000 drunken driving arrests in 1997, 347 were jailed or on probation. This represents a steep increase from 151 in 1986 (Yost, 1999). The decrease in the number of arrests may be partially explained by the ages of licensed drivers. In 1997 there were more licensed drivers aged 35 to 54 than in 1986.

The lack of national attention to the role of alcohol in crime may be the result of an interplay of several factors. First, alcohol is a "legal" drug in this society. As a result, the alcohol industry wields a tremendous amount of influence in the United States through contributions to political campaigns, scholarship funds, and other causes; advertising; and tax dollars generated through the sale of its product. Although the Bureau of Justice does not report alcohol-related crime statistics according to race, I believe that most of the arrests related to alcohol may involve white, non-Latino males, and they do not capture the public's attention and ire.

Drugs, Crime, and Incarceration of People of Color

Drug involvement must be viewed from the perspectives of personal consumption (use) and distribution and sale (Moon, Thompson, and Bennett, 1993). The typical drug user in the United States is white, male, in his twenties, and lives in the suburbs (Staples, 1999). A 1992 series of articles published in the *Hartford Courant* reported that 70 percent of the drug-addicted prostitutes in the series were white, much to the dismay of the general readership (Staples, 1999). Racial profiling as a practice is well understood in most of the nation's cities. Law enforcement in the states of Maryland and New Jersey, for example, stops African American motorists five times as often as white motorists. The practice is often justified by the argument that it leads to valid arrests; yet it exempts from scrutiny white drug users and traffickers.

Nevertheless, there is little dispute that drugs have played an important role in the growing presence of African Americans in the nation's prisons: "Between 1980 and 1990 the proportion of drug offenders among those admitted to federal prisons in the U.S. rose from 22 percent to 40 percent, while over the same period the proportion of blacks among those arrested nationwide for drug offenses grew from 24 to 41 percent, and the percentage of blacks among persons admitted to state and federal prisons rose from 39 to 53 percent" (Loury, 1996, p. 23). In 1996, 37 percent of African American offenders, 40 percent of Latinos, and 39 percent of females admitted to prison had committed a drug offense—African Americans and Latinos were almost two hundred times more likely than white non-Latinos to be incarcerated for a drug offense (Bureau of Justice Statistics, 1999b).

Incarceration, not surprisingly to human services providers, does not have a dramatic effect on drug markets in low-income urban communities of color. Low-level drug dealers are routinely replaced upon their imprisonment (Blumstein, 1995; Curtis et al., 1994; Egan, 1999b). There seems to be an ever-expanding labor supply to fill the voids left by arrests.

The violence created by crack cocaine during the 1980s hit large cities across the United States particularly hard. Small and midsize cities did not feel the same effect of crack until the late 1990s (Inciardi, Pottieger, and Lockwood, 1993; Lipton, 1995; Mieckowki, 1990). Nevertheless, they too have since experienced similar tragedies and devastation, particularly murder (Janofsky, 1998). Publicity generated by increases in murder rates resulting from drug wars, youth killings related to crack, and mothers addicted to crack has created an atmosphere of zero tolerance of drugs and the crimes associated with addiction (Donnelly, 2000a).

The increase in the number of women imprisoned, as with their male counterparts, has been due to drug offenses. Women prisoners, when compared with men, are more likely to have used drugs (cocaine and heroin) in the month prior to their arrest, daily, and at the time they committed the crime that led to imprisonment (Moon, Thompson, and Bennett, 1993). There is, as a result, a tremendous need for women inmates to receive treatment (Kassebaum, 1999). According to the U.S. Department of Justice (1994), drug offenses accounted for 68 percent of all offenses committed by women, compared with 59 percent for men. Ironically, women may receive longer prison sentences than the drug-dealing men they are in a relationship with (Stodghill, 1999). In 1991 approximately 33 percent of women in prisons were there as a result of a drug offense, an increase from 10 percent in 1979 (Donziger, 1996).

There are indications that women are receiving more severe sentences than male counterparts arrested for the same offense: "A rise in the number of arrests of women would be a fairly reliable indicator that crime by women is increasing. If arrests rise but imprisonment rates rise even faster, then it suggests that women offenders are being treated more harshly and/ or being given longer sentences. This is precisely what is happening" (Donziger, 1996, pp. 148–49). Between 1984 and 1993, women in prison almost doubled (181 percent), but the number of arrests only increased by 37 percent (Donziger, 1996). This does not suggest a female crime wave!

California, as noted in chapter 2, has been among the leaders in the nation in the number of offenders imprisoned. Many of those offenders have been men and women of color. Currie (1998), in examining the composition of the California prison system, notes the disproportionate number of men of color who are imprisoned: "In California today, four times as many black men are 'enrolled' in state prison as are enrolled in public colleges and universities. More than anything else, it is the war on drugs that has caused this dramatic increase: between 1985 and 1995, the number of black state prison inmates sentenced for drug offenses rose by more than 700 percent. Less discussed but even more startling is the enormous increase in the number of Hispanic prisoners, which has more than quintupled since 1980 alone" (pp. 13–14).

There is little debate in this country that people of color bear a disproportionate burden in current national efforts to fight crime and substance abuse (Gilbert, 1999). African Americans, for example, constitute approximately 13 percent of the nation's monthly drug users, yet they account for 75 percent of the group imprisoned for drug offenses. This disparity becomes even more glaring when examined at the local level. In Baltimore in 1991, of the 12,956 arrests made for drug offenses, 11,107 (85.7 percent) were of African Americans and 13 were of white non-Latinos. Of those 11,107 African Americans, 1,304 were arrested for drug sales (Miller, 1992).

Deaths resulting from drug use also fall disproportionately on people of color. African Americans, for example, have the highest rates of death attributed to drug use with 8.3 per 100,000 deaths in 1997, compared with white non-Latinos with 5.8 per 100,000 (Donnelly, 2000b). A comment by the president of Common Sense for Drug Policy, a group supporting drug abuse treatment, highlights the racism and classism in U.S. policies: " 'It's never focused on by the drug czar's office or by the media. The underclass, the black and brown people, don't get the focus they deserve. If you had 15,000 deaths every year for five years among middle-class white people, there would be an outcry' " (Donnelly, 2000b, p. 23)

Mauer (1999) makes an important observation when comparing the problem of substance abuse in middle-class and low-income families. Middle-class families recognize substance abuse as a problem and do not hesitate to find the best treatment program available with the aid of their health insurer. However, the outcome is significantly different for low-income families of color: "In contrast, for nearly two decades the nation has been engaged in a very different 'war on drugs' to respond to drug abuse and its associated ills among low-income and minority families. Treatment programs are likely to be in short supply, so the problem of abuse is much more likely to fester and eventually result in actions that will define it as a criminal justice problem" (Mauer, 1999, p. 7).

Lack of Availability of Substance Abuse Treatment

Although data indicate that offenders have a need for substance abuse treatment, barriers to such treatment persist: (1) treatment is perceived by prison officials as an opportunity and not a punishment; (2) the criminal justice offender is often unwanted in the treatment system; and (3) volunteers are widely considered to be more motivated than offenders (Taxman, 1998). These barriers, unfortunately, have been particularly strong within the criminal justice system and have seriously limited the potential of substance abuse treatment for those who are imprisoned on drug offenses (Feucht and Keyser, 1999).

Ironically, drugs are widely recognized as one of the primary reasons for the commission of crimes: "Legislators' punitive responses to drug abuse, furthermore, created new issues for courts and prison systems during the 1980s. At the beginning of the decade, violent crime accounted for 48.2 percent of new commitments to state prisons, compared with only 6.8 percent for drug crime. But by 1992 the figure for drug offenders had more than quadrupled to 30.5 percent, exceeding the 28.5 percent figure for prisoners convicted of violent crimes" (Anderson, 1998a, p. 70). Consequently, the need for substance abuse treatment in prisons and community programs that are alternatives to prisons takes on greater prominence. However, it is estimated that less than 15 percent of inmates receive some form of treatment, and most of those interventions fall into the categories of self-help groups and drug/alcohol abuse education (Taxman, 1998).

The use of methadone maintenance as a treatment intervention has a long history in the treatment field. Its use to treat heroin addiction has been widely considered to be very successful. Methadone maintenance does have its share of critics because of its substitution of one drug for another, and its use in prisons is considered rare: "Methadone maintenance programs are rare in prisons and jails, and their use in these settings [are] much more controversial than in the country. Few corrections officials are willing to make a narcotic drug available to inmates. In addition, the medical supervision necessary to administer a methadone program makes it more expensive" (CASA, 1998, p. 129). Thus, a very successful treatment method, albeit controversial, is widely ignored in prisons.

The economic benefits of turning an incarcerated substance abuser into a productive member of society are remarkable. Treatment is considered to be a viable intervention in addressing drug use and criminal behavior among the correctionally supervised (Taxman, 1998). Interestingly, contrary to popular belief, offenders who receive treatment have a higher success rate of staying out of trouble with the law when compared with those offenders who do not participate in treatment programs (Taxman, 1998). One study reported that provision of drug treatment for inmates, when combined with job training, education, and health care, would cost approximately $6,500 per inmate in the first year. However, the economic benefits, not to mention the social benefits, would result in a financial benefit of $68,800 per inmate in the first year after completion of treatment (CASA, 1998).

However, treatment in prison is not readily available (CASA, 1998; Taxman, 1998). The number of inmates receiving residential substance abuse treatment increased from 1,236 in 1991 to 10,006 in 1998 (ONDCP, 1999). In 1998 approximately 34,000 federal inmates received drug treatment services. From 1994 to 1998 the number of prisons offering residential treatment increased from thirty-two to forty-two (ONDCP, 1999). However, these increases have not kept up with a demand that estimates the number of arrestees at more than two million per year. Ironically, the inability of "supply" to meet "demand" is typical of this nation's goal when it comes to interdiction—preventing drugs from entering the country. However, in the case of treatment, that goal is simply irrelevant. It does not take an astute policymaker to realize that if substance abuse is the primary reason someone commits a crime and is incarcerated, and that if the abuse is not treated while in prison, then most likely he or she will return to abusing drugs upon release. The cycle of abusing drugs, crime, incarceration, release, and re-abusing drugs will occur again and again. It is only through a concerted and therapeutic approach to treating substance abuse that this cycle has any chance of being broken (Donnelly and Chacon, 2000).

In 1992, there were 945,000 individuals in specialty substance abuse treatment programs in the United States, or 432 per 100,000 of the general population 12 years of age or older. However, only 3.2 percent of those people were getting help in correctional facilities: "Oddly enough, although drug offenders had become much more prevalent as prison inmates since the late 1980s, in 1980 correctional facilities accounted for a higher share—4.8 percent—of the drug and alcohol treatment clients, compared to only 3.2 percent twelve years later, meaning that prison-based drug treatment had fallen behind the expansion of other types of treatment" (Christianson, 1998, p. 289). Drug treatment slots have declined by over 50 percent since the early 1990s (Bureau of Justice Statistics, 1999i; DiMascio, 1995; Schlosser, 1998).

Lack of treatment increases the likelihood of recidivism: "Incarcerating offenders without treating underlying substance abuse problems simply defers the time when they are released back into our communities to start harming themselves and the larger society. Between 60 to 75 percent of untreated parolees with histories of cocaine and/or heroin use reportedly return to those drugs within three months of release" (ONDCP, 1999, p. 63). Lipton (1995), in a review of the research and literature, found that drug treatment in prison does work, although its effectiveness may vary according to modality and setting. Why, then, isn't treatment made more available as a means of reducing recidivism? Lipton writes:

> It is evident, however, that senior State-level correctional executives have another overriding concern: ensuring adequate space to house inmates. Their budgets reflect that priority: additional space takes priority over rehabilitation programs. . . . Some prison administrators believe that prison-based treatment programs make it difficult to manage inmate housing. Programs occur when a facility is overcrowded and, in an attempt to separate program residents from general population inmates, a separate housing unit has been dedicated to a treatment program. This sometimes leads to filling unused treatment space with inappropriate inmates. (p. 11)

Lipton goes on to note the role of the legislature in the decision-making process: "Legislators, as well as correctional authorities, are often skeptical about the effectiveness of correctional treatment and reluctant to spend tax dollars on efforts that net no votes and are likely, in their minds, to produce little change in behavior" (p. 11).

A Bureau of Prisons study of drug treatment outcomes found that inmates who successfully completed a residential drug treatment program were less likely (3.3 percent) to be rearrested in the first six months after release, compared with 12.1 percent of inmates who did not receive treatment. Those who received treatment were also less likely (12.1 percent) to use drugs in the first six months after release compared with those (36.7 percent) who did not receive treatment (ONDCP, 1998). The use of drug courts, established specifically to address the increase in drug-related arrests, have shown promising results. Drug courts exist in thirty-eight states, the District of Columbia, and Puerto Rico (ONDCP, 1998). Further, drug courts have shown they can save taxpayers money in the process.

I believe that two editorials, one appearing in the *San Jose Mercury News* and the other in the *Chicago Tribune*, capture the dilemmas facing this country regarding how best to address substance abuse–related crime:

> Despite study after study showing the societal savings of drug treatment, Congress would rather spend money on new high-speed patrol boats and high-tech surveillance equipment than on new treatment facilitates and drug courts. If it's common knowledge that treatment saves money, why does California spend more than $4 billion to catch, prosecute and incarcerate substance abusers and just $400 million to treat them? Because lawmakers are afraid of looking soft on crime if they divert money from prisons to treatment beds. It would take a bold move for the governor and the Legislature to divert money from prisons and law enforcement to drug and alcohol treatment. . . . Perhaps if

the fear of crime relaxes its stranglehold on the public, we will be able to move toward a more rational approach to the drug war. ("Drug War Is Failing," 1998, p. 25)

Virtually all credible research on addiction shows treatment programs are the most effective antidote to drug and alcohol abuse. Likewise, study after study has shown that our criminal justice system places entirely too much emphasis on the capture, trial and incarceration of minor drug offenders . . . incredibly, state and federal funding for [treatment] . . . has been dwindling—penny-wise, pound-foolish budgetary choice if ever there was one. Treatment is no panacea. It's not cheap, and readdiction rates are discouragingly high. But it's the best anti-drug weapon society has, and the courts are wise to make greater use of it. ("Treatment, Not Jail," 1998, p. 15)

Grassroots Responses to Drug-Related Incarceration

Grassroots efforts to advocate for change in the nation's prison systems or assist prisoners vary in focus and the nature of the services provided. However, with some notable exceptions, such efforts have been undertaken on very small budgets and are generally the work of one or more individuals who are essentially volunteering their efforts for this cause. Further, social workers do not play prominent parts in these initiatives.

Several national organizations have sprung up to address the issues related to incarceration due to substance abuse. The Sentencing Project has undertaken numerous research projects and actively lobbied to bring about changes in sentencing. Another such organization, the November Coalition (1999), typifies the approach toward incarceration:

We are a growing body of citizens whose lives have been gravely affected by our government's present drug policy. Our goal is to make our voice heard, expose the folly of America's War on Drugs and demand change in current policy. . . . We see the drug war as the primary reason for the exploding prison population with its attendant societal and monetary toll and these costs are too high: there are currently 1.7 million Americans behind bars in this country, a rate that is seven times that of Europe, and these monstrous incarceration rates, and the results on marriages and families is a national disgrace. The war on drugs promotes violence and social instability. There are now millions of "drug orphans" with one or both parents in prison. (p. 1)

Conclusion

This chapter has painted a picture difficult to imagine in a country that professes to be the world's leading democracy. A national effort to curtail substance abuse has resulted in a national effort to incarcerate and punish drug abusers. Treatment, as a result, is considered "soft" and not to serve as a deterrent to substance abuse and crime, even though the evidence and economic savings indicate otherwise (Lille-Blanton, 1998). The issues related to substance abuse and the criminal justice system can easily be framed in terms of class, race, and gender. There is clearly no social service system that is not affected by this nation's substance abuse policies.

At a national law enforcement conference General Barry R. McCaffrey, the White House director of national drug policy, publicly acknowledged that the nation's law enforcement strategy of incarcerating substance abusers has failed: "General McCaffrey told them that the present criminal justice system was a 'disaster' that had put thousands of drug offenders behind bars without treating the addictions that had put them there. . . . Refining an argument that he has been advancing for months, General McCaffrey said an estimated 50 percent to 85 percent of the 1.8 million inmates in American prisons and jails were there fundamentally because of compulsive use of psychoactive drugs or alcohol" (Wren, 1999, p. A20). General McCaffrey noted at the same conference that the country's prison system is costing the nation $38 billion a year to operate and unless the problem is addressed, the cost will continue to escalate and the number of prisons will exceed two million in the very near future.

Some critics also argue that "nothing works." However, that myth can easily be dispelled by research studies: "The generalized belief that nothing works has been a major factor in the reluctance of many policy makers to support prison-based treatment. . . . The current reemphasis on providing drug abuse treatment in prisons and jails appears to be anchored in the need to do something about the large numbers of drug abusers who are incarcerated. The emphasis is also driven by recent research findings that reveal the effectiveness of drug abuse treatment" (Lipton, 1995, p. 15–16). Nevertheless, current efforts to provide drug treatment in prison can probably best be categorized as "too little" and "too late." A substantial impact on substance abuse and incarceration cannot be achieved without treatment, not to mention probation.

The impact of the U.S. war on drugs and crime has fallen disproportionately on youth and adults of color from the nation's cities, large and small. Yet the country's drug problem shows no evidence of abating. In essence, the nation's efforts at addressing this social problem have failed by everyone's account. On the other hand, studies have shown that every dollar invested in substance abuse treatment saves taxpayers $7.46 in societal costs (Rydell and Everingham, 1994). Further, the addition of domestic law enforcement efforts results in costs that are fifteen times as much as those of treatment in order to achieve the same reduction in societal costs (Rydell and Everingham, 1994). These resources can no doubt be put to better and more humane use through the funding of treatment on demand.

Some critics argue that more resources must be allocated to stop the supply of drugs before they enter U.S. shores. Drugs, in turn, can only be restricted through increased use of incarceration and an emphasis on punishment rather than treatment and rehabilitation. Those who argue against these policies do so by pointing to the continued demand for drugs in the United States and the social injustice of incarceration and mandatory sentencing at the expense of emphasizing prevention and treatment. One U.S. Department of Justice (1994) study of recidivism found that the amount of time inmates serve in prison does not affect the likelihood of recidivism. Treatment is considered to be ten times more cost effective than interdiction in curtailing the use of cocaine in the United States (Rydell and Everingham, 1994). It is estimated that the federal government spent more than $17.1 billion, or $634 per second, on the drug war in 1999, with state governments spending an additional $20 billion (Drucker, 1998). Is this money well spent in preparing the nation for the challenges ahead in the twenty-first century? No! Chambliss (1999) makes a powerful comment on the forces that shape domestic policy in this realm:

> We are becoming a country obsessed with an imaginary plague, spending scarce resources on failed remedies while refusing to recognize both the reality of the problem and the social policies that do work. We must bring about a revolution in our thinking lest, too late, we realize that our fears generated policies that created the plague we feared. It is the law enforcement bureaucracy, the politicians, the media, and the industries that profit from the building of prisons and the creation and manufacture of crime control technologies that perpetuate the myths that justify wasting vast sums of taxpayers' money on failed efforts at crime control. (pp. xi–xii)

The media's efforts to cover prisons have met with barriers to reporting. Reporters wishing to interview inmates in person, for example, have had to resort to creative ways of conducting such interviews. For instance, newsroom telephones accept collect calls from prisons, and three-way calls are created by lawyers or inmate family members (Green, 1998). Increased costs, fraud, and prisoner abuses all combine to create an atmosphere restricting reporters' access to prisoners.

4

The Impact of
Correctional Supervision

A Multifaceted Perspective

The consequences of correctional supervision, particularly imprisonment, can be felt at multiple levels of society: the individual who is imprisoned, his or her children and family, the neighborhood and community, and the nation. Within each of these levels are sublevels that bring additional dimensions and considerations to bear on the event of imprisonment. Several of these perspectives, however, are rarely discussed or written about in the media or professional literature. A comprehensive examination, particularly of imprisonment, would require several books to do justice to the topic. Thus, the goal of outlining for the reader a multifaceted perspective on the consequences of correctional supervision is a daunting task. There are numerous publications examining various dimensions of correctional supervision and its ecological impact on society. Thus, this chapter does not intend to be an exhaustive review of the literature; it seeks only to highlight major issues and considerations.

The chapter does provide the reader with an understanding of the prodigious impact of incarceration and other forms of correctional supervision on families and communities, as well as on the prisoners' and former prisoners' experience within institutions and in their adjustment to life outside of a correctional facility (Arax, 1999a, 1999b; Dowling, 1997; Parenti, 1996). A special aspect of this chapter is its attention to the effect of incarceration on communities and the nation. All too often the focus of research on the subject of correctional supervision eschews this perspective.

I was struck in my review of the literature by the commonality of the needs and issues identified by a wide range of professionals in other disciplines, not just in social work. Numerous newspaper articles and editorials across the United States have addressed the consequences of incarcerating a parent and not fostering a connection with his or her children in the process: "Mr. Eng's [an inmate] experience reflects a side of the nation's prison-building boom that is only now gaining attention: there are seven million children with a parent in jail or prison or recently released on probation or parole. Those numbers alarm experts who say that having a parent behind bars is the factor that puts a child at greatest risk of becoming a juvenile delinquent and adult criminal" (Butterfield, 1999d, p. A1).

Studies have shown that more than 50 percent of all juveniles in custody have had a father, mother, or other close relative in prison. Parental prison experience, however, is not restricted to youth of color but cuts across racial and ethnic lines, and this historically has been the case (Butterfield, 1999d). The consequences of multigenerational experiences with prisons, as a result, necessitates that society view incarceration through a multifaceted perspective.

Consequences of Correctional Supervision

At first glance, the uninformed reader will focus only on the consequences of incarceration for an individual convicted of a crime. That person has his or her rights terminated and is incarcerated to pay society for a crime and to act as an example to deter criminal tendencies in others. However, such a picture is simplistic and does not begin to capture the consequences associated with being in prison or on probation or parole. Correctional supervision, particularly incarceration, is a life-altering event. Nothing will ever be the same for the offender or his or her family and community. Numerous economic, psychosocial, and sociopolitical needs of individuals, families, and communities need to be examined in order to more fully grasp the consequences of involvement with the criminal justice system: "The sense of loss is *the* central experience of the family when a family member is incarcerated. The losses that must be grieved include emotional and financial supports, and the roles that person played, as well as that person's physical presence" (Girshick, 1996, p. 11).

Prison

There are few people in the United States who have not watched a film or documentary pertaining to prison life. Generally, such films stress the brutal reality of a life that is under the constant control and supervision of authorities, its violence, and the despair that surrounds a prisoner inside a total institution—that is, an institution where all needs are met within.

These elements, although sensational in nature, are not without validity. Themes related to loneliness and missing family members or stories of significant family members dying and being buried without the presence of the prisoner to pay final respects are not out of the ordinary. Nor are stories of divorce, children being placed in foster care, and the ultimate breakup of the family. However, less obvious and possibly more powerful aspects of prison life rarely get highlighted or even mentioned in the film script. Stories of prisoners overcoming incredible odds to make a comeback, with some exceptions, generally do not have an audience in this society.

Relatively few studies have specifically focused on health care needs and utilization within prisons (Fitzgerald, D'Atri, Kasl, and Ostfeld, 1984; Twaddle, 1976; Young, 1999). More specifically, the relationship between health service utilization and ethnicity has largely gone unnoticed by the professional literature (Young, 1999). Women in prison present a higher likelihood of entering the system with unmet needs, and their health status is further compromised once in the prison (Chandler and Kassebaum, 1994; Ingram-Fogel, 1991, 1993; Shilling et al., 1994; Wilson and Leasure, 1991). Inmates who are HIV-positive or who have AIDS represent the latest challenges to providing health care within prisons. Most federal and state prison systems do not test for HIV, with one reason being the difficulty of maintaining inmate confidentiality (Pugh, 1998). Estimates based on the last survey of HIV and AIDS in prisons found that the rate of AIDS among inmates was six times that in the total U.S. population (Pugh, 1998).

Inmates who are monolingual in a language other than English face incredible challenges during their incarceration. They are limited in getting services because of language barriers and cultural barriers (New York Department of Correctional Services, 1986). This lack of access to services further enhances the possibility that transition back to society after prison will be jeopardized.

Women in prison face many of the same challenges that their male counterparts face. However, the extent of rape and sexual assaults is far greater than that experienced by men and makes their experience that much more traumatic: "The stories of these women are not unique. The National Prison Project of the ACLU reports that once women enter prison, they are frequently the target of sexual abuse by the staff. According to the Project, this is particularly traumatic because many women prisoners have previously been sexually or physically abused" (National Prison Project, 1996, p. 24). For women inmates who also happen to be mothers, such trauma further limits their ability to carry out parental roles and places them at greater risk for returning to prison because of another violation.

With some exceptions, the rehabilitation of prisoners is not a widely held value in U.S. society. Justice often warrants that prisoners "pay" for their crimes against society, often resulting in "time" that is, at best, unproductive. In some cases such time is spent learning or refining a trade that is illegal and will in all likelihood result in reincarceration. Several scholars have noted that time spent in prison can result in offenders learning anti-social values and beliefs or joining gangs and continuing this affiliation after release (Hunt, Riegel, Morales, and Waldoff, 1992; Moore, Garcia, Garcia, Cerda, and Valencia, 1978; Tonry, 1995; Vigil, 1989). Loyalty to gangs can replace loyalty to families, increasing the likelihood of recidivism.

Probation and Parole

The number of people on probation and parole in the United States is at an all-time high. Both of these types of correctional supervision have an impact on the ex-offender. Their rights are severely restricted, and they are required to account for movements and actions. Criminal justice personnel wield a tremendous influence on whether an offender violates the contract he or she has with the courts. As noted in chapter 2, violation of parole and probation conditions is a key factor in the number of individuals returning to prison.

The release from prison is both joyous and fraught with anxiety and concern for the "ex-con." In all likelihood, the transition back to the outside world does not mean freedom from correctional supervision, since a high number of former inmates must now report to a parole officer on a regular basis in accord with the terms of their release. The transition process is best conceptualized from a multifaceted perspective, one that includes family and community.

Life after prison, and the challenges associated with it, can euphemistically be called "transition challenges." However, this term does not do justice to the leap a former prisoner, his or her family, and community must make for him or her to succeed. Priestley et al.'s (1992) comments concerning the challenges inherent in going from prison to community were made approximately twenty years ago and are still relevant today:

> The problems which confront the newly released prisoner are different for each individual but the most common and immediate of them are the practical difficulties of finding somewhere to live, getting and keeping a job, and negotiating the social security system in order to keep afloat financially. Behind these tangible problems lie the less visible but no less real ones of reestablishing relationships with family and friends and neighbors. To the tackling of these dilemmas many ex-prisoners bring a deeply rooted sense of belonging to a legally disadvantaged and socially stigmatized minority. (pp. 2–3)

The transition back to community and society is further compounded for people of color because of the added stress associated with racism. The stereotype of an "ex-con" is rarely one that is white in complexion. Thus, the stigmatization identified by Priestley et al. (1992) often represents an insurmountable barrier for the newly released prisoner. Nevertheless, as this book points out, ex-offenders are not without skills. The story of Frank Sweeney reported in *Newsweek* (Reibstein, 1997) is a case in point: "Frank Sweeney has spent 23 of his 53 years in prison. . . . [The] unbroken losing streak would seem to qualify Sweeney to do very little except maybe lift weights. But Sweeney, a reader of Nietzsche when he's not concocting scams, has intuited that one of the most robust markets these days is the booming prison population. So having spent quality time in some 17 federal prisons, Sweeney has turned himself into the Dear Abby and Dr. Ruth for people about to enter prison or those who are already there. . . . At the moment . . . Sweeney may be the only consultant in it as a full-time business" (p. 64). Although stories like this are few and far between, ex-offenders do possess talents. It is not a question of whether they do. It is a question of what they are.

Impact of Incarceration on the Child Welfare System

Prison life can have a devastating impact on inmates, their families, and their communities. Life simply does not stand still until an individual can return home. Much transpires between the time a man or woman is incarcerated and then released. In the case where an offender's children are very young at the time of incarceration and the sentence is several years in length, children may not recognize their parent upon release. Places that traditionally employed members of the community may have closed or moved away, severely limiting employment possibilities, particularly if the former prisoner does not have an automobile or public transportation is restricted.

Why is incarceration considered a child welfare problem? Simply stated, there is a high likelihood of prisoners having children given the average age of who is typically imprisoned (Johnston, 1995a). A 1991 study found that almost three-quarters of imprisoned mothers and approximately one-half of imprisoned fathers lived with at least one minor child prior to being incarcerated (U.S. Department of Justice, 1993). The impact of substance abuse goes far beyond the consequences associated with incarceration of a parent. It is estimated that over two-thirds of the more than half million children in foster care in the United States have one or both parents who have a substance abuse problem (ONDCP, 1999). However, despite this number, in 1996 only 10 percent of the child welfare agencies were able to locate treatment within a thirty-day period for clients who needed it. That year, lack of available treatment was considered a serious barrier to having parents reunited with their children—4.4 to 5.3 million people needed treatment and less than 2 million received it (ONDCP, 1999). Further, women of color who use illicit drugs during pregnancy are ten times more likely to be reported to a child welfare agency when compared with white, non-Latina women, regardless of similar or equal levels of drug use (Chasnoff, Landress, and Barrett, 1990; Neuspiel, 1996).

Unfortunately, the compilers of criminal justice–related data have focused almost exclusively on gathering information related to individual inmates and eschewed most information regarding inmates' families and communities (Bloom, 1995; Johnson, Selber, and Lauderdale, 1998; Johnston, 1995b). That bias has made the systematic gathering of information on an inmate's social network prior to incarceration difficult, if not impossible, to obtain. Johnson, Selber, and Lauderdale (1998) also point out the need for further research on child welfare issues: "The growing number of incarcerated adults has drawn attention to the children and families who are affected when family members are imprisoned. Children of incarcerated parents are at increased risk of out-of-home placement as well as intergenerational patterns of incarceration due to the increased poverty, trauma, and stigmatization, and inadequate quality of care that often accompanies the incarceration of a parent. These risks remain understudied" (p. 612).

Numerous barriers limit or completely cut off children's visitation with their incarcerated parent. The following barriers are the most frequently cited and are not mutually exclusive—that is, more than one can and usually does exist: (1) geographical distance; (2) reluctance or inability of caregivers to facilitate visits; (3) frequent and excessive inmate transfers between prisons; (4) an incarcerated parent actively discouraging visits— shame being one of the primary reasons; (5) children may not want to visit; (6) out-of-home visits are arduous; (7) correctional settings may actively discourage visits; and (8) communication is limited to writing for those who can write, because of high costs of telephone calls (Seymour, 1998). It is estimated that more than 60 percent of children with incarcerated parents live more than a hundred miles away from their parents, making it expensive to visit and logistically arduous when relying on public transportation.

The U.S. child welfare system has witnessed a tremendous demand for services caused by the absence of fathers and mothers who have been incarcerated (Block and Potthast, 1998; Hairston, 1998a; Katz, 1998; Martin, 1997; Seymour, 1998; Watterson, 1996; Weissman and Larue, 1998). Families have also experienced prodigious stress as a result of a member or members being incarcerated (Beckerman, 1998; Genty, 1998; Phillis and Bloom, 1998). Social work's involvement in the child welfare system, more so than in the criminal justice arena, has thrust the profession into the "front lines" of this social problem.

Familial Roles and Responsibilities: Substance Abuse, Child Maltreatment, and Correctional Supervision

As already noted in chapters 2 and 3, the impact of substance abuse and correctional supervision, particularly the incarceration of mothers, has been immense. There is no aspect of child welfare that has not been touched by substance abuse and the criminal justice system. A recent report by the Columbia University National Center on Addiction and Substance Abuse highlights how communities and child welfare have been transformed in the last decade: "A devastating tornado of substance abuse and addiction is tearing through the nation's child welfare and family court systems leaving in its path a wreckage of abused and neglected children, turning social welfare agencies and courts on their heads and uprooting the traditional disposition to keep children with their natural parents" (CASA, 1999, p. i).

The relationship between drugs and neglect is very strong. CASA estimates that almost 70 percent of all cases of child abuse and neglect can be attributed to substance abuse by one or both parents (CASA, 1999). Children from homes where alcohol and drugs are abused are at least 2.7 times more likely to be abused and 4.2 times more likely to be neglected than children from non–substance abusing families. Many of the children entering the child welfare system come from families of color and face the additional burden of being placed in families and institutions that do not reflect the ethnic or racial background of their biological families. Further, once they have entered the child welfare system, they face an increased risk of not returning home in a period of time that can be considered optimal. Those children who are eligible for adoption are rarely adopted. In 1995, of 107,000 eligible children only 27,115 were adopted (CASA, 1999). Foster homes, too, are in short supply relative to the need, particularly homes that match a child's racial or ethnic background and that are located in the community in which the child lives.

Lack of readily available treatment for substance-abusing parents is widely recognized as a major barrier to reunifying children with their parents. One estimate notes that only 31 percent of parents seeking treatment and 20 percent of pregnant women seeking treatment have access to services. The lack of treatment availability in prisons further compounds the problem of delivery of services to this population group.

The social stigma associated with incarceration is great when a parent is incarcerated, and even greater when the parent is a mother, although the imprisonment of a father is not without its undue implications, particularly related to the changes in social roles for the mother. In situations of an incarcerated father, 90 percent of the children continue living with their biological mothers. However, there is little denying that the imprisonment of the mother has far-reaching implications within the community and society.

One of the major consequences for inmates who are mothers is in regard to their ability to sustain parenting functions (Dowling and Nyary, 1997; Huie, 1992). The words of a current inmate named Michelle provided by the November Coalition (1999) do a wonderful job of stressing the importance of parenting roles:

> I have just finished my second year in federal prison, guilty of the greatest crime of all: I had no information to barter my freedom, and so I was of no use to the government. . . . When my nightmare began, I expected to encounter hardened prison women and

vicious criminals. Instead, I've met daughters, mothers, grand-mothers, and even great-grandmothers. I've met women of great strength and courage, dignity and grace. . . . Our children suffer greatly within this unthinking frenzy of mass incarceration. How do you explain to a 2-year-old that Mommy won't be around for a long, long time? . . . This madness touches us all. Mothers like myself are kept so far from home that our children can never visit. Christmases, Easters, Thanksgivings and birthdays come and go as we miss out on the first loose tooth, first steps, first words, first day of school, first slumber party and first school dance. We live our lives through photographs, but photos can never come close to being really there for our children.

Michelle's comments raise numerous issues and considerations for society. The punishment of the offender, in Michelle's case, has been broadened to her children, family, and community (Bloom and Steinhardt, 1993).

A mother's loss of parental functions can often mean a long and difficult road to reclaiming her children, particularly if a state agency has taken over responsibilities for the parenting functions (CASA, 1999; Norman, 1995; Seymour, 1998). In cases of incarcerated mothers, a family member often takes over the parenting role, and it tends to be the maternal grandmother (50 percent), followed by other relatives, foster parents, and friends (Seymour, 1998). Fathers accounted for 17 percent of the caregivers (Bloom and Steinhardt, 1993). The role of grandmothers, particularly those who are African American, has increased in importance in the community because of the role of drugs and the arrest and incarceration of parents due to violation of drug laws. A focus on African American grandmothers is the result of their traditional role in the African American family (Minkler and Roe, 1993).

Why aren't parental roles reinforced through increased access to family and children? Simply put, prisons have as a primary, and very often only, role the maintenance of security within their institutions. Increased access of inmates to children and family increases the likelihood of drugs being smuggled, requires a disruption in routines, and requires greater attention and security from guards. Guards, in turn, may have to deal with the emotional consequences that visits create. In essence, it is a nuisance (Butterfield, 1999d)!

Consequences for the Community

Inmates who manage to maintain family ties while incarcerated have a higher likelihood of successfully reentering the community (Fishman and Alissi, 1997). However, incarceration invariably means that the inmate, be it a father or mother, will have contact with his or her children terminated. Giving up children, physically and emotionally, may well eliminate one of the most powerful motivators for an inmate's engaging in productive and prosocial behavior.

Individuals under correctional supervision, particularly those who are imprisoned but also those mandated to community programs, sever ties with their community and society. As noted in chapter 2, they are effectively disenfranchised from voting in local and national elections (Sentencing Project, 1998a). Even if they are placed in a program based in their community, the relationship between the correctionally supervised and the rest of the community is seriously altered. Life after prison can prove even more challenging for former inmates as they struggle to reenter their community and family. Interestingly, with some exceptions the problems associated with release from prison have rarely been looked at from a community-wide standpoint.

There is a growing awareness that an abrupt release from prison at the end of a sentence does not lend itself to an easy transition back into the community. One possibility that has received some degree of discussion has been the development of a reentry program lasting approximately eighteen months. This program actively seeks to involve local houses of worship (Broder, 1999). Connecting released prisoners with ministers, who then function as counselors and "case managers," will help in marshaling local resources (formal and informal) to help in the transition.

The impact of imprisonment on communities, particularly those of color and low income, is striking both from a historical and a contemporary perspective (Sisson, 1979). Currie (1998), in commenting on just one dimension of that impact (unemployment), notes how statistics on employment would change dramatically if they included those who are imprisoned:

> Thus, in 1996 there was an average of about 3.9 million men officially unemployed in the United States, and about 1.1 million in state or federal prison. Adding the imprisoned to the officially unemployed would boost the male unemployment rate in that year by more than a fourth, from 5.4 percent to 6.9 percent. And that national average obscures the social implications of the huge increases in incarceration in some states. In Texas, there were about 120,000 men in prison in 1995, and 300,000 officially unemployed. Adding the imprisoned to the jobless count raises the state's male unemployment rate by well over a third, from 5.6 to 7.8 percent. If we conduct the same exercise for black men, the figures are even more thought-provoking. In 1995, there were 762,000 black men officially counted as unemployed, and another 511,000 in state or federal prison. Combining these numbers raises the jobless rate for black men by two-thirds, from just under 11 to almost 18 percent. (p. 33)

The Bureau of Justice noted that 36 percent of all inmates were unemployed during the month preceding their arrest, with 20 percent actively looking for work and 16 percent not doing so (Bureau of Justice Statistics, 1998b).

The impact of the criminal justice system goes beyond the inmate and his or her immediate family, as noted by Moore (1999):

> Although the criminal justice system can help reduce violence and fear, it can and has become itself a source of violence and fear as well as a protector. In many of the nation's most desperate communities, agencies of the criminal justice system are hardly seen as important sources of security. They are instead considered either irrelevant (because of their neglect and indifference to the people who live in these communities and the problems they face) or worse, as additional threats (that is, strangers who are as likely to victimize as to protect), and to do so without the victim's having any real recourse. (p. 299)

Communities that are economically marginal in this society cannot afford to have "able-bodied" men not be in the workforce supporting their families. This lack of income has a ripple effect in a community. An ecological perspective will identify numerous consequences, some not so visible, for a community. An ecological view of a community forces a practitioner to expand his or her vision of how a problem is conceptualized, as in a caseload of a clinician; or sector, as in the case of a community organizer. This perspective may at first overwhelm a practitioner who is used to a narrow view of issues and interventions.

From a social fabric perspective, communities with an unusually high percentage of residents in prisons face the prospect of having a higher-than-expected number of households headed by women, because of their husbands and significant others being "away." Ex-inmates, upon release and return to the community, face the challenge of finding work and or making constructive use of their time if not gainfully employed. Lack of employment possibilities, in turn, means that "extra" time is available with limited opportunities to be gainfully occupied. Lack of employment among ex-offenders may not be restricted to them as a group; unemployment may be an integral part of life in a community.

The chances of former prisoners engaging in substance abuse is considerable if they have no gainful employment and did not receive help with their addictions while in prison. Consequently, the likelihood of abusing drugs and recommitting a crime is high, and so is the likelihood of being sent back to prison. This cycle is not out of the ordinary in many low-income urban communities of color in the United States.

Role-modeling by adult men, particularly since their absolute numbers in prisons are greater than those of women, cannot inspire confidence in helping youth to grow up to be productive members of their families, communities, and society.

Communities also suffer severe consequences when women, such as mothers, are imprisoned. As already noted, other family members, particularly grandmothers, are thrust into caregiving for youngsters at a point in their lives when their own physical and psychological needs may be significant.

Over- and Underpolicing

Communities that have historically supplied high percentages of their residents to prisons can suffer from over- or underpolicing (Bruni, 1999). Overpolicing may seem as if there is an "occupying army" in the community: "These officers have been told that they form the front line in a 'war' on crime and a 'war' on drugs, that they have been enlisted in special 'operations' and drafted for bold new 'offensives.' 'We use all these paramilitary terms' . . . 'and we have promoted somewhat of a siege mentality among police: The enemy is out there, and there are more of them than we thought.' . . . 'When you have this sort of mentality, excessive brutality and improper actions are more likely to occur' " (Bruni, 1999, p. 1).

Excessive use of force, violations of constitutional rights, and frequent police raids result in tremendous disruption to daily and family interactions and may seem like a "community-wide crisis" (Barstow, 2000; Flynn, 1999a; Fritsch, 2000; Gorov, 1999). Even if the raids result only in the arrest and eventual release of residents after the local district attorney determines that the "case" will not stand trial because of lack of evidence, the community still suffers under a siege mentality. This form of policing also generates a tremendous amount of negative publicity for a community.

I remember working in a New England community where the local newspaper published a daily list of those who had been arrested the previous day. The Latino community, which happened to be the largest group of color in the city, had a negative reputation for accounting for the majority of the arrests in the city, particularly violations of drug laws. The newspaper, in turn, had a practice of bold lettering Latino names on the list and not doing so for non-Latino names.

Latino community leaders approached the newspaper and protested this practice, which was stopped. I, in turn, in collaboration with a Latino community-based outpatient drug-treatment organization, undertook a study of all the names of those arrested in the course of a year and found that approximately fifty Latinos were arrested and rearrested over and over, accounting for the majority of the Latinos arrested during that time period. These Latinos, in turn, lived in two segregated sections of the city. On occasions, there were publicity-generating raids that resulted in large numbers of Latino arrests and front-page pictures and news stories, further reinforcing the negative image of the Latino community.

Underpolicing, on the other hand, has a tremendous impact on a community by allowing illegal activities to flourish without consequences for perpetrators. Lack of law enforcement essentially turns the state's authority to govern over to the criminals. They, in turn, dictate what is morally acceptable behavior, control the allocation of jobs, which essentially are drug related, and reward and punish residents. The general absence of law enforcement essentially serves to help a drug-based economy flourish. This extreme case, in turn, causes communities to avoid reporting crimes when they occur and eschew cooperating with law enforcement officials when approached; such communities consider the police and the courts enemies.

Informal Community Settings

Communities consist of much more than people. Open spaces, institutions, and geographical proximity to the "outside" world also figure into the equation called "community." Consequently, imprisonment and other forms of correctional supervision affect more than just families, neighbors, and other residents in a community. They affect all institutions within a community. Informal settings, too, are affected in ways very rarely thought of by human services providers and funders.

Informal settings can be defined as places in a community where residents can either purchase a product or service or congregate for social purposes. However, in the process, residents can seek assistance to meet their informational, expressive, or instrumental needs, and do so in a manner that is culturally affirming (Delgado, 1999). These settings play an instrumental role in the social fabric of the community and can easily be affected by what happens when a member of the community is imprisoned.

The consequences of correctional supervision are felt in informal settings. Houses of worship, for example, often are called upon to pick up the pieces when a member of the congregation is imprisoned. Support groups, counseling, advocacy, financial assistance to the family, and even provision of transportation so that family members can visit prisoners are not unusual. These efforts take away from resources that could be used to address other issues or even put toward enhancement-oriented activities.

Business-centered informal settings, too, are affected when community members are incarcerated. Local businesses such as grocery stores, restaurants, beauty parlors, and the like do not have the benefit of increased business. Their owners, in turn, do not have the necessary funds to reinvest in their businesses, which limits their opportunities to expand or upgrade equipment. Community economic enhancement, as a result, is artificially limited, and so is the influence the community can wield in the political process of a city. If the residents do not vote or contribute financially to political campaigns, where is their influence? The only influence available to these communities is to act as a target for political rhetoric and metaphors.

Impact on the Nation

The economic costs of imprisonment, as already noted in previous chapters, can be staggering as dollars are reallocated away from education, health, and social programs. In 1986, for example, California allocated

12.6 percent of its budget for higher education and 2 percent for prisons. In 1994 the percentages had shifted to 9 percent for both. It is projected that if the trend continues at that pace, in the year 2000 California will have 1 percent allocated for higher education and 18 percent for prisons (Moore, 1999).

The economic pressures to shift funding from education and social programs to prisons are not unique to California (Parenti, 1999). Resistance to raising taxes to cover both areas necessitates that legislators, and indirectly taxpayers, make these choices that are very difficult for elected officials to make. Their decisions, in turn, are greatly influenced by lobbying forces that can provide financial contributions and deliver votes. Unions and corporations, as a result, are in a strategic position; communities, particularly those that are undervalued in this society, are rarely in such a position.

Police corruption as a result of drug-related money is another dimension that is rarely talked about but that has an impact on the nation (General Accounting Office, 1998). When police are actively involved in facilitating drug trafficking or are themselves sellers of illicit drugs, it seriously undermines the power and influence of law enforcement. Although data related to police corruption in drug enforcement are difficult to obtain, well-publicized arrests of police officers involved in the drug trade seriously undermine the public's faith in police being able, or willing, to stop the drug business within communities (Purdum, 1999).

The Unique Circumstances Involving Death Row

For inmates on death row, the unique circumstances surrounding their incarceration make their "time" in prison that much more extreme and oppressive ("Forty-three Women," 1998; Light and Donovan, 1997; "The News from Death Row," 1990). The impact of a state or nation having a death row is difficult to comprehend because of the message sent to its citizenry and the world. However, a nation with more than five thousand inmates on death row means that it can execute approximately fifteen inmates every day for a three-year period. A killing machine, or in this case multiple killing machines, is necessary to accomplish this goal in a cost-efficient manner. I sincerely do not believe that a nation with this capability wants to be a role model for other nations.

Inmates on death row face a unique set of challenges, as do their families and loved ones. A death sentence can mean being on death row for many years before the sentence is carried out. In the meantime, inmates on death row cannot continue business as usual, planning for the future or for bettering their chances upon release and so forth. In essence, these individuals cannot have a "normalizing" experience, or as close to that as can be expected within a total institution, because they are separated from other inmates, have a different daily routine, and essentially have a future than can be measured only on a day-by-day basis. On death row the "routine" is an essential part of the execution (Light and Donovan, 1997).

Conclusion

This chapter has outlined the incredible challenges posed by incarceration and correctional supervision for individuals, families, communities, and the nation. It seems as if no sector of society—no age, gender, race, or socioeconomic group—escapes the impact of substance abuse and corrections. The impact varies from indirect, through increased taxes, to direct, with actual imprisonment, parole, or probation. The challenge of measuring the implications of such a social problem for the nation can be met only by viewing the problem from a multifaceted perspective.

Although all people who are imprisoned suffer tremendous losses, women, particularly mothers, seem to suffer the greatest losses. But there is no sector of society that escapes the consequences of increased rates of imprisonment. Some communities are more greatly affected than others. Others, still, are affected by turning open space into prisons in the hope of generating jobs and income for the community. Such communities, I believe, have essentially tied their futures to the U.S. prison system. It is not unusual for communities that are home to state correctional facilities that bear the name of the community they are located in to lobby their legislatures to change the names of these prisons because of the stigma associated with them. Names may change. However, these communities will forever be associated with prisons.

The social and financial costs of correctional supervision cannot easily be measured in dollars, or any other way, although dollars seem to be the favorite language used in lobbying for a de-emphasis on prisons. However, the costs resulting from children who embark upon lives of crime, their lost potential for family, community, and society, cannot easily be measured in dollars. A lost dream cannot easily be recaptured again. However, a lost dream in the midst of a family or community can wield a tremendous impact on others. When youth stop dreaming about their future, the country suffers, too. Prisons, after all, have become a very distorted rite of passage in some communities.

An abundance of adult role models who are in prisons or belong to gangs, for example, serve as testaments of what is and is not possible within a community. Institutions that serve such communities, such as schools, eventually give up trying to make a difference and simply accept what appears to be an inevitable future for their young people—one that, unfortunately, has as an outcome death at an early age or prison. Neither of those outcomes is attractive. Sadly, they do not have to happen!

The impact alcohol and other drugs have on society can only be appreciated and understood if viewed from multiple perspectives, starting with the individual who abuses drugs and progressing all the way through the family, the community, and the nation as a whole. The challenge former convicts face in becoming productive members of society may seem overwhelming to the average person. They must make a successful transition to the work world, family life, and community, all at once. They do not have the luxury of putting on hold any one of these worlds in order to concentrate on another. Their challenge, simply put, is to completely forget the time spent in prison and move forward as if that experience never existed. Needless to say, this is simply impossible. Unfortunately, post-traumatic stress disorder has been recognized only for war veterans and those who have suffered trauma at some point in their lives resulting from abuse or witnessing a cruel or unjust act. The experiences associated with prisons simply are not thought of in this manner, even though there are significant parallels.

As noted throughout this chapter, there is no lack of barriers to providing services to ex-offenders, their families, and communities. The challenge, however, is to take into account these barriers and still identify and mobilize the capacities of the correctionally supervised in the creation of a future that is productive and "normalizing." We cannot ignore barriers or challenges and focus just on capacities. Ironically, barriers and capacities are closely tied together in practice. Thus, one of our greatest challenges becomes how to successfully overcome the barriers without losing focus on the ultimate goal. Unfortunately, it is not uncommon for practitioners to become overwhelmed by the challenges and simply forget what we were originally trying to accomplish.

Success stories abound and need to be looked at carefully, and the lessons learned applied in practice. Unfortunately, many of us simply have not developed the sensitivity and ability to hear the success stories. When success is achieved because the individual has certain capacities, we simply accept it and move on. Some of us may even attribute the success to luck or circumstances without seriously looking at the intervention and what made an individual succeed.

Somehow, the failures always seem to stand out in our minds. In essence, we need to "train" ourselves to listen for the successes, analyze why those individuals succeeded, share the stories with others, and learn from them. In the field of corrections, failure seems to be the name of the game, and as a result, we do not question the methods or systems that routinely result in failure. I seriously doubt that there is another system where failure is the norm and where the public, who pays for these systems, does not question how its tax dollars are being wasted.

The consequences of correctional supervision, particularly imprisonment, can be quite devastating to an offender. Yet there are many alternatives to prison that do not completely ignore the crime. It is only fitting to end this chapter with an observation concerning the nation's experiment with imprisonment:

> By the early 1990s, these skewed priorities had brought us what was arguably the worst of all possible worlds when it came to crime and punishment. We had attained a level of violent crime that, in some places, was the highest in this century and that threatened to destroy the social fabric of many American com-

munities. At the same time, we had created a bloated penal system whose uncontrolled growth had helped deprive our most vulnerable communities of urgently needed social investment. It seemed painfully clear to most who studied these problems that the experiment was not working. (Currie, 1998, p. 36).

Capacity Enhancement Concepts, Principles, and Practice

Section 2 consists of two chapters that specifically address the concept and practice of capacity enhancement with the correctionally supervised. Chapter 5, "Capacity Enhancement Practice: Key Values, Principles, and Goals," provides a conceptual foundation for this paradigm. Chapter 6, "A Framework for Capacity Enhancement Practice with the Correctionally Supervised," provides the reader with a tool, or framework, to apply to social work practice with the correctionally supervised.

5

Capacity Enhancement Practice

Key Values, Principles, and Goals

The challenges human services professions face, and for that matter the nation as a whole, in addressing the needs of those who have been incarcerated or are under some other form of correctional supervision necessitate a new approach to conceptualizing interventions. The ever-spiraling costs of building and maintaining prisons, not to mention the human toll on prisoners, their families, and communities, require the development of bold initiatives that serve both to prevent crime and to effectively address the needs of offenders in U.S. society.

Helping professions, and not only social work, must reach out to offenders, and do so in a manner that systematically builds upon their assets. Although this chapter focuses on the social work profession, much, if not all, that is addressed is also applicable to other helping professions interested in better serving those under correctional supervision. Thus, every effort is made to broaden the appeal of the chapter to non–social work audiences without losing the focus on social work, the book's primary audience. There is little question that social work must form working alliances with other helping professions in order to be successful in the criminal justice arena. The profession, for example, has successfully achieved that goal in the law enforcement arena. However, the correctional field will prove to be a greater challenge.

Many people no doubt share a general perspective on the correction-ally supervised—namely, that they are born criminals who have no respect for human life or private property. As a result, rehabilitation is virtually impossible without "turning the keys of the prison" over to the prisoners. The punishment inflicted, according to this line of thought, is one of choice. Namely, those who violate the law know the consequences and therefore have a choice to make—break or not break the law. The prospect that offenders could possibly have strengths of any kind exists in the "dreams" of progressives, liberals, and radical thinkers (Chevigny, 1999). A shift in the paradigm from one based on punishment and incarceration to one that uses community-based alternatives to prison and focuses on capacity enhancement may just be too great a leap to be made in this society and for the profession of social work!

This chapter provides a multifaceted perspective on capacity enhancement and its potential for use with undervalued population groups and communities. The reader is exposed to values, principles, goals, concepts, and theoretical material related to how capacity enhance-ment–focused interventions can be shaped to address those who are cor-rectionally supervised inside and outside prison. The reader, in turn, is provided with examples from work with other population groups as a means of broadening the use of the approach and increasing its appli-cability for the human services field. This chapter also seeks to identify the challenges practitioners will face in using capacity enhancement prac-tice with the correctionally supervised. In essence, the information pre-sented in this chapter will serve as a foundation that the reader can apply to work with the correctionally supervised and other marginalized groups.

Finally, this chapter will use a series of field-based illustrations where inmate and former inmate strengths and assets have been tapped in pro-gramming of various kinds. A sizable number of programs or interventions stressing a variety of dimensions related to enhanced capacities can be found in all regions of the United States. Case illustrations, as noted in chapter 1, are not meant to provide the reader within an in-depth analysis but are just suggestive of what is possible when utilizing a capacity enhancement perspective. The reader is advised to read chapters 8 through 17, which consist of case studies, for an in-depth examination of various programs throughout the country.

I was able to locate numerous programs and services that were actively based on capacity enhancement missions and principles. I found examples in the professional literature, on the Internet, and through word of mouth when staff at one program mentioned another program somewhere else in the country. Thus, at times I and my research assistants felt like "inves-tigators" seeking leads, following up on suggestions, and "nagging" pro-gram administrators to send materials. However, the reader will no doubt be enlightened by the examples provided in this chapter and other chap-ters, and will hopefully be inspired to copy or create some of his or her own as a result.

Need for a New Practice Paradigm

Any advocate of a new paradigm must be prepared for a long and hard journey in getting his or her perspective "on the table," so to speak. The need for a new paradigm is very often fueled by a series of ideological, sociodemographic, and practical factors and considerations. Whether the new paradigm is widely accepted, however, is very much contingent on "who" is advocating for the paradigm, their position in being able to do so, data available on the results of interventions using the paradigm, and funding availability encouraging its use. Thus, there really is no mystery concerning why one paradigm receives attention and another dies a "lonely death." It is no mistake that academics are usually the ones championing a new paradigm. We seem to have the time, energy, and resources to take on this task. However, this is not to say that practitioners are not using highly innovative approaches toward practice, many of which may be capacity enhancement in nature. However, the writing of articles, book chapters, and books invariably falls upon academics because that is part of our job description—advance knowledge in the field.

A number of scholars have identified a series of critical issues confronting social work practitioners in the next century (Holmes, 1996; Kreuger, 1997; Murdock and Michael, 1996; Pozatek, 1994; Weinman and Smith, 1996; Wellons, 1996). Social work scholars, thus, have not simply "put their heads in the sand" and not acknowledged key issues confronting the profession in the twenty-first century. I would add to those issues the need for the profession to embrace a paradigm that has particular relevance for, and seeks to identify and mobilize indigenous assets within, urban communities of color. A paradigm focused on poor, white, non-Latinos living in the rural United States, for example, may share many of the same principles with one addressing urban communities. However, how such principles get operationalized, measured, and ultimately evaluated will differ considerably based upon context and the social forces impinging on the community.

In simple terms, a paradigm can be described as a way of, or approach to, looking at an issue or need. The relearning of new approaches for practice within undervalued communities is critical if social work is to be successful in the twenty-first century. Efforts to strengthen communities and enhance their capacity to provide help for their members must be a central goal for the years to come (Poole, 1997). However, the author is under no illusion concerning the difficulty of introducing a new paradigm into practice. New paradigms, by their very nature, upset the status quo. Consequently, they are not without their share of skeptics and critics. To a certain degree, this is to be expected and welcomed since no paradigm should be beyond question. Nevertheless, new paradigms bring with them an increased sense of excitement and importance that is rarely matched in the field of practice. The hope associated with a new paradigm serves to engender a healthy dose of energy and drive to apply the paradigm to new situations, population groups, and settings.

Garbarino's (1983) use of the metaphor of a hammer and nail illus-trates wonderfully the importance of social work's broadening its approach to service delivery by actively exploring alternative paradigms:

> We must begin by reorienting our perspective because our train-ing and culture impose conceptual baggage that stands in our way. One of my favorite metaphors is the saying, "If the only tool you have is a hammer, then you tend to treat every problem as if it were a nail." . . . Our principal tool is one-to-one intervention, professional to client. . . . few professionals have reoriented their basic thinking about helping. . . . They continue to see most, if not all, of their clients and their problems as nails for which the hammer of direct didactic intervention is the appropriate tool. . . . The hammer and nail metaphor is powerful because it highlights how our investment in professional roles and practices blind us to other tools and resources for improving the quality of life. (pp. 16–17)

The lack of vision and political will to explore new forms of service delivery and new settings are the "hammer" and "nail" counterparts to Garbarino's example. Work with the "correctionally supervised" presents social work with an opportunity to find new and creative approaches to engaging this population group. These approaches, however, cannot rely on deficit-based premises if they are to make a contribution to work in this field of practice. I cannot think of a population group—with the possible exception of the homeless, who may also have criminal justice backgrounds—that is so widely distrusted and perceived by society to be without assets of any kind. Consequently, the development of a paradigm focused on the correctionally supervised will prove a challenge. It will also generate excitement, questioning, debate, and ultimately a more effective and social justice–based approach toward practice. Social work education and scholarship, in turn, must play an active leadership role in paving the way for capacity enhancement practice with the correctionally supervised. We in social work education cannot stand by while practitioners seek to develop innovative forms of practice on their own. We can play a collab-orative role to facilitate the creation of this form of knowledge.

No field of practice is without its share of critics, both from within and without, and social work is no exception. A number of social work scholars have been very critical of the profession and have argued that the mission of social work has not been implemented fully when addressing undervalued population groups. Some inherent tensions have been iden-tified that have served to prevent the profession from maximizing its actively engaging with certain groups and actively seeking a social justice agenda. Galper (1975) criticized the social work profession in the 1970s from a radical perspective. He argued that the profession had focused too much attention on delivery of services that were uncontroversial and had abandoned efforts at achieving reform. Social work, in effect, had abandoned its roots in favor of being more widely accepted in U.S. society. Consequently, it had exerted more energy and resources in maintaining the status quo than threatening it. Longres (1996), in turn, has raised questions about where the radical "voices" have disappeared to. He notes that progressive thinkers have couched their perspective in writings about multicultural, diversity-based, or feminist frameworks. This approach, as a result, has served to increase the value of focusing on one's favorite group and abandoning collective efforts at bringing groups together in search of social justice for all.

Specht and Courtney (1994), in their widely discussed book, have argued that the profession of social work has lost sight of its historical mission of helping the undervalued and tapping indigenous assets in the formulation of community-based services. Instead, the profession has relied too heavily on a medical model that refuses to identify and mobilize indigenous strengths. The prevalent model is disempowering and further undermines a community's capacity to help itself. Correctionally supervised groups typify this approach because of the emphasis on deficits and the de-emphasis on assets. It is necessary to reconceptualize how the profession views itself, and its mission, before meaningful progress can be made to work with those who are undervalued in a manner that is both affirming and liberating. The profession has missed a golden opportunity to align itself with communities, set social and economic justice goals, and seek major social change.

Iglehart and Becerra (1995), on the other hand, have examined the profession from the viewpoint of communities of color and have concluded that social work has not taken into account or involved people of color to any significant extent. Communities of color, with some notable exceptions, are still viewed by the profession as being deficient. Scholarly contributions by scholars of color have not received the attention they deserve and are often overlooked in the literature (Delgado, 2000a). The professional literature, with notable exceptions, still heavily favors a deficit, and ethnocentric, perspective toward communities of color.

Trolander (1988) cites social work's quest for professionalism, the demographic changes in urban population composition, and a decreased emphasis on advocacy as key factors in the movement of social work away from social change. These factors essentially make the profession unsuited to effectively work with undervalued groups and seek to redress the consequences of oppression. Margolin (1997), in turn, believes that social work's embrace of social control functions has made it impossible for the profession to undertake reform efforts involving people of color or the poor. Margolin's thesis raises important points of consideration concerning the role of social work in a society that systematically seeks ways to control marginalized groups. Imprisonment of low-income groups is one way society exercises this form of control.

I, in turn, have looked at the problem from the perspective of geographical setting and argued that social work has systematically limited itself in serving undervalued groups and communities in urban areas of the country, even though its history can be traced back to urban-based practice (Delgado, 1999). The profession has been too passive in challenging itself to develop models of service delivery that effectively have social workers in partnership with the communities they seek to serve, and that seek to maximize community strengths. I also advocate that social work should embrace new paradigms with strengths/assets underpinnings in an effort to reach undervalued communities, particularly those that are of low income, of color, and urban based (Delgado 2000a, 2000b). Use of asset-based interventions would allow social workers to branch out in the field of practice and work in settings such as community development corporations, for example.

In *New Arenas for Community Social Work Practice with Urban Youth: The Use of the Arts, Humanities, and Sports,* I argue that the profession has essentially abandoned part of its historical mission of using the arts, humanities, and sports as vehicles for providing services to youth and other age groups (Delgado, 2000b). This shift in practice has essentially resulted in social workers not playing an influential role in youth development programs. Ironically, settings such as the YMCA, YWCA, and Boys and Girls Clubs used to employ many social workers; however, it is rare to find social workers employed in these types of agencies now.

Youth development is rarely covered in social work curriculum and is generally not part of child welfare concentrations—abuse and neglect, juvenile delinquency, and social work in schools are usually the focus of this type of curriculum. Community-based settings, when specifically targeting low-income consumers, offer the potential and opportunity to refocus social work's mission on undervalued groups such as people with disabilities, newcomers, and people of color, to list but a few types.

Finally, I have previously summed up the difficulty of a profession taking a risk by embracing new approaches and paradigms for practice, and those thoughts are very applicable to capacity enhancement work with the correctionally supervised: "I am aware that any shift in paradigms results in an uneasy feeling for a social worker or any other helping professional. This uneasiness will lead to questioning past actions, possible guilt over why an old paradigm was not the most liberating and culturally competent way of helping undervalued communities, fear of what embracing a new paradigm will bring (politically, professionally, socially), and possibly concern that the new quest will result in a 'dead end'; in wasted time, energy, and 'political capital.' Change is never possible without risk, both personal and professional" (Delgado, 1999, p. 219). Before capacity enhancement practice is possible, the profession of social work must be willing to question previous assumptions and approaches; discarding, modifying, and adopting new paradigms is inevitable if we are to make the necessary decisions and take the necessary actions that will strategically position the profession for the next century.

What Is Capacity Enhancement?

The concept of capacity enhancement has emerged slowly in the human services field and in the scholarly literature. Like any other new paradigm, capacity enhancement owes a great deal of credit to many individuals, practitioners as well as scholars. New paradigms, after all, are rarely, if ever, the result of one scholar's work. The history of how this concept emerged is beyond the scope of this book. The work of McKnight and Kreztmann (1990) is widely acknowledged to have provided currency to the concept. However, the wide acceptance of the strengths perspective also played an important role in the birth of capacity enhancement within the profession of social work (Saleebey, 1992; Weick, Rapp, Sullivan, and Kisthardt, 1989). Its theoretical roots, nevertheless, can be traced back to the introduction of social networks and social and natural support systems in the 1970s and 1980s (Delgado, 1999). During those decades social workers and other professionals actively sought to develop ways of intervening in groups and communities in a manner that built upon and actively used their indigenous resources in the construction of services and programs.

Although various ideological and theoretical underpinnings of capacity enhancement have been around for many years, the concept is only now receiving the attention it deserves. As noted in the introductory chapter, capacity enhancement can be defined simply as the systematic identification and use of indigenous assets in the construction and implementation of intervention strategies. Poole notes that the primary goal of capacity building (enhancement) "is to foster conditions that strengthen the characteristics of communities that enable them to plan, develop, implement, and maintain effective community programs" (1997, p. 163). However, as the reader is probably aware, simple definitions can be quite complex in meaning, and concepts often entail multidimensional ways of operationalization. Capacity enhancement typifies this complexity.

Further, intervention strategies, in turn, not only actively seek the involvement of those they target to play instrumental roles, but also serve to enhance competencies (individual, institutional, and community) in the process (Delgado, 2000a; Poole, 1997). Interventions address two time frames—the here and now and the future. Further, capacity enhancement initiatives, as to be expected, can be successful only if they take into account cultural competence and base services within the cultural context of the population being targeted (Delgado, 2000b).

Capacity enhancement is a philosophical stance, a goal, and a method for practice. Capacity enhancement, like empowerment, does not have to enjoy a universal meaning with its boundaries clearly defined. This approach is sufficiently broad and flexible to allow local circumstances, and not to mention practitioners, to be incorporated into the design of an intervention based on its principles. Capacity enhancement takes a very broad approach to looking at a community's assets. It takes into account not only individual strengths but also community intangibles such as availability of open space, geographical location, and natural resources.

The broadening of the strengths perspective beyond individuals is essential in order to maximize available resources, local circumstances, and opportunity.

In a previous review of the literature on capacity enhancement, I identified eight instrumental aspects of capacity enhancement initiatives targeting undervalued communities: (1) participation and indigenous leadership, (2) access to and efficient use of formal and informal resources, (3) social and interorganizational networks, (4) the creation of a community spirit, (5) a community history of various kinds of collective actions, (6) community power, (7) shared core values, and (8) the capacity to engage in critical reflection (Delgado, 2000a). The interplay of these eight dimensions brings community capacity enhancement to life by giving it meaning, purpose, and direction.

A capacity enhancement perspective is very important to better provide a balanced view of undervalued populations and to identify areas, services, and programs where social workers can help initiate or collaborate on service to a community.

Values and Principles of Capacity Enhancement

It would be artificial to separate values from any proposed recommendations pertaining to interventions. Values form the core of an intervention and as a result shape the principles and guide how an intervention is conceptualized and implemented. Although capacity enhancement practice is relevant when working with any population group, it has particular appeal for use with undervalued groups—groups that, understandably, have historically been told by society that they have no strengths or assets. Such groups include the poor, people with various disabilities, people of color, women, elders, gays, lesbians, and the transgendered. When a group has multiple jeopardies—such as low-income women of color who have prison records—a need to "rediscover" and "reawaken," and a need to have hope for the future and to believe in themselves, then capacity enhancement practice takes on added significance in any form of intervention.

The fundamental belief that all human beings, institutions, and communities have strengths and assets forms the core of the values that inform capacity enhancement practice: "Social work is in need of a paradigm that builds community capacity as a central goal. Such a paradigm requires a philosophical foundation that embraces the belief that communities are capable of helping themselves if provided with the opportunity to do so" (Delgado, 1999, p. 25). Although social work and other helping professions have had no difficulty embracing these values, the reality is such that practice based on such values is not often found in the field, particularly when it involves undervalued groups such as the correctionally supervised. Few practitioners would argue publicly that individuals or communities do have strengths—otherwise why would they need a social worker?

I remember one of my students who upon covering the material on assets in class went back to her field placement with suggestions about how to better tap community assets and was told by her field supervisor that "this is the real world." In other words, material on assets was much too theoretical and not practical enough to warrant integration into practice. Indirectly, the field instructor was saying to the student that her professor had lost touch with reality! Attitudes toward capacities, assets, strengths, and the like may well be the most significant barrier facing interventions that actively eschew deficits as a basis for practice.

Many of the principles presented here are not unique to capacity enhancement. In fact, practitioners may well already use some of these principles in the creation of interventions. However, in combination the principles reinforce each other and maximize intervention goals. A total of nine capacity enhancement principles will be presented with particular relevance to work with the correctionally supervised in urban areas of the United States. These principles, it should be noted, have been written specifically with people of color in mind, and they are based on my review of the literature and practice in this field:

1. All individuals, regardless of background and circumstances, possess strengths and abilities. It is never a question of whether a person has strengths. It is only a question of what they are! Strengths come in various shapes and types, and this must be understood by all participants, particularly practitioners. Efforts to "categorize" strengths according to "narrow" types are foolhardy and misleading.
2. Interventions rarely follow a predictable and linear path. Thus, flexibility in design and implementation is essential to allow for local circumstances to influence the process and outcome. An understanding of this principle can allow all parties in the change process to proceed at a pace that is realistic and can contribute to a high likelihood of success in the long run.
3. Process is as important as, if not more important than, outcome. Every effort must be built into an intervention not only to encourage but to require active and meaningful participation by those the intervention seeks to help. Planning with, rather than for, is the norm. An emphasis on the importance of process highlights the importance of engagement, or "buy in," by all parties.
4. Cultural context cannot be separated from social and economic context. These spheres overlap, interact, and alter each other. Interventions, as a result, must take into account the circumstances influencing perceptions and behaviors. This principle ensures the relevance of an intervention.
5. Interventions must address a current need or concern, while systematically preparing participants, organizations, and communities for the future. This duality is necessary in order to be responsive to current and future needs and considerations.

6. A community's quality of life must be bettered as a result of an intervention. This change can be instrumental, as when physical changes are made in the environment, or expressive, as when perceptions of a "safer" and more "welcoming" community are created. Capacity enhancement interventions do not have the luxury of targeting only an individual or group of people. Interventions must change both individual participants and the community in which they live.

7. Social and economic justice themes must be integrated into capacity enhancement interventions as a means of bringing about societal changes. Capacity enhancement cannot achieve its true potential without also considering how undervalued groups in the United States face a disproportionate likelihood of being imprisoned.

8. Interventions must provide participants with an opportunity to have their voices heard—to express their hopes, fears, and concerns. A safe setting and climate is essential if these emotions are to be expressed. Interventions must also provide opportunities for participants to follow creative impulses. The correctionally supervised rarely have opportunities to express their innermost thoughts and feelings and, as a result, must be provided with a vehicle to do so in a manner that is affirming.

9. Reconnecting ex-offenders so that they may participate meaningfully in the life of family and community is an essential element of any capacity enhancement intervention. The correctionally supervised often find themselves disconnected from support systems—both formal and informal—yet their ultimate success in the outside world rests with their capacity to form and maintain relationships. Reconnecting forms the basis for current and future relationships.

Goals of Capacity Enhancement Social Work Practice with Prisoners and Former Prisoners

I am very fond of describing goals as "inspirational statements of what one hopes to achieve by designing an intervention." Objectives, in turn, "are measurement statements of what you hope to accomplish by a given point in time." The goals of capacity enhancement practice fall into five categories: (1) collective action/participation, (2) strengths and assets, (3) empowerment, (4) cultural competency, and (5) collaboration.

Collective Action/Participation

The goal of achieving meaningful participation and collective action is as old as social work itself. Both micro- and macropractice methods have identified the importance of clients and communities playing an active and meaningful role in determining what is best for them. Collective action, or consumer participation, in programs is widely accepted within the human services and educational fields. However, in the field of corrections, participation on the part of the correctionally supervised has few advocates. Ownership of interventions is simply not possible when major decisions are made on behalf of someone rather than with someone.

Collective action is often accomplished by providing consumers with an understanding of the avenues available to them, including the consequences of certain choices, and by fostering the development, or enhancement, of the necessary tools (knowledge and skills) to carry out their decisions. Self-determination is a central goal of any form of intervention. However, having said this, I am well aware that in many instances—such as when social workers are hampered by funding and agency restraints— a consumer may be given the "illusion" of determining his or her fate when the options are either not fully available or nonexistent. Consequently, the goal of collective action and participation can prove very perplexing to consumers and troubling to social workers.

If ownership of a decision, or program, is ultimately to rest with consumers, they must play an active and significant role in all phases of the process, from design and implementation to evaluation. Capacity enhancement practice, as a result, requires the consumer to have ownership of the decision and outcome. There is a dramatic difference between planning for and planning with a consumer. Actively seeking input from the consumer is significantly different from decision making. Decision making with the correctionally supervised, however, will require that practitioners walk a thin line between artificially offering alternatives, since coercion may be the underlying factor in the relationship, and offering "true" choices within a set of boundaries that are understood by all parties. In essence, true choice for the correctionally supervised may be made impossible because of legal requirements.

Social work scholars have generally tackled the subject of collective action and participation from a variety of perspectives. Burke's (1978) framework viewed participation from the perspective of the party seeking community participation and stresses how an agenda may facilitate or hinder participation and outcomes. Rothman (1974), in turn, looked at participation from the perspective of the consumer and the gains that can be derived by participation: (1) experiential (psychological) and (2) instrumental (concrete benefits such as access to privileged information and material gains).

Strengths and Assets

Although the concepts of strengths and assets have been around for many decades in the social work profession, they have only relatively recently received the attention they warrant, particularly as they relate to undervalued populations in this country. Undervalued groups have historically been viewed from a deficit perspective by many in this country, and, I would argue, by the profession of social work as well. Consequently, it is not a "major leap" to see the need to bring these concepts into a capacity enhancement paradigm.

A focus on strengths and assets is central to any capacity enhancement practice and effectively differentiates capacity enhancement from paradigms stressing deficits, pathology, and needs. A strengths/assets perspective is much more than a change of vocabulary—"Is the glass half full or half empty?" Nevertheless, vocabulary is an important aspect of any paradigm. We shape language and language shapes us. For example, the reader is challenged to come up with terms that use the word "black" in a positive way and "white" in a negative way. This exercise is a powerful way to highlight how language helps to shape attitudes and how attitudes shape language.

A strengths/assets approach to capacity enhancement requires the acquisition of new forms of knowledge and new skills. Interviewing to identify strengths, for example, requires a new approach to asking and sequencing questions because most people, the correctionally supervised among them, are much more skilled at answering questions that look at faults or needs. In addition, one must allocate more time to getting answers to strengths types of questions. I often recommend to students and practitioners to triple the time used to do a needs assessment in order to do an asset-based intervention.

Unfortunately, assessment methods used for identifying strengths and assets are, on the whole, inadequate because of social work's reliance on assessment methods that have emphasized deficits, pathologies, and needs. These methods, in turn, have been reinforced in social work education and further reinforced in the field by funders. Assessment of strengths requires a different language, as well as different ways of asking questions, making observations, and putting together all the information to reflect a positive perspective.

A capacity enhancement paradigm allows practitioners to consider a wide range of types of strengths and assets. Strengths, for example, have historically been viewed as belonging to the individual. In the corrections field, for example, practitioners seek to identify qualities in an individual that have served to help him or her survive in a hostile world. Assets, on the other hand, provide practitioners with an opportunity to bring into consideration indigenous resources such as open spaces, geographical location of a community, and cultural and community traditions—resources that do not fall into the category of "individual" strengths. The combination of strengths and assets, as a result, provides a capacity enhancement paradigm with sufficient options to "mix and match" resources in the development of interventions.

Empowerment

The literature on empowerment reflects that concept's rich tradition in social work, and as a result it will not be reviewed in any great depth in this section (Gutierrez and Lewis, 1999; Lee, 1994; Simon, 1994; Solomon,

1976; Staples, 1984). Empowerment can be defined as the process through which individuals and communities acquire the beliefs, knowledge, and skills necessary to exercise control over their destinies. This process, or journey, so to speak, will vary depending on local circumstances. Empowerment, then, is a complex construct that involves values, beliefs, and capacities. Like capacity enhancement, it too can be a philosophical stance, an intervention, or a goal. Depending upon how empowerment is conceptualized and implemented, it can look dramatically different yet still be considered empowerment.

Empowerment, as a result, has a multidimensional aspect. It first must have an attitudinal basis. Individuals, groups, and communities must believe that they have been offended in an unfair manner and believe that they have the right to effectively seek redress to alter the situation. The belief in their rights and power to act, however, is no small accomplishment for undervalued groups who have been socialized to believe that they are "powerless." Any degree of change starts with the belief that it is possible. The achievement of this belief is never easy, but it is essential if a transformation is to occur.

Knowledge is also an important element of empowerment. Knowledge, in this instance, can apply to a wide range of subjects. However, the most important knowledge area is possessing the know-how to target a system for change and possessing the requisite cognitive competence to design and implement a change strategy. Skills, in turn, flow from having the right attitude and possessing the requisite knowledge. The skills to implement a plan of action represent the third critical element of empowerment-based interventions. I have, unfortunately, witnessed too many empowerment workshops where the emphasis is on knowledge and skills without paying adequate attention to attitudes and beliefs. Thus, attitudes form the foundation of intervention, and all sources of knowledge and skills rest upon that foundation.

Cultural Competency

The concept of culture can be operationalized in a multitude of ways. However, perhaps the most common in social work is to use culture as the context for explaining attitudes and behavior. Using an ethnic/racial lens further focuses a cultural viewpoint. Culture, as I am fond of saying, is like a moving cloud. We call all see and track it; however, good luck in trying to grab it. The cloud metaphor highlights culture's beauty and significance, as well as its elusive nature—it challenges us to define it. The use of culture in a capacity enhancement perspective brings an important and much needed dimension to the paradigm. Natural support systems have played a critical role in bringing culture to life with various groups. I have applied such support systems in my work with Latinos, particularly Puerto Ricans.

A cultural perspective on behavior provides practitioners with a context to assist them in both assessment and interventions. This perspective must also take into account historical factors, reasons for migration, and other influential factors. In essence, a cultural perspective seeks to identify how key values are represented and how communication is conducted. Communication styles, for example, influence verbal and non-verbal language. An understanding of how culture influences communication informs a practitioner on how best to ask questions and interpret responses.

The dramatic demographic changes that are occurring across the United States, particularly in urban areas, cannot be ignored by the profession in the twenty-first century. The country is not only "browning" in terms of the composition of its residents, but it is also "graying," resulting in a population shift unprecedented in our history. Leigh notes that cultural competence necessitates being "aware that any helping situation must be consistent and consonant with the historical and contemporary culture of the person, family, and community . . . [and] take into account the nature of exchange relationships which characterize and give objective and subjective meanings to helping encounters" (1998, p. 173).

Interestingly, most of the literature on cultural competence has eschewed its application to the correctionally supervised. Ogawa's (1999) book on cultural sensitivity focuses on treatment of victims of color and does not examine to any great degree offenders and their assets. The lack of scholarly material on cultural competence and the correctionally supervised may be the result of the stigma associated with working with this population and of prevailing national sentiments on punishment versus rehabilitation. Nevertheless, I believe that cultural competence is as relevant with the correctionally supervised as with any other group, and deserving of attention from scholars, practitioners, and policymakers (New York Department of Correctional Services, 1986).

Collaboration

The concept of collaboration has been widely accepted in the helping professions. There is wide agreement that service delivery can be enhanced and resources maximized only when organizations are willing to enter into collaborative partnerships. The broad and often complex nature of consumer needs, whether at the individual or community level, requires that organizations enter into formal or informal agreements with other organizations. Rarely will one organization possess the necessary expertise and resources to meet all the needs of a consumer.

To ensure that new groups can access services, it is necessary to conceptualize accessibility very broadly. Social workers, as a result, will have to be flexible in carrying out their functions. This will necessitate that services are no longer based in or on agency, setting, geography, or time (day or hour). Such flexibility will no doubt raise serious operational questions. Nevertheless, "standardized" ways of doing business may not "work" to the best interests of those they seek to help. Partnerships between organizations may minimize the strain on any one organization, thus sharing the onus of delivering services, as well as the rewards.

Collaboration as a service delivery strategy is near and dear to me both as a practitioner and a social work educator. Rarely will practitioners learn in school that partnerships are detrimental to the mission of their profession or organization. Nor will they learn in the field that collaboration must be avoided at all costs in seeking to reach and meet the needs of consumers. We often preach the virtues of cooperation and teamwork as ideal goals in service delivery or program development. However, rarely do we seriously speak about the difficulties in developing partnerships or about the labor intensive aspects of doing so. It is almost as if by magic we decree collaboration partnerships. Life in the field, unfortunately, is rarely that way.

I often ask my students about their experiences with collaboration, and rarely do I hear examples of positive experiences. Most of the time the discussion centers on horror stories and situations where the best of intentions were just not good enough to overcome organizational rivalries, jealousies, poor planning, poor communication, and just plain distrust. Collaboration within and between organizations, simply put, is difficult to achieve, although very rewarding when it is accomplished.

However, this does not mean that collaboration is impossible. As the saying goes: "The truth shall set you free. But in the meantime, it makes you feel horrible." One must acknowledge the challenges of achieving collaboration before attempting it. Capacity enhancement practice requires that practitioners and organizations enter into various forms of partnerships in order to maximize the possibilities of achieving their goals.

Capacity Enhancement Arenas with the Correctionally Supervised

Capacity enhancement strategies come in different shapes and sizes. However, capacity enhancement interventions with the correctionally supervised need to address as many of the following areas as possible in order to maximize success: (1) increase control over stress and behavior, (2) foster participation in and input into programming, (3) maintain and enhance contact with families and community, (4) increase self-esteem, (5) increase ethnic and cultural pride, (6) provide opportunities to give back to the community (community service), and (7) enhance feelings of empathy and wanting to care for others. These seven arenas for success are not mutually exclusive and very often are found in various combinations.

Increase Control Over Stress and Behavior

An individual's having control over his or her behavior and reducing stress serves multiple purposes within and outside of prison. Control over one's actions is critical in an effort to become a productive member of a community. The reduction of stress, in turn, is a common goal in most people's lives. This reduction serves to free up energy for other worthwhile pursuits.

Consequently, any intervention that actively seeks to provide offenders with "tools" for reducing stress and controlling behavior will be well received by the correctionally supervised and those charged with supervising them. Achievement of the above, however, does not have to be expensive and highly complex, as evidenced by the programs highlighted in this section.

PrisonSmart Foundation, a program that originated in Massachusetts, uses breathing techniques to help change prisoners' lives (Tarcy, 1999). The program started in 1992 in a county jail and has since expanded to involve approximately six thousand inmates in fourteen prisons in eleven states. The breathing exercises have served to reduce stress and minimize confrontations between prisoners. A prisoner's acquisition of breathing control serves to provide him or her with necessary skills that can be transferred to other areas of his or her life. The newly learned techniques do not require the purchase, storage, or maintenance of equipment. This "equipment," in essence, resides within oneself.

Foster Participation in and Input Into Programming

The goal of helping offenders gain control over their lives and their environment is never easy when the correctional system is charged with a mandate to monitor and control them. Nevertheless, one should not conceive of this goal in all-or-nothing terms. Instead, it can best be thought of as a continuum ranging from *no freedom to make choices* to *no restraints on making choices*. There is a tremendous amount of variability depending on the setting and the individuals involved. However, having said this, the practitioner must be sensitive to the realities of criminal justice systems and programs.

A program coordinator in the Bexar County (Texas) Adult Detention Center shared the following example, and it highlights what a capacity enhancement perspective on fostering participation can look like:

> One thing I have learned in my six years of working in the Bexar County Jail is that inmates can be very resourceful when the need arises. For example, in our program, there is a particular inmate that has grown spiritually. He wanted to share his faith in God with the other inmates. But, in order to teach others, he acknowledged that he needed to create something that would keep their attention. This particular inmate invented a Christian board game that resembles the famous game "Trivial Pursuit" (except that the questions are about Bible characters and stories). He uses the game in the unit, and from what he has told me, it is a success. This could be an example of an inmate teaching or mentoring another inmate, which you mentioned in your letter. (Camero, 1999, p. 1)

The creativity this inmate displayed could not have occurred had the detention center not provided him with the opportunity to be creative and the "space" in which to carry out the game. The example illustrates that you do not have to have a "program" fostering participation; it can be done on a case-by-case basis according to individual talents and goals.

Maintain and Enhance Contact with Family and Community

The ability to engage with family and, to a lesser extent, community provides ex-offenders with an opportunity to redress the consequences of past acts that resulted in their correctional supervision. Contact takes on added importance when incarceration was the consequence of violating a law. The increased awareness of the importance of children being with their parents has resulted in a number of prison and community alternative programs that stress parent-child unification, particularly for female offenders. The goal of reunification with children is widely recognized as possibly the most important motivation for mothers to enter and successfully complete treatment for substance abuse.

One such program is the Mother-Offspring Life Development (MOLD) program in the Nebraska Correctional Center for Women in York, Nebraska: "Here in Nebraska, innovative programs—a prison nursery, overnight visits for older children—are breaking down the bars between prisoners and their children. Larry Wayne, the warden for eight years, says that even if he didn't like children, even if there were no pressing reasons to strengthen the connection between inmates and their children, he would approve of their presence on the grounds. 'Children bring humanity into a situation that's otherwise pretty tense, hostile, volatile' " (Dowling and Nyary, 1997, p. 84).

MOLD was modeled after the program developed in Bedford Hills, New York (see the case study in chapter 8) and is one of only two prisons in the country with nurseries. Special nursery cells are situated next to sitting rooms with televisions, toys, and rocking chairs. Programs such as MOLD minimize the disruption to caring that results from imprisonment, facilitate bonding and the maintenance of relationships, and ultimately help the ex-offender make the transition back to family, community, and society. Capacity enhancement necessitates that relationships be made stronger as a result of an intervention. These relationships, in turn, serve to build a foundation in the community and society.

The MATCH/PATCH (Mothers and Their Children/Papas and Their Children) program, based in San Antonio, Texas, is another example of a program that actively seeks to maintain parental participation at the county jail level. Established in 1984, it is considered to be the first in the country to offer parenting contact visitation services for inmate mothers in a county jail. A social worker, Ms. Julianna Perez, is credited for creating the program. The program's mission is "to modify behavior of incarcerated parents with parenting and life skills training to strengthen the parent-child relationship during incarceration; to lessen the trauma of separation for the children; to involve community agencies in the rehabilitation of incarcerated parents; and to assist family reconciliation efforts upon the parent's release from jail" (MATCH/PATCH, 1999, p. 1). Participation in the program is considered a privilege and is voluntary. This program's success is based on an understanding of the importance of children in the lives of most inmates and the need to encourage community-based organizations to participate in all aspects of the program. This team approach minimizes the disruption that inmates who have lost ties to their community can cause.

Increase Self-Esteem

A high measure of oneself is contingent upon having sufficiently high self-esteem. Low self-esteem severely limits the accomplishment of worthy deeds for oneself and others. Consequently, capacity enhancement must seek, directly or indirectly, to increase the self-esteem of ex-offenders in order to achieve a high level of social competence. Capacity enhancement, like empowerment, cannot succeed if the person being helped does not believe he or she is capable of being successful in society. Knowledge and skills must be built upon the right attitude.

The Prison Pet Partnership program at the Purdy Treatment Center for Women in Washington state serves as an excellent example of the importance of increased self-esteem. Providing inmates with the requisite skills to prevent them from resorting to crime to generate income is an important aspect of the program. However, skill acquisition without confidence, willingness to trust, and perseverance is not enough to ensure success, as attested to by the following inmate's story:

> Leslie is the most recent graduate of the grooming program. In September, she entered a work release program and started her new job as a groomer at a Seattle pet store. She confesses that she had no interest in dogs when she decided to apply for the program. Her motivation was strictly self-centered. She was scheduled to move from medium to minimum security and the thought terrified her. She was comfortable where she was, where she knew the routine and the people. Searching for a way to stop the transfer, she discovered the Prison Pet Partnership program only accepted inmates in medium security. She worked hard to pass the entrance exam and was offered a position in the program. She began working with the dogs, and her life changed. For the first time, she has found something she loves to do. Her self-confidence has soared. Far from being a timid young woman afraid to leave her unit, she is now eagerly awaiting her final release this spring so that she and her twelve-year-old daughter can begin their new life. Her future goals include helping to establish a Prison Pet Partnership program in another prison. Excitement shines in her eyes as she declares. "I can do it." (Shilstone, 1998, p. 34)

The Cell Door, an Internet magazine, provides a different perspective on the importance of individuals having an opportunity to increase their self-esteem through provision of outlets for creativity. Written by prisoners, the magazine provides avenues for outsiders to meet men and women behind bars. The topics of discussion, although heavily prison related, do not have to address the subject of imprisonment.

The Cell Door's mission statement reads as follows: "Our goal is to draw an audience who reads *The Cell Door* for its entertainment value and quality, learning in the process that prisoners are intelligent, personable, talented human beings."

The Cell Door provides prisoners such as Michael Tenneson and Calbraith MacLeod an opportunity to tell their stories, which are very often told in highly literary fashion. "The typical convict could also be accurately compared to a state of the art computer system with a very poorly written, virus-laden program," writes Tenneson. "Even though the 'computer' is not faulty, it appears so to the layman. In frustration, we may trash the computer, because it malfunctions, but a wise person, able to properly diagnose the malady would simply install a new, tested and proven program. Then the computer would function as it is supposed to." Calbraith MacLeod: "None of us wanted to be criminals. We did not sit in our fifth grade social studies class and dream of spending our lives in conflict with the law. We dreamed of having homes and jobs and grown up toys. We dreamed of leading serene, sane, non-destructive lives. Although many people, both in and out of prison, do not want convicts to be at peace in prison (some convicts refuse to even think of becoming at peace while incarcerated), it is our early dreams of serenity we as prisoners need to rediscover. It is only in developing a feeling of inner-peace, we can hope to live in society for long as nondestructive citizens."

Tenneson and MacLeod provide a rare glimpse of the lifelong capacities prisoners possess. These perspectives, dreams, angers, and hopes will find a voice if they are allowed to be aired. Using the Internet and *The Cell Door* publishes these sentiments and provides a venue for reader responses. The increased self-esteem that results from finding their voice goes a long way toward helping the correctionally supervised, in this case prisoners, take necessary steps toward finding their place in society.

Thus capacity enhancement practice brings with it gains at multiple levels—increased self-esteem for former inmates and, in the case of Leslie, new skills, reunification with family, and last, and certainly not least, a desire to give back to society—that is, her desire to replicate the Prison Pet Partnership program in another prison. Capacity enhancement is much more than the "enhancement" of skills. It is the creation of a belief in one's sense of self and one's ability to create new, and more positive, circumstances.

Increase Ethnic and Cultural Pride

In many ways it is artificial to separate self-esteem from pride in ethnic and cultural heritage. I, and other like-minded individuals, would argue that it is impossible to have high self-esteem and be ashamed of one's cultural heritage. In this society, if you are of color, you have had to contend with a lifetime of negative stereotypes of your ethnic or racial group. Factor in socioeconomic status, sexual orientation, and gender, as in the case of women, and the struggle to survive a negative self-image takes on monumental proportions. I believe that one's understanding and acceptance of cultural heritage forms the cornerstone of high self-esteem. However, for the purposes of this discussion, ethnic and cultural pride refers to individuals, in this case offenders, having a profound understanding, appreciation, and sense of their cultural heritage—a heritage that emphasizes positive contributions to society and values that have meaning in a cultural-historical context. Namely, "You are someone!" Needless to say, a concerted effort at building self-esteem through cultural pride will encounter tremendous resistance in American society. I remember having a heated discussion with someone who found the phrase "Black is beautiful" offensive. My reaction was that no one was saying that "white is ugly." Why must only one group be beautiful? Mind you, this same person had no issue with the phrase "white is right." Consequently, a systematic effort at building self-esteem through the use of cultural heritage will frighten people in authority.

Few organizations, religious or social service–based, have been as successful as the Black Muslims in developing the racial/ethnic pride of prisoners, a key dimension of capacity enhancement practice (Christianson, 1998). The example of Malcolm X, formerly known as Malcolm Little, stands as vivid testimony to the role religion and race (Nation of Islam) played in bringing about the transformation of a convict into a national leader: "By 1961 or so the Nation of Islam had attracted as many as a hundred thousand members, many of them urban males who had been in prison and who now eschewed drugs and other vices and were supposed to give as much as one-third of their legitimate earnings back to Black Muslim temples and schools" (Christianson, 1998, p. 247).

Malcolm X frequently spoke about his experiences in prison as part of his political message: "Don't be shocked when I say that I was in prison. You're still in prison. That's what America means: prison" (Malcom X and Haley, 1951, p. 45). The politicization of the prison experience built upon the importance of racial pride, history, and the contributions of Africans to society. It provided African American inmates with a deep sense of self-worth at a time when they were supposed to feel worthless. This achievement was no small feat for a group of people who were stigmatized and rejected by society.

Provide Opportunities to Give Back to the Community (Community Service)

The act of giving back to the community, or making amends for prior actions, is significant in capacity enhancement interventions, regardless of what population group is being addressed. The opportunity to make a difference in a community through focused work with individuals, families, and groups allows ex-offenders to practice new forms of knowledge and enhance skills. However, it is widely acknowledged that before individuals can give back to their community, they must first acknowledge to themselves and others that through their deeds they have harmed their community. This "ownership" of previous acts places responsibility on themselves. The giving back is a means of making restitution.

Service to the community has enjoyed a rich and long tradition in American society, and particularly in the youth development field (Osterman, 1995; Partee, 1996; Pennington, 1995; Scales and Leffert, 1999; Smith and Jucovy, 1996; Youniss and Yates, 1998). However, the concept of community service has not received the attention it deserves in the correctional justice field. Some residents may object strenuously to ex-offenders working with children, for example. Nevertheless, the experiences ex-offenders have had in the correctional field puts them in an excellent position to describe to youth what prison life is all about, a lesson that is not based on readings from a textbook.

There is a tremendous difference between experiential expertise (being able to "walk the walk," so to speak) and educational expertise (having a credential from a university saying one has pursued a certain line of educational inquiry). Needless to say, the person who has both has a powerful advantage in the human services field. It provides an individual with an opportunity to share experiences with both other providers and a client or community. Having both experiential and expertise legitimacy allows the possessor of this knowledge to act as a bridge between the two worlds.

Enhance Feelings of Empathy and Willingness to Care for Others

The willingness and ability to empathize and care for others forms the cornerstone of any set of emotions. Capacity enhancement, after all, is much more than strategies and techniques; it has an emotional component that is rarely touched on in the professional literature. One cannot, I believe, be effective in this society without the ability to empathize. Consequently, the practitioner should elicit from the client this aspect of being "human," or enhance it, before emphasizing the client's obtaining technical knowledge and skills. The People Animals Love program, discussed in greater detail in chapter 12, places animals with prisoners, providing inmates with an opportunity to care about others, in this case animals, as part of their rehabilitation and preparation for reentering the outside world.

Some would argue that focusing on enhanced feelings is another way of looking at what is commonly referred to as spirituality. Spirituality, after all, cannot be limited to religion; it is operationalized in a variety of ways and is receiving increased recognition in the profession of social work. Empathy and willingness to care for others brings a dimension to social work that is equally applicable to both micro- and macropractice. This "core" dimension, so to speak, also can serve to bring together practitioners from these two very different worlds, worlds that often use language that is foreign to each other and where mind-sets with sharply different perspectives can interfere with collaborative endeavors.

The Challenges of Capacity Enhancement Social Work with the Correctionally Supervised

I would love to say that capacity enhancement practice with the correctionally supervised can be implemented with minimal or no resistance, that the only barrier is our lack of imagination. However, I cannot honestly say this. The practice of capacity enhancement is challenging enough without adding a population that frightens the general public. Thus, practitioners have to be prepared to encounter, and counter, negative public opinion concerning their work with the correctionally supervised. Unfortunately, such negativity is an inherent aspect of any type of work involving undervalued groups.

I remember conducting a training session with human services workers and asking them about the stigma associated with working with undervalued people. Several workers noted they worked in the corrections field. I asked them how they coped with meeting strangers and being asked what they do. One worker responded that he would say he "worked for the state" and would refuse to elaborate any further. Another worker said that she would "mumble" the response and "prayed" that the person asking the question would be "kind" and not pursue the matter further. Another would tell the questioner that the nature of his work was confidential and he was not "at liberty" to discuss it publicly. In essence, the stigma associated with the correctionally supervised is "contagious," and this must be taken into account in any effort at developing an intervention based on capacity enhancement principles.

National debate about "punishment" versus "rehabilitation" will also play an influential role in how capacity enhancement principles get operationalized in daily practice. If advocates for the punishment and control of offenders win the debate, as is the case today, capacity enhancement practice as envisioned in this book will not see the light of day. However, if rehabilitation gets a fair opportunity to be tried, as I expect it will have to, then capacity enhancement can play an influential part in policy and practice development. Its potential for bringing about positive change in the field is limitless.

Social workers interested in capacity enhancement practice with the correctionally supervised may encounter significant resistance from other social workers not versed in the approach or resistant to working with the correctional population. Such resistance may well be the most painful kind to accept because it comes from one's own profession and colleagues. This fact should not come as a surprise to anyone with extensive experience in the profession. However, having said that, it still is a painful experience and one that I cannot get used to.

Resistance can take various forms from gratuitous statements such as "That is nice that you work with offenders" or "I am sure glad you can do it because I cannot" to more blatant resistance such as "Don't you have better things to do with your time and effort, such as devoting it to more worthy individuals?" Finally, resistance may also come from significant others and family. Rarely will a day go by when someone near and dear to us doesn't encourage us to seek other employment! In essence, some degree of resistance will be a part of our lives because of who we wish to help and the fact that we believe in their capacities. Such a "novel" approach, unfortunately, will make us appear "naive" (believing in "pie in the sky") or even "unprofessional" in the eyes of others.

Practitioners will face the challenge of having to prove to funders and administrators that interventions based on capacity enhancement principles and goals are effective. This challenge should not come as a surprise to anyone in the field. Advocating a "new" approach toward work with the correctionally supervised will bring with it increased pressure to quantify and measure all aspects of intervention—never an easy task. Nevertheless, the challenge must be met head on, and hopefully academics and others interested in research and evaluation will play an instrumental role in putting capacity enhancement on the national map.

As noted in chapter 1, a number of other professions have made concerted efforts to enter the field of corrections, with social work being one of the last and probably the least energetic of these efforts. Developing a collaborative practice with other professions may prove challenging because concerns over "turf" may act as barriers to partnerships. Nevertheless, I do not believe any profession, including social work, can effectively reach out to the correctionally supervised by itself. It will take an immense lobbying effort that crosses professions and citizen groups to change U.S. policies toward the correctionally supervised and to prevent future imprisonment. It will take a coalition made up of the social work profession and other disciplines to change the nation's policies.

Conclusion

I am under no illusion that the values, principles, goals, and concepts addressed in this chapter are the exclusive domain of social work. These values and concepts also can be found in the professional literature and education of other human services professions. However, the author believes that such an approach toward practice is more representative of social workers, although other professions may argue otherwise. Nevertheless, although few students of social work can graduate from a social work program without having been exposed to this material, most, unfortunately, have had difficulty translating this new form of knowledge into practice.

The structure and funding of services in the field has, with some exceptions, not embraced capacity enhancement principles and goals. Consequently, practitioners wishing to design and implement capacity enhancement initiatives will find numerous obstacles in their path. These obstacles are attitudinal as well as structural in nature. Capacity enhancement requires the creation of new ways of funding and evaluating activities, not to mention employing staff with the political will and skills to carry out interventions with this focus. To achieve the potential inherent in a capacity enhancement approach requires that the community, organizations, the correctionally supervised, and social workers come together as a team. The unifying philosophy that is capacity enhancement goes a long way toward providing the framework, language, and mission to accomplish this lofty goal we call a "team."

The field-based examples interspersed throughout this chapter cannot help but inspire hope for undervalued communities, and for that matter, the nation. Some of the examples even have social workers playing important roles in the creation and operation of programs. The examples clearly reflect a major paradigm shift concerning how best to serve the correctionally supervised. The case illustrations, in addition, show how communities and organizations with minimal "formal" resources have managed to mobilize themselves to reach out and engage the correctionally supervised. In so doing, they not only have increased the self-esteem of those they seek to reach, but also have systematically enhanced their capacities in the process. The clients' newly enhanced capacities, in turn, have strengthened the communities in which they live.

Some of the case illustrations are controversial, such as the example of the Black Muslims. Some practitioners, and the general public for that matter, would argue that this group preaches hatred and has systematically sought to separate black people from others, and as a result, has set back racial relations in America. Nevertheless, there is no denying that the Black Muslim movement has had a major impact on thousands of people whom society has largely, and unceremoniously, written off. I know of no other group, religious or otherwise, that has specifically reached out to inmates in such a systematic and deliberate manner.

Other case examples create less controversy, although they represent nonmainstream thinking in the field of correctional supervision. Such efforts have nevertheless pointed out the possibilities for success with the correctionally supervised. They show the rewards and challenges in store for providers in their efforts to reach out to the imprisoned and ex-offenders through the use of capacities and strengths.

The interventions discussed in this chapter entail budgets of various sizes. Some depend on grassroots fund-raising; others depend on multi-million-dollar budgets involving grants from foundations and federal and state sources. Capacity enhancement practice is not based on having a certain sized budget or a particular number of staff. In other words, it is not contingent on money. It represents a philosophical approach that can be implemented in any context, setting, or circumstance—from cases involving one person to those involving a large organization or community. This flexibility is one of the strengths of capacity enhancement work with the correctionally supervised.

6

A Framework for Capacity Enhancement Practice with the Correctionally Supervised

Practice is never without its share of challenges for a practitioner regardless of discipline or years of experience in the field. In fact, such challenges are what makes practice so exciting and meaningful as a line of work. Practice with the correctionally supervised, regardless of ethnic or racial considerations, is no exception. As a student, I was always struck by the difficulty of applying theory covered in class to actual situations in the field. The concurrent nature of having academic classes and field simultaneously was supposed to facilitate the application of theory to practice. However, although it looked good on paper, in reality it was a different story. It took me many years of postgraduate experience to realize that theory cannot be accepted as "truth," and that one is expected, if not required, to modify it to take into account local circumstances and one's abilities, knowledge, and capacities. In essence, the dynamic nature of practice necessitated the development of this "wisdom" in order to succeed in the field.

The disparity between theory and practice was even more striking when it involved communities of color. It seemed like it was never an effortless task to apply theory, particularly when the examples used in class with certain population groups did not "translate" to other population groups, with work with the correctionally supervised being one example. That group of clients always seemed to be faced with insurmountable barriers and multiple needs and to be distrustful of authority figures. These challenges, so to speak, increased the importance of using a practice framework that was sufficiently flexible to take into account unforeseen situations and circumstances, a framework that lent itself to modification, and could be so modified in a short period of time. This, as a result, required that the practitioner be willing to develop his or her own framework based on theory, past experience, and local circumstances.

The implementation of theoretical concepts is facilitated when practitioners have a tool (framework) to guide them in their intervention decision-making process. Thus, the importance of a framework is well understood by practitioners and scholars alike. A framework is more important than an "outline" for practice: it provides practitioners with sufficient guidance to help them in assessing, planning, implementing, and evaluating actions. There are numerous types of frameworks in the field of social work and other helping professions, allowing practitioners to select the one that best represents their approaches to intervention. I, like other practitioners and scholars, have developed what I believe is a workable framework for practice with undervalued groups and communities. It has evolved slowly over the years to include a series of steps, or stages, that are conducive to use with a capacity enhancement perspective, incorporating the philosophical and theoretical concepts covered in chapter 5. This framework, in addition, is not limited for use in either micro- or macropractice. It lends itself to either—with the requisite modifications that are necessarily influenced by method used. Mind you, this "discovery" is not unique to me. Practitioners, in order to be effective, also develop frameworks that are applicable to their job functions, organizations employing them, and communities or issues being addressed. The framework provided here may well serve as a foundation that can be modified and built upon by practitioners. The "license" to do so is openly acknowledged and encouraged. I use examples from the field of corrections whenever possible to highlight how this framework can be implemented.

Functions of a Practice Framework

A framework, as already mentioned, is a tool that practitioners use to help them to carry out interventions. A framework has four primary goals: (1) provide practitioners with overall direction for an intervention, (2) assist them in making decisions concerning approaches, (3) systematically break an intervention into manageable components, and (4) facilitate assignment of tasks within a team. A framework integrates interactional (sociopolitical) factors and theoretical material. The former stresses the gathering of information and decision making based on local circumstances and other political considerations—for example, what the funding source will allow and what language needs to be used to communicate with funders, the community, and so on.

Theoretical concepts, in turn, are just that—use of theory to inform the practitioner. Theoretical concepts can be derived from a variety of sources. However, when they are combined with interactional aspects of a framework, the practitioner has a solid understanding of what he or she wishes to accomplish throughout all phases of an intervention, contingency plans should anything go wrong, a time frame, and an understanding that there are certain key functions that must be accomplished to bring about a desired change in an individual, organization, or community. A framework, as a result, should be a tool that is flexible enough to be as simple or as complex as a practitioner wants it to be. Each stage of a framework can be operationalized according to the demands of time and the availability of funding, as well as the level of "sophistication" a practitioner may have with theoretical concepts.

Framework for Capacity Enhancement Practice

I rely on a framework that seeks to ensure that groups and communities play an active role in shaping the intervention based on local circumstances, cultural context, and goals. Thus, the reader is advised that any framework that actively seeks meaningful input and direction from constituents will prove challenging, labor intensive, and at times, frustrating, particularly when the practitioner must develop an intervention without sufficient time and resources, or when she or he cannot operationalize important principles such as self-determination because the organization employing her or him, such as is often the case with prisons, does not encourage self-determination. However, I am hard pressed to develop another framework that is less intensive.

The capacity enhancement framework that I advocate consists of five distinct yet highly interrelated phases, or stages, with each having two important dimensions—interactional (sociopolitical) and analytical (theoretical). The phases are (1) identification and assessment, (2) mapping, (3) engagement, (4) intervention, and (5) evaluation. The reader will come across frameworks that may use different terms than the ones used here, or a different number of stages. Some frameworks place greater emphasis on different stages, while others do not openly state their bias. Further, as I have noted elsewhere, a framework having multiple phases necessitates that all are considered while focusing on the one at hand: "A practitioner does not have the luxury of focusing exclusively on assessment, for example, without keeping in mind how to undertake a map, actively seeking support (engagement), noting what kind of service will be widely received, taking into account implementation considerations, and thinking about evaluation factors. An effective practitioner can consider one phase as foreground and the others backgrounds, but never lose sight of the importance of the other phases" (Delgado, 2000a, p. 36).

I realize that no practitioner is equally adept at all phases of a framework. Some of us may have a favorite phase, and I certainly do, and some phases may prove more challenging than others. That is quite natural in practice. I seriously doubt whether there is a practitioner who not only is an "expert" at the phases of an intervention but also favors all of the phases. Some of the more challenging phases may require that a practitioner seek advice, consultation, supervision, or even active assistance. On the other hand, we never have the luxury of working on only one phase of a framework to the exclusion of other phases. There are always aspects of a framework that require further thought, work, and mastery, and that is what makes for educational growth!

Identification and Assessment

The identification and assessment phase is undoubtedly my favorite. The initiation of this stage brings about a tremendous amount of excitement and uncertainty. All the hopes and fears associated with an intervention are an integral part of this phase of the framework. When properly planned and implemented, it sets a strong foundation for an entire project or intervention and can help the practitioner weather the uncertainties and trials and tribulations that are to follow during the other stages of the framework.

The initial phase of any framework takes on added importance because it not only sets the stage, or foundation, but also serves to engage the individual or community being worked with. The literature, fortunately, has slowly started to reflect examples of asset assessments and the thinking that goes into conceptualizing and implementing them, particularly in urban communities and with population groups that are marginalized. As a number of scholars have noted, it is essential for practitioners not to rely on existing data, which in all likelihood are deficit driven. A capacity enhancement approach requires that practitioners generate data, qualitative in nature, as a means of developing a more well-rounded picture of a community's capacity to address issues affecting it. These data may be derived from interviews or conversations with offenders and community residents.

Unfortunately, typical assessment-related data such as those gathered by law enforcement and criminal justice organizations tend to focus on recording the nature and extent of illegal-based activities. These data serve to further stigmatize and demoralize communities because of the constant need to highlight the dysfunctional aspects of the community and because they are used as a means of substantiating grant-related funds. In essence, there is money to be had by stressing deficits, needs, dysfunctions, and so on. Funding sources, with some exceptions, are not really interested in learning more about how those who are oppressed manage to survive the trials and tribulations of life in "distressed" communities.

Asset-driven data are generally not valued by funding sources, the media, or policymakers and, as a result, are not gathered. When gathered under exceptional circumstances, such data are limited to a certain geographical location and do not benefit from systematic gathering across several geographical boundaries. Thus, it is impossible to compare assets from one community to another when relevant data are not available. Nevertheless, it is relatively easy to compare along deficit lines. This bias serves to reinforce stereotypes of marginalized communities in our society. Thus, generally there is a need to generate primary data when developing capacity-enhancing initiatives targeting the undervalued. This process is labor intensive and expensive for an organization; however, it is critical if an initiative is to be capacity enhancement driven. Further, identifying and assessing assets serves an important engagement goal in enlisting the support of the community from the initial phases of an intervention project.

For example, how many community-based institutions, such as houses of worship, are employing staff with criminal justice experiences? Individuals with firsthand knowledge of prison, for example, very often find that their experience is valued by community-based social service organizations, particularly those who actively do outreach and serve those who have been or currently are in correctional supervision situations. These same individuals can play important roles as neighbors, friends, and "informal" providers of service in the community in which they live. Some may even act as "consultants" to the community by helping individuals and families "navigate" the criminal justice system. In fact, there are a number of consulting businesses, established by former prisoners, to help those in need through advocacy and provision of information (Reibstein, 1997).

Houses of worship are excellent nontraditional settings that have historically reached out to offenders and ex-offenders and, in some cases, employed them in programs targeting ex-offenders and their families. In some cases, ex-offenders have played important volunteer functions involving the congregation and the community at large. Unfortunately, programs run from houses of worship rarely get listed in agency resource directories, requiring contact with each individual church within the community in order to identify relevant programs. For example, I have found that communities generally have certain places, or spaces, where former offenders feel comfortable going and where they are accepted. I remember one such place, a bar, that seemed to have a high number of employees with prison records. The community, needless to say, did not hold this place in high esteem because it did not hold any bar in high esteem. Yet this bar was different from most other bars: it served as a place where bartenders would provide consultation to recently released inmates as to where they could go to get different types of social services in the community. In situations where a former inmate could not speak or read English, one bartender in particular would translate letters from English to Spanish and, on occasion, would make telephone calls on behalf of the former inmate. This experience parallels very closely my experiences with a local restaurant that fulfilled many of the same functions, but for people who were not former offenders (Delgado, 1996). However, the restaurant did not have a stigma attached to it. The bar did!

The social stigma associated with having a prison record makes an asset assessment ever more challenging to accomplish, particularly in communities distrustful of any form of research. Families very often seek to hide the fact that one of their members has served time in prison. Sometimes they may even make up stories about an individual moving to another part of the country in search of employment.

The stigma for the family, as noted in chapter 4, can be sufficiently strong as to mask the true impact of imprisonment on families and communities. Ex-offenders, in turn, who have managed to put their life on track and are productive members of the community may not want to share their past with strangers. Unfortunately, distrust of researchers is very often founded on a past experience, or experiences, with "researchers" coming into the community under one pretense and then unveiling a hidden agenda—an agenda that is likely deficit based and that ultimately results in a report that further stigmatizes the community being studied. Community residents with correctional experiences will rarely "open up" and share their personal backgrounds with outsiders. Many ex-offenders may wish to hide their past in an effort to start new lives—or in the case of those who are widely known to have been in prison, to rekindle new community feelings. The process of identifying and assessing the contributions made by such people to a community may be incomplete unless practitioners specifically take these factors into account in the design and implementation of the assessment.

The identification and assessment phase may be labor intensive, requiring a considerable amount of time and energy. This phase will be greatly facilitated if the people doing the assessment are ex-offenders and share similar ethnic or racial backgrounds with those in the community being studied. Obtaining the sponsorship of community organizations and leaders will also serve to minimize distrust of outsiders. Every effort must be made to have community residents do the interviews as a means of effectively reaching out to all sectors of the community and minimizing miscommunication. Also, involving residents as interviewers provides important income to the community, and when training of interviewers is undertaken, that enhances their capacities in the process.

Mapping

The process of mapping community assets to be used in the development of capacity enhancement interventions is both exciting and frustrating. The lack of existing data on community assets in general, not to mention the correctionally supervised, can frustrate organizations and practitioners. The identification and assessment phase of the framework prepares the practitioner to be better informed and appreciative of the assets available in a community and potential obstacles to overcome in developing an intervention, be it micro or macro centered; it helps identify potential sources of assistance in the community; and lastly, it informs the practitioner about how best to design an intervention. It is important to note, however, that having done a "solid" identification and assessment is no guarantee that the design of an intervention will be 100 percent certain of success. The odds of being successful do go up dramatically, however.

The process of mapping, it should be noted, is not restricted to macro-practitioners, although it lends itself very well to that type of practice. Clinicians, too, can use mapping strategies and techniques based upon their caseloads and those of the organization employing them. Most of us are very familiar with identifying groups of individuals from existing case-loads. Sharing of information between providers has served as a means of helping to shape the focus of a group and has facilitated the recruitment process—no small feat. However, similar principles regarding capacities are generally absent in those types of settings. Nevertheless, because it has not happened in the past does not mean it cannot happen in the future under the right circumstances.

The actual process of mapping can cover a wide range of possibilities depending on the goals of the practitioner, his or her time and resource constraints, and the level of sophistication required of the practitioner. The process of mapping does not have to be very expensive. Sometimes it only requires an actual map of a geographical area, as in the case of macro-focused interventions. Such maps can be enlarged to facilitate the input of group members and to provide sufficient community details—or, as in the case of micro-focused interventions, to facilitate a listing, or inventory, of the capacities possessed by individuals in a caseload.

Different-colored pins can be used to mark certain qualities or conditions that must be taken into account in the development of an intervention. Red pins, for example, can be used to mark places in the community where the correctionally supervised "hang out" and feel comfortable. Another color can be used to indicate indigenous resources, such as houses of worship, where programs exist targeting the particular population group. After a systematic process of marking off key factors comes a process of analysis. There may be a place in the community that attracts the correctionally supervised, but upon closer examination, no resources (formal and informal) may exist there to do outreach and provide services.

Engagement

The engagement process, as already noted, does not necessarily start and end with this phase. If properly conceptualized and implemented, engagement starts during the initial phase of identification and assessment and continues through all the other phases. It is of sufficient importance, however, to warrant a phase of its own as a means of focusing attention and resources on developing supportive relationships between community and practitioner.

The process of engagement seeks to obtain a commitment from all interested parties to either the development or facilitation of an intervention. This sociopolitical process stresses communication and interpersonal skills. Communication, in this instance, refers to much more than the ability to speak the languages of the community being addressed. In essence, if a practitioner attempting to involve a Latino community spoke Spanish, and particularly the dialect of those being targeted for intervention, communication would mean to facilitate engagement. But communication is more than this. Competencies in speaking and understanding language refers to nonverbal communication, slang, and other forms of communication.

An ability to read murals serves as an excellent example of what I mean by possessing communication competencies. Murals are endemic in most low-income urban communities of color in the United States. It would be rare for a practitioner not to notice them and their images and the story they seek to tell the public (Delgado and Baron, 1998). Yet few practitioners actually stop and try to "read" the messages expressed in this art form. Memorial murals, for example, present a story of a premature death or tragedy to the public (Delgado, in press). Such stories often highlight how the death occurred and the date it occurred, and references are made to the deceased's talents, hobbies, and aspirations. These murals are essentially a message board that can provide outsiders with a historical view of a community, its major struggles, and hopes for the future.

Intervention

Capacity enhancement programming offers practitioners a wealth of opportunities to actively build upon individual assets—in this case, those of inmates—and community assets. These two arenas should never be conceptualized as separate. In addition, interventions based on capacity enhancement principles cannot be dismissed according to the setting. Prisons, for example, may be quite a formidable establishment in which to bring about capacity enhancement, but they cannot be written off as being too arduous a project and too resistant to change. Capacity enhancement can take place in total institutions as well as community alternatives. Practitioners, as a result of the previous phase's related activities, will be able to select the intervention that best maximizes capacities by taking into account local considerations and circumstances.

Interventions utilizing capacity enhancement can cover a wide range of types and population groups ranging from individuals to couples to families to organizations and communities. This wide range makes it possible for all practitioners, regardless of their methods of practice, to use capacity enhancement. Educational and career counseling, for example, lend themselves to building on the talents and aspirations of inmates and ex-offenders. Although social workers historically have not been involved in this arena, there is no reason why we cannot be. Serious efforts to reduce recidivism, for example, must address issues of transition, one of which is obtaining gainful employment. This goal has concrete and emotional components, and social workers can effectively address both.

Educational programs, not surprisingly, provide a viable and effective vehicle for preparing an offender for release and increase the likelihood of success (Duguid, 1997; Gehring, 1997; Halstead, 1997; Semmens, 1997).

The issues raised by Gehring (1997) in initiating educational programs within prisons, however, must seriously be considered by practitioners: "Successful correctional educators know that students can sometimes function as teachers, and teachers can certainly participate in learning along with students. GOBs [good old boys] disdain these parallel interests. They always try to keep students and teachers separate" (p. 21). A thorough identification and assessment process will highlight for the practitioner possible helping and hindering forces to be taken into account in planning this form of intervention. The identification and assessment phase provides a practitioner with a solid understanding of how an intervention will be received and how it has to be framed in order to maximize engagement and support; it also serves to better prepare the practitioner for obstacles.

Correctional education, however, needs to have a solid philosophical foundation that does not treat the offender as a subhuman and actively prepares him or her for life in the community: "Providing offenders with education which merely parallels that available in the outside community was never enough of a goal. Our core activity must be education for living productively in the community and for the protection of potential victims" (Halstead, 1997, pp. 33–34). There is little question that correctional education has the potential to be empowering and actively build on innate capacities in the process.

Interventions seeking to achieve capacity enhancement goals will require active efforts to bring about collaboration between organizations—both formal and nontraditional. These partnerships not only seek to share the responsibility and ownership of an intervention; they seek to enhance the capacities of all the parties involved in the endeavor. No organization, regardless of its capacities, cannot benefit from the resources, information, and knowledge other organizations may possess. Consequently, capacity enhancement interventions must seek to enhance the capacities of all those involved in the process. The reciprocal nature of this relationship also strengthens the relationship among all parties involved in a collaborative intervention.

Evaluation

The subject of evaluation is one that is widely recognized as important and needed, but it is also one that is fraught with challenges for both practitioner and evaluator alike. However, there is no disputing the importance of practitioners having an ability to either design or carry out evaluations. Funding sources and social service organizations alike have increased their reliance on evaluation-generated data as a means of helping in the decision-making process concerning the funding of programs. These decisions ultimately affect the type of programs that are funded. Programs based upon noble ideals but poorly operationalized (demonstrating an inability to create objectives that are amenable to measurement) will not fare well.

Evaluations of interventions have generally focused on recidivism, a topic of wide importance in corrections and one that is well understood by policymakers. However, evaluation of how well interventions prevent recidivism are not without challenges, particularly when interventions are community based and considered "outside of more conventional incarceration approaches" (Gendreau, 1994, 1996; Johnson, Selber, and Lauderdale, 1998). The ability to take into account community characteristics and circumstances plays a critical role in helping evaluators better understand process objectives. A focus on outcome, although important, is not sufficient without an in-depth understanding of how the process of carrying out the intervention was influenced by local circumstances.

The paucity of professional literature on assets, strengths, and enhancement perspectives is not surprising (Johnson, Selber, and Lauderdale, 1998). Unfortunately it makes the tasks associated with evaluation that much more arduous to implement since a substantial body of literature cannot be used as a foundation from which to borrow and build upon. This lack of data, however, cannot be used as an excuse for not undertaking an evaluation or for using approaches that may have extensive literature written about them but essentially are deficit based or are not conducive for evaluating work with the correctionally supervised.

The evaluation of capacity enhancement initiatives invariably requires that practitioners use qualitative methods for gathering data. As noted by Patton, "The more a program aims at individual outcomes, the greater the appropriateness of qualitative methods" (1987, p. 19). Capacity enhancement initiatives are very much about achieving individual outcomes; they stress individualizing interventions whenever possible. However, they cannot be limited to just individual outcomes because part of what makes this approach so important is that it has broader applications.

Qualitative methods usually consist of three basic approaches: (1) in-depth, open-ended interviews that encourage probing and allow the "voice" of the individual to be highlighted, (2) direct observation, and (3) review of written documents such as records, questionnaires, and personal logs or diaries (Patton, 1987). These approaches to evaluation lend themselves well to either micro- or macropractitioners' efforts to assess the effectiveness of their work. Further, they are not capital intensive. Namely, they do not require elaborate methods for gathering data that can be expensive for a practitioner and his or her organization. "User-friendly" methods, in turn, can be modified to reduce any feelings an individual or community may have about "invasive" research.

At minimum, capacity enhancement evaluation should seek to answer six questions: (1) Did the intervention achieve its stated objectives? (2) Who (sociodemographic characteristics) best benefited from the intervention? (3) Are there ways of strengthening the intervention in a manner that is cost effective? (4) Are there ways of increasing the involvement of the community in the decision making and implementation of interventions? (5) To what extent can greater acceptance of capacity enhancement principles be built into the intervention? Finally, (6) How did the intervention materially change the community? The answer to this last question may uncover only relatively minor changes in the environment.

These six questions should serve as a core set that each practitioner and his or her organization should address in an evaluation. There is ample opportunity to develop other questions or questions that further operationalize these six to make them more relevant to local circumstances and considerations and take into account what being under correctional supervision means.

Conclusion

The importance of a framework can never be underestimated. It provides us with a tool that can play an influential role in helping us develop and evaluate an intervention. Further, it facilitates our communication with other practitioners by specifically outlining how we conceptualize our approach to intervention. Consequently, a framework helps us to develop a systematic "outline," if you wish, of how we hope to achieve a change in an individual, organization, or community.

Frameworks, however, are never apolitical in nature, nor are they rigid in structure. Human circumstances require flexibility on the part of a practitioner, whether he or she is micro or macro focused. Theory cannot be examined and implemented outside of a political context. It is not unusual for me to hear that macropractice "is political in nature" and that clinical practice is not. I would argue that all forms of practice are political in nature, and this needs to be recognized. It is an important lesson that all practitioners must learn. What do I mean by this? It is not possible to address the correctionally supervised, for example, in an urban community of color without incurring a great deal of anger and suspicion from residents. Distrust of authority figures, after all, is quite natural.

I remember working in an English and jobs-training program with the Latino community in a New England city, and the group was suggesting places it could visit as part of the field visit component of the program. One of the primary goals of the program was to expose participants to possible places of employment that they were unaware of or would not possibly consider. Upon finishing the process I commented on the fact that the local police headquarters or the courts were not mentioned by the group, and I asked whether anyone had any guesses as to the reasons for this omission. The group spent the next thirty minutes sharing stories about experiences they had had, or their relatives had had, with law enforcement and the legal system. Needless to say, the group did not want to visit these places or consider possible jobs in these systems. Ironically, the need for bilingual and bicultural staff in these settings made them excellent places for future employment. However, the stigma attached to working in such settings and the participants' fears of discrimination and racism effectively ruled out work in the criminal justice field. That experience left a lasting impression on me.

The framework presented in this chapter is not the "definitive" framework! In fact, I hope the reader can take it and modify it accordingly to best match his or her approach. Frameworks, after all, are dynamic in nature and must be open to change to take into account changes in context. Such changes, incidentally, may reflect findings from the latest research on how "best" to design and implement an intervention with a certain population or subpopulation. Work with the correctionally supervised of color is one example. Work with upper-middle-class ex-offenders who were imprisoned for embezzlement or fraud will look significantly different than work with a woman of color who is imprisoned for prostitution in order to "feed a habit" and has several children being cared for by a close relative.

3

Reflections from
the Field

Section 3 gives the reader an opportunity to apply the themes reviewed in chapters 1 through 6 to cases. The chapters in this section address a variety of settings. Chapter 7, "Case Study Method," introduces the considerations and methods involved in case selection and construction. Ten case studies (chapters 8 through 17) have been strategically selected to reflect a wide range of settings, services, and population groups. The capacity enhancement principles and methods at work in each are highlighted and detailed in hopes of bringing this concept to life in work with the correctionally supervised. These cases specifically focus on people of color, both male and female, young as well as adult. Chapter 18, "Reflections on Case Studies," summarizes key aspects of the case studies.

7

Case Study Method

The introduction of a new way of thinking, or paradigm, cannot rest squarely on theory alone. The concept also needs to be presented in a manner that brings it to life for the reader. This method of presentation, in addition, cannot emphasize the positives or the rewards without equal consideration of the challenges and consequences often associated with a new idea. Thus, the use of case studies to illustrate practice principles and techniques is not out of the ordinary in the field of social work and human services, and it is often the preferred method for illustrating how practice theory and principles get operationalized in the field. Further, a new perspective related to practice will evolve slowly over time, sometimes for longer than others, while practitioners start reading theoretical papers and books. The material works its way into the curriculum in schools of social work, and practitioners graduate ready to initiate practice interventions based on the concepts. Conversely, the concepts may originate in the field of practice and scholars hear and witness their use and decide to write about them. In essence, new perspectives related to practice may originate in the field or in the minds of scholars; however, regardless of their origins, new concepts require application and scrutiny in the field.

Case studies give practitioners an opportunity to witness an intervention, examine the rewards and challenges, and draw lessons for their practice. Thus, case studies very often represent the second best opportunity to learn, after actual practice. However, in order for case studies to achieve "educational success" in teaching practitioners, they must be "realistic," provide sufficient details to allow in-depth examination, and integrate theoretical material. Last, but certainly not least, they must be presented in a fashion that facilitates reading and the reader's eliciting of important factors and lessons. Readers, in turn, can select certain cases to read and study based on their interests and opportunities to implement the principles in their practice. Other cases may, or may not, be read with close attention to detail. I hereby give the reader license to do so in the following chapters.

The chapters on case studies were without question my favorite chapters of the book to write. They provided me with an opportunity to "venture out" into the field and talk to practitioners and consumers of services. In many ways, that process brings to life the subject of capacity enhancement practice with the correctionally supervised. The interaction that transpires in the creation of a case study is exhilarating and challenging at the same time. My sincere hope is that the reader, too, will experience these sentiments in reading these chapters. Although there is never a perfect substitute to actually "being there," case studies may prove to be good substitutes.

This chapter gives the reader an opportunity to examine how the case method has been conceptualized for use in this book, with its advantages and disadvantages. Following that, the reader is presented with ten cases, representing seven states (California, Maryland, Massachusetts, New York, North Carolina, Pennsylvania, Washington), Washington, D.C., and several regions of the country in an effort to be geographically responsible. Further, these case studies illustrate practice with men and women, juveniles as well as adults, and incarceration and postincarceration situations. One case (chapter 16) specifically looks at prevention. The cases have been purposefully selected, as will be explained later in this chapter, and they do not represent every possible setting involving the correctionally supervised.

Approaches to Field Studies

A multitude of research methods can be employed in examining practice and related issues. Social work research no longer lies within the domain of one approach or method. The complexity of the issues examined necessitates that researchers be sufficiently flexible in their selection of research approaches and methodologies. Goals and circumstances should inform the research method, and not the other way around. There is wider recognition, for example, that both qualitative and quantitative methods have much to offer and, as a result, are not mutually exclusive (Allen-Meares and Lane, 1990). Further, within each of these orientations toward data gathering are numerous approaches, each with certain advantages and disadvantages. Thus, the issues social work traditionally researches can benefit from multiple approaches and methods, with case studies being but one method.

The nature of the subject matter lends itself very well to using qualitative and, more specifically, ethnographic research (Burawoy, 1991; Martinez-Brawley, 1990; Sells, Smith, and Newfield, 1997; Spradley, 1979). Hardcastle, Wenocur, and Powers summed up quite well the relevance of ethnography for community social workers: "To grasp the hidden, a social worker, like an ethnographer, must search for the 'meaning of things' that a full participant in a separate culture 'knows but doesn't know he knows' " (1997, pp. 82, 84). A study of prisoners and former prisoners requires an approach that allows the researcher, and in this case the reader, to obtain the perspective of those who live with the subject matter on a daily basis. This perspective can best be obtained through an ethnographic approach to research. Such research, as a result, can best be compared to a journey without scheduled stops along the way. Enough unscheduled stops may require that the traveler change destinations as a result of new-found knowledge, experiences, and goals.

I have elected to use the case study method. This method, although not without limitations, provides the best window through which to examine new forms of practice. The case study method offers me a tremendous amount of flexibility in staging the case into which the reader will immerse him- or herself. This immersion, as a result, allows the highlighting of practice-relevant information, details, and conclusions. Nevertheless, many social work researchers have avoided this method: "The case study is a neglected and maligned approach to social work research. Rejected more for how uninformed researchers have used it and less for flaws intrinsic to its nature, the case study is compatible with many forms of social work practice and policy research. Although case studies are not useful for estimating prevalence rates or for probabilistic generalizations, they are useful to study problems in depth, to understand the stages in processes, or to understand situations in context" (Gilgun, 1994, p. 371).

I have made extensive use of this method in researching and writing about undervalued groups. The paucity of published research on the subject and the nature of the subject matter makes quantitative-based research of limited usefulness. Consequently, a method that is sufficiently flexible to take into account the voices of the people most affected by the subject matter is ideal for use in this book. A four-pronged approach was used in the studies: (1) review of existing literature—professional and popular press; (2) interviews with key informants in cities throughout the United States; (3) analysis of the content and methods used in reaching out to and serving former prisoners; and (4) profiles of exemplary programs that specifically seek to serve prisoners, former prisoners, and their families by using a capacity enhancement paradigm.

Effective use of case studies provides the reader with a great opportunity to bear witness to the experiences of others, and it allows him or her to enter a particular situation without actually having to do so in real life. In essence, a good case study helps the reader develop an in-depth understanding (Stake, 1995; Yin, 1994). The voices of these social workers in these fields of practice are very important in this book because they are in the best position to advise other social work professionals and educators about the importance of their work, the challenges they face in these new settings, and the strategies they have used to fulfill their mission. Case studies illustrating such efforts will aid the reader in translating theory into practice. Every effort will be made to draw on a diverse sample, taking into account types of settings, functions, sociodemographic characteristics of the correctionally supervised, and geographical sections of the country in order to increase the relevance and appeal of the book to a wide range of sectors.

The case method, however, has important limitations that must be acknowledged up front. Failure to do so will give the reader a misguided sense of the case study method. Its weaknesses, unfortunately, are notable, and the case studies presented in this book are no exception. A tremendous amount of information was gathered, but only a small percentage found its way into the written case studies. Limitations of time and resources did not allow me to gather greater in-depth information on a variety of aspects involving a case: (1) data provided by the organization examined were not checked for accuracy; (2) consumers of services were not interviewed because of issues related to confidentiality—their perspective, as a result, is missing; (3) only a limited number of key informants were interviewed, although every effort was made to obtain the views of those having concerns about an intervention; and (4) although every effort has been made to minimize author bias, total elimination is impossible. Nevertheless, although these limitations are ever present in the cases, the advantages, I believe, far outweigh the disadvantages.

Each case has enough detail to provide in-depth information, but it is not so long as to overwhelm the reader with unimportant information. The reader wishing to obtain information on the rationale for case selection and a review of the literature on the population group addressed in a case study can do so by going to the appendix. This strategy is intended to aid the reader by eliminating what some readers may call extraneous material. Readers who want this information have access to it.

Establishing the context is critical in a case study. The reader needs to contextualize the case, and this necessitates that I provide enough information to aid him or her in determining the setting and the conditions leading to the establishment of an intervention. Only then can the reader be in a position to extrapolate the case experience and apply it to his or her circumstances. Program-specific information, in turn, allows the reader to be able to examine the details surrounding practice and how the program is operationalized in the field. This, as a result, allows the reader to accept, modify, or reject program aspects that are either not feasible to his or her circumstances or politically difficult to achieve. Finally, the lessons-learned aspect of a case provides the reader with an opportunity to "listen to the voices" of the actual participants. This information, nevertheless, cannot be provided without addressing the previous two aspects of the case study.

It is important for the reader to know that none of the programs reported on in chapters 8 through 17 used the term *capacity enhancement* in its literature. Most had not heard of the concept when they were initially contacted about the writing of this book and its focus. This revelation should come as no great surprise since "professional jargon" often has more currency in research and scholarship than in the field of practice. As a result, I had to explain what was meant by capacity enhancement. Once the concept was defined and operationalized, practitioners were able to identify aspects of it that related to their programs. No program, however, had all the elements of capacity enhancement covered in chapter 5. Nevertheless, the case studies still reflect the philosophical thrust of capacity enhancement practice and serve as excellent field-based examples of how to build capacity enhancement–based services.

Key Informant Questions

Case studies are best constructed when a series of open-ended questions guide the data-gathering process. These questions, although obviously biased in their selection and construction, are an essential element of case study construction. In this spirit, a series of open-ended questions were developed to guide the key informant interviews used in the construction of the cases. These questions, in turn, were followed by subquestions that were used to elicit more definitive answers. The subquestions, however, will not be provided here, since they were tailored to the specific setting.

1. What motivated you (program director or executive director) to take a capacity enhancement perspective toward the correctionally supervised?
2. What do you look for in identifying capacities in the correctionally supervised?
3. How do you get individuals to believe that they have capacities and a desire to change their lives?
4. How do you use capacities in programming?
5. What are some of the strengths most people overlook in working with the correctionally supervised?
6. What kind of special skills do you look for when hiring staff to work in your program?
7. What are the biggest challenges that you face in having services and programs built upon a capacity enhancement perspective?

The preceding questions were purposefully constructed to help guide the interview without imposing undue structure on the informant. Further, the questions served to help my analysis of the responses with specific reference to capacity enhancement. Clearly, all the programs reported on in this book were complex and multifaceted in nature and lent themselves to analysis from a variety of perspectives. Nevertheless, a capacity enhancement perspective served to focus the questions used as a foundation in the key informant interviews.

The reader would undoubtedly have constructed another series of questions based upon particular interests and circumstances regarding practice. That, I believe, is quite natural and healthy. Ideally, the reader will examine the content presented in each of the cases and develop new interpretations, insights, and directions for practice. In essence, the case studies are intended to spark a curiosity and desire to attempt new methods for achieving the same goals of intervention.

Case Study Outline

How a case study is organized is important. Structure is needed to bring about uniformity between cases representing dramatically different population groups, settings, and geographical areas. The case studies are divided into five sections as a means of providing the reader with various perspectives and information on a case, and thus facilitating the reading of the material. Some of the sections lend themselves to presentation of facts while others lend themselves to interpretation:

1. *Context.* Information is provided on the factors and circumstances leading up to the creation of the program or service.
2. *Program specifics.* Information is provided on the nature of the work and program and responsibilities of staff.
3. *Capacity enhancement methods.* This section specifically highlights material related to capacity enhancement, such as approaches to identifying capacities, types of collaborative partnerships involving indigenous community resources, and samples of forms with particular relevance to the topic.
4. *Individual story.* This section, although it does not appear in every case study, provides a study of a successful intervention in order to help the reader concretize what is meant by capacity enhancement principles, goals, and methods. I was able to construct some of the case studies from already published material. Not every setting was able or willing to provide a case study of a success story. Some settings were reluctant to provide a case because of issues of confidentiality. Other settings were willing but it would have required a considerable amount of time and resources to either construct one or have one constructed. Yet others were willing, but because of publication deadlines, it was not possible to do so.

5. *Lessons for social work.* Finally, this section addresses the lessons learned and how they can be applied to social work practice.

Some sections of some cases are more fully developed than others because of greater availability of documentation and access for interviews. Nevertheless, each case can stand on its own, so to speak, with sufficient contextualization and details to both engage and challenge the reader.

8

AIDS Counseling Education, Bedford Hills Correctional Facility, New York

Bedford Hills Correctional Facility opened in 1901 and is located about forty-five minutes north of New York City. Bedford Hills houses 750 of a total of 3,500 female inmates in the state of New York. An additional 2,000 women are housed in New York City jails (Engle, 1999). The vast majority (approximately 80 percent) of female inmates in New York state prisons have histories of substance abuse, 75 percent are mothers, and 50 percent have suffered from a major psychiatric disorder (Engle, 1999). This profile does not differ dramatically from that reported in the literature and found in other states across the United States.

AIDS Counseling Education (ACE), established in 1988, serves as an excellent example of how capacity enhancement comes to life in a maximum security prison. Women in prison face tremendous challenges, one of which is AIDS (ACE Program, 1998). This program was developed by women inmates, primarily of color, of the Bedford Hills Correctional Facility in response to the devastating impact of AIDS on their and their families' well-being. The program is multifaceted and directed by leadership from the inmates themselves, but with close collaborative relationships with social service and health organizations, some of which are staffed by social workers.

In 1992 approximately one of every five women inmates in the New York correctional system tested positive for the HIV virus, indicating a tremendous need for education and services related to the disease. In 1998 more than 18 percent of women incarcerated in New York state prisons and more than 25 percent of women inmates entering Rikers Island, New York City, were HIV-positive (Engle, 1999). In contrast, only 7 percent of male inmates in New York state were HIV-positive (Boudin et al., 1999). New York state led the nation in the number of HIV-positive inmates and inmates with AIDS in 1996 (AIDS in Prison Project, 1996). It is estimated that intravenous drug use is the primary risk for HIV transmission in more than 90 percent of AIDS cases among New York state prisoners (AIDS in Prison Project, 1996).

Not surprisingly, AIDS is the leading cause of death in New York state prisons. As of 1997, two-thirds of AIDS cases among Latino women were the result of the injection of drugs—approximately 43 percent contracted AIDS by injecting drugs, while an additional 23 percent contracted it through sexual intercourse with male injecting drug users (National Coalition of Hispanic Health and Human Service Organizations, 1998). In 1982 in New York state four prisoners died of AIDS; in 1993 the number of deaths attributed to AIDS increased to 224. Overall, more than 1,600 inmates, or 62 percent of all known AIDS cases in New York state prisons, have died (AIDS in Prison Project, 1996).

One inmate eloquently described the impact of AIDS as follows: "Living with AIDS anywhere is difficult. Being in prison brings added fears and problems. Although the illness is the same, our conditions are different. Perhaps the most important factor that helps people endure HIV/AIDS is love and support, yet in prison we are separated from our friends and families on the outside" (ACE Program, 1998, p. 24). Another woman in a Pennsylvania prison describes a similar sense of being:

> My name is Kimberly Morris #OB4212. I'm an inmate at SCI-Muncy, a maximum institution for women, in rural Pennsylvania. I'm 28 years old and I've been HIV positive for seven years. I'd like to say a few things about the way that women with HIV and AIDS are being treated at this institution. Since my arrival here at SCI-Muncy with a 1 to 3 year sentence, I've finally discovered what it means to be a woman with AIDS. We aren't treated as human beings but [as] outcasts within a prison system. There is no one to help us, or give us moral support. We're being treated like sub-human caged animals and have no one to defend us. We endure daily humiliation and demoralization. We are constantly being asked a thousand questions by prison employees and inmates in order to relieve their fears about contracting this disease. ("Women Prisoners," 1994, p. 1)

Separation and stigmatization, as a result, increase the need for the provision of love and support by fellow inmates, which is an arduous task when there is fear and stigma related to being HIV-positive or having AIDS. The ACE program came into being in direct response to this need for support, education, and advocacy on behalf of HIV-positive women or their loved ones.

Program Specifics

Not surprisingly, ACE started out as an infirmary support program involving "friendly visitors" (visitors with no relation to prisoners before the initial meeting) to women in the late stages of AIDS. It slowly transformed, however, into a multifaceted program involving peer education and peer counseling focused on AIDS. Women who are HIV-positive or have AIDS require comprehensive services to help them manage the disease. However, being integrated with peers is probably one of the most effective measures in helping to break down their isolation, alleviate their self-doubts and anxiety, and answer questions they may have about AIDS. ACE identified four goals for itself: (1) educate inmates on prevention, (2) establish care standards for those who are HIV-positive, (3) provide education and support to women with HIV/AIDS, and (4) act as a liaison to community-based groups to assist HIV-positive women in their reentry into the community.

ACE subscribes to five key principles in guiding its efforts to reach women inmates. These principles systematically address the multifaceted needs of women who are HIV-positive or who have AIDS and take into account the context in which these women find themselves—namely, a maximum security prison:

1. *Support.* The provision of mutual support represents a critical cornerstone of the program. The availability of peer support takes on greater significance when women inmates feel isolated or cannot communicate because of language differences. The support provided within the group takes on instrumental, informational, and expressive dimensions.
2. *Confidentiality.* Freedom to share information and stories is possible only if participants feel that confidentiality will be protected from the authorities and non-ACE members. Being in a total institution increases the need for a forum where there is little or no fear of confidentiality being breached.
3. *Empowerment/Giving each women her own voice.* Empowerment can be achieved only to a certain degree when women are imprisoned. This is a reality. However, it does not mean that there isn't sufficient opportunity for program participants to be empowered within the program. Deciding what information to share and act upon is one example of how empowerment can take hold for ACE participants.
4. *Respecting and protecting ACE.* Participation in the ACE program is a privilege, and every effort must be made to ensure that the program's name, space, access, and materials are respected.

Failure to do so may jeopardize the program's existence and the well-being of its members.

5. *Coming to ACE activities able to work.* Participation in ACE activities requires the ability to focus completely on the issues being addressed. This means that participants must be in a "drug-free" state of mind.

The multifaceted program developed by ACE seeks to address a multitude of needs through service provision, walkathons, parties, celebrations, rap groups, videos, a puppet show (summer program for children having extended visits of five days), quilts, workshops in Spanish and English, hosting conferences, HIV testing, and collaboration. There are enough activities to accommodate the competencies and interests of virtually any inmate. A medical social worker from Montefiore Hospital played an instrumental role in the program's inception by providing consultation. Support and education provided by peers can help women inmates with the HIV virus or AIDS find their voice. Such mutual support groups can be very powerful:

> Learning about the disease and learning about symptoms that might occur intrigued me. It made me think that the more I know about HIV, the more able I am to fight it, and I wanted to be surrounded by the knowledge, to know everything so that I could master it instead of it mastering me. In some aspects it makes a difference that someone infected by it has a relationship to it, to what is being taught, because in some aspect you're dealing with feelings and you know you're talking with someone who has been there, who's been struggling with the same issues. It's like looking at an addict looking at another addict, who's done it, who's been through the struggle, and it's inspiring. I could get where they're at and that's a goal. (Boudin et al., 1999, p. 92)

Another participant brought a different dimension to support and education:

> The struggle with adherence is hard. If you've made it to the point of accepting that you're HIV positive and you're learning to live with it, and you have your hopes and dreams and then you constantly have to take the medications to remind you that you're sick, that can be depressing. I was finally free of the denial, and then I was free of constant thoughts of being HIV positive, and yet then I had to constantly be reminded of it, taking 20 to 30 pills [a day]. I was mentally free of the disease yet then I was back with it all the time. The group helps with the support because when you're struggling with it, it helps to have others going through it, looking at it from this side, looking at it from the other

side—having people that take them, looking at people who aren't and then making your own decision. (Boudin et al., 1999, p. 92)

Workshops

Education pertaining to HIV and AIDS, for those infected with the virus and for those who fear contracting it, forms a critical and central component of the program. This method of reaching out to inmates is non-threatening and supports women in search of information and assistance. ACE offers several types of workshops. However, those related to HIV and AIDS clearly form the central core of their educational efforts.

The workshops address attitudes, knowledge, and skills and use a variety of techniques to engage and educate participants—small group discussions, didactics, and small group exercises. Workshop topics include HIV/AIDS: A Shared Concern; HIV/AIDS: The Social Disease of Stigma; What Is HIV/AIDS?; HIV/AIDS: Social and Medical Issues Regarding Treatment; HIV/AIDS: Transmission; HIV/AIDS: Sexual Transmission; HIV/AIDS: Testing; Women and HIV/AIDS; and Living with AIDS.

Capacity Enhancement Methods

A program that systematically seeks to empower participants can be considered capacity enhancement driven. Empowerment refers not only to a goal but also to a method for inmates to regain control over their decision-making process, and therefore, their actions. Education and decision making are but two of the essential vehicles for operationalizing the principle of empowerment. The ACE program illustrates the work of multiple capacity enhancement principles. However, five principles in particular stand out: (1) all individuals, regardless of background and circumstances, possess strengths and abilities; (2) process is as important as, if not more important than, outcome; (3) interventions must address a current need or concern, while systematically preparing participants for the future; (4) social and economic justice themes must be integrated into capacity enhancement interventions as a means of bringing about societal changes; and (5) interventions must provide participants with an opportunity to have their voices heard, to express their hopes, fears, and concerns.

Rehabilitation is enhanced when inmates are given opportunities to enter into roles that allow them to assist others. Service on behalf of others provides participants with an opportunity to help shape the lives of others. Participants, in addition, not only learn critical skills pertaining to conducting workshops, leading, listening, and advice giving, but also learn how to set up and maintain a schedule. Peer education and counseling are "jobs" in the best sense of the word:

Seemed like the only way I could keep what I have is to give back every chance I get. Just to have the education and give it back, to have someone look at me and know that I've been where they are, that helps me. I go through the tunnels here and people call me, ask me for help, almost like I could be [a] savior and it makes me feel good that I can give it back to them, and I think once people [who] are HIV positive can unify in this way we can be a powerful force to get something done, find a cure. It takes unification. Stigma is a big thing in the way of putting a stop on this disease. (Boudin et al., 1999, p. 93)

Women who have adopted ACE peer roles have been very successful in obtaining employment in AIDS-related jobs upon release (Boudin et al., 1999).

Capacity enhancement can take place in any setting. The case of ACE, however, highlights how capacity enhancement practice can occur even in a maximum security prison. Although the importance of decision making is highlighted in the literature on empowerment and capacity enhancement, it takes on a higher degree of importance in a maximum security prison, where the power to make decisions usually lies within the province of guards and prison officials, not with the inmates. Nevertheless, prisoners do exercise decision-making powers in electing whether to participate in ACE activities, and when they do, they have the power of deciding to what extent they wish to participate. The latitude of decision making is greater in society and community alternatives to incarceration; nevertheless, it still exists in a maximum security prison.

The use of workshops as a central vehicle for reaching out to inmates holds much promise for capacity enhancement. When properly planned and implemented, this method provides participants with an opportunity to engage to the limit they feel comfortable, as well as providing them with a chance to contribute to others through the sharing process. Workshops, as a result, need to have a strong experiential component in order to facilitate exchange. Leaders must always be able to both offer assistance and facilitate assistance being provided by group attendees.

Individual Story

The following story was published on the Internet (O'Leary, 1999), and it is included in this case study because it is a well-written piece typifying how a capacity enhancement perspective has tremendous implications for service delivery that targets women prisoners both inside and outside prison:

The women of Bedford Hills maximum-security prison in New York state get to wear one article of clothing that is their own. When I meet Francine Rodriguez, 29, in the office of the prison's ACE (AIDS Counseling and Education) program, she is wearing a silk shirt with her state-issued olive-drab pants. A ringlet of her perfectly coifed hair falls over her right eye. It's Mrs. Rodriguez to you. She married the love of her life—and codefendant—Anthony Rodriguez, in 1994, seven years after testing positive. The pair was charged with assault after beating a man she says attacked her first. The incident occurred in the same Brooklyn park where she had first met Anthony three months before. Home for him is now 45 minutes away, where he's serving a longer sentence in Otisville. "At least we know where each other is," she says. A serodiverse relationship can be tough enough, but imagine when the walls between you have barbed wire. "We write all the time, and we get to call each other every six months," she says, "on our anniversary in June and for the December holidays." They get 20 minutes on the phone.

She points to two large boxes on the mail cart. "That's pamphlets and study for him," she says. "He's doing AIDS education now, too." Rodriguez says that Anthony was the first person (not excluding her family) not to reject her upon finding out she had HIV. But Anthony just seemed like a special case, the one person who could love her, virus and all. It was only after she went to prison and joined the ACE program, that she found others who would not reject her. Then she bloomed.

"At first, I was afraid to come to the ACE office," she recalls. "I was still in denial. But I thought I had every symptom I'd ever heard of." Rodriguez confided in fellow inmate Kathy Boudin, whose trailblazing AIDS activism behind the walls had become legendary. Boudin urged her to get involved in ACE. You get the sense that when Rodriguez commits to something, she holds on for dear life. She joined ACE this past February as an HIV wallflower, silent and shy. But soon she put out feelers and, after a few months, had launched a prison newsletter on AIDS and women's health. ACE NEWS is now a sophisticated, sisterly forum for women behind bars to discuss AIDS treatment, resources and stigma. Rodriguez's editorials have put her in the limelight: She is often stopped in the hall for advice or encouragement. "I also work in the mess hall part-time as an assistant cook," she says. Asked if having their dinner made by one of the most out HIV positive women at Bedford Hills has caused any problems with inmates, Rodriguez raises her chin and says: "Just once. It was count time in the mess hall. I was sitting with Karen Ely, whom I call Mom. This loudmouth across the room points at me and says something about an 'AIDS-infected bitch.' " That, Rodriguez decided, would not do.

"I gave my glasses to Mom and said, 'I have to hit this girl.' I had to. So I marched over there and hit her. Then I said, 'I don't have AIDS. I have HIV.' " The other inmates, recognizing an underdog, readily cheered her on; afterward even the guards supported her.

Once Rodriguez came out about her serostatus, getting adequate antiretroviral treatments wasn't a problem, but the side effects were. "I was on Viracept for six months," she says. "I was right out of The Exorcist, a mess. Then I noticed wasting in my legs, and I was getting the stomach thing, too. I got off it. Now I'm on a hydroxyurea combination. No side effects."

Like many women in the ACE program, Rodriguez worries about life after prison. She has found not only a self but a community behind bars, so she naturally fears the future: "I think about going home, and it scares me. I'm up for parole in 2000 but it probably won't happen. Too soon." One thing she does look forward to on the outside is skydiving. At night in her cell, she thinks about jumping out of an airplane and flying. "It's total freedom," she says. "I can't wait."

The case story of Francine Rodriguez is inspiring, yet it touches on the fears and challenges facing women behind bars. The future, in many regards, is very scary, yet the potential of making a contribution to family and community is ever present. Mrs. Rodriguez was able to take a stigmatizing condition and turn it into an empowering experience. In so doing, she was able to encourage others to claim their rightful place in a community—in this case, a prison-based community. A capacity enhancement perspective has ramifications that go far beyond the individual participant. In the case of Mrs. Rodriguez, she was able to enlist the support of her spouse to distribute materials related to HIV and AIDS in his prison.

Lessons for Social Work

It is hard to imagine a situation carrying a greater stigma for a woman of color than to be in prison and to be HIV-positive or have AIDS. HIV and AIDS have profound social and medical implications that can easily result in someone with the diagnosis withdrawing from society in shame, and thereby limiting her potential contributions to self, family, and community. ACE's contributions must, as a result, be placed within the context usually associated with maximum security prisons—namely, a total institution that places a primary emphasis on controlling inmate behavior. Inmates in maximum security prisons, women being no exception, have few opportunities to exercise their rights and to have their voices heard by prison administration. The Bedford Hills ACE program has managed to surmount numerous barriers to achieve widely acclaimed success within and outside the prison system.

The prison leadership of Bedford Hills must be congratulated for its wisdom in taking a situation that could easily be custodial in nature and providing inmates with a chance to make a contribution to their colleagues. Maximum security prisons, after all, generally just focus their attention on controlling inmate actions. Putting "power" in the hands of inmates, be they male or female, is not the usual circumstance in these correctional facilities.

Capacity enhancement social work practice with female offenders diagnosed with HIV or AIDS is possible, as proven by ACE. Individuals diagnosed with HIV or AIDS can play influential roles in helping other female offenders and ex-offenders meet the challenges associated with prevention and intervention. ACE has provided these women with roles that are empowering for themselves and others, in and out of prison. One peer educator put it quite eloquently:

> I see that women still even in this day and age of the epidemic want to trust and believe that their sexual partners will be faithful and never hurt or cause them harm. . . . I hear in the questions they ask, that many have never even so much thought about using protection nor quite know how to begin the change due to fear, stigma, and most of all, rejection. As I teach, I realize that most of the women have a low self-esteem along with a drug addiction which I believe in many cases led them to make unhealthy choices and not think of the disease [as] a threat. (Boudin et al., 1999, p. 95)

Social workers can play influential roles in helping to establish and maintain peer support and education groups within and outside prison, as in the case of ACE. Few social workers have not experienced and witnessed the power of peer-led groups in practice. Mutual support brings an added dimension to work with the correctionally supervised. The offender's opportunity to serve others cannot be easily dismissed in implementing capacity enhancement initiatives with the correctionally supervised:

> Having peers providing this service facilitates the process of communicating key information in a culturally, ethnically, and gender-sensitive manner and in a language that can be understood. . . . their role as a peer support group complemented our work [medical staff] in the medical area. They were in many ways an important part of our outreach effort by maintaining an alert eye among the population to identify women in need of medical care who were not accessing available services because of fear, distrust, misinformation, language barriers, or pure hopelessness. They would empower other women to begin taking control of their lives by making informed decisions about their health and lives. (ACE Program, 1998, pp. 137–39)

Social workers, and for that matter other helping professionals, can act as brokers between inmates and prison authorities. Knowledge of external resources, in turn, can help peer-led programs by connecting them with outside agencies and providers. Prisons can be settings where effective treatment and prevention strategies related to HIV and AIDS can be implemented with what many would consider to be a "high-risk" population (MacDougall, 1998). Prison time, after all, allows those who are drugging and engaging in other risk-taking behaviors to slow down and reflect upon their lives and future (Kaplan, 1998). Prison time can also be a time for individuals to become more hardened in their outlook on life and learn new trades that will enhance their capacity to benefit financially from their crimes. Unfortunately, the choice between these two extreme perspectives is very often out of the hands of inmates, particularly in situations where viable alternatives are not available within a prison.

9

Reading Academy, Maryland Correctional Institute–Jessup

The Reading Academy was established in the early 1980s as a result of an identified need to use education as a vehicle for achieving various goals related to life within and outside prison for inmates with limited academic skills in reading, writing, and math. However, like most literacy programs that have been successful in helping individuals from poor and working-class backgrounds, the Reading Academy also addressed a multitude of other needs in the process. In 1984, the state of Maryland established mandatory education for certain inmates in the adult prison system. After initial screening, inmates with a below-eighth-grade equivalency in reading are required to participate in a school program for a period of ninety days (Steurer, 1991). In 1980 with the aid of a federal grant, the Johns Hopkins University Reading Center developed a peer tutoring program at the Maryland house of corrections in Jessup. The success of this program led to its expansion to every major prison within the Maryland correctional system.

Program Specifics

The Peer Tutoring Reading Academy operates among the educational programs of the Maryland correctional system. The Reading Academy specifically targets inmates who are reading below a third-grade level. The Reading Academy stresses mutual support as a central tenet: "The reading academy is a fine example of 'people helping people.' This is the premise on which the Peer Tutoring Reading Academy was built. It has been the basic philosophy and overarching goal of the Maryland correctional education program that educational attainment is not enough. Educational attainment coupled with basic consideration for the needs of other people facilitates the (re)habilitation of offenders. Educational skills and the development of positive attitudes go hand in hand in correctional education" (Steurer, 1991, p. 133).

The program uses the motivation of a reduced sentence as an incentive. Both tutors and students receive five days of reduction in sentence for each month of sentence served in the program. The project uses inmates as tutors to work with other adult inmates reading below a third-grade level. The goal of empowerment, although it may not be specifically stated, is inherent in an intervention where individuals being served increase their ability to exercise control over their lives. In this case, control is operationalized through an increased ability to write and read. Inmates with a high school diploma or GED are encouraged to apply to be tutors.

The tutors, in turn, take on mentoring roles in the process of teaching academic subjects: "The program is designed to develop basic skills and self-esteem by using real-life materials such as newspapers, sports magazines, driver's license booklets, mail-order applications, legal documents, or whatever a student chooses as the basis for initial instruction" (Steurer, 1991, p. 136). A variety of teaching methods are used such as the Fernald technique, directed listening language experience, the neurological impress method, word attack, sustained listening, and comprehensive skills instruction (Steurer, 1991).

Under the guidance of a certified reading teacher, tutors help students understand the nature of their reading problems and help develop educational goals that are realistic: "In the literacy lab setting the student works with a highly trained inmate-tutor for the entire class period five days per week. . . . Most classrooms are large enough to accommodate from ten to fifteen tutor/student pairs as often as three times per day. In this context, it is easy to see that many more students can be accommodated" (Steurer, 1991, p. 137). Tutors work closely with the reading teacher through ongoing meetings and continuous training. Student files and records are maintained and kept in the classroom as a means of making them accessible. After reading and discussing the material together, the student conveys to the tutor his or her understanding of what he or she has read. The inmate's version is translated into three to five sentences, which the tutor writes down for the student to read (American News Service, 1998).

Capacity Enhancement Methods

The enhancement of one's ability to read and write is in itself a form of capacity enhancement. This skill gives former inmates an opportunity to educate themselves and, once they have gained confidence, to educate others. By giving inmates and former inmates the chance to serve their community—in this case it may be a prison-based community—capacity enhancement takes place at a variety of levels. Former or current inmates who tutor are in the unique position of helping tutees with instruction, as well as providing advice and listening to their concerns, hopes, and fears. The relationship between the two parties can be powerful and transformative.

The following three capacity enhancement principles are highly operative in this case study: (1) all individuals, regardless of background and circumstances, possess strengths and abilities; (2) interventions rarely follow a predictable and linear path—thus, flexibility in design and implementation is essential to allow for local circumstances to influence the process and outcome; and (3) the quality of life in a community must be bettered as a result of an intervention. A strong community service component, within and outside the prison, brings an important and often overlooked dimension to capacity enhancement strategies.

The discovery of one's potential to read and write is powerful. It takes on greater importance for someone who has been led to believe that he or she does not have the cognitive abilities to do so, as in the case of many ex-offenders from low-income or working-class backgrounds. The spark that literacy brings to an individual can open doors that historically have been closed to him or her. The teaching of literacy must be flexible enough to incorporate different methods and styles, however.

The potential that teaching has to offer is well understood in social work. It takes on added importance when teacher and pupil share similar backgrounds and circumstances. Teaching in these situations transcends didactic material and lessons and takes on greater meaning—namely, preparation for life outside the criminal justice system, with all its rewards and challenges. Thus, flexibility in the design and implementation of a literacy program is essential in carrying out such efforts with the correctionally supervised. Finally, the opportunity to contribute to the quality of life in a community, even if it is in a total institution, represents an important dimension.

Lessons for Social Work

Practitioners can provide much assistance to consumers, empower them, and enhance their capacities through the use of education (Baird, 1997; Valentine, 1998). In fact, few methods hold as much promise as teaching does to bring about significant changes in the lives of marginalized people. Baird, although referring to women, touches upon the role of education if creatively used: "Survival, for incarcerated women, depends on their being able to hold their minds intact despite regulations on every act of their bodies. Poetic discourse is a powerful survival strategy for them. Even without bodily freedoms, some discover again, in one small classroom, and in their imaginative creative writing, the lost sense of fun, curiosity, intelligent talk, and free expression" (1997, p. 4).

The ability to read and write provides inmates with an avenue through which they can educate and express themselves to others. This voice, so to speak, is essential in the rehabilitation process, as is well articulated by one tutor: "Gerald Pompey, who is serving 20 years for second-degree murder, became a tutor to earn 'good days' credits. But four years later, Pompey has found more reasons for sticking with it. 'Immediately, I witnessed men apply themselves with dedication and determination to improve their lives. My efforts are a major influence on their successes. That gave me a feeling of accomplishment' " (American News Service, 1998, p. 8). Tutors do earn $1 a day and ten "good days" credits toward reducing their sentences. However, as in Pompey's case, the benefits of tutoring far outweigh the reasons that led to volunteering.

Social workers can play the role of educators, too. In fact, we play virtually all other roles, and the role of educator is a natural extension of much of what we do on a daily basis. The role of educator, however, can be transformative in a manner different from other roles. This role is non-stigmatizing and, in order to be effective, must successfully be conceptualized as broad and multifaceted. Consequently, numerous types of interventions resting on educational goals are possible both within and outside prison.

A successful intervention focused on reading and writing, for example, necessitates that the facilitator be prepared to address a whole series of emotional responses. Past negative experiences in school invariably emerge and need to be listened to and validated. Deep-seated feelings of shame will also be present and, no doubt, the offender's inability to read and write will have resulted in occasions of being mocked or shamed. This history, as one would expect, has a profound impact on the present and an influence on perceptions of the future.

The teaching of literacy by those who once were illiterate can be a transformative experience for both teacher and pupil (McPherson and Santos, 1997). When the individual who is teaching shares a prison background with the pupil, the interaction between the two goes far beyond teaching and learning reading and writing. Life's lessons are also shared— lessons that few social workers can share. Nevertheless, social workers can work closely with ex-offenders in leading groups, providing support to group leaders when needed, obtaining resources, and brokering with institutions. In short, the possibility of establishing a partnership is not out of the realm of possibility.

Mutual support programs have a long and distinguished history in social work, as already noted in chapter 8's case study—ACE. Mutual support in prisons presents us with another setting and another set of challenges in applying the concept. The profession may be in a position to foster the growth of these types of groups within and outside prison. Of course, there will be settings where this isn't possible. However, when a support group is tied to a program that is capacity enhancement driven, its feasibility is increased. Steurer (1991) sums up the importance of a prison-based literacy program for students, tutors, and society:

> The Peer Tutoring Reading Academy recognizes the worth of every human being. Most offenders are generally written off by a . . . disgusted public, but they will return to society within the very near future, as the vast majority serve about two to three years behind bars. If the criminal justice system does not equip those returning to society with the skills to acquire jobs and contribute to the welfare of their fellow citizens, they will continue to commit more crimes. The Peer Tutoring Reading Academy is a partial, yet important answer to breaking the crime cycle—people helping people. (p. 139)

10

Experimental Gallery, Children's Museum, Seattle, Washington

Programs such as the Experimental Gallery owe their inception to many different people. However, they are usually the brain-child of one in particular. In this case, that person was Ms. Susan Warner, who is currently the curator of education at the Children's Museum in Seattle, Washington. Warner developed a link between the work and activities associated with museum exhibit development and their potential to reach out to and engage youth. Multidisciplinary, experiential, and team-oriented activities can have a place in work with youth, just as they do in the development of exhibits. Rehabilitation of youth requires the collaboration and involvement of many different areas, community being one:

> The institutions in which these young people are housed employ many dedicated and wonderful people. The responsibility for these young people lies, however, with all of us. It is unrealistic to expect the institutions to rehabilitate youth without community support and real involvement. The Experimental Gallery serves as one such example. We believe that some of these young people are talented, and could potentially become contributing members of our society. For them it should never be too late. In this program, we therefore choose to focus our efforts in the arena of juvenile justice. We work with kids who have gone astray rather

than in a traditional prevention approach because the programming void is huge and no child should ever be given up. (Experimental Gallery, 1997, p. 1)

The Experimental Gallery integrates the arts and humanities and targets juvenile offenders in Washington's juvenile rehabilitation system. The use of these methods as interventions has successfully reduced the rate of recidivism to 50 percent from the state average of 80 percent. This program teaches youth painting, sculpture, creative writing, and video production (Rook, 1998). The Experimental Gallery in Seattle takes a strengths/resiliency approach toward youth inmates and seeks to provide avenues for their expressing themselves that are not conflict driven. This perspective serves to better prepare them for eventual release back into society.

The success of the Experimental Gallery has not gone unnoticed, judging by the number of awards given to the program: Coming Up Taller Award, President's Committee on the Arts and the Humanities (1998); Surviving Arts Partnership, Harvard University, Project Zero (1998); Golden Apple award for excellence in education (1997); semifinalist, Innovations in American Government (1997); Washington Museum Association award for outstanding exhibition (1996); Model Program, President's Committee on the Arts and the Humanities (1996).

Program Specifics

The Experimental Gallery was founded in 1992 and generally has an operating budget of approximately $150,000 per year, derived primarily from the state (Department of Social and Health Services, Juvenile Rehabilitation Administration). Experimental Gallery projects are present in all six of Washington's juvenile detention facilities (Echo Glen Children's Home, Green Hill, Indian Ridge, Maple Lane School, Mission Creek, Naselle Youth Camp), and the gallery reaches more than 1,550 youth in these facilities. Approximately 400 youth are active participants in various aspects of the program. The Maple Lane School project has historically played, and continues to play, a particularly influential role in the program.

The Experimental Gallery's A Changed World program addresses three major goals and nine objectives (Ezell, 1998, p. 2). Its goals are (1) to reduce criminal behavior by building self-esteem and by providing a follow-up mentorship program, (2) to visibly and tangibly illustrate appropriate prosocial success through the exhibit process, and (3) to encourage other cultural organizations to use their resources in the effort to find a solution to youth crime and violence by providing educational materials in the form of videos, panel discussions, and workshops. These three goals translate into nine program objectives:

1. Inculcate cultural and community awareness—tangibly expressed in the written and visual imagery created by the students

2. Lessen the risks of inappropriate behavior within the institutional environment
3. Develop vocational and academic skills that will motivate and assist the student with the search for employment/career
4. Develop students' understanding of good decision-making processes—through material selected and written for the general public
5. Develop students' cognitive and analytical thinking skills as demonstrated in research on the selected theme
6. Create a safe and supportive environment in which juveniles can explore unrecognized or unappreciated talents
7. Develop students' sense of responsibility by giving responsibility through participation in the exhibition and advisory committee
8. Work closely with all project partners to development a suitable outreach prevention component geared to at-risk students still connected to mainstream/alternative schools and detention centers
9. Allow, when appropriate, family comment and participation in the exhibit development (Ezell, 1998, pp. 1–2)

The A Changed World program consists of various types of workshops that range in duration from two weeks to two months and stress experiential learning and the use of stories, poems, sketches, videos, murals, sculptures, and other types of activities. An interactional and experiential format helps participants in the processes of connecting, expressing, learning, and discovering. Youth participants acquire competencies, values, attitudes, and work habits. Artists are hired to conduct the workshops who not only provide expertise in their individual artistic areas but also serve as mentors and role models for participants (Warner, 1999).

Executive Director Susan Warner emphasized the importance of youth finding outlets for expression and tapping individual strengths:

> We have found that a high percentage of young offenders who participate in our program have a strong need to express themselves, and learn through the arts. . . . The Experimental Gallery strives to present the positive, the strengths, the talents, and the achievements of institutionalized youth to our community through sophisticated projects that give something back. These publications are a testimony to what can be achieved given the right educational environment. We ask you to take another look. This is not an "untouchable" but a real person with hopes, and needs, and in many cases huge potential. (Experimental Gallery, 1997, pp. 1–2)

The opportunity for youth participants to exercise control over their experience in prison highlights how empowerment can be conceptualized and carried out in a total institution. In one facility, for example, youth participants manage an art gallery and serve as board members. Youth also receive training on the ethics of governance. All six centers have workshops offering creative writing, painting, drama, graphic design, sculpture, and videography. These workshops, in turn, are led by community artists and humanities scholars.

The themes and projects involving the arts and humanities are selected by the participants and very often reflect major issues they have or expect to confront upon their return to the community. Subjects such as substance abuse, violence, disease, abuse, and neglect are not unusual in the lives of these youth. These projects, in turn, are shared with the community. Participants developed a film that was aired by a local PBS station (KCTS TV). The film's central theme was the fear youth have of returning to the community after incarceration and the community's fear of them. Participants were actively involved in writing the script, filming, creating the musical score, and developing the catalog that accompanied the film. Projects such as this provide participants with a voice, a sense of achievement, and pride in their efforts and talents. The Experimental Gallery also gives a select group of graduates an opportunity to continue their progress in the arts and humanities through an apprenticeship program.

A three-year evaluation of A Changed World found that program participants gained new vocational skills, increased levels of pride and confidence, and reduced rule breaking and misbehavior within the institution (Ezell, 1998). One program participant (anonymous), in a short but eloquent statement, summed up the importance of being a part of the Experimental Gallery: "I'm now currently going to be leaving shortly and I will be leaving with hope now. A year ago today if you asked me [where] I saw myself in ten years I would have said dead or in prison now that's changed. I now thank those whom [sic] have stood behind me with the humor and their kindness and I hope they will continue to share that with the others who will follow long after I leave. I now thank the Lane" (Experimental Gallery, 1997, p. 35).

Capacity Enhancement Methods

A number of capacity enhancement principles are strikingly evident in the programming the Experimental Gallery sponsors: (1) all individuals, regardless of background or circumstances, possess strengths and abilities; (2) interventions rarely follow a predictable and linear path—thus, flexibility in design and implementation is essential to allow for local circumstances to influence the process and outcome; (3) process is at least as important as, if not more important than, outcome; (4) interventions must address a current need or concern, while systematically preparing participants for the future; (5) the quality of life of a community must be bettered as a result of an intervention; and (6) interventions must provide participants with an opportunity to have their voices heard, to express their hopes, fears, and concerns. The influence of these principles, like that of the principles at work in other case studies in this book, is enhanced because of their interrelationship with each other.

A client's ability to express highly charged emotions is an important step in any form of capacity enhancement—in this case it involves drama and youth who are incarcerated. The volunteer participants were required to exercise decision-making skills in the design, implementation, and evaluation of the activities that they created and staged. Scripts, for example, were not handed to them. They had to be developed based upon their life experiences and with the input and direction of a director.

Mentoring, not surprisingly with a youth-focused program, plays an important role during program activities. Staff are not "labeled" as the participants' mentors. The role comes naturally, and it takes on added significance as the participants engage in activities and mature through the process. Mentors, after all, do not get up in the morning and decide that they will be "mentors" today. The willingness of participants to view staff as mentors evolves over time; in that respect it is not dissimilar from what occurs in other programs that may be community based.

Lessons for Social Work

As noted in chapter 2 and earlier in this chapter, juveniles are increasingly being viewed by society as a serious threat, and as a result, they are being punished for their crimes as if they were adults. In the long term a correctional policy of treating juveniles as adults in the courts will have profound implications for communities and society. Higher incarceration rates for juveniles raise important social, economic, and political issues for our society. The social work profession, in turn, will no doubt be thrust into addressing the family and community issues associated with incarceration of youth in adult prisons. These offenders, upon release from prison, will have life histories that will make it particularly challenging for the rehabilitation process to be successful. Human services providers will be called on to work with individuals who have spent a significant portion of their lives in prison.

The use of the arts and humanities in social work is not new. Psychodrama, for example, is a technique with a long and rich tradition in social work. However, drama as conceptualized in the Experimental Gallery has enjoyed no such tradition in the profession. Drama provides a structured and destigmatized manner in which people—in this case youth who have histories that are stigmatizing—can express their thoughts and feelings. Under the right supervision and guidance, this structured activity can allow youth offenders to find their voice, to express painful experiences and feelings. Other arts and humanities–driven activities provide practitioners with the necessary flexibility to accommodate local circumstances to programming. Not every participant can be expected to be interested in drama. Thus, using other methods increases the potential of a program engaging all youth depending on their interests and abilities. However, regardless of the types of activities used, the emphasis is still on the potential and need for participants to seek to express themselves in a manner that is affirming.

Further, the prospect of a children's museum offering a program such as the one discussed in this chapter opens up venues for social work practice. Museums have historically not been thought of as places for social workers to work in or with—volunteer, yes, but not work. In fact, museums have developed a reputation in this society as catering to the various needs of the elite. However, the thrust toward a more "open" policy has resulted in many of these settings establishing active outreach efforts into communities that have historically not been patrons. The success of these efforts, in turn, rests with the ability of the sponsoring institution to initiate programming that meets the needs of the community.

Thus, the case of the Experimental Gallery has much to offer the social work profession. There are numerous venues in a community that can be considered "new frontier" settings, where important, and what can be considered to be "social," work can be practiced. Social work can transpire in any setting; however, its potential is greatly increased when it takes place with an undervalued community, in a setting that can be considered less-than-optimal for potential growth.

The use of a youth development paradigm with a strong arts and humanities foundation affords practitioners, whether they are social workers or not, a method that is not threatening to prisons, not expensive to initiate and maintain, and that can result in an end product—such as videos, photographs, writing, and painting—that can be shared with the community at large. This form of service benefits not only the participants but also the community.

11

Delancey Street
Foundation,
San Francisco, California

Delancey Street Foundation was established in 1971 by
John Maher (Sales, 1976), a former substance abuser and ex-prisoner, and
Dr. Mimi Silbert, a psychologist. John Maher has since passed away (1988),
and the organization is run by Dr. Silbert. Delancey Street is widely considered to be the nation's leading self-help residential education center for
former substance abusers and ex-prisoners (Rodarmor, 1990; Wilentz,
1996; Whittemore, 1992). Although headquartered in San Francisco, it has
facilities in New Mexico, New York, North Carolina, and Los Angeles.

It currently has a budget of $3 million per year and is almost totally
self-supporting:

> Its business enterprises, run by residents, net $3 million a year.
> Silbert was approached in 1971 by John Maher, a former felon
> who invited her to join him in creating a center for criminal reha-
> bilitation and vocational training. It would be for ex-cons and run
> by ex-cons. When they joined forces Silbert and Maher agreed on
> a system of total self-sufficiency. All residents would work to sup-
> port the group, with no outside funds. They would follow strict
> rules of behavior and self-governing. Each resident would develop
> at least three marketable skills as well as earn a high school equiv-
> alency diploma. Named for the section of New York City's Lower

East Side where immigrants congregated at the turn of the century, Delancey Street started with four addicts in a San Francisco apartment. By late 1972, about 100 former felons were jammed into that single space. Yet through the efforts of the residents, they were able to buy an old mansion in fashionable Pacific Heights. After Maher's death in 1988, Silbert became Delancey's driving force. The construction of a new complex in San Francisco was conducted entirely by residents, and cost only half the estimated cost of $30 million. (Delancey Street Foundation, 1999a, p. 1)

The population served by Delancey Street Foundation is almost equally divided along racial/ethnic lines with one-third being African American, one-third Latino, and one-third white non-Latino. The age range is 18 to 68. Approximately 25 percent of the residents are women. Approximately 30 percent were homeless prior to entering the program. Almost 70 percent come from the courts, either probated, paroled, or sentenced as an alternative to prison. As of 1999, there were 1,000 residents in the program, 500 of whom were at the San Francisco site. Participants are prohibited from using alcohol or drugs and from engaging in threats or acts of violence.

Program Specifics

Although no magical period of time can be specified as how long is needed to bring about a complete transformation in a former inmate, Delancey Street has developed a time frame based on its experiences. The minimum stay at Delancey Street is two years, and the average stay is four. The program is open to both women and men. Residents are required to learn academic, vocational, interpersonal, and social survival skills. These skills are interdependent and as a result influence each other in the process of rehabilitation. The inculcation of all these competencies is facilitated when the opportunity to enhance them is centered in one location. A variety of activities are used to help residents enhance their interpersonal skills, with various rituals used to mark significant milestones. The first anniversary involves an extensive session called "dissipation," during which a resident is helped to rid himself or herself of the guilt accumulated over the years. A life of drugs and crime does not come without the infliction of pain and loss on many loved ones. A tremendous amount of guilt surfaces during the recovery phase; ex-offenders and drug abusers must find a therapeutic outlet for it before they can move on in their recovery. Community service requires residents to volunteer community or social work, and that can involve them in numerous community-centered projects, as a way of giving to the community.

Delancey Street is a multifaceted organization that is almost totally self-sufficient as a result of running a series of revenue-generating programs. Program residents are involved in every aspect of Delancey's operation. There are no paid staff; Dr. Silbert lives on the grounds and is unpaid as the agency's president and CEO. Delancey Street's focus on self-sufficiency permeates all aspects of programming, staff hiring, and relationships between staff and residents. When Delancey Street's current San Francisco complex was constructed, residents made up the main workforce. Ex-convicts learned, by doing, how to lay the building materials, how to install plumbing and electric, doing most of the work themselves. If a wall went up crooked, they tore it down and rebuilt it.

Residents must learn at least three trades before graduating, and they are the sole employees of the many businesses the agency owns and operates, which include a high-tech print shop, a moving and trucking company, paratransit services, an advertising specialty operation, catering services, interior and exterior decorating, and a restaurant. The income from these businesses keeps Delancey Street almost entirely self-sufficient—the rest of its budget comes from private donations. Residents take on jobs from entry-level to corporate management positions in exchange for housing and food. "Newcomers start at the bottom, living . . . with eight or nine roommates and taking on daily maintenance chores such as sweeping, mopping and caring for the facilities [parks]. Operating on an 'each one teach one basis,' participants quickly move up the ladder, taking on more responsible jobs . . . where they oversee newer arrivals" (Garr, 1995).

Housing

The 370,000-square-foot complex of Delancey Street contains 177 residential units. As already noted, residents were responsible for erecting their own complex. The cost of the building was estimated at almost $30 million, but by having residents build most of it, that cost was lowered to $15 million. The two-bedroom apartment units, located in the top three stories of the four-story complex, house up to 700 residents. The first floor consists of shops and businesses owned and operated by Delancey. From the street outside the triangle-shaped complex, only the businesses are visible; the apartments all face an internal courtyard.

Approximately a quarter of the residents come from the ranks of the homeless, while the remaining 75 percent are involved in the criminal justice system. Life begins as it does in a large authoritarian extended family. Newcomers live in eight-person dorms and gradually move up to one-room-per-person roommate suites as their responsibilities grow and they progress in learning skills. Each person is assigned to a big brother or big sister, who mentors him or her, and to a "mini van," a single-sex group of ten to twelve people, and to a larger group called a tribe. Mini van leaders are charged with providing day-to-day supervision for the group. They assign jobs, determine what telephone calls can be made, visiting schedules, promotions, and so on. With time and growth comes greater responsibility and leadership opportunities.

The Life Learning Academy

In an effort to prevent youth from embarking on a criminal career, Delancey Street has instituted an academic program that specifically targets youth "at risk" for a life of crime. The Life Learning Academy is Delancey Street's latest program, and it specifically addresses the importance of youth having the requisite academic skills to succeed in society. Many of the principles used in other programs are applied in the academy. Formal schooling of youth enhances Delancey Street's commitment to prevention and early intervention rather than waiting for youth to be imprisoned before qualifying for participation in the program.

The Life Learning Academy is based on Treasure Island: "This charter school helps students develop healthy, productive, independent lives by teaching rigorous academic, social and vocational skills coupled with positive community values. Students 'learn by doing,' engaging in hands-on vocational projects, including site renovation and establishment of a cafe. Academic programs are highly individualized, tailored to the strengths and needs of each student and lead to a high-school diploma. Peer leadership, earned responsibility and privilege, community service and environmental education are cornerstones of the Academy's foundation" (Delancey Street Foundation, 1999b, p. 1).

Drop-In Intake Center

The availability of a place ex-mental patients can drop in to when they are in need is not unusual in the human services field. However, in the criminal justice field this is not a commonplace. This type of setting fulfills many important goals, one of which is to allow participants an opportunity to interact in a place where they feel comfortable.

Delancey Street Restaurant

In operation since 1991, the Delancey Street Restaurant is probably unlike any restaurant the reader has ever patronized. It is wholly staffed by program participants who work in exchange for rehabilitation services and housing. They have an opportunity to learn any aspect of running a restaurant business—on both the business and creative sides. The Delancey Street Restaurant has been named one of San Francisco's "delicious dozen" by *Image Magazine*. The American cuisine is designed and tested by Mimi Silbert, and the menu changes weekly. Customers are mostly repeat diners, and the restaurant draws a variety of clientele ranging from students to businesspeople to politicians due to its location and reasonable prices.

The waitstaff dress professionally and trade their street lingo for professional conduct and quick service. As one critic writes, "[The waiter] works at the incredibly fast pace you would expect in a chic restaurant in San Francisco's upscale South Park neighborhood, but for a moment he slows down at our table to advise me on what to order. . . . Sure, you can show somebody the value of hard work and they can take it all in. But what Delancey Street is really about is pride. The men and women work all day at this restaurant. . . . they put everything into making this come off, so they're proud when you enjoy their food" (Gross, 1989).

The *Digital Lantern*, an Internet guide to restaurants, describes the restaurant as follows: "This large bright room with linen tablecloths, fresh flowers and a gorgeous view of the bay provides a nice, relaxing environment. This smaller outside patio, with tabled umbrellas and a plexiglass wall shades diners from sun and wind. Nice quick service and interesting range of American food at a good value" (cited in Gross, 1989, p. A32) The descriptions of Delancey Street Restaurant provided by these two critics could easily be ones of typical mainstream restaurants found in most cities across the country. However, the philosophical underpinnings of this establishment are anything but typical.

Delancey Street Moving and Transportation

Delancey Street Moving and Transportation, like all Delancey businesses, is completely staffed by ex-felons. It is hired by both businesses and residential customers and even advertises on the Internet (www.marmsweb .com/giving/delancey2.html). Established in 1973, the moving company is a member of the California Moving and Trucking Association, the California Trucking Association, and the Better Business Bureau. It now considers itself one of California's largest independent moving and trucking firms.

Delancey Street Decorating and Catering

The decorating and catering businesses are full-service operations that organize and complete a diversity of large and small projects both on and off the Delancey property. The catering business includes an on-site ballroom that can hold 325 people. The facility also has a disco and several conference rooms. A business or group of people can order essentially any kind of food for its functions, and Delancey delivers a high-quality product. These functions are strictly black-tie affairs and include corporate luncheons, fund-raising parties, and weddings, although Delancey tries to focus most of its business on serving corporate clientele. Neither the catering nor the decorating business does any kind of formal advertising; all business is generated by word of mouth, and this speaks well to the reputation of the organization.

The decorating business primarily specializes in Christmas tree and winter ensembles, doing large and small projects for corporate clients, businesses, and public places in San Francisco and the vicinity. The holiday scenes are generally nondenominational Christmas scenes that often include animals. Each year, Delancey fully decorates a downtown complex in San Francisco using an average of twenty trees and thirty laborers. This downtown project is Delancey's biggest client. Another regular project is the installation and decoration of an outdoor thirty-foot tree in Long

Beach. For all of Delancey's decorating projects, the agency supplies the trees and decorations. The size of trees varies from client to client, and Delancey recommends what decoration materials and color schemes to use. Estimates are free. Finally, this service is popular with clientele such as real estate offices and property management buildings. Again, there is no formal advertising; all referrals are generated by word of mouth and repeat customers.

Capacity Enhancement Methods

Delancey Street could not possibly operate and succeed without relying on a wide range of capacity enhancement principles and strategies. It is rare to find an organization devoted to serving a marginalized group that is totally self-reliant. Self-reliance is not only taught but practiced on a daily basis. Self-reliance is not possible without a fundamental belief in one's capacity to succeed in today's world.

The following five principles have particular meaning in the day-to-day operation of the organization: (1) all individuals possess strengths and abilities; (2) process is at least as important as, if not more important than, outcome; (3) interventions must address a current need or concern, while systematically preparing participants, organizations, and communities for the future; (4) interventions must provide participants with an opportunity to have their voices heard; and (5) meaningful participation in the life of a family and or in the community requires that participants be reconnected with support systems.

Individual Stories

Delancey Street Foundation, with its rich and diverse history, has a countless number of success stories. Nearly ten thousand people have graduated from Delancey Street since it was founded. The number of graduates has continued to grow over the past ten years. The following stories provide the reader with a clear sense of how people's lives have been dramatically changed by their experiences at Delancey. Rugged street pushers and criminal offenders, out of their own merits, visions for the future, and determination to change have fashioned a new image and new sense of self; they have come to embody the values and commitment to make productive contributions to society.

Amy Wilentz (1996), in the *San Francisco Examiner*, profiled one resident named Gerald. Gerald grew up with alcohol- and drug-addicted parents in Harlem, New York, and had a rough life from the start. His mother was killed when he was 12 years old, and his father died when Gerald was 15. As Gerald himself noted, "I don't really remember not doing drugs, smoking weed. In school, I'd be trying to get kids' lunch money off them." His role models were drug pushers and pimps. Gerald was selling drugs and running scams throughout his teens. He had numerous arrests for fights. At 25, he moved to California on his own. As Gerald notes, "I shot up and sold . . . never got anywhere. I knew a lot of people, though. . . . I could get anything I wanted: passports, guns. I was usually armed, and I was paranoid."

In his 20s and 30s, Gerald was arrested and convicted numerous times for armed robberies and assaults. He served several prison sentences that were under ten years each. Each time he was released, he immediately went back to the same crimes, and he went back to prison. His attitude was hardly that of a person who could survive in the community. When first offered a chance at Delancey, he believed that "work was for suckers. You have to get up early in the morning, cut your hair. The people at Delancey Street were weak; if you can't make it in prison, you're weak." He did more prison time.

When he was told about Delancey Street the second time, Gerald was facing twelve years in prison. At first, he just told them "what I thought they wanted to hear" in order to get into the program. He was immediately surprised by the people he met there, several of whom he had known in prison. "One guy in particular looked healthy, was respected. He'd talk to me every day. . . . My whole code was being broken." At first, he did not want to be with other people, choosing instead to feel angry and hurt. "I had to sit with people from other races . . . gangs. . . . I had to work with people. I couldn't stand it." Delancey was different from prison in that anything he did that was wrong was reported to Mimi Silbert or the higher-ranking residents. Gerald was not allowed to get away with anything, and learning that responsibility was important. He began to learn from his mistakes and made friends. Picking up on a strong habit of reading from his prison days, Gerald read scholarly books and got a GED.

Gerald's view of Mimi Silbert was one of respect. "I've always been in awe of Mimi; she had that presence. I was respectfully nervous around her. She's someone you can trust; she is going to be there no matter what. And trust was never my thing." This view of others is in stark contrast to the world inside prison, where no one trusts anyone else. After two years at Delancey, Gerald moved up to being an administrative assistant to Mimi Silbert; he interviews new applicants, earned an education, got a driver's license, and has been in charge of maintenance. His new view of Delancey changed his life: "I was planning on leaving in two years, but I got pulled in. I enjoyed things. I do not want to walk out, I have a life here." At age 38, Gerald has taken the opportunity to restart his life, and has done well with it.

Another ex-offender's story is that of Robert Rocha (Whittemore, 1992). In his teens, Robert was selling drugs in San Francisco and was homeless. His mother was a repeat felon convicted of bank robbery. Rocha was charged in his teens with twenty-seven armed robberies and finally was sentenced to San Quentin Prison. As Rocha notes, "I'd lost touch with everything . . . and had no belief in myself. No hope. No trust in nothing or nobody. . . . I wanted to go to prison . . . because that's where I could be somebody" (Whittemore, 1992, p. 4).

Rocha finally began to think about changing his life, but he was still living the same life of crime. Finally, arrested for selling drugs to an undercover police officer, he was introduced to Delancey Street. For the first eight months there, he "didn't believe in anything that Mimi and the others were saying. I had such a hard attitude that nobody could tell me nothing. . . . there was no way that I could trust anybody with my feelings. Nobody had ever cared about me, so why should I care about anyone else?" (Whittemore, 1992, p. 5). As time passed, the new rules and mutual interdependence began to wear on Robert's way of thinking. One day, a resident was planning on quitting and leaving Delancey Street. Rocha, without thinking about it, started shouting at the resident and trying to get the resident to listen to him. Rocha realized at that moment that he had begun to care for others. "And when I realized that it was true—that I did care—I almost broke into tears." (Whittemore, 1992, p. 5).

Rocha's life changed dramatically at age 26: "The same young man is well-groomed, wears a business suit and carries himself with quiet pride. He wears the warm, confident smile of a person with solid ground under his feet along with a future. In the four years since he went on parole, he has learned eight construction trades. He takes college courses in criminology. He tutors other ex-convicts in geometry, helping them to earn high school diplomas. He has transformed his life on every level—not in some magical way, but through a painful process of taking one small step after another" (Whittemore, 1992, p. 4).

Lessons for Social Work

It is fascinating to see Delancey Street in action and how it sponsors a self-sufficient, multifaceted approach to rehabilitation of the correctionally supervised. Anyone examining the range and type of services delivered by Delancey Street without looking at the staffing pattern would think of this organization as a social service agency with a specific focus on ex-offenders and substance abuse treatment. Rehabilitation, as already indicated, requires a multipronged, comprehensive approach. Few organizations currently exist that provide comprehensive services themselves. However, such services are possible if interagency collaborative partnerships are established.

Delancey Street's success lies in its teaching the values of hard work and self-sufficiency, teaching important life skills and job skills for long-term gainful employment, and fostering a strong, trusting mutual relationship between agency and clientele. It is important when reaching out to those recently released from prison to create programs that necessitate a total investment in the community and people being reached by staff, so that an ex-offender is not merely receiving services but also being mentored, trained, encouraged, supported, and destigmatized in the most nurturing and the least restrictive environment possible, with ready access to the resources necessary for economic and physical survival. At Delancey

Street, virtually the entire world of the ex-offender is centered in one location. It is rare to find another situation other than a prison where that is the case.

The importance of having role models who work with a stigmatized and undervalued group cannot be overestimated. In work with ex-offenders this takes on added importance. Much can be learned from the study of criminal justice, but "walking the walk" is critical. This is not to say that social workers must have been an offender in order to successfully work with this population. However, programming that systematically incorporates ex-offenders and has important roles for them is going to be much more successful than those programs that serve ex-offenders but have no intention of including them as staff.

12

People Animals Love, Washington, D.C.

People Animals Love (PAL) was established in 1992 by Dr. Earl Strimple and Reverend William Wendt, both of whom realized that animals can be effective vehicles for addressing many human needs. In particular, the needs of those who are marginalized in U.S. society because of health, age, or prison status require special attention.

PAL consists of four programs, only one of which—PAL and Prisons—will be addressed in detail in this case study. In the Pet Visiting Program, volunteers and their pets (dogs, cats, rabbits, guinea pigs, and birds) visit elderly residents in nursing homes and sick children in hospitals on a monthly basis. In the Farm-on-the-MOOve program, farms animals such as cows, ducks, turkeys, goats, rabbits, llamas, and pigs, among others, are transported to school playgrounds for gatherings with children. Teachers are given educational materials to use before and after each visit. In the PAL Camp and Clubs, children are provided with an opportunity to learn more about animals from a scientific and personal perspective. Under the guidance of a mentor, children learn new skills, unconditional love, and a sense of belonging and responsibility during the summer (camp) and during the school year (clubs). The last program, PAL and Prisons, is described in this chapter. These four programs target different audiences yet share a common basis—namely, the importance of using animals to help foster bonds of caring and acquisition of new knowledge and skills and to facilitate the rehabilitation process in cases where that is needed.

Program Specifics

PAL and Prisons has experienced considerable success and longevity since its inception in 1982 (Shilstone, 1998; Strimple, 1998). In its first two years, ninety-nine men enrolled in the program. At the end of that time, thirty-one inmates had completed the program but were yet to be released from Lorton Correctional Facility in Lorton, Virginia. Sixty-eight of the program participants had been released from prison, and nine of those had been arrested and reincarcerated, for a recidivism rate of 13 percent compared with a rate of 62.5 percent in the U.S. prison system (Strimple, 1995). One of the program participants wrote a poem that captures the importance of animals in his life and draws comparisons between inmates and caged animals (Strimple, 1995, p.7):

> It's like opening a book and finding
> This meaning on every page
> We're not too much different from
> The animals we have in a cage
>
> Look at the fish we have in our tanks
> They're not at liberty to swim the sea
> Is that any different from us down here
> Not being able to live in society
>
> Take the birds we have in the cages
> They're not free to fly all about
> Like some of us here in this big cage
> May never have a chance to get out
>
> But we still generate enough love
> To give these animals T L care
> And through this program may we generate enough love
> For each other
> To which, hopefully, nothing can
> Compare
>
> *Anonymous inmate, 1986*

The primary objective of PAL and Prisons is to assist in the rehabilitation of inmates. To be rehabilitated, inmates must have a desire and "reason" to change. Inmates' histories of less-than-positive relationships or the lack of opportunities to establish and maintain relationships based on mutual trust and respect seriously impede the rehabilitation process upon release from prison. Rehabilitation, after all, is much more than having employable skills and a desire to stay "clean" upon leaving prison. Relationships are critical in helping ex-offenders commit to a change in lifestyle. However, inmates initially may be unable to develop a relationship with and empathize with another human being. Consequently, pets may be used in the rehabilitation process to foster empathy, responsibility, and a desire to change.

Inmates may see many parallels between themselves and the dogs they take care of and train: "The parallels between the inmates and their dogs are not lost on the women. Dogs used in the program are rescued from local animal shelters, where many of them were scheduled for euthanasia. Some are victims of abuse and neglect. Others were abandoned when they became inconvenient. Before being selected for the program, many were considered untrainable and not worth saving. These parallels make the inmates even more determined to give the dogs a second chance" (Shilstone, 1998, p. 55). Being given an opportunity to exercise responsibility while within the walls of a prison is rare in today's criminal justice system. Thus, a program that fosters the development of skills and the capacity to act responsibly is valuable to the rehabilitation effort.

Programs such as PAL and Prisons and a program at the Massachusetts Correctional Institution–Framingham's Hidden House Women's Prison provide an opportunity for inmates to make community reparation as well (Sweet, 1999). Giving back to the community is accomplished at the same time that a skill is learned, and an inmate finds the ability to feel and care for others. The Framingham Prison program focuses on dogs that are trained to assist the physically challenged. The dogs turn on lights, pick up dropped objects, open doors, and retrieve portable telephones, among other activities. Giving a dog to the community, or community reparation, is one of the primary objectives of the program. Service to community, then, can take a countless number of forms.

Capacity Enhancement Methods

The capacity to empathize with and care for others forms the cornerstone principle of PAL and Prisons. Unlike some of the other programs highlighted in this book, the program utilizes animals as the primary vehicle for establishing these critical qualities in the participants. Harsh prison conditions combined with prolonged separation from families make the development of empathy an arduous process. Feelings of love and caring cannot be fostered in systems where empathy is viewed as a weakness. However, the failure to empathize makes relationship building and maintenance impossible to accomplish.

Thus five principles of capacity enhancement play particularly prominent roles in this program: (1) all individuals, regardless of background and circumstances, possess strengths and abilities; (2) process is of equal importance to, if not more important than, outcome; (3) cultural context cannot be separated from social and economic context; (4) the quality of life in a community must be bettered as a result of an intervention; and (5) interventions must address a current need or concern, while systematically preparing participants for the future.

Lessons for Social Work

Capacity enhancement social work practice is not limited to a select few types of interventions, and it is not the exclusive domain of human beings.

This orientation toward practice necessitates that practitioners broaden their horizons and be creative in selecting approaches and methods that can effectively be modified to reach the correctionally supervised. The use of animals, long acknowledged in human services as mechanisms for helping people with various disabilities, can be used for rehabilitation. Any way that we can enhance a person's capacity to empathize as part of an intervention should be pursued. If the intervention, in turn, prepares an ex-offender to reenter society—in this case, to obtain gainful employment—then it is hard to come up with a "better" intervention.

The case example of PAL does a wonderful job of bringing to life the importance of empathy. Offenders, particularly those with histories of violent crime, are very often written off in our society because of their inability to care for others. In this case, however, animals are used to foster and enhance emotion in the hope that the process facilitates the inmate's application of that emotion to fellow human beings. The community service component, as already mentioned, provides ex-offenders the chance to give back to society within the confines of a prison system. This component, in addition, gives participants a chance to practice on the job as a means of enhancing their competencies.

Social workers can accomplish successful interventions using "unorthodox" approaches, and use of animals is such an example. Collaborative efforts between animal clinics, the Society for the Prevention of Cruelty to Animals, local pet control programs, and social service agencies is not out of the question. All communities have these entities. However, collaboration involving social workers and other human services providers is rare. The People Animals Love program illustrates the potential of animals to play instrumental roles in the rehabilitation of former offenders. When programs involve unwanted animals and inmates, the needs of both parties are addressed in a manner that is creative and affirming for both.

The flexibility to use different types of animals is a programmatic strength that cannot easily be ignored. This flexibility allows local circumstances to dictate how an animal-inmate program can be established. For example, availability of a large number of cats and dogs allows staff to tap this resource. However, different types of animals require different types of care. Costs, as a result, can be greater in programs that involve dogs and cats than in those that involve birds. Consequently, allowing programs to incorporate different types of animals facilitates the use of this method in prisons.

The responsibilities that are inherent in taking care of someone else can be found in taking care of an animal. The skills associated with communication, physical and emotional care, tenderness, and attachment all are instrumental in helping ex-offenders rehabilitate and reenter the community. Not surprisingly, the opportunity to create and maintain relationships represents a strength that can easily be used as a foundation from which to address other areas of competency.

13

Summit House, Greensboro, North Carolina

Summit House was established in 1987 in Greensboro, North Carolina, under the name Guilford County Residential Day Center. Its name was changed to Summit House in 1989. Since then, Summit House has been established in Charlotte, Piedmont, and Raleigh. The initial effort at establishing an alternative to imprisonment for women was motivated by a group of community leaders in Greensboro who saw a crisis in what happens to children when their mothers are arrested and incarcerated (Chapple, Cox, and MacDonald-Furches, 1997a, 1997b). Greensboro citizens, in combination with the North Carolina legislature and judicial system, played an instrumental role in the establishment of the program (Helms, 1995).

Program Specifics

Summit House's mission statement addresses many themes and factors identified in this book as pertaining to capacity enhancement: "The Summit House program strengthens the family by intervening in the lives of non-violent women offenders and their children. Comprehensive services are administered to the women and their children through the efforts of a public-private partnership in a highly structured and controlled environment. The program strives to break the cycle of crime. Summit House also advocates nationally for community-based sentencing programs" (Summit House, 1998, p. 2). The goals that Summit House sets for its participants are discussed in the following sections. The third and fourth sections discuss goals that are most in line with capacity enhancement principles (Chapple, Cox, and MacDonald-Furches, 1997).

Improve Parenting Skills

Parenting is not a natural skill. Thus every effort needs to be made to help parents, in this case mothers, acquire the necessary skills. The fundamental belief is that these women do have the potential for positive mothering. They just need an opportunity to learn the skills and apply them within a supportive environment.

Identify and Manage Self-Defeating Behaviors

A successful rehabilitation program cannot ignore risk-taking behaviors that increase the likelihood of someone's entering the criminal justice system. Such behaviors and attitudes have to be identified, analyzed, and addressed throughout the course of programming. Female offenders themselves are in the best position to understand what motivates them to engage in risk-taking behaviors. They, too, are in the best position to exercise alternative strategies when provided with viable options to do so.

Practice Self-Supporting Behaviors

It is not sufficient to say "no" to certain behaviors without substituting what we can say "yes" to. Just saying no to risk-taking behaviors is too simplistic and doomed to fail if viable and productive alternatives are not available. Thus, the acquisition of new behaviors to substitute for the old counterproductive ones needs to fostered. These alternative behaviors, in turn, need to build upon the inner strengths and capacities of women in order to succeed.

Develop a Healthy Sense of Self, Family, and Competency in Relationships with Others

Competencies are usually associated with job performance, but the concept of competency also can be applied to interpersonal relations involving oneself and significant others. Relationships form the cornerstone of a successful capacity enhancement strategy. As a consequence, female ex-offenders who are mothers must reestablish their roles with their children and the significant adults in their lives. In some cases involving adults, it may mean developing new relationships.

The ability to practice self-supporting behaviors has prodigious short- and long-term implications, and it touches on a central aspect of capacity enhancement goals. An offender cannot successfully take control of his or her life without self-supporting attitudes, knowledge, and behaviors. This does not mean that support cannot or should not be provided. Summit House provides a highly structured environment in order to support participants.

Development of a healthy (physical and psychological) sense of self, family, and competency in relation to others is a critical component in any programmatic effort seeking to enhance competencies. Success in this regard benefits a multitude of individuals and the broader community. If family is readily accessible, then the development of competencies related to parenthood is greatly facilitated.

Approximately 80 percent of Summit House participants have a history of substance abuse, with crack cocaine being the drug of choice. Approximately 50 percent of the participants are white non-Latinas, and 50 percent are women of color, primarily African American. The average participant is from 18 to 35, has two children, has not completed high school, and has been convicted of a nonviolent crime. Their children's well-being is the primary motivator for women to enter Summit House:

> The women who attend Summit House are a unique group, indeed. While they come with a lifetime of factors that have put them on a trajectory of crime and self-denigration, and come with a history of significant, nonviolent offenses, they are truly a testament of the human desire to rise above adversity. They come primarily for the sake of their children, who have paid the highest price for their mothers' addictions and criminal behaviors. These women come willing to live in the highly structured environment, and under the great demands placed on them, for self-enhancement and successful living. They come seeking better lives for and better relationships with their children. Often, they feel tempted to leave Summit House, but love for their children anchors their stay. (Chapple, Cox, and MacDonald-Furches, 1997b, p. 111)

Summit House participants spend an average of twelve to twenty-four months in the program before graduation, depending on their competencies prior to entering the program. All graduates must meet the following requirements: (1) complete an individualized treatment plan; (2) complete counseling; (3) complete a general equivalency diploma if appropriate; (4) obtain employment with an income above minimum wage and arrange child care; (5) establish a savings account and budget; (6) locate appropriate housing for one's family; (7) develop a homebound plan, a resource guide, and an aftercare plan; (8) agree to be actively involved in aftercare through one's probation period or for a minimum of six months if not on probation; (9) begin paying restitution; and (10) perform community service (Chapple, Cox, and MacDonald-Furches, 1997a).

Capacity Enhancement Methods

Capacity enhancement is rarely focused on an individual. The broader the scope of an initiative, the greater the impact on an offender, his or her family, and the community. Community alternatives to incarceration provide the field of criminal justice with greater potential than if its efforts are based solely within the walls of a prison. Under exceptional circumstances, prison-based capacity enhancement initiatives reach into the broader community, as in the case of ACE (see chapter 8). Community alternatives, in turn, by their very nature, require capacity enhancement initiatives to be broad.

The case of Summit House illustrates the importance of broadening an intervention. When the intervention is community-based, a ripple effect is seen along a multifaceted perspective. Summit House focuses on these principles: (1) all individuals, regardless of background and circumstances, possess strengths and abilities; (2) interventions must address a current need or concern, while systematically preparing participants for their future; (3) the quality of life in a community must be bettered as a result of an intervention; (4) interventions must provide participants with an opportunity to have their voices heard; and (5) meaningful participation in family and community requires that an ex-offender be reconnected with his or her support systems.

Lessons for Social Work

The importance of reuniting families is not a new concept for social workers. However, the profession has generally applied this goal from a child welfare perspective, not from a correctional supervision perspective. The reunification of children with mothers who are offenders is not only desirable but possible under the proper circumstances. Housing, without question, forms the cornerstone of any effort to rehabilitate women offenders. Once this service is in place, other services can be marshaled to facilitate the reunification of children with their mothers. That is not to say that acquisition of housing is easy. In many instances, community opposition and the marketplace make this goal difficult if not impossible to achieve.

Services should not be defined so narrowly as to focus solely on mothers. Children, too, need services to foster their relationships. Families of offenders, unfortunately, are generally overlooked in the process of reunification. Immediate and extended family members, particularly grandmothers, are often the primary caregivers for children while their mothers are in prison. However, upon inmates' release, programs tend to focus on them and their children, relegating other caregivers to a secondary or nonexistent role. An important source of support, as a result, is simply overlooked!

The disturbing prison-for-profit trend raises serious concerns for society. This tendency can be characterized as follows: "At its heart, privatizing prisons is really about privatizing tax dollars, transforming public money into private profits" (Bates, 1998, p. 15). Social workers are a "luxury" in private prisons. Our ultimate success in the correctional field will undoubtedly rest on our ability to work in the community environment.

Community alternatives to incarceration probably provide social workers with the best opportunity to work with the correctionally supervised and their families. Agencies not necessarily targeting the offender can be brought into a treatment situation. Programs such as the Girl Scouts, for example, can play important roles in helping children of incarcerated mothers. The Girl Scouts Beyond Bars program, developed by the National Institute of Justice in New Jersey, has proven very effective in strengthening relationships between women prisoners and their children (Moses, 1995). Similar community-based alternative programs can be developed to address mothers.

Social workers interested in working with substance abusers can also be actively involved in community alternatives to incarceration. It would be a rare social worker working in the field of substance abuse who has not had as a client someone with a correctional experience, or one pending in the courts. Some may even be actively working with this population in noncorrectional types of settings. Addressing the individual substance abuser in a community alternative program can bring about a dramatic increase in the number of social workers working with the correctionally supervised.

14

Moving Ahead Program, St. Francis House, Boston, Massachusetts

The composition of the homeless has undergone a dramatic change in many U.S. cities over the past two decades. The homeless were traditionally thought to be men who abused alcohol and other drugs; however, they are now families, women, and the formerly institutionalized such as mental patients and inmates. In New York state, approximately 33 percent of women leaving jail or prison are homeless (Engle, 1999). There is also an increasing number who are undocumented immigrants. The homeless, as a result, comprise men, women, children, adults, elders, citizens, noncitizens, and more. In essence, this population group is heterogeneous. Nevertheless, former inmates are increasingly overrepresented among the homeless as the result of record numbers of people being incarcerated in America's prisons and eventually released onto the streets.

One 1997 study of Massachusetts's homeless shelters found a significant upsurge in the number of guests who were ex-convicts and young adults, resulting in a record number of individuals seeking shelter. Results showed that out of the 1,920 beds available in ten shelters, 423, or 22 percent, were occupied by guests who were directly released from the correctional system to emergency shelters (Walker, 1998). This statistic, when generalized to the entire Massachusetts shelter system, translates into 919 guests who were ex-convicts. Another study found that from 1997 to 1998 the number of ex-convicts in homeless shelters in Massachusetts increased by 17 percent (to 1,100) (Kahn, 1999).

A separate study sponsored by the Boston Rescue Mission (1997) found that 49 percent of guests in shelters self-reported that they had criminal records. Thirty-two reported having been incarcerated, and 12 percent stated that they had been discharged directly from prison to the shelter. The Massachusetts Housing and Shelter Alliance recommended, based on its 1997 study of homeless shelters, that state agencies allocate greater resources to prison discharge and after-release planning to reduce the number of ex-offenders being discharged into shelters (Eno, 1998). The Bethesda Mission (1999), based in Harrisburg, Pennsylvania, reported that 21.9 percent of local shelter guests who were women had been in jail or prison on an average of 2.1 occasions. Men, in turn, showed a higher percentage, with 76.6 percent having been incarcerated an average of 6.8 occasions.

Larivee's (1999) comments on the trends in prisoner release in Massachusetts provide an overview of the extent of the problem in that state:

> Thirty-three thousand inmates were released from Massachusetts state and county prisons last year, but only 10 to 15 percent received any kind of reintegration services. That's no supervision on the streets, no mandatory drug treatment or counseling, no job training, no employment assistance. . . . There are troubling signs in almost every direction. Parole rates have dropped precipitously since 1989, when 63 percent of inmates leaving lockup received some parole oversight. By 1996, just 27 percent received supervision and counseling when they walked out. Halfway house beds, which help bridge the transition, fell from 693 in 1990, when state prisons held 7,600 inmates, to 375 beds today, with a population of 11,000. That's a 46 percent drop in prerelease beds while the prison population jumped 45 percent. And, in 1998, there were 906 ex-offenders going directly from prison to homeless shelters, according to the Department of Corrections. (p. A19)

The introduction of a greater number of former prisoners, in turn, presents programs working with the homeless with greater challenges in helping consumers find housing and obtain the requisite services to facilitate their reentry into the community. These former inmates very often have backgrounds of substance abuse and are increasingly of color. These shifts in population groups necessitate that organizations carefully think about staffing patterns, service provision, and how to best meet the needs of people who may not speak English as their primary language and whose culture is different from that most commonly encountered in society.

Homeless people with a history of substance abuse are often caught in a double bind. They can enroll for a twenty-eight-day stay in an addiction program; however, upon release, they either return to an emergency shelter or go homeless. There is a need for a program that provides shelter while a formerly homeless person is in recovery. Successful recovery, in turn, requires that participants develop a daily routine that has work as a central feature.

St. Francis House was established in 1984 as a nonprofit, nonsectarian agency providing comprehensive and basic rehabilitation programs for the poor and homeless. Guests range in age from 18 to over 65. St. Francis House has slowly evolved over the years into a multifaceted organization with a budget of approximately $4 million, with multiple sources of funding. The Moving Ahead Program, the focus of this case study, has a budget of approximately $700,000. Volunteers, however, have and continue to play instrumental roles in virtually all key facets of the organization. Further, St. Francis maintains an interagency collaborative agreement with numerous organizations throughout the city and state.

Program Specifics

Shelters play a unique role in this country's efforts to reach out to the homeless, regardless of their background and circumstances for being homeless. However, shelters, by their general welcoming nature, make access by the homeless with a criminal justice background much easier than most "conventional" human services agencies. St. Francis House is a case in point.

St. Francis House's mission is "to work in service to the poor with the heart, mind, and spirit of Saint Francis of Assisi." St. Francis House's statement of purpose reads as follows:

> We are committed to providing necessities: food, clothing, shelter, showers and medical care, and other emergency services to building mutually enriching relationships with the community among the homeless. We attempt to break down the isolation that is a part of their lives. We are also committed to helping those who are able to take steps to move themselves up and out of poverty, unemployment, and homelessness to lives of self-respect and hope. "Being aware of the fragile humanity we all share we accept God's invitation to respond to the guests who come to our House with gracious hospitality, respect, kindness, patience, trust, and hope so as to encourage and support them in lives of greater dignity and self-worth." (St. Francis House, 1998, pp. 1–2)

The story of Jose, a Latino male, illustrates the potential of a capacity enhancement perspective, and how individuals who are perceived as not having assets can play a role in achieving social change in this society. The story of Jose was shared with the general public in the fall 1998 issue of *The Spirit of St. Francis Newsletter:*

Jose Ramos had a dream, and a newfound voice to proclaim it with. It is his goal to educate his homeless peers on the importance of voting, and eliminate many of their fears about the registering process. For Jose, this is the first time he will vote since he became homeless eight years ago. Jose is helping with St. Francis House's first Voter Registration Drive, initiated at a Guest Council meeting after guests voiced their need for affordable housing, livable income, public restrooms and adequate storage facilities. What better way to make change than to use the power of the vote?

Questions arose about the feasibility of registering the homeless community for the 1998 elections. Could a person with no address register to vote? Leaders in the San Francis House homeless community gathered information from City Hall and from the State House, where they found the answer. The National Voter Registration Act of 1993 makes it easier for the homeless to vote. The Act provides that if a homeless person is staying at a shelter, they can register under that shelter's address. If they are sleeping on a bench or a grate, they may register using that location as well. For Jose, these are golden words. "Voting for me is important. If you don't vote, you don't have rights. We, homeless, have the right to be part of society." "When you want to build a house, you need talent, effort and hope. With these three, you will finish it."

St. Francis House, although technically considered a day shelter for the homeless of Boston, can best be conceptualized as a settlement house, in the social work profession's conventional sense of the term. A settlement house orientation is one that seeks to address the individual in need of assistance from a holistic perspective, with a wide range of services. For example, there is in general a tremendous need to expand the services targeting the homeless to include assistance with immigration—this is the result of a shift in the composition of the homeless population. It has been estimated that 20 percent of the guests at St. Francis House are undocumented and in need of legal assistance regarding their immigration status. St. Francis House helps in this area.

The Moving Ahead Program, or MAP, founded in 1995, seeks to help participants with four major life transitions: (1) from homelessness to personal and community support; (2) from addiction to recovery; (3) from hopelessness to self-efficacy; and (4) from isolation to job, career, economic self-sufficiency, and valued community roles (Education Development Center, 1999). MAP targets the formerly homeless with histories of substance abuse and is modeled on the HOPE program in New York City. Many of the men and women that MAP serves are also former offenders with histories of incarceration. The program has made a special effort to serve the homeless with prison backgrounds. This special effort has resulted in "word on the streets" concerning MAP's welcoming of homeless participants with criminal justice backgrounds. Participants must be

18 or older, be in a residential substance abuse program or residing at a shelter or temporary residence, and be willing to undergo training related to employment (Bilt, Raynovich, and Shaffer, 1999). Employment is considered a critical element in helping formerly homeless individuals with substance abuse backgrounds to succeed in society. MAP is a fourteen-week program that seeks to prepare participants for work upon completion of the program. St. Francis pays for up to six months' residence in "recovery homes" in Boston.

MAP is built upon a set of holistic concepts that reinforce independence and resiliency:

> MAP is a much broader concept of recovery than what is normally considered in the field. MAP is a holistic model, addressing the needs of the whole person. MAP is a bridge to society, taking a stigmatized, disenfranchised group into the mainstream culture. Addiction recovery is viewed as a process that cannot happen in isolation, but must be anchored in a new, positive work-life and lifestyle. MAP is a "no-blame" approach, stressing the positive aspects of the individual. While many social programs view homelessness and addiction as a weakness—following a social deficit model—MAP holds high expectations for the participants to succeed. (Education Development Center, 1999, p. 2)

Participants are given a stipend during the period of enrollment. The program integrates counseling, self-assessment, skills development, and work experience. In addition, it utilizes a participant-centered approach. Participants learn about themselves in addition to how to seek employment, write a résumé, interview, and other job-related skills. Participants gaining an increased awareness of who they are and of their past struggles and successes plays a central role in the program.

The MAP curriculum consists of nine modules that vary in intensity and duration over the fourteen-week period:

1. Orientation to MAP spans a three-day period (two half days and a third full day of classes).
2. Life transition skills and career readiness consists of eight units that span a twelve-week period and focus on better preparing participants for the world of work.
3. Studio Shine seeks to alter the external appearance of participants through the use of clothing, hair styles, and so on.
4. Cultural literacy provides participants with new pastimes by introducing, or reintroducing, healthy and constructive activities that help them in their transition back to society.
5. Legal rehabilitation helps participants resolve issues related to the legal system that may hamper employment and recovery.
6. Introduction to information technology (transpires over an eight-week period) assists participants in obtaining skills

related to word processing, databases, spreadsheets, and graphics.

7. The workplace readiness and internship component involves participants in a six-week internship or trial work period and takes place during the seventh week of the program. Participants are required to undertake an internship in their area of specialty and interest, during which their progress is monitored and supported by program staff. Participants are expected to spend twenty to thirty hours per week at the internship site.

8. Graduation ceremonies highlight the accomplishments of the participants. Upon successfully completing the program, graduates participate in formal graduation ceremonies, which serve as testimonies to the capacities of participants. It is not unusual to find relatives and other loved ones attending these ceremonies and sharing in the festivities.

9. The alumni program provides graduates with an opportunity to obtain emotional, social, career, and practical support as needed—graduates of MAP have ample opportunities to maintain contact with program staff.

There is an understanding among program staff that graduates often encounter difficult periods in maintaining sobriety, jobs, housing, and the like. These stressors can easily result in relapse. Consequently, avenues for graduates to contact staff are maintained. Graduates do not have to be facing stress in their lives in order to reestablish contact with the program. In numerous instances graduates have come back to share their successes and even volunteer.

Approximately 58 percent of MAP participants are male. White non-Latinos make up the highest percentage (46.7) of participants followed by African Americans (23.7 percent), Latinos (15.8 percent), Asian/Pacific Islanders (3.4 percent), Cape Verdean (1.7 percent), and others accounting for 8.7 percent (Bilt, Raynovich, and Shaffer, 1999). The majority of participants have had some involvement with the legal system—35.6 percent were on probation, 6.8 percent had court cases pending, 5.1 percent had outstanding warrants, 3.4 percent were on parole, and 5 percent had other legal-related issues (Bilt, Raynovich, and Shaffer, 1999).

Capacity Enhancement Methods

MAP has develop a set of principles that serve to guide programming: (1) view addiction and recovery within the context of the person's life map; (2) establish positive expectations that will enhance commitment to future growth; (3) develop supportive, long-term relationships as a foundation for supporting recovery; (4) integrate program activities that support both recovery and vocational development as part of a comprehensive approach; (5) ensure that the program environment engenders respect for each individual; (6) focus on skill development rather than deficit reduction; (7) develop work readiness and self-efficacy; (8) create bridges to mainstream culture; and (9) subscribe to the formula "success breeds success."

The following five capacity enhancement principles can be found integrated with the methods of the Moving Ahead Program: (1) social and economic justice themes should be integrated into an intervention; (2) participants should be given an opportunity to have their voices heard and to express hopes, fears, and concerns; (3) process is as important as, if not more important than, outcome; (4) cultural context cannot be separated from social and economic context; and (5) interventions must prepare participants for current and future needs.

The MAP program utilizes a series of methods that can be thought of as capacity enhancing. Self-discovery is central to the program and is operationalized in a variety of ways, one of which is having participants develop a better understanding of their lives. A fundamental belief in the inherent capacities of the participants builds upon their strengths through this self-discovery method. Further, the group-sharing process serves to build group identity and an appreciation of how participants have encountered and coped with many of life's challenges and tragedies.

Clearly, capacity enhancement can take place only when the participant has had an opportunity to better understand the context that led him or her to engage in criminal activities and drug abuse. The process associated with this insightfulness is both time consuming and quite painful. However, it is also enlightening and transformative. Capacity enhancement, in addition, does not take place in a vacuum historically; nor does it take place in a vacuum in the present. Efforts to connect the participant to the outside world through work and cultural connections assist him or her in becoming part of a larger social network that is positive in nature. Unlike his or her network in the past that often consisted of people who were also involved with criminal and drug-abusing activities, this network offers hope and builds a set of relationships with a "new" participant, a participant who believes in his or her self-worth and capacities to take control of his or her life and environment.

MAP activities, as a result, can be viewed developmentally—that is, as preparing a participant for his or her new life and journey into recovery and as an outstanding member of the community and society. It is important that a focus on capacity enhancement not overwhelm a participant. Many, if not all, have internalized very negative images of themselves. It would not be unusual for them to tell stories of how they were considered "losers" and not capable of making important and sustained contributions to their family, community, and society. Thus, any effort to identify and draw upon capacities must seriously consider years upon years of negative images that have become an integral part of a participant's life.

Programming involving the homeless who have criminal justice and substance abuse backgrounds, as a result, must be carefully planned with the understanding that there is no question about whether participants have strengths or assets. They would have died years ago if they did not. Programming must be based on identifying the capacities the participants have. That may seem like semantics. However, it is a fundamental premise that is operative in MAP's activities and adhered to by its staff. The degree to which capacity enhancement is integrated into an activity very much depends on the ability of the participants to understand and embrace their capacities or strengths.

Lessons for Social Work

Work with the homeless in this society—and Boston is certainly no exception—requires dedicated staff with a keen understanding of the issues and challenges facing this group. The story of Jose highlighted earlier brings to the foreground the importance of hiring as staff members individuals who were formerly homeless and have been under correctional supervision. Such people bring a unique perspective to the job and, as a result, are able more easily to win the trust and respect of ex-inmates who are homeless. As evidenced by MAP, the work is long term, requires extensive knowledge of existing area resources in order to be comprehensive, and requires an understanding of cultural factors. The program places a tremendous amount of emphasis on participants having an in-depth understanding of who they are and of the challenges ahead in seeking to regain control over their lives. Relapse, although not desirable from an individual and programmatic perspective, is an important aspect of recovery.

MAP has been immensely successful in helping participants make the transition from homelessness to maintaining sobriety and jobs. Benefiting from MAP's collaborative partnership with Harvard Medical School's Division on Addiction, which has evaluated the program, 79.4 percent of the MAP graduates have met program objectives. This compares very favorably with the national average graduation rate from a recovery home of 26 percent.

Social workers who have worked with the homeless in major cities across the country know how the sociodemographics of homelessness have changed over the years. The percentage of homeless with correctional backgrounds continues to increase, and they are very often of color. The number of undocumented newcomers has also increased in U.S. cities. These individuals, in turn, often do not speak English as their primary language and face considerable barriers in adjusting to life in U.S. society, and more specifically, to life on the streets during the winter months in northern cities. Women, a group that historically was not part of the homeless community, have shown greater presence in homeless-oriented programs. Many of these women, too, have prison backgrounds, further stigmatizing them among the homeless population.

The Moving Ahead Program underscores the importance of collaborative relationships between programs in order to meet the complex needs

of the homeless who have substance abuse and criminal justice backgrounds. Few organizations possess the requisite resources to meet all the
social, economic, medical, and legal needs of the homeless. Thus, there is
a tremendous need to develop and maintain active collaborative partnerships between multiple organizations. The homeless with criminal justice
backgrounds, like former mental patients who are homeless, require organizations to actively advocate for their needs. Advocacy at the national,
state, and local levels serves to ensure that we do not ignore the needs of
this population group. The criminal justice system, like the mental health
system, has the responsibility to ensure that when offenders are released
a plan is in place to minimize the chances of their returning to prison.

15

Women's Prison Association, New York City

Barriers established by male-dominated reform organizations resulted in women reformers seeking to create their own organizations in the nineteenth century (Morton, 1995). The Women's Prison Association (WPA) was established in 1844 in an effort to facilitate women making the transition from prison back to the community. The women who established the WPA were very unusual for their time: "WPA is a wonderful organization with a very rich history. It was founded in 1844 by a group of visionaries who were associated with the Quakers, and concerned about prison conditions. One of the things they did was to found the first halfway house for women in the country. . . . The women originally involved in the organization did everything from running this house as a volunteer labor of love, to getting on the train and going to Albany to advocate for legislation to create a separate prison for women" (Jacobs, 1997, p. 44).

The WPA is widely considered one of the leading organizations in establishing services for female ex-offenders in the country. The organization has a staff of approximately one hundred and a budget of $5.5 million, with 20 percent of that derived from foundations and donations and the rest from government. The establishment of the Isaac T. Hopper Home provided housing and training for women during the nineteenth century, helping more than 450 women offenders during the first three years of operation and more than 37,000 since its inception (Conly, 1999). The WPA's mission is "to create opportunities for change in the lives of women prisoners, ex-prisoners, and their families. The WPA provides programs through which women acquire life skills needed to end involvement in the criminal justice system and to make positive, healthy choices for themselves and their families. . . . We emphasize: Self-reliance through the development of independent living skills. Self-empowerment and peer support. Client involvement in the community. Assistance from dedicated staff, advisers, and volunteers" (Conly, 1999, p. 5).

Program Specifics

The WPA estimates that between 30 and 50 percent of women released from prison are homeless, and that 80 percent of the women in the criminal justice system are mothers (Jacobs, 1997). These two sets of statistics play important roles in how WPA services are conceptualized and structured: "A lot of what WPA has done has been to focus on the huge gap between how the child welfare system operates and how the criminal system operates, and figure out what it would take for both of them to work more collaboratively in the best interests of the kids. So besides the direct services that we offer the woman as mother—recognizing that sometimes her kids are her biggest motivating factor to get sober and get straight— we also try to work at a systemic level to help the two systems get to know each other better and work together better" (Jacobs, 1997, p. 44). Services to women offenders, therefore, must be multifaceted and comprehensive whenever possible, including the active use of outreach. The form of outreach that is necessary, however, is not one that is limited by geography or by day of the week or time of day.

The Women's Prison Association's mission statement translates into a series of goals that, as to be expected, have a direct influence on all facets of programming. Those goals are (1) the importance of learning and adopting independent living skills, (2) the need to obtain permanent living arrangements, (3) the need to receive appropriate preventive and medical care, (4) the importance of gaining financial independence and support, (5) achievement and maintenance of sobriety, (6) development of support relationships, and (7) reunification of children and families. These goals are indicative of the need for comprehensive services and of the importance of meeting the needs of female offenders as early as possible.

Five major programs constitute the programmatic thrust of WPA services: (1) the Transitional Services Unit, which provides intensive support and housing placement services for women who are HIV-positive both inside the corrections system and upon release; (2) the Hopper Home Alternative to Incarceration Program, which is a community alternative transitional residence with intensive support services for women who would otherwise be in jail or prison; (3) the Sarah Powell Huntington House, which is a transitional residence for homeless women offenders who are reuniting with their children, including women with HIV or AIDS; (4) the Incarcerated Mothers Law Project, which in partnership with the Volunteers of Legal Service, Inc., provides workshops on family law to groups of incarcerated and formerly incarcerated women within and outside the correctional system; and (5) the Steps to Independence Program, which provides job placement, housing placement, and independent living skills and training services to participants in the other four programs.

Women are referred to the WPA from a wide variety of sources, including self-referrals. The WPA programs target women who are 18 or older, have a past or current involvement with the criminal justice system, have not been diagnosed with severe mental illness, are detoxed and able to participate in a day-treatment program (for residential programs), and have not been charged with arson (for residential programs). The WPA accepts approximately 85 percent of all those who are referred, and the average participant spends almost eighteen months in a program (Conly, 1999).

Recent efforts at welfare reform will have a devastating impact on female ex-offenders and their quest to reunite with their children and stay out of the criminal justice system:

> Welfare reform is going to be devastating for women in the criminal justice system. The new rules say that people convicted of a drug felony aren't eligible for public assistance (TANF), which means that an enormous number of women with drug convictions now have no way of supporting their families (though the federal welfare reform act does give states the option of ignoring this rule). . . . They're being punished twice over. We're inflicting this additional punishment through the welfare system, but we're not giving it to convicted rapists, or convicted murderers. Just convicted drug felons. Why? It's a way of looking tough on crime at the expense of women and children. (Jacobs, 1997, p. 45)

Capacity Enhancement Methods

Capacity enhancement principles are integrated throughout most of the WPA programs and activities. Three of the WPA's methods typify the potential of capacity enhancement practice with offenders (in this case, women): (1) building on strengths, (2) developing skills, and (3) peer support. The strategies for building on client strengths incorporate several of the principles of capacity enhancement practice with the correctionally supervised covered in chapter 5:

> WPA seeks to build on client experiences and strengths (as opposed to merely addressing deficiencies) and to recognize small successes. Clients are encouraged to assume a variety of respon-

sibilities that contribute to their viewing themselves as capable. Each client is required to define and refine her own case plan and encouraged to assume increased responsibility for accomplishing her specified goals. In addition, clients participate in the development of WPA programs. They also serve as public speakers, peer educators, trainers, and assistants in the Child Center at the Sarah Powell Huntington House. (Conly, 1999, p. 9)

The principle that all individuals, regardless of background and circumstances, possess strengths and abilities applies; it is important that the staff has the ability to both identify these competencies and encourage the ex-offender to recognize and own them.

The embrace of a strengths perspective is manifested in a variety of ways ranging from participants playing an active role in decision making to opportunities to serve fellow offenders and communities. Participants must take responsibility for their decisions and actions. This goal, however, may be difficult to accomplish for women with histories of being dependent on others, particularly men who have not played positive and enriching roles. Because some women will accomplish this goal more easily than others, there needs to be a tremendous amount of flexibility in the programming of activities seeking to enhance capacities.

The principle that the quality of life in a community must be bettered as a result of an intervention is evident in the community service program. Participants can play a critical role in giving back to their communities and in so doing can transform themselves. Being given such an opportunity may be a rare occurrence in an ex-offender's life. Community service broadens a participant's understanding of commitment and responsibility. In addition, it allows the community to see the participant in a role other than that of "ex-offender." The ex-offender role is usually very stereotypical and destructive to the process of rehabilitation.

The development and enhancement of skills represents an important strategy for capacity enhancement. The principle that interventions must provide participants with an opportunity to have their voices heard and to express their hopes, fears, and concerns necessitates the embrace of an empowerment perspective. The empowerment of women is not possible without providing them with the requisite skills to control their own destiny: "Each WPA program includes workshops and skills-building exercises to help women improve their abilities to participate productively and healthfully in their roles as parents, students, employees, tenants, and friends. Information presented spans a broad range of topics including health (e.g., substance abuse, HIV prevention and treatment), mental health, vocational training, parenting, and independent living" (Conly, 1999, p. 10). When skills development and training workshops are conducted by peers, they take on added significance in the transformation of participants. The skills addressed by the WPA cover a wide range including vocational and personal. It is not rare to see participants presented with a wealth of opportunities to enhance their lives. Thus, much work and attention must be devoted to essential tasks that must be accomplished before participants make significant progress.

The WPA's focus on peer support addresses two capacity enhancement principles: that the quality of life in a community be bettered as a result of the intervention and that all people, regardless of background and circumstances, have strengths and abilities. WPA participants are considered as having innate capacities and are encouraged to use them in service to others: "WPA's programs help women offenders build healthy relationships through peer support. Reportedly, most WPA clients arrive with very poor self-images and little sense that they can make a positive contribution. Through group workshops, support groups, household work assignments, and recreational assignments, participants support each other in recovery and in accomplishing their goals. This redefinition of their relationships with each other can be very transformative" (Conly, 1999, p. 9).

Peer mentors, many of whom are former incarcerated women themselves, very often meet program participants at the door of a prison or jail. Not surprisingly, recently released women offenders are considered to be at their most vulnerable upon their release, which is often done at night. A peer mentor is well versed in the anxieties associated with release and is well aware of the resources in the city to help women offenders find a place to sleep. The mentor's ability to "connect" with the released offender enhances his or her value and effectiveness in gaining the ex-offender's trust and providing the advice and resources necessary to help the newly released confront the many questions and insecurities associated with leaving a total institution after an extended stay.

Lessons for Social Work

The concept of empowerment has been operationalized by the social work profession in a multitude of settings and with a multitude of population groups—the latest of which is women offenders. Efforts to empower women inmates, advocate on their behalf, and bring national attention to the unique set of challenges they face in the nation's prison system are not without their rewards and challenges. The increasing number of female prisoners has caused human services agencies—child welfare and non–child welfare—to examine how best to reach and assist them. The WPA has a long tradition of service to women prisoners; however, the increasing number of women being released from prison with a host of major problems such as HIV and AIDS has necessitated the development of new services and methods for reaching out to and engaging them upon release. This effort is facilitated in cases where women have been fortunate enough to have received treatment and education before being released from prison.

Evaluation of services has increased in importance in the human services field in the last twenty years. More and more, funders are requesting, and often demanding, that programs prove that they are in fact serving who they profess to be serving and achieving stated objectives, and that they are cost effective. This information plays an important role in determining who gets funding, for what services, and for what costs. Evaluation is not an easy task in any form of service delivery. However, it takes on added challenges when it pertains to programs addressing the service needs of ex-offenders.

The trend toward evaluation, as a result, is forcing organizations that serve difficult-to-reach population groups to develop methods of evaluation that are unintrusive, valid, and inexpensive to administer.

One of the major challenges facing the Women's Prison Association is evaluating and documenting how its work has transformed participants. The challenge of maintaining contact with former participants often necessitates the expenditure of considerable energy and resources. This should not come as a surprise to any organization wishing to service marginalized groups in urban areas of the country. The increased number of incarcerated and released women has placed considerable demands on organizations to meet their needs. When HIV and AIDS are entered into the equation the challenges become even greater. The attempts of an organization to gather necessary but very sensitive information on program participants is often not welcomed by women who are very guarded of their lives.

Many former women inmates who are mothers want to be reunited with their children, who more often than not have been placed in non-kinship foster homes. But before they can take custody of their children, they must first prove that they have a stable home life, which means having a home of their own. However, a woman cannot qualify for family rental and income assistance without her children. Sarah Powell Huntington House was developed to address this catch-22. Barriers such as this can be surmounted; however, it requires a considerable amount of staff time and resources. Once they have reunited with their children, women then face the challenge of reestablishing their roles as mothers when their children may have spent most of their lifetimes with some "other" mother. Adjustment to parenthood, as a result, is a two-sided affair—for mothers as well as children.

Successful reentry into the community will require that social workers first identify the capacities of these women to maintain an independent lifestyle. Independence, however, does not mean that no form of instrumental or expressive support is allowed. Support in the form of housing assistance and social, psychological, and economic aid is very often needed in order to prevent recidivism. In cases where a woman also has an HIV or AIDS diagnosis, she will need assistance in negotiating the complex, ever-changing health care system in this country. Having capacities, as a result, does not mean there are no needs. It does mean that these women must tap their strengths, and that in so doing they can play an instrumental role in all facets of their service provision.

The importance of comprehensive service delivery often places social workers in the role of broker, or case manager, because few organizations have the capability to provide comprehensive services. An in-depth knowledge of community resources, both formal and informal, is critical in helping female ex-offenders. Advocacy, as to be expected, will have to be exercised almost daily in order for these women to receive the resources they both need and deserve. Failure to exercise advocacy skills means that some important need will go unmet, and therefore the chances of recidivism go up dramatically.

Finally, system change is necessary, a concept not foreign to social workers. While advocacy at the individual level is a necessity in working with female ex-offenders, social reform is also necessary. Few organizations can afford to do one without doing the other. The increasing number of women who are being incarcerated combined with persistent efforts at the local and national level to alter the safety net will have a profound impact on whether women ex-offenders have a legitimate chance at rehabilitation and reunification with their children. Social work, as a result, cannot afford to focus on one arena to the exclusion of the other.

16

Bliss Unlimited, Glendale, California

We Care for Youth (WCFY) was established in 1991 under the leadership of codirectors Linda Maxwell and Jose R. Quintanar; it was incorporated in 1994. The organization's mission statement reads: "We Care for Youth offers unconditional love as the path and employment training as a vehicle toward improving youths' self-respect and competency. Programs engage teens in the learning process and provide life skills that enable them to plan their future with hope." This mission statement highlights the importance of viewing youth from a capacity versus deficit perspective and underscores the importance of self-respect and competency. WCFY has a fourteen-member board, which includes two youth members. The organization uses six key philosophical principles to guide its development of programs:

1. The philosophy of We Care for Youth and its subdivision, Bliss Unlimited, is that our work is rooted in peace, guided by compassion, and conducted in teamwork, striving for impeccability.
2. Unconditional love is the path we follow to treat all people equally with respect, to accept everyone as they are at that moment. Those who work with us interact with young people out of compassion.

183

3. Peace is seen as the wellspring of inspiration, strength and hope for the work that we do with teenagers. If youth can contemplate a future of non-violence, they are more likely to set and accomplish goals.
4. All projects and partnerships are inspired by youth, made with integrity and sold with love. Other values we teach and model are commitment, trust, respect, responsibility, tolerance, honesty and determination.
5. We are constantly influenced by and seek opportunities with national and global organizations and individuals who share our vision.
6. All activities, programs, and ideas are run through the filters of the WCFY mission and philosophy before engaging. (Bliss Unlimited, 1998)

We Care for Youth runs a series of programs in addition to Bliss Unlimited, the focus of this case study. School-based and other trainings focus on job-readiness and skill-oriented trainings. Participants are shown how their actions can have a positive influence on their futures. These programs seek to better prepare youth to become independent, caring, and productive adults. Training of Trainers is a program that focuses on identifying and preparing youth to assume positions of presenters and to bring the job-readiness program into a larger number of Los Angeles area schools. Peace Conference is a forum through which youth can discover alternatives to the use of violence in resolving conflicts (Huffaker, 1999a, 1999b; Robinson-Jacobs, 1999; Tanaka, 1998, 1999).

Bliss Unlimited was developed in response to a perceived need to provide youth with a sense of hope for the future, to provide them with an alternative to joining gangs, and to provide them with an opportunity to both learn and do in the work world. Police had identified more than three hundred gang members who lived in Glendale, and gangs were actively recruiting youth. In 1995 a business partnership with the coffee company Piacere International evolved into the creation of Bliss Baskets. That year the operation produced $4,500 in sales revenues and broke even financially. The success of that venture eventually led to the creation of Bliss Unlimited. In 1996 the operation generated $19,000 in revenues. In 1997 Bliss Unlimited, in collaboration with Glendale Galleria, established a retail operation (Rivero, 1997).

Program Specifics

Bliss Unlimited was established in 1995 and is a business enterprise inspired and directed by youth themselves. Through a gift store in the Glendale Galleria Mall, youth are given an opportunity to learn by doing— in this case, running a business. The young people create a number of gift items that are sold through the store—gift baskets, hand-painted greeting cards, painted gift boxes, message stones, potpourri sachets and containers, ornaments, gift wrap, and other items.

All youth that are referred to Bliss Unlimited are accepted. Referrals come from a wide variety of sources, including schools, community-based organizations, police, and former graduates. The program has been so successful that it does not undertake recruitment efforts to enroll youth. Youth participants, aged 13 to 21 and of equally mixed gender, represent a wide variety of ethnic and racial groups (African American, Armenian, Chinese, Japanese, Korean, Latino, Pacific Islander, and white non-Latino). More than four thousand youth have graduated from the We Care for Youth programs, and approximately twenty-five students are involved annually with Bliss Unlimited (Fox, 1995; Steinman, 1997).

Bliss Unlimited's mission statement reads as follows: "Bliss Unlimited (a subsidiary of We Care for Youth, a California not-for-profit Corporation) is a youth-directed global enterprise built on a foundation of humane values, teamwork and impeccability. Our gift products and services are inspired by youth and dedicated to the empowerment of youth and designed to cultivate world peace" (Bliss Unlimited, 1999). Bliss Unlimited (1998) developed a set of guiding principles that provide direction for the program:

1. The Employees and Volunteers will have the quality of youth. To define "youth" as people, some of whom are young in age, that are learning, capable of being influenced in a positive way, energetic to do their personal best, remain willing to be challenged, and are unique individuals.
2. Unconditional Love. To treat people equally with love and respect, to accept everyone as they are at that moment and to express compassion to all who cross our path.
3. Commitment. To acknowledge our heartfelt desire to serve, succeed and work, we will keep our word unconditionally.
4. Teamwork. To work together in harmony and strive for the success of one another.
5. Trust. To accept each others' strengths and weaknesses, we graciously agree to treat one another with the highest level of human decency and respect.
6. Standing for the Greatness of Others. To always see the best in each other and defend the truth. To acknowledge each others' greatness without jealously or envy, and wish them the best.
7. Respect. To honor oneself and the opinions, actions, differences, ethnicity and personalities of others with love and tolerance. To honor our environment with mindfulness.
8. Responsibility. To keep our word, acknowledge when we do not, and to honor the agreement.
9. Impeccability. To mindfully do our very best at every moment.

10. Inclusion. To value everyone.
11. Opportunity. To allow everyone an equal chance to succeed, improve and learn.
12. Positive Energy. To focus on the best of each person or situation.
13. Tolerance. To accept oneself and others, just as we/they are.
14. Honesty. To at all moments speak and walk our personal truth, knowing it is the best place from which to operate.
15. Determination. To commit to live these guiding principles.

Bliss Unlimited involves youth in three major organization-related strategies: (1) product strategy, (2) sales and marketing strategies, and (3) business operation. Product strategies necessitate that youth design and create high-quality products that will be sold through the store. Under the guidance of the Bliss director, youth research and purchase supplies and make their gift products, on- and off-site. During the busy holiday season, youth create and distribute hundreds of corporate gift baskets to clients.

Sales and marketing strategies require that youth be exposed to and learn all aspects of the business—purchasing, production, marketing, sales, promotion, and accounting. Gross sales during the holiday season through mid-January can amount to $55,000 or greater. When expenses are subtracted, a profit of more than $5,000 can be generated, which is reinvested into the program. Finally, the operations of the business require that youth develop teams. They elect team managers to supervise them. This facet involves adult managers and some experienced youth managers staffing the cash register, keeping track of receipts, and supervising the payroll. Youth receive above the minimum wage for their efforts. Those involved through a school program receive class credit and are paid a monthly stipend (Fox, 1998).

Youth participate in training programs that stress life skills and employment readiness. Workshops cover subjects such as self-love, goal setting, problem-solving strategies, prejudice reduction, conflict management, power of appearance, résumé skills, and interview and application processes. Mentoring, in addition, plays an important role in the operation of Bliss Unlimited. Adult mentors supervise and train youth in activities such as marketing, sales, product development, quality control, and use of art mediums. Several major corporations, such as American Express and Time Warner/Turner Broadcasting, and local businesses provide mentors.

Bliss Unlimited seeks to accomplish six major objectives: (1) expand the job training program to offer graduates an educational experience in the business world, (2) create a program that mentors youngsters and establishes partnerships with community leaders, (3) secure $65,000 in donations and grants to cover operating expenses, (4) raise awareness of the program among the public and potential business partners by generating $50,000 in publicity, (5) encourage merchant involvement in the program, and (6) instill pride and a sense of ownership in the Glendale Galleria among teens (Bliss Unlimited, 1998). In 1998 Bliss Unlimited had profits that totaled close to $84,000, was able to secure more than five thousand volunteer hours from teens, generated almost $94,000 in corporate donations, and gathered $74,000 in publicity. Profits were reinvested into the program (Bliss Unlimited, 1998). The holiday season, as to be expected, is the most profitable and busy, generating more than 50 percent of a year's revenues.

Bliss Unlimited could not possibly succeed without entering into collaborative partnerships with many other organizations. The following partial list serves to illustrate the types and range of organizations actively working with Bliss Unlimited: (1) Glendale Galleria—provides free retail and warehouse space and assistance in placing youth in jobs at the mall, with merchants also playing an influential role in directing customers to the store for gift wrapping; (2) Glendale Unified School District—provides assistance in recruiting youth for training, provides meeting space, grants credit to youth completing courses, and pays WCFY to conduct training in the schools; (3) Glendale High School Construction Academy—provides tables and screen dividers for the store; (4) Piacere International—provides coffee at cost and lessons about the history, economics, and politics of coffee to youth; (5) Boy Scouts of America—has provided, through the Explorer program, insurance for youth and space at its headquarters; (6) CNN and Turner Broadcasting—purchases products and donates technical equipment; (7) Glendale Chamber of Commerce—provides membership privileges to two youth leaders, contacts for networking, and potential customers; (8) American Express Financial Services—provides mentoring and purchases products; (9) Glendale Youth Alliance—hires WCFY youth to act as trainers and provides volunteers to work in the store; (10) Glendale Infiniti—donates a van for delivering gift baskets and provides consultation; and (11) De Vries Imports—this local import company donated free gift-basket-making classes and business consulting classes.

Capital requirements for the year on which this case study is based (December 30, 1998, through December 31, 1999) incorporated Bliss Unlimited's twin focuses on the enhancement of youth capacities and on business (Bliss Unlimited, 1999). Funds were used to expand educational curriculum; increase production and inventory to maintain yearly operations; employ two full-time program directors; create full-time and part-time employed youth staff to support and sustain prolonged growth under the new marketing plan; expand product lines for both the corporate and retail segments; maximize sales with an extensive campaign to promote products and services, especially via the Internet; invest in additional business equipment and expand operations to maximize efficiency; and increase research and development to find or create new product lines and improve existing ones.

Evaluation of the program is multifaceted with an emphasis on pre- and postschool performance, attendance, and participant reactions and suggestions, as well as a focus on business-related factors such as profits and sales. The program, in addition, monitors its collaborative agreements quite carefully. A more comprehensive evaluation of the program is desired, but costs associated with such an effort necessitate obtaining funds specifically for this activity.

Capacity Enhancement Methods

A commitment to learning serves as a foundation for Bliss Unlimited. Such a commitment, as to be expected, must foster values, beliefs, knowledge, and skills to be successful (Griffin-Wiesner and Hong, 1998–1999). Bliss Unlimited actively seeks to identify the strengths youngsters bring to the program, and it does this through a variety of methods, including asking participants what they like and are good at doing.

A spiritual dimension also plays an important role in the program. Many participants, although they might identify themselves as belonging to a particular denomination, do not know much about religion. It should be added that the program does not tie spirituality exclusively to religious affiliation. Qualities of spirituality are fostered in the program as a means of providing youth with inner strengths that are not tied to possessions or achievements. Program staff believe that the identification and foster-ing of spirituality provides youth with an asset that will help them make a successful transition to adulthood, and specifically help them in times of crisis. The program also gives youth who have graduated the opportu-nity to return to the program and provide service to participants and the community.

As noted in the above descriptions, Bliss Unlimited incorporates many of the capacity enhancement principles outlined in chapter 2. However, the following principles stand out from the perspective of this book: (1) all people possess strengths and abilities; (2) interventions rarely follow a predictable and linear path, and thus require a considerable degree of flexibility; (3) cultural context cannot be separated from social and eco-nomic context; (4) interventions must address current needs while pre-paring participants for the future; and (5) interventions must provide par-ticipants with an opportunity to have their voices heard.

Individual Story

The case of Amanda (pseudonym) reflects both the rewards and challenges associated with working with youth who are involved in gangs and in perpetual trouble with law enforcement. Amanda was 13 when she was referred to Bliss Unlimited by the principal of a local junior high school that the program had "adopted." She was one of twenty youth who were members of two rival gangs at the time. She had a lengthy history of vio-lence and low school grades, and was a leader of one of the gangs.

Initially, she displayed very little motivation for being in the program. She was in the program because she had to be and was not willing to actively engage in activities. Although she attended as required, she remained very much on the outskirts of the group. She provided no posi-

tive feedback to program staff throughout the initial period of her involvement, yet she attended on a regular basis. Staff needed to provide her with
sufficient "space" to be there on her terms, but they never passed up an
opportunity to invite her to take part in program activities.

Amanda eventually started to feel more comfortable in the program,
and she began actively to participate in projects. She eventually left the
gang and put more of her energies into Bliss Unlimited and school. She
always had an innate ability to work with computers. In 1996 she managed
to start and complete the job training program at Bliss Unlimited and also
to graduate from high school with a B average. Just when it seemed she
was ready to make a long-term commitment to changing her life, she disappeared from the program. One of the program codirectors ran into her
in the community and found that Amanda was pregnant. She had always
said that she wanted to have a baby, so the pregnancy did not come as a
total surprise to staff. Unfortunately for Amanda, the father of the child
was not well liked by her family, and this caused a tremendous amount of
friction between her and her family.

Amanda went through a series of emotionally painful experiences during the next few years that culminated in a life-changing path. She witnessed the death of a close friend who was sitting next to her during a
drive in one of Los Angeles's toughest neighborhoods. Her friend was shot
and killed instantly while she drove her car, and Amanda was very lucky
that she was not an injured "innocent" bystander in this incident. Another
time she had a terrible fight with her parents about the father of her child.
Shortly after the fight she was involved in an altercation with two other
girls, which resulted in her being sentenced to five months in county jail
at the age of 18. Her experience in jail made her realize that she could lose
everything she valued in life.

After her release from jail she went to work with Bliss Unlimited as a
business manager. After a brief period, she left Bliss Unlimited for another
job where she received on-the-job training on computers. She is now 23
years old and earning $35,000 a year working for a business resource com-
pany. Amanda wants to give back to Bliss Unlimited and is volunteering
to help the program design a Web page.

Lessons for Social Work

Although in principle identifying youth capacities may seem like a
straightforward task, in reality it is not. Many youngsters, particularly
those from marginalized groups, have rarely been asked what they were
good at or liked. Shamefully, these youngsters are much more capable of
identifying their deficits than their strengths. Thus, any effort to identify
capacities is an arduous, time-consuming process that cannot be relegated
to an intake session. This process is evolutionary in nature, filled with
periods of discovery.

Work with youth who are designated "at risk" requires a tremendous amount of patience, dedication, and flexibility in programming. In essence, the programming needs to flow from the participants' assets and needs; participants must not strictly conform to the program. This is a dynamic relationship between the client and the nature and structure of programming. Many youngsters enter Bliss Unlimited with few formal achievements in life. In fact, many have systematically been told by persons in authority that they are "losers." Thus, years of hearing negative messages cannot be overturned in a few days, weeks, or even months, depending upon the severity of the socialization.

Progress toward achieving productive lives is rarely linear in nature. Namely, once a decision is made to move forward that does not mean that relapse is not possible. In Amanda's case, she seemed well on her way to being a positive member of the community upon graduating from high school. However, much happened after that period that would not "qualify" as a success—out-of-wedlock pregnancy and prison, for example. Having a place to which she could return and where she would be accepted was very important in Amanda's life.

Prevention programs subscribing to youth development concepts and principles cannot succeed without a dedicated effort to develop partnerships with other organizations. The field, however, has generally not emphasized developing partnerships with business. Nevertheless, the business arena is sufficiently broad to lend itself to collaboration, as evidenced by Bliss Unlimited's success. Yet this arena is not without its share of challenges and obstacles when applied to youth.

Reaching out to the business sector is not without its difficulties for human services workers. First, we need to overcome some of our biases toward the for-profit world. Many of us have a long-standing suspicion of the corporate world, myself notwithstanding, and as a result, we need to be willing to reach out to this sector with an open mind. Our failure to seriously explore this prejudice will result in our being at a distinct disadvantage in the identification and assessment phase of the framework presented early on in this book (chapter 6). We, in addition, must acquire a new language—business talk—that is critical in helping us translate to a new arena concepts that have deep roots in the human services.

Entering the world of business presents program staff with challenges in developing evaluation mechanisms and strategies. On one level, quantifying costs and profits is relatively easy. There are established methods for doing so. Secondly, numerous places can provide advice and consultation on the best methods to cut costs and maximize profits. These places, however, rarely get the opportunity to consult with youth and to have youth carrying out established business practices. Collaboration with community is also an important aspect of programming. Bliss Unlimited, as a result, has actively sought partnerships with community-based organizations. One collaborative venture with a nonprofit community-based organization helped Bliss Unlimited obtain space in which to build gift-filled baskets for two corporate customers, as well as storage and training for youth, during a particularly stressful period in the organization's development.

The evaluation of business practices, as a result, should be a straightforward process. However, youth development requires that interventions take a two-pronged approach—the enhancement of business practice skills and the enhancement of youth in the process. The knowledge and skills learned in the process of conducting business must be placed in a youth development context. Youth must play an active and meaningful role in all aspects of a business operation. The bottom line, so to speak, is that process is as important as, if not more important than, outcome. As you might expect, this is out of the realm of usual business practice. Evaluation of youth enterprise efforts must encompass youth development.

17

Program for Female Offenders, Inc., Pittsburgh, Pennsylvania

The Program for Female Offenders was established in 1971 through the vision of Charlotte Arnold, who worked in the Pittsburgh office of the Pennsylvania Program for Women and Girl Offenders. Arnold was visiting female prisoners in state custody to talk with them individually about their needs. As women prisoners have specific needs that often go unmet in a male-run prison system, the prisoners often asked Arnold to help them meet immediate instrumental needs such as obtaining clothes for court appearances, tracking children who had been taken away from them by the state, and getting information to family members: "I smoked in those days . . . as they told me what they needed. I would write it on the cover of my matchbook" (Harris, 1997, p. 54). The women's greatest need was getting help finding employment upon release from prison. In 1974, Arnold opened a storefront office to place newly released women in paying jobs either directly or through job training programs. The original goal of the Program for Female Offenders, as a result, focused on employment. According to the organization's newsletter, *The Program News*, its mission "is to provide programs for the reintegration of female offenders into society with the goal of reducing the number of offenders returning to criminal behavior, and to promote criminal justice programs which will increase community awareness and improve the criminal justice system" (Program for Female Offenders, n.d.-b, p. 1).

Program Specifics

Over the years, as incarceration trends have changed, so too have the needs of incarcerated and newly released women. The staff of the Program for Female Offenders created new services to meet these needs as they emerged. These new needs centered on several facts: younger women were being incarcerated and lacked the daily living skills to survive on their own when they got out; more mothers were ending up in the criminal justice system; and issues such as substance abuse and a family history of involvement in the system created, and perpetuated, the cycle of involvement in the system. "The female offender typically is a teenage mother and single head of household, from a background of abuse, a substance abuser, undereducated, unskilled and poor, dependent, with a poor self image, and depressed when incarcerated and separated from her children" (Program for Female Offenders, n.d.-a). In 1979, a second office of the program was opened in Harrisburg, Pennsylvania, at the request of the state attorney general. Today, additional affiliate agencies exist in Greensburg, Allentown, Philadelphia, and Tel Aviv, Israel (Harris, 1997).

New services that were developed to meet the needs of female prisoners and ex-prisoners include a life skills training course, counseling, HIV/AIDS education, substance abuse case management, mental health services, GED and adult basic education programs, and programs that serve as alternatives to incarceration. Alternatives to incarceration include day programming, residential services, and children's programming. Each of these services was established for various reasons. Alternatives to incarceration programs were developed in an effort to alleviate prison overcrowding. Children's programming, in turn, arose out of the finding that many women prisoners needed to develop their parenting skills and that, while in prison, they had no opportunities to do so. Alternatives to incarceration provide such opportunities in a setting that preserves the family with the necessary supports. Further, both mother and child can receive education and services to help break the cycle of intergenerational incarceration: "In the past few years, the agency staff has counseled two and sometimes three generations of women in the system. In order to proactively intervene in the intergenerational nature of crime . . . programs were designed to impact children of women in jail" (Program for Female Offenders, n.d.-c, p. 2). In essence, the Program for Female Offenders believes that "the answer is creating productive, cost-effective alternatives to incarceration, breaking the cycle of crime, violence and abuse, teaching life management and job skills and preparing women for the labor market, reuniting families by instilling responsibility, values, positive parenting practices and work ethics, and stabilizing the lives of children [by] intervening before it is too late" (Program for Female Offenders, n.d.-c, p. 1).

At the heart of the Program for Female Offenders is the belief that the family is all important in development and success and an important source of strength. The program provides supportive services and a "second chance" for women and a "first chance" for their children. Prerelease services include prison activities and life skills groups. These services are provided for incarcerated women at Dauphin County and Cumberland County prisons in Pennsylvania: "These women receive individual and group counseling services and are helped to prepare themselves for release. Information is provided to assist with housing, employment, transportation, child care, relapse prevention and other problems they may face once released from prison" (Program for Female Offenders, 1998–1999, p. 2). In addition, participants are encouraged to continue seeking the program's services in the community, so that they are not without a positive support system. Life skills groups include topics such as communication, stress and anger management, problem solving, decision making, relapse prevention, and others. One hundred thirty-three different agencies employ women who complete the Program for Female Offenders, at an average wage of $6.25 per hour.

Employment and job training is provided to women who are making the transition from prison prior to community living. This is accomplished in the community upon release. Job training includes life skills, GED tutoring, typing and computer training, and job-readiness/job-search training. Some participants go on to college as well. An internship program was also developed "to promote proper professional behavior along with hands-on-training. Clients have an opportunity to learn first-hand from professionals within their chosen career" (Program for Female Offenders, 1998–1999, p. 6).

Community centers provide services such as HIV/AIDS education, which is mandatory, seed money for new graduates starting out on their own through the START Project, and program evaluation and client data. Many alternatives to incarceration exist in community-based agencies founded and run by the Program for Female Offenders. Woodside Family Center is a work-release program funded by taxpayers and by the women in residence. It serves as a court-referred alternative to incarceration. It affords the offender an opportunity to resolve those issues that resulted in her coming into conflict with the legal system (Program for Female Offenders, n.d.-c). "The Center provides work release, educational training, counseling, life skills training, involvement in community programs, visitation, recreation and a Level of Earned Privileges Program. Finally, Woodside Family Center also seeks to provide a stable foundation for the acquisition of requisite knowledge and skills for eventual return to the community. The offender has the opportunity to build her life by maintaining secure housing while finding work, building savings, and learning skills that will help her avoid conflicts with the criminal justice system."

Women who have substance abuse histories and are recently released from prison can take advantage of Promise Place, a residential community program. This program provides a safe and supportive living environment with staff and peers while the women attend programming geared at reducing recidivism. This programming includes life skills, case management, support groups, HIV/AIDS prevention and education, career coun-

seling, employment assistance, counseling, aftercare, spiritual development, community service opportunities, and vocational training and
referrals. Counselors spend much of their time locating employers willing
to hire women with criminal records. This entails visiting potential
employers making presentations and telephone calls explaining the Program for Female Offenders. Women in the surrounding community volunteer to become peer mentors and guides, and they provide a supportive
network on which the participants can rely. These volunteers work with
the staff and participate in various activities. Friendships are created and
continue beyond the doors of the program and into the community once
the participants leave. Participants are referred from prisons, probation
officers, the community, and other agencies.

Three programs are also offered for children of female offenders. These
programs seek to help children develop personal insight, knowledge, and
skills to bring about positive change in their lives. Started in 1994, the
LINK program mentors children of incarcerated mothers by providing a
community volunteer who serves as a positive role model in the life of the
child and in the parent's life. The children, through work with the mentor,
are encouraged to be creative and individualistic in after-school and summer camp activities. This program is funded through a Children's Trust
Fund grant.

A sister program to LINK, KIDS (Kids Interacting and Discovering Self)
Are the Key, was created in 1995. This ten-week after-school program
teaches children of incarcerated mothers the importance of an education.
The third program is Saturday Sessions, where mothers and children work
together to develop better study habits, gain computer experience, spend
quality educational time together, and gain exposure to community
events. Staff and community volunteers provide assistance and support.
Both parent and child develop an appreciation of a good education. Goals
include confidence building and helping mothers to see themselves as a
positive influence and as advocates for their children. Through these sessions, the Program for Female Offenders reports that many children leave
the program reading two grade levels higher than when they came in.

Capacity Enhancement Methods

This case illustrates multiple capacity enhancement principles; however,
four principles particularly stand out: (1) all people, regardless of background and circumstances, possess strengths and abilities; (2) ex-offenders
must reconnect with support systems in order to meaningfully participate
in the life of a family and community; (3) interventions must provide
participants with an opportunity to have their voices heard and to express
their hopes, fears, and concerns; and (4) interventions must address a current need or concern, while systematically preparing participants for the
future.

The Program for Female Offenders has operationalized these four capacity enhancement principles in a multitude of ways. However, it is very striking that only a community alternative to incarceration could provide the setting and conditions to allow these capacity enhancement principles to be realized. The gradual process through which participants in the program earn their privileges is instrumental in helping them discover their capacities to be mothers as well as capable adults.

The Program for Female Offenders seeks to preserve the family system by recognizing that incarcerated mothers are often the sole caregivers of their children, as data show that the fathers are often either incarcerated themselves or absent from the family. Thus, the presence of the mother is seen by the program and by its participants as an asset to be cultivated and promoted. That the agency recognizes these highly stigmatized people as mothers and not just as "felons" or "criminals" is worthy of note, as it provides a vehicle for empowerment beyond such labels. This is the driving philosophy behind the agency's mission of "offering a second chance."

The design of the services has a far more normalizing effect than prison bars, prison uniforms, and cell blocks. Women are able to live together, socialize, and share meals. With women often being the sole caregivers of their children and often entering prison pregnant, the Program for Female Offenders allows women in the residential programs to keep their children with them. In addition, the agency provides day care for working participants. Former director Charlotte Arnold reports, "If you want healthy mothers and healthy children; if you want to break the cycle of crime, you have to let mothers and their children spend time together" (Harris, 1997, p. 53). In addition, many of the agency's programs, such as the Woodside Family Center, provide opportunities for learning and achievement that are not available in a confinement environment, such as participation in the community while learning skills and developing positive relationships with peers and community residents.

Life skills are taught to the women because of their previous experience relying on men. Past reliance on men for such basic needs as shelter, money, and lifestyle choices has not prepared participants for basic job skills outside of the home. Mothers take parenting classes to learn skills and then put these skills into practice in a private day care facility, under the supervision of counselors. The skills are put into practice by the women in as real-life situations as possible. Privileges are earned, such as extended passes, for good behavior. One resident states that "I didn't have time for my kids when I was taking drugs. . . . The Program is giving me the time to be with them" (Harris, 1997, p. 57). The counselors also see the children as instrumental to the mother's recovery.

Aside from learning, the women have the opportunity to give something back to the agency and to their peers. Support groups and biweekly sharing groups are run by graduates of the program. The latter involve participants talking and supporting each other without counselors being present. Participants also give back to the Program for Female Offenders through the agency's newsletter, *The Program News*. This is also a place for creative expression and to affirm the changes one has made in one's life since coming to the program. The first issue contained a "client's corner" where consumers published their own works. Later issues, however, became more devoted to the consumers, as more articles were written by participants and these articles were placed in the front pages of the newsletter. The newsletter acknowledges on its cover that all articles are written by participants. The rest of the newsletter is devoted to program announcements. Some examples of participant writings in *The Program News* follow:

I do not want people to fear me. I do not want people to pity me. And if I don't seem to fit the description or profile of a common criminal, it's because there is none. I am a young, pretty, well-raised, intelligent, multi-racial female who made . . . a whole lot of dumb mistakes and got caught for two of them. I do not blame my environment, society, or anyone for the poor choices that I have made, because no one has made them for me. I can only learn from them and move on, hopefully a wiser person for it.

Catherine G.

Here, I feel that I can finally succeed and become the woman I know I was meant to be. Becoming a resident at the Woodside Family Center means finally getting the opportunity for my children to be proud of me. It means learning to love myself, knowing who I am, and being a responsible person. I will always remember where I came from and will strive to never go back that way again.

Anonymous

Today I am able to think clearly. Today I know that I can get help when I need it. I don't want to leave [my daughter] alone in the world, the way my mother (who was an alcoholic) left me. I love (my daughter) and I want to be a role model for her. I want to show her the right way to live instead of the way I lived for the past sixteen years. I let her know that it's okay to cry when you're sad. I was always told that only babies cry. Today I know that it takes a big person to cry and to say I'm sorry. Ultimately, I've learned that it's okay to make mistakes . . . as long as you learn from them!"

Theresa S.

The goals set out by the individual programs sponsored by the Program for Female Offenders underscore how staff work to be capacity enhancing agents in the lives of participants. Volunteers are called upon to "go with these women as they make their way back into our community to find their place, their home, their future." This statement is highly destigmatizing in comparison with the notion that offenders deserve what they get and should be punished, or that incarcerated women or drug abusers are unfit mothers. Promise Place requires that women demonstrate capacity enhancement in their own lives. It is expected that participants will within one year be able to maintain employment, secure appropriate housing, and demonstrate stability and reliability in their lives. These are qualities that, through lives of dependence on men, drugs, and criminal behavior, have grown stagnant and foreign to the women before they come to the program to redevelop them.

The goals of the Saturday Sessions program reflect the innate capacities of women to be good mothers and good role models through positive behavior and to enrich their children's lives. These goals include to bond mother and child, build confidence in mothers, teach mothers to be a positive influence and advocate for their children by daily participation with homework assignments, and teach mothers and their children to understand the importance of an education and to apply that knowledge. The mothers, who previously have had minimal time for their children in light of their maladaptive living situations, now are provided the environment to invest in their kids, guidance in learning and practicing these skills, and the chance to succeed, to feel confident and able as mothers, and to recognize their own powers for enriching the lives of others. They no longer become burdens to the criminal justice system and society but proud mothers who learn to make dramatic changes in their lives to stay clear of the criminal justice system, hopefully for good. And, judging by a recidivism rate of 13–15 percent, it works for most of them. Children, as well, learn capacity-enhancing skills and attitudes. The purpose of KIDS Are the Key is to help children embrace differences between themselves and others as a strength and to help each child to realize his or her specialness, individual assets, and ability to make positive choices. Program goals include helping children to (1) measure success, (2) increase self-esteem, (3) develop self-worth, (4) develop social skills, (5) understand the value of an education, (6) become productive individuals, and (7) develop and have a positive attitude toward life.

When children are stigmatized by having an incarcerated parent or parents, and they are being perceived by others as only eventually becoming criminals themselves, such differences from "the norm" are seen by the child and others as negative. No child in such an oppressive and stigmatizing situation can feel proud and special. And, as these children often do indeed become involved in the criminal justice system, it becomes important for them to learn to make positive choices early on in their lives. The Program for Female Offenders thus seeks to counter these early problems by fostering a positive self image, creativity, and success. Some of the most important work is in the mothers and their children learning to feel good about themselves and to believe that they can make positive changes in their lives. Their own empowerment to make these differences is capacity enhancing.

Individual Story

The story of Ms. X, a 35-year-old African American single mother of five children and long-time drug addict, does a wonderful job illustrating the challenges, processes, and rewards associated with being placed in a community alternative to incarceration. Ms. X was arrested for parole violations. She showed signs of recent heroin use and had already served a prison sentence in the Allegheny County Jail for a drug offense. In today's prison system, many drug offenders are subject to mandatory sentences or to a "three strikes and you are out" policy. However, the judge ordered her to spend her two-year sentence in the Program for Female Offenders. She was admitted to the program in 1996. "Consumed by her addiction, she had been spending so little time with her five children that signing over custody to her mother was mostly a formality. 'Using [drugs] was hurting me, and it was hurting my kids,' she says" (Harris, 1997, p. 54). Ms. X was placed in the Allegheny County Treatment Center (ACTC), a community residence for offenders with extensive histories of substance abuse.

The first step was drug rehabilitation. The ACTC utilizes a step-down approach, where residents undergo gradually decreasing intensive treatment over a six-month period. This treatment includes community meals, multiple daily group therapy sessions, one-on-one therapy with a counselor, weekly twelve-step meetings in the residence and in the community, educational sessions on addictions, and support groups run by peers and absent counselors, where the women learn to help each other. At first Ms. X resented the intensive rehabilitation: "I didn't think I had a problem at first" (Harris, 1997, p. 55). However, as she continued treatment, she developed a new attitude, stemming from her experiences in the peer support groups: "She saw her own experiences mirrored in those of the women who talked about wanting to shoot up, how hard it was to deny the urge, and how their drug use had hurt their families" (Harris, 1997, p. 56). Once Ms. X acquired the skills she desired, she was able to move on to work with counselors in planning for job placement.

Through guidance and support, Ms. X learned how to conduct a job search properly, how to prepare a résumé, ways to seek more desired training through community resources, and how to interview. In this way, she learned not only the skills she needed immediately in order to obtain a job but also how to work on her own to find a different or better job in the future, if she so desired. Ms. X found her first job through a temporary agency packing boxes of literature for a printing company, earning $5.50 an hour one day per week. She was informed that the job could become full time. The money she made was divided by the Program for Female Offenders as follows: 20 percent to the agency to help pay room and board expenses; 20 percent to a mandatory savings account for use upon discharge from the program; 10 percent to court-ordered restitution payments for merchandise she had stolen; and the remaining 50 percent to a personal account that Ms. X could use on occasion (Harris, 1997).

Ms. X was given much greater freedom in her daily routine compared with someone who is imprisoned and under constant supervision. She had to meet the expectations associated with community alternatives to incarceration—meaning she signed out and in and was subject to drug search and screening. Ms. X met these requirements and as a result earned privileges. The privileges entailed weekend passes allowing her to spend time at home with her children (Harris and Clines, 1997).

Ms. X spent time with her children both in program activities and outside in the community. These activities included parenting classes, arts and crafts, outdoor play equipment, and trips to museums. As Ms. X noted: "We look forward to seeing each other and being together. The hardest thing I have to do every week is seeing my kids on a 24 hour pass and then having to leave them" (Harris, 1997, p. 57). At that point, Ms. X had spent the majority of her six-month minimum sentence at the Program for Female Offenders, and the agency was preparing to submit papers to the judge recommending her release back into the community. The agency staff saw the key to her success as maintaining her support network, which she had developed over the past few months, and avoiding old friends in the community who use drugs.

Did Ms. X put into practice the things she learned at Program for Female Offenders after she was released? She certainly did. She has moved back with her mother, takes her children on outings, helps them with their homework, and continues her work at the printing plant. She is still not working full time, so she is also looking on her own for a job with more permanence. She continues to attend substance abuse recovery meetings in the community, just as she did at the program. While tempted sometimes, she avoids her old friends and works on developing the growing and deepening relationship with her children. She continues to remain off drugs. These aspects of a "normal" and legal life simply did not exist for her before coming to the Program for Female Offenders, but now they are internalized. Is she a convict? Or is she a hardworking and capable mother doing typical things and actively seeking to better her life through full-time employment, self-care, and community involvement? Ms. X, by drawing on her inherent capacities, has been able to turn her life around and has made significant strides in recovery through her commitment to her children and family.

Lessons for Social Work

Many significant lessons for social work practice with the correctionally supervised can be drawn from the success of community alternatives to prisons. Identifying the capacities of women offenders who are also mothers is very often a slow and tedious process. Opportunities need to be provided with the necessary structure and support for ex-offenders to be able to realize their inherent capacities in the community. The process through which they learn about their capacities may slowly evolve through closely monitored opportunities where privileges are earned and lost, depending upon their actions.

The range of methods the Program for Female Offenders uses to enhance the capacities of program participants may not be possible for other community alternative programs to incarceration. Nevertheless, the multiple services provided by the program illustrate the power of capacity enhancement interventions and the flexibility that is available to other agencies to carry out such initiatives. Successful rehabilitation depends on a comprehensive set of services that systematically address key issues and take into consideration the unique needs of women ex-offenders who are mothers and who wish to assume a parental role. Not every woman ex-offender who is a mother may wish to reestablish her parental role. Recovery, after all, can be both helped and hindered by assuming a parental role. Social workers are in unique positions to provide comprehensive services through case management roles as well as directly in counseling situations. Our knowledge of community resources and possession of advocacy skills combine to make our contribution to the correctionally supervised that much more effective. An embrace of empowerment principles, in turn, allows us to be directive and supportive in helping ex-offenders, in this case women, enhance their capacities.

18

Reflections on the Case Studies

The programs highlighted through the case studies illustrate a wide range of types, settings, missions, and goals. However, they all seek to use capacity enhancement principles and strategies to achieve their mission. Each program brings an innovative and highly relevant service to the field of correctional supervision, yet they all highlight the importance of identifying and tapping some aspect of capacity enhancement in the structure and delivery of services. Some of these programs do their work within prison walls, probably the most challenging setting in which to undertake capacity enhancement practice; others take place in various community-based settings and involve both youth and adults, men as well as women. Regardless of setting, these programs illustrate for the practitioner the potential of believing in the abilities of offenders, their families, and communities.

The individual stories reported as part of each case study bring a needed dimension to the study—namely, the importance of individuals in bringing the concept of capacity enhancement to life. The individual stories also highlight the ripple effect of capacity enhancement interventions—significant others, families, and communities all benefit by unleashing the potential of ex-offenders. The case studies also serve the important function of grounding this book in the operative reality of day-to-day practice. The cases, as a result, effectively serve to prevent this book from being "too" theoretical in orientation and losing sight of what capacity enhancement means in practice.

Garr (1995) argues that the nation must look at poor people from a strengths perspective rather than assume that their "weaknesses" will prevail. The efforts outlined in the previous chapters demonstrate that private groups can make a difference. However, they do not replace the role of government and often do better when they enter into equal partnerships with government. Government, at both the federal and state levels, created the prisons, communities did not. Consequently, it is the responsibility of government to ensure the safety of society, but to do so in a manner that is respective of the rights of the victims as well as those of the perpetrator. The ability to tax citizens is a very powerful mechanism and can be mobilized to the betterment of all communities, and not just those that are wealthy and powerful.

As evidenced by the case studies, important work is being undertaken in the field based on principles that are empowering and capacity enhancing in nature. The principles that undergird capacity enhancement can be operationalized in a variety of settings and with various population groups. However, it seems programs such as these, with some exceptions, have not enjoyed the publicity they deserve: "A quiet revolution is going on, all right, so quietly that hardly anybody outside the grassroots organizations themselves knows it is happening—and they aren't talking much about it. The media, the government, even most funding organizations don't get it at all. This is a shame, because some of this stuff is working, and way too many of the traditional welfare programs aren't. Are there lessons here? The more I traveled and the more I saw, the more I thought so" (Garr, 1995, pp. 8–9). There are many lessons to be learned from the cases presented in Section 3. Chapters 19, "Lessons for Social Work Practice," and 20, "Lessons for Social Work Education," present but a few related to practice and education.

I have reported on only a handful of case examples where significant work was being undertaken at the national, state, and local levels in the lives of the correctionally supervised using various principles of capacity enhancement. An entire casebook specifically devoted to capacity enhancement practice and the correctionally supervised could have easily been written highlighting case studies. For example, I included only one study that focused on a program operating from the perspective of prevention and youth development—i.e., Bliss Unlimited—yet countless other examples of programs taking a prevention orientation were available. The reader, too, may be familiar with programs in his or her own neighborhood where capacity enhancement is being practiced.

However, as argued by Garr (1995), the word on these grassroots efforts is not being heard in the public and professional arenas across the nation. Thus, we must make every effort to give voice to these efforts in the circles in which we travel. In providing a voice for these efforts, we also open up more possibilities for social workers to actively get involved in this field. Some of us may have no difficulty working in total institutions. For others of us who cannot practice in such a setting, community alternatives are more viable. An ability or willingness to work in one and not the other does not make one "better" or worse than his or her counterparts. We, however, need social workers who are willing to embrace capacity enhancement principles in all settings that address the correctionally supervised.

4

Lessons, Recommendations, and Reflections

The two chapters in this section focus specifically on translating the material covered in the previous two sections into social work practice. Many changes are required in both social work practice and social work education in order to bring the potential of capacity enhancement to bear on the field of correctional supervision. Chapter 19, "Lessons for Social Work Practice," draws implications for practice with the correctionally supervised and identifies a series of challenges we must surmount to be successful in the correctional field. Chapter 20, "Implications for Social Work Education," in turn, addresses similar issues with regard to social work education.

19

Lessons for Social Work Practice

Social work practice has a rich history of incorporating new changes resulting from new knowledge and research. Practice, regardless of the population group or modality, seeks to bring about change in behavior and social circumstances. I believe that the profession, when addressing undervalued groups, does not have the luxury of focusing on narrow clinical issues and needs to the exclusion of efforts to bring about social and economic justice. This dual focus, I believe, separates social work from other counseling-related professions. Consequently, my recommendations for clinical, or micro-focused, practice are biased in favor of this duality of focus. Any chapter that specifically prescribes changes in practice will not be without its share of critics and controversy; it seems as if changes and criticism go hand in hand in any profession, and that is to be expected.

Capacity enhancement practice with the correctionally supervised requires that social workers be prepared to modify existing forms of intervention and create new ways of serving groups and communities; thus it requires new types of competencies. These new competencies necessitate the acquisition of new knowledge content in the classroom and the creation of field placements to facilitate translation of theory into practice. Social work practice settings will require social workers to use a wide variety of methods and approaches to reaching consumers. Knowledge of the community and community resources will play an important role in helping social workers to carry out their functions. It should not be unusual, for example, for social workers to visit homes and reach out in houses of worship and other community-based settings. Outreach, a lost skill, will takes on added importance when seeking to engage youth in malls, nightclubs, or arcades, for example.

This chapter provides the reader with a set of competencies that he or she will need to achieve the goals of intervention in work with the correctionally supervised. The principles associated with capacity enhancement covered in chapter 5 lend themselves to be operationalized into practice competencies. Further, they are flexible enough to take into account capacities of practitioners and local circumstances.

What Are Competencies?

There are a variety of ways of addressing practice-related changes, one of which is to focus on a set of competencies that facilitate the translation of theory into everyday forms of practice. These competencies, if you wish, serve to highlight what are the essential tasks that must be performed in order to achieve intervention goals. The term *competency* has entered the everyday vocabulary of human services practitioners and educators alike. Although the term is being used more and more, it can mean different things depending upon the person using it and the context in which it is used.

However, simply stated, competence is the ability to perform work activities to the expected standard (Vass, 1996b). Vass defines competence within a criminal justice context as "the ability to perform in diverse contexts and with offenders from diverse backgrounds, sentences, dispositions and needs. It is the ability to understand, assess, and make choices (hence reach decisions) by utilizing and combining knowledge, values, skills and experiences" (1996a, pp. 133–34). In essence, competencies are minimum levels of abilities needed to bring about desired outcomes. These levels of abilities, in turn, require acquisition of knowledge and adherence to a set of values and attitudes.

An emphasis on competence serves to focus attention on the knowledge and skills that are necessary to accomplish a job and that thus lend themselves to measurement. I am very fond of telling students that one way of looking at competencies is to view them "as the bare essentials needed to accomplishment a goal." Thus, in respect to working with the correctionally supervised who are of color from a capacity enhancement perspective, competencies cover all the stages of the framework presented in chapter 6. To achieve the "bare essential tasks," practitioners must be prepared to bring a multicultural context into assessment, planning, intervention, and evaluation. If practice is influenced by context, and context is influenced by culture, then cultural competence is required. Such competence is premised on taking into account the unique characteristics and circumstances of the people being targeted for interventions of various types.

Supervision is greatly facilitated when competencies are clearly delineated and lend themselves to performance evaluation. Few workers in the field would argue that supervision is nothing but a drain on their energies—it becomes a drain when it is irrelevant to the situation being addressed. When supervision is relevant, it becomes a source of strength and support for a worker in the field. Supervisors, as a result, can identify practitioner strengths and areas for improvement. This is important information in helping organizations better serve consumers. Organizations, as a result, are in a better position to establish workshops or obtain consultation in a more deliberate and systematic fashion.

The process of arriving at the requisite competencies to achieve the stated goals of an intervention is not easy, and very often it is labor intensive, requiring practitioners to seek and take into consideration various perspectives and competencies. These competencies, as to be expected, are not just skill oriented. To achieve a level of skill one needs also to possess a basic level of knowledge and to have the right attitude, as well. Competencies, as a result, rest upon "proper" knowledge and attitudes.

I take the stance that job-related competencies in the field of correctional supervision can be achieved only if they take into account cultural factors. The large number of people of color in the prison system, for example, bring to the experience their cultural heritage and background. Any effort to rehabilitate them, in turn, must be made within the cultural context of the prisoner. The prisoner, after all, does not leave her or his culture at the door of a prison, just as we do not leave ours at the door of the school we attend or the agency in which we practice.

The field of multicultural practice has been quick to embrace the concept of competency, as evidenced by the number of books addressing the subject. Service delivery competency can best be defined as possession of the skills necessary to carry out the functions associated with a job description. Cultural competence, in turn, refers to possession of the skills necessary to bring about positive change, and the ability to do so by incorporating, and taking into account, the cultural values and beliefs of the individuals and communities being addressed.

The issue of the practitioner's need to be "comfortable" while working with the correctionally supervised must be raised and addressed. Not everyone is at ease working with this population group. In fact, I am suspicious of any social worker who says he or she is comfortable working with any and all population groups. The label *correctionally supervised* covers a wide range of offenses. Some of us may have no difficulty working with someone with a record of assaults, but we will find it difficult to work with someone convicted of a sexual crime. Others, in turn, may prefer to work with people of a particular gender, ethnicity, and age. This is not unusual. However, these sentiments necessitate that we have a keen understanding of ourselves and of why we wish to do this type of work, including our concerns and fears.

Work with the correctionally supervised will place workers in the position of being "tested" regarding their commitment to this field. As a practitioner this always proved to be my greatest challenge. Although I very often represented institutions that were not held in high esteem in the community, and very often rightly so, my primary task was not to report infractions but to help. Further, my clients were very often Puerto Rican—similar to my background. Yet testing was almost always part of the relationship-building process.

Competencies related to establishing and maintaining collaborative partnerships can be considered both micropractice and macropractice skills, with the focus varying according to the method of practice used. Collaborative competencies, however, must be developed with a specific focus on nontraditional settings such as houses of worship and other settings that the correctionally supervised patronize. As I've noted elsewhere (Delgado, 1999), collaboration with these types of settings is both rewarding and challenging. Such settings exist in the community, but they may not appear on the surface to be addressing the needs of the correctionally supervised and their families. Thus, staff must visit the community in order to assess the availability of this resource.

Collaborative relationships, or partnerships, with nontraditional settings take more than the usual amount of time to establish and maintain. It is important to remember, too, that these are not your conventional agencies with conventional operating procedures and professionally trained social workers on staff. Process—which in this instance refers to establishing a dialogue, common goals, and procedures—may often require numerous meetings over an extended period of time. Formalization of partnerships, in turn, may involve a letter of understanding versus a detailed contract outlining terms of engagement and termination. Thus, flexibility will be an important attribute for staff involved in these forms of partnerships.

As one of the goals of an intervention, practitioners should seek to establish collaborative partnerships in which ex-offenders are equal members of a team. An intervention should take advantage of opportunities to enhance the knowledge and skills of the individual who has intimate knowledge of prisons and other forms of correctional supervision. This can only enhance the capacity of that individual and of the community in the long run. In essence, it represents an important investment.

To effectively change U.S. policies toward increased incarceration, social workers need to develop advocacy skills. Advocacy-related competencies are almost as old as the profession of social work itself. The ability to advocate on behalf of a client or community is often part of one's job description, although how and how often this transpires very much depends upon the practitioner and his or her setting. Advocacy skills are not specific to macro- or micropractice, and depending on the method of practice, they will take on different forms. What is meant by advocacy? Simply stated, advocacy refers to an intervention that systematically seeks to ensure that a consumer's rights are not violated by an organization or community. The criminal justice system is one of the primary targets of this form of intervention.

Skills related to effectively working with correctional personnel form a category of their own. In working with prison guards, police officers, and other law enforcement and correctional personnel, I often had to exercise a tremendous amount of patience, and I had to develop a thick skin regarding offensive comments that somehow seemed to work themselves into conversations and meetings. I had to decide which comments I would simply ignore and which ones I needed to address. Addressing these comments very often required careful selection of words, intonation, and so on. In essence, there were instances where I had the patience to work with certain staff, and there were also times when I did not, and those required a considerable amount of what I called "psychic energy."

Finally, competencies related to substance abuse are essential, particularly since drug-related offenses are the primary reason for offenders' court involvement. To practice effectively in the field, it is not enough to simply be aware of the particular issues confronting the correctionally supervised with substance abuse backgrounds. A knowledge of existing resources to help in this area is needed if the practitioner is going to marshal the requisite resources to provide comprehensive services to this population. Knowledge of resources that are culturally competent takes on added value and significance.

Micropractice Competencies

Micropractice-focused competencies must not only address a wide range of modalities such as individual, couples, families, and groups. Competencies related to age, such as work with the children of those who are incarcerated, add another dimension to practice. Settings, too, must be taken into consideration. Office-based practice is not possible in this form of work. Capacity enhancement practice requires social workers to be able to deliver services in a variety of settings, the least of which may be their offices. Consequently, social workers must welcome the challenge of providing services in people's homes and in their communities. Practitioners may spend considerable time traveling through the city or neighborhood in an effort to facilitate geographical access for consumers. Accessibility, as I have already mentioned but which bears repeating, is multidimensional—geographical, cultural, psychological (trust), and operational. Being able to venture into the "real world" of the correctionally supervised is not without its challenges, but it is unavoidable if we are to make the impact we are quite capable of making.

Assessment of capacities will form the cornerstone of any microintervention strategy. This approach will prove particularly challenging for practitioners accustomed to, and trained in, eliciting information on deficits. That is not to say that practitioners cannot ask questions pertaining to needs and difficulties that a client or community may be experiencing.

However, the focus of an interview must never lose sight of capacities. This takes on added importance in an assessment because most clients or communities are very used to talking about needs, problems, and so on, and they may feel much more comfortable being engaged in this line of questioning. Of course, there may be some problems or needs; however, the assessment process must also seek to identify capacities. Interviews, as a result, will require not only additional time to complete but also a skilled practitioner who is able to mix in different types of questions. Intake forms and related data-gathering instruments must be developed to facilitate this process for both the worker and consumer of services.

Community Practice (Macropractice) Competencies

Competencies related to community practice (macropractice) must be sufficiently flexible to take into account the goals of the organization employing the practitioner, the nature of the setting being targeted (prison or community alternative), the characteristics of the population group (gender, age, ethnicity/race, etc.), community, and last but not least, funding source requirements. I am not saying that community social work practice is more complex or challenging than clinical practice. However, there are many more options involved in macropractice.

My experience doing intakes in a clinical setting provided me with an opportunity to recommend certain types of interventions. However, I also had an intake form that dictated the nature of the questions that needed to be asked and intake procedures specifying time and process considerations. In macropractice I would be given an assignment and very little guidance, or supervision for that matter—unlike my experience as a clinician. The ambiguity associated with macropractice lent itself to my being creative and taking chances—much more so than as a clinician. This arena of practice offers practitioners much flexibility in conceptualizing interventions. This can be exciting and overwhelming at the same time.

Reeser (1996) has noted the importance of future social work practitioners possessing both micropractice and macropractice skills in order to effectively and holistically address the needs of their constituencies. Social work practice with the correctionally supervised will no doubt have similarities to and differences from practice in more conventional settings. Management of social work units, for example, will no doubt test a social work manager's creativity, flexibility, and ability to apply social work knowledge and values to new circumstances. Clinically trained social workers, in turn, will need to expand the nature of practice to take into account new considerations of "goals" for clinical intervention. Clinicians must be prepared to actively engage in advocacy efforts and participate in coalitions to bring about requisite changes in funding and programming. These skills are not restricted to macropractitioners. Consequently, although this section specifically focuses on macropractice competencies, it should also have relevance for clinicians. Community practice, a more focused form of macropractice, can be defined as "the application of practice skills to alter behavioral patterns of community groups, organizations, and institutions or people's relationships and interactions with these entities" (Hardcastle, Wenocur, and Powers, 1998, p. 1). Community practice requires the development of skills that are typically associated with community organization, community and program development, social planning, management, and social action (Hardcastle, Wenocur, and Powers, 1998).

I believe that to be an effective community practitioner, one must have solid interpersonal and clinical skills such as those associated with interviewing or meeting with various types of groups. Conversely, an effective micropractitioner must also have solid macro-related skills, such as those associated with designing and conducting key informant interviews. My educational and experiential background as both a micropractitioner (M.S.W. in clinical) and a macropractitioner (Ph.D. in social welfare) has reinforced the importance of having some degree of competence in both methods. Obviously, one's primary method is the strongest; however, having a secondary method is not only attractive but essential in the field. The broadening of one's competencies in what is often regarded as two distinct worlds is essential for practice in the twenty-first century.

A provider who is flexible enough in his or her approach to work with the correctionally supervised will prove invaluable to his or her employer and a valuable asset to a community. The situation, as a result, dictates the best approach rather than be limited to what the practitioner is "good at." Consequently, organizations that wish to reach out to the correctionally supervised must not only hire social workers who are flexible in their approach but also emphasize the provision of training, consultation, and supervision in order for staff members to be able to fully carry out their responsibilities.

In situations where an organization has no history of working with the correctionally supervised but has decided to do so, the organization will undoubtedly face a host of challenges internally and externally because of the stigma associated with this population group. Mind you, this is not to say such an initiative should not be attempted, because that is after all the central purpose of this book. However, it should be undertaken with deliberate speed and careful attention to potential barriers and roadblocks.

The continued number of women entering the criminal justice system will necessitate the development of services that are either gender specific or highly sensitive to gender issues. Historically, correctional supervision has been associated with men. However, some issues are unique to women, or more highly related to women, and this requires that the characteristics of women and the unique barriers they face be taken into account in programming and delivery of services. Although the need for gender-specific programming is self-evident, there is also a great need for development of transitional housing that allows mothers to be reunited with their children, for example. The involvement of children in the recovery of women offenders presents macropractitioners with a set of challenges that are not normally associated with male offenders. When women offenders who are also mothers and are HIV-positive or have AIDS are released from prison, it adds another dimension to programming. Macropractitioners must possess competencies in programming and obtaining funding, and they must have an increasingly specific target group in mind.

Conclusion

Social work practice in the criminal justice arena is an excellent opportunity to reconnect with a sector of society that very few helping professions wish to be associated with. The needs and challenges associated with the correctionally supervised provide a wide range of possibilities for interventions—from individual to community capacity enhancement. The practical implications of adopting a capacity enhancement paradigm toward the correctionally supervised are profound for the social work profession in the twenty-first century. Policy debates at the local and national level will undoubtedly occur more often when the astronomical costs associated with correctional supervision, particularly imprisonment, require government to make hard choices in what gets funded.

Capacity enhancement, as already noted on numerous occasions, lends itself to work with undervalued groups, particularly those with multiple jeopardies, such as ex-offenders. Some of the changes required in implementing a capacity enhancement perspective are quite dramatic— others less so. Being a realist, I know that capacity enhancement work with the correctionally supervised faces an uphill battle for "air time" in the national forum. Nevertheless, even the longest journey starts with the first step.

Ideally, I would like to see all the practice implications addressed in this chapter implemented. But the operative reality pertaining to changes in the field of practice is that this will probably not happen in my lifetime. Some of the recommendations require considerable changes in ways of thinking and conceptualizing service provision; yet others do not require such drastic rethinking. As the concept of capacity enhancement gains greater and greater currency in the field of human services, the recommendations put forth in this chapter will seem less and less radical. The contextualization of capacity enhancement, as a result, will serve to reinforce the viability of this approach to working with the undervalued in our society. Nevertheless, such a shift will require a concerted effort on the part of the profession and other professions, not to mention communities.

The reader must realize that the review of competencies in this chapter is not exhaustive. However, it does capture the core elements of capacity enhancement practice with the correctionally supervised in urban areas of the country. As will be noted in the next chapter, social work education must play a pivotal role in leading and guiding the profession in the acquisition of these skills. In order for social work education to achieve this lofty goal, it must enter into partnerships with communities and practitioners. This relationship is crucial for all parties to be able to function to their maximum capacities.

The importance of having competencies that transcend the usual macro- and micropractice methods should not be lost on the reader. It seems that, more and more, practice is becoming highly specialized and more focused as a result. Practice with the correctionally supervised, however, necessitates that social workers be flexible in their approaches to interventions. This necessitates knowledge of and competence in carrying out multiple roles—roles that historically have been relegated to either macro- or micropractice.

20

Implications for Social Work Education

A book of this type must ultimately provide the field with implications for social work education. Practice with the urban-based correctionally supervised will necessitate that social work education be responsive to the needs of future social workers working in such a setting. Frankly, it would be irresponsible to place the entire challenge of addressing the correctionally supervised from a capacity enhancement perspective, or for that matter a deficit perspective, on practitioners without social work education's playing a critical role in helping the profession to shift toward this field of practice. The success of any new form of human services practice rests on a collaborative effort between providers, consumers, and academics.

This chapter, as a result, provides a series of recommendations that systematically address the need for social work instruction in the classroom and in the field. These recommendations, however, are probably not going to be fully accepted without considerable debate, and in some cases, active resistance.

Social Work Education

I am well aware that very few schools of social work have courses, or for that matter modules, specifically focused on correctionally supervised juveniles or adults. If the subject is addressed, it most likely will be in passing or as part of some discussion, without the requisite reading assignments. Although field placements may address the needs of this population group, in all likelihood, they are few in number. Correctional settings can be found in virtually every U.S. community. However, how many actually have students placed there is a different question. This is probably the result of policies related to placing students in settings where they can obtain M.S.W. supervision or of an unwillingness to expose students to this population group because of the challenges it presents in practice. Further, relatively few students may be interested in pursuing a career in the corrections field, limiting the attractiveness of these settings for field placements.

Schools of social work, nevertheless, are in excellent positions to provide leadership in establishing programs of study on criminal justice needs and issues and to "legitimize" this form of practice by offering courses, using readings, providing field placements, holding conferences, and conducting workshops on the topic (Wormer and Roberts, 1999). Further, taking a capacity enhancement perspective toward the correctionally supervised fits well within the mission of most social work programs. Nevertheless, the challenge for the profession is far greater than one might imagine, even though the benefits may far outweigh the costs. Much groundwork must be done before a social work program can provide a coherent and comprehensive educational program involving practice with this population, and before it can support social work practitioners in the field. Thus, all facets of the profession must engage in a noble and sustainable effort at producing social workers with the necessary skills to practice in this arena. If the social work profession is to wield the influence it is capable of, it must actively seek out settings that can accommodate social work interns and can employ social workers, particularly those with interests in working with undervalued groups. Such settings can open important doors to practitioners working in organizations that have historically not employed social workers. Further, settings involved in working with the correctionally supervised offer much potential for social work scholars and researchers interested in expanding the nature of practice. There is, after all, a tremendous amount of research that is awaiting to be undertaken in this arena.

Ideally, I would recommend that at least one required course on the correctionally supervised be offered in every social work program; however, this is certainly not feasible. Consequently, there may be creative ways of introducing content on the subject into a curriculum. Content may be integrated into class sessions through lectures, exercises, and assigned readings whenever advisable. For example, a course on child welfare policy or practice can easily lend itself to integration of content on various needs and issues associated with incarcerated parents. Course assignments, too, can be modified to integrate some aspect of criminal justice. Lastly, students wishing to pursue topics involving the correctionally supervised can undertake independent studies in this field. In essence, there are countless ways that course instruction and assignments can be changed to examine some facet of the subject without completely changing content or assignments in the process.

Special lectures and workshops can be offered throughout the academic year or through continuing education courses. Lecture series lend themselves very well to most social work programs because of their flexibility in scheduling and not being tied to administrative requirements often inherent in courses taken for credit. Field placements in correctional settings can be supplemented through field-based seminars and workshops that bring together students and field instructors in various settings to discuss subjects of mutual interest.

Hiring faculty with interests in the correctional field can no doubt play an important role in galvanizing a social work program's efforts in this field. However, programs may already have faculty with some form of interest in working with this population group, and those interests can be fostered through faculty development workshops at annual social work conferences. In essence, the intent of this recommendation is not to "divert" faculty from interests in other fields to interests in the correctional field. Instead, the goal is to expand current interests to include the correctionally supervised.

There is little question that the group of social work scholars currently writing on the correctionally supervised needs to be expanded. These individuals do very important work; however, a critical mass of social work scholars is needed to enhance this form of practice in the profession. My "formal" interest in work with the correctionally supervised started during a second-year field placement in Manhattan's Family Court more than twenty-five years ago. The subject of the correctionally supervised has consistently emerged in my work with substance abusers, families, and communities. The focus of my work on this subject, however, did not clearly emerge until my work on youth of color (Delgado, 2000b) and the challenges they face in either staying alive or avoiding prison. In essence, it is difficult enough making it through adolescence without also worrying about dying or imprisonment!

The creation of field placements in a variety of correctional settings can play an influential role in changing both these institutions and schools of social work in the process. Such field placements will not be easy to create when these correctional settings do not employ social workers to provide needed supervision. New models can be created whereby social work supervision can be provided back at the school.

Finally, I am a firm believer in social work students receiving some form of financial incentive to get them to seriously consider a career in working with the correctionally supervised. As a matter of fact, that was how I initially got interested in the field. I was very fortunate in receiving a federal grant specifically targeted to get social work graduate students interested in the juvenile justice field. Some form of financial assistance with tuition or in the form of a stipend may be a great recruitment mechanism for the field of social work. Field-related stipends can go a long way toward opening doors for interns. These interns, then, would be in excellent positions to be employed upon completing their education.

Conclusion

Practice with the correctionally supervised and the communities in which they live cannot possibly succeed without the active cooperation and encouragement of the major professional social work organizations. The magnitude of the task will require considerable marshaling of resources to bring it to the attention of, and maintain pressure on, elected officials. The criminal justice system has been rightly referred to as the "prison-industrial complex" as a means of highlighting the formidable force behind this system. Thus, practice with the correctionally supervised will require that social work education, for example, respond positively to the needs of social workers in these new service delivery systems. Competencies are built through acquisition of knowledge and adoption of necessary values and beliefs. The competencies addressed in the preceding chapter speak for themselves. Social work education must, in turn, play an influential role in providing the basic skills necessary to succeed in practice and undertaking the requisite research to ensure that the best practices are shared in the classroom and discussed in the scholarly literature. Field support, in turn, is also necessary if practitioners are to fine-tune these skills in order to carry out their functions within an organization and a community-specific context.

The process of providing supervision, for example, will require that supervisors are able to venture into the field to meet with their supervisees and are actively involved in problem solving whenever it is advisable. Technology will help facilitate communication in the field—nevertheless, there is no substitute for in-person contact. This venturing out not only helps the student in the field but also sends a message to field instructors and organizations that issues related to correctional supervision are very important to the social work school or program. Further, an added benefit falls to the faculty adviser, particularly when he or she is also a full-time instructor: valuable experience and information that can be integrated into classroom teaching.

Increased field contact will also help faculty in undertaking scholarly endeavors related to the correctionally supervised by providing them with access to staff and organizations undertaking this form of work. Access, after all, is critical in the undertaking of any field-based research and scholarly writing. Field placements in correctional supervision settings will also provide these settings with access to university-based resources. Such resources can take a variety of forms such as access to consultation, workshops, grant activity, courses for supervisors, and so on. Consequently, field placements offer tremendous benefits to all parties.

Learning can take place in a variety of settings and through the use of a wide range of methods. Content related to correctional supervision from a capacity enhancement perspective can be delivered formally, such as through an academic course specifically on the subject, through the invitation of outside speakers, through participation in field-based conferences, or via assignments, in-class exercises, field placements, and so on. Learning can also take place through volunteer opportunities in local agencies and community-based settings and through the provision of videotapes and materials to interested students, without any formal assignment attached to these materials. This flexibility is wonderful and gives schools of social work the opportunity to modify learning goals based on local circumstances. Some schools, for example, have correctional supervision as a focus—all too few, unfortunately. Yet others may have concentrations, elective courses, and field placements, to note but a few of the approaches.

On the surface the recommendations made in this chapter do not appear radical. However, upon closer examination, they strike at the heart of a set of values concerning how the nation in general and many helping professions view the correctionally supervised. When this population also happens to be a group of color, such views are compounded by racism. Social work, through its educational component, can play a proactive and influential role in getting the correctionally supervised on the "agenda" of human services. However, it will not suffice to get them on the agenda if we are to take a business-as-usual approach—namely, further stigmatizing and maginalizing them by focusing on their deficits. A capacity enhancement perspective radically changes how we as social workers, and as other helping professionals, view our role in this field. This perspective requires that we join in partnership with those who have been through the U.S. correctional system. Anything less than an equal partnership will subvert the fundamental thrust of capacity enhancement initiatives.

Appendix

The case studies in chapters 8 through 17 did not include rationales for why they were selected for this book. Nor did they contain literature review sections that would serve to ground the respective organization and service in the key issues in the field of correctional supervision. The reader was spared this content to maximize the readability of the studies. However, some readers would like more thorough grounding in the context of the cases. Thus, this appendix is intended to address the needs of readers who want, or need, as the situation may be, more details and context. The organization of the following material is rather simple—for each case study there is (1) the rationale for its selection and (2) an overview of relevant literature.

AIDS Counseling Education, Bedford Hills Correctional Facility, New York

Rationale for Selection

Prisons have historically been associated with men, although women prisoners have been present in this country dating back to the colonial times. Still, the association between prisons and men is quite strong. However, over the past two decades women, as a group, represent the greatest growing sector in state and federal prisons. More specifically, women of color (African Americans and Latinas) make up the most significant portions of this increase, as noted in chapter 2. The trend of women's rapidly increasing numbers in prisons is projected to continue well into the twenty-first century.

The needs and issues confronting women in maximum security prisons rarely receive the attention and resources they warrant. The public probably doesn't even realize that in the United States there are approximately thirty maximum security prisons specifically targeting women. Thus, women inmates in maximum security prisons experience the trauma and issues associated with extreme isolation from family and friends and they face the challenges of successfully reentering their community. Successfully returning to the community is further complicated if the woman offender is HIV-positive or has AIDS.

This case example, as a result, focuses on the isolation, stigma, and challenges associated with inmates who are HIV-positive or have AIDS in a system that marginalizes those with this disease. Innovative efforts at reaching such women bring an added aspect to capacity enhancement practice with the correctionally supervised and are therefore worthy of a case study. Lastly, a case study involving the state of New York was in order because of the high number of inmates currently in that state's prison system, the high percentage of inmates of color, and the importance of examining a case involving a maximum security prison.

This case study, as a result, highlights the importance of giving female prisoners a voice within the system—a voice that allows them to express themselves as well as gives them an opportunity to listen to each other. Such opportunities can be very powerful in helping to transform lives both within and outside prison. Zaitzow (1999) summed up the current trends and why HIV/AIDS education and treatment should play a greater role in prisons in the twenty-first century:

> As the population ages, and as determinate sentencing and strict sentencing guidelines continue, inmates—women, in particular—will age within our facilities. We will see more women of childbearing age who are infected. The historic differences between the federal offender versus offenders within state, city, or county systems have become blurred by the issue of drug trafficking. These offenders tend to be less educated and from predominantly urban and depressed socioeconomic backgrounds. The frequent victimization of these female offenders also increases the risk for heterosexual disease transmission. HIV infection and resulting AIDS cases pose particular problems for corrections in terms of staff and inmates. (p. 90)

Overview of Literature

As noted in chapters 2 and 3, women have experienced imprisonment at an accelerated pace, particularly for nonviolent or drug-related offenses.

Prisons, as a result, that have historically been constructed to serve male inmates, create tensions and challenges to better serve the needs of this group. Prisons, particularly those classified as maximum security (which are intended for the more serious offender), seem to have increased in popularity in the past ten years and may well continue to increase numerically well into the twenty-first century. The increased number of women entering prisons with histories of substance abuse also increases the likelihood of women who are at risk for HIV entering these penal institutions.

The subject of AIDS is not foreign to most low-income families of color (Kaplan, 1998; Levy, 1997; Maldonado, 1999; MacDougall, 1998; Zaitzow, 1999). Few urban-based families residing in low-income neighborhoods have escaped the consequences of this disease. The disease, however, is not confined to the outside world and can be found inside prisons housing both males and females. In 1997 an estimated 8,900 inmates had AIDS and 35,000 to 47,000 were HIV-positive (Altman, 1999). Those released from jails and prisons accounted for 17 percent of the total number of Americans with AIDS (Altman, 1999). That same year saw 907 inmates in state prisons die from AIDS, or 29 percent of all deaths in state prisons (Altman, 1999). However, when present in the female inmate population, the disease takes on added significance because it often involves a woman who is a mother. Estimates of HIV prevalence among prisoners note that inmates have a rate of infection that is almost thirteen times that of the nonprison population (Mauer, 1999).

Drug-related activities among those who are incarcerated are widely considered to be the primary causal factor—sharing needles, intravenous drug use, prostitution. AIDS has had a particularly devastating impact on women of color, particularly African American and Latina women, youth as well as adults (Bok and Morales, 1997; Carbone, 1996; Maldonado, 1999). The National Institute on Drug Abuse estimates that there are one and a half million injecting drug users in the United States, with almost 50 percent of all new HIV infections occurring among injecting drug users (Maldonado, 1999). African Americans, in turn, accounted for 58 percent of the total adolescent/adult AIDS cases attributed to injection drug use, with African American women being responsible for 60 percent of the new female AIDS cases among injecting drug users in 1997 (Maldonado, 1999).

Youth who are HIV-infected do not represent a significant problem from a statistical point of view; however, this will change dramatically in the coming years:

> The problem is disguised by a statistical artifact: compared with other age groups, the number of adolescents reported with AIDS is relatively small (2,028 cases by the end of 1995). Because it often takes a number of years after infection before a person develops AIDS-defining symptoms, these figures underestimate the severity of the problem of HIV disease among adolescents. Since approximately one-fifth of all cases of AIDS are diagnosed in individuals aged between 20 and 29 years, we can conclude

that the time of these infections can be located during the teen years. (Carbone, 1996, p. 2)

It should not come as a great surprise to anyone working with the correctionally supervised that AIDS is a serious threat to that population. The impact, however, extends far beyond the individual who is infected, reaching to their family, friends, and community (Adam and Sears, 1996; Long and Ankrah, 1997).

In the 1980s, approximately 20 percent of women entering the New York state prison system were infected with HIV or had AIDS. In 1997, the number of inmates with AIDS stood at approximately 7,500, and the New York state prison system is considered the largest setting specializing in AIDS patients in the country (Kaplan, 1998). The social, psychological, and health consequences of being HIV-positive add a different and very often devastating dimension to the prison experience for these women. The social stigma of being HIV-positive or diagnosed with AIDS further isolates women prisoners from each other, and it seriously limits the type of relationships they can have with their significant others and families on the outside. It is safe to say that the U.S. prison system has been, and currently is, ill prepared to address this epidemic, just as it is ill prepared to address substance abuse. However, AIDS can be potentially devastating to the families of those who are released back into the community without proper education and treatment (Engle, 1999; Viadro and Earp, 1991).

Cultural differences, linguistic differences (in the case of those who are monolingual in a language other than English), and lack of access to quality health care are formidable barriers in helping former inmates seek and receive quality services (Diaz-Cotto, 1996; Garcia, in press). One Latina peer educator noted the influence of culture: "In our culture we were raised to feel that talking about sexual issues is like a taboo topic, you don't talk about it at home. If you do, it means you're either having sex, and if you're a woman, they might consider you a loose woman. Because of AIDS, some of these things have changed. But many are still in denial and don't want to accept the circumstances. Or they're so proud or afraid of being stigmatized and they don't want to admit that this could happen to them" (Boudin et al., 1999, p. 95).

Unfortunately, it has been estimated by the National Institute of Justice that only 13 percent of state and federal prisons had peer-led HIV programs in 1997 (Kaplan, 1998). It is estimated that there are approximately 25,000 HIV-positive inmates in state and federal prisons (Kaplan, 1998). Fortunately, there are alternatives to prison for HIV-positive offenders, but not many (Levy, 1997). Compassionate release is one such approach; however, release of the terminally ill is widely considered to be more of a political than medical issue (MacDougall, 1998). Women prisoners with HIV or AIDS face the additional challenges in receiving quality health care for their illness. Most of them reside in relatively small prisons, making quality care that much more difficult and expensive to access: "Correctional systems are experiencing financial pressures concerning the care of AIDS-ill inmates. The increasing number of AIDS symptomatic inmates has resulted in a major escalation in medical costs as a budget item for institutions. This increased financial burden is the result of the fact that inmates are not eligible for Medicaid, which is the prime public health care method of financing AIDS-related treatment; hence, the costs of health care for HIV/AIDS inmates must be born entirely by the system in which they are incarcerated" (Zaitzow, 1999, p. 86).

The possibility of ex-offenders being further stigmatized by the disease severely limits their potential reintegration with their families and their regaining custody of their children. The following interchange took place in an ACE peer-run group at Bedford Hills Correctional Facility, and it highlights the struggles inmates who are mothers and have AIDS face: "At today's gathering, all the women happen to be mothers, and their children quickly eclipse health concerns once one woman confesses her biggest fear; that she won't make it out alive. The conversation heats up. Pearl Richardson, a mother of five whose youngest is HIV positive, says the state is seeking to terminate her parental rights. From across the table, Karen 'K. K.' Loftin, a mother of two and one of the group's charismatic leaders, issues a challenge. 'My attitude is, I'm not dead yet! and I plan to live and take care of them' " (Kaplan, 1998, p. 1).

Thus, the needs of female ex-offenders who are HIV-positive or have AIDS are considerable, and their efforts at rehabilitation can be considerably undermined if their health needs are not taken into account and addressed. Successful rehabilitation necessitates instilling a sense of hope and future. A female ex-offender who believes that her future is limited to the here and now has little incentive to be law abiding.

Reading Academy, Maryland Correctional Institute–Jessup

Rationale for Selection

Capacity enhancement with the correctionally supervised requires that they acquire educational content that they can translate into marketable skills when they enter society. These skills, in turn, can cause a profound transformation in individuals that involves shifts in attitudes and values about themselves and their surroundings. The ability to read and write carries benefits that go beyond what many providers can reasonably expect. Education is widely understood to have tremendous potential in transforming marginalized people in this society and the world; consequently, it can be an empowering mechanism that can enhance the capacities of ex-offenders. Time spent in prison, for example, can be time spent reflecting on life's choices and circumstances, and it can present opportunities to make life-altering changes (MacDougall, 1998). Baird summed up the importance of learning while in prison quite well when he wrote: "For incarcerated women of all races and ethnic groups, the mandate is that, within a relatively short period of time following release from prison, 'whether [they] like it or not' they better have learned something that will enable them to find 'socially acceptable' employment; otherwise, the door to prison becomes a revolving one." (1997, p. 1). Although the preceding comment refers to women prisoners, the statement also applies to men and to the young and old alike.

Acquisition of a formal education is one of the decisions an individual can make. The belief in oneself is the cornerstone of capacity enhancement. This belief is enhanced when one is able to use a set of skills, in this case reading and writing, to better understand the world around him or her. The shame and embarrassment many people who are illiterate experience in this society is not well understood by providers. Efforts to mask this inability often interfere with the establishment of relationships and other important aspects of life, such as obtaining gainful employment, a key element in any successful effort at keeping ex-offenders from reentering the criminal justice system.

The importance of academic skills such as reading and writing cannot be underestimated by the practitioner who wants to help an ex-offender seek and maintain employment. Participation in learning can also help offenders stay out of trouble while in prison (Baird, 1997). Reading and writing, in addition, plays a central role in the development of self-esteem. Consequently, this ability must never be underestimated. Any effort to help offenders learn how to read will go a long way toward helping them make a successful adjustment once released. A prisoner's willingness to self-identify as someone with limited reading and writing skills may well be the first step in the process of his or her self-identifying other needs in his or her life. The abilities to read, write, and do math may be taken for granted by a countless number of people. However, these abilities are not shared by all!

Overview of Literature

The prison population in the United States, as noted in chapter 2, can generally be classified as coming from low-income neighborhoods and having very limited formal education, and this profile applies to both males and females (Diaz-Cotto, 1996; Palmer, 1999; Smith, 1998). In California, for example, five African Americans are incarcerated for every one that attends state college, and three Latinos are in prison for every one in a four-year college (Casa, 1999). Thus, prisons can be considered the institution where "higher" learning is taking place for many people who are poor and of color in America.

Most prisoners in state and federal facilities do not have high school diplomas, and their educational experiences in public school have been of poor quality. It is estimated that approximately 13 percent of adults in the United States are illiterate; however, 65 percent of all prisoners are functionally illiterate and 85 percent of all juvenile offenders are functionally illiterate (Siegel, 1997). Limited formal education and its consequences make for limit employment opportunities in a society that increasingly stresses high formal educational attainment. Most jobs, particularly those that pay a livable wage and offer various forms of fringe benefits, require at a minimum a high school diploma and comparable reading and writing abilities. After all, it is possible to graduate from high school and still not be able to read, write, and comprehend beyond that of an elementary-level education.

Thus, an inmate with a functional reading level of a grade-schooler will have a hard, if not impossible, time finding a decent job. Increasing inmates' ability to read and write becomes a critical component of any effort at rehabilitation and increases the likelihood of success in their transition back to the community and society. There are estimates that approximately 40 percent of all prisoners can be classified as illiterate, or unable to read, and that more than two-thirds are functionally illiterate, or unable to write a brief letter explaining a billing error (Elikann, 1996). Consequently, any effort that successfully helps an inmate increase his or her literacy skills will also result in an increase in self-esteem.

The provision of correctional education has largely been possible through the Adult Education Act, as amended by the National Literacy Act of 1991 (Public Law 102-73). The act mandates that at least 10 percent of a state's grant be allocated for educational programs for criminal offenders in correctional institutions and for other institutionalized adults. Correctional educational programs have as a goal changing the behavior of offenders through instruction. They seek to either develop or enhance, as the case may be, the knowledge, skills, attitudes, and values of the imprisoned. Literacy, as a result, is viewed as a method of instruction that not only enhances an inmate's quality of life but also serves to decrease the recidivism rate in the process.

Adult education and literacy can consist of many different types of programs and modalities, including but not restricted to instruction in the core, or basic, skills of reading, writing, math, speaking, listening, and problem solving. However, education with offenders cannot strictly limit itself to educational subjects. It must also seek to help students become better acquainted with themselves, with their circumstances, dreams, and fears, and with reality. Education must be a transformative experience if it is going to be true to its mission (Batiuk, 1997; Moreno, Garrido, and Esteban, 1997; Semmens, 1997).

Helping a student achieve the goal of democratic citizenship, for example, requires a teaching style that should resonate for most social workers: "A teaching style most appropriate for achieving the curriculum goals of democratic citizenship would encourage student participation in a problem-solving approach to vocational, political, cultural, and interpersonal issues. The model suggested here is not prescriptive, nor detailed, but is intended to provide . . . a style of teaching designed to engage students actively in their own learning as preparation for citizenship in a democratic society" (Semmens, 1997, p. 82). Providing inmates with education that parallels that found outside prison, with no regard for the unique circumstances prisoners find themselves in, should never be a goal (Halstead, 1997).

Writers and scholars in the field of corrections have given a fair amount of attention to the subject of education as a key factor in helping former inmates make a successful adjustment back to society (Siegel, 1997; Taylor, 1996). The results of the following studies will not come as a great surprise to the reader, or to the average person in the street, and they show the influence of formal education prior to and during the incarceration experience. Beck and Shipley (1989), in an Illinois study, found that former inmates with a formal educational level of eighth grade or lower were more likely (61.9 percent), when compared with those who were high school graduates (57.4 percent) or had college-level education (51.9 percent), to be rearrested. Eisenberg (1991), in a Texas-based, five-year, longitudinal study, found that formal educational attainment influenced recidivism— the higher the attainment, the lower the likelihood of rearrest. Holloway and Moke (1986), in their study of former inmates who hold associate of arts degrees, found them to have a higher likelihood of finding employment and not being rearrested than former inmates who were high school graduates, followed by non–high school graduates.

Gainous (1992), in an Alabama-based study, found that inmates who were offered job placement and postrelease counseling, had a lower likelihood of being rearrested when compared with those who did not receive those services. Harer (1994), in a study of federal prison releases in 1987, found that the higher an inmate's formal education upon entering the prison system, the less likely the inmate was to be rearrested.

The relationship between unemployment and crime has not escaped public attention (Mauer, 1999). Wilson (1996) comments specifically on the interrelationship between the two and the impact it has on communities:

> Neighborhoods in which adults are able to interact in terms of obligations, expectations, and relationships are in a better position to supervise and control activities and behavior of children. In neighborhoods with high levels of social organization, adults are empowered to act to improve the quality of neighborhood life. Neighborhoods plagued by high levels of joblessness are more likely to experience low levels of social organization: the two go hand in hand. High rates of joblessness trigger other neighborhood problems that undermine social organization, ranging from crime, gang violence, and drug trafficking to family breakups and problems in the organization of family life. (p. 20–21)

Provision of employment by itself may not be the solution to rehabilitating offenders with a history of drug-related crimes, particularly trafficking in drugs. One study in Washington, D.C., found that two-thirds of African Americans arrested for drug dealing were gainfully employed at the time of arrest. Moonlighting, as noted by Mauer (1999), to supplement low wages was the primary reason for selling drugs. Consequently, an effort simply to provide "legitimate" forms of employment may not be sufficient to prevent recidivism.

The inability of social institutions such as houses of worship to play a mediating role in communities facing incredible challenges in maintaining social order makes the task of other institutions, in addition to the family, that much more arduous. Rehabilitation, after all, requires a concerted and coordinated effort in order to increase the odds of success. Any efforts to better prepare prisoners for the transition back to society while they are prisoners will go a long way toward making the efforts of institutions on the outside more fruitful. The case of Michael is an example:

> On August 11, 1987, I was arrested. It was the beginning of the end of nearly two years in the drug industry and all that followed was a long trial, and a 45-year prison sentence. I was 23 then; I am 29 now. Most of my adult life has been spent and most of my maturing has taken place behind prison walls. This may sound surprising, and it may even lead some to believe that the correctional system was responsible; instead, I must attribute it to self-determination, and to the commitment and help of my family and my mentors have provided. (McPherson and Santos, 1997, p. 121)

A 1994 national survey undertaken by the Judiciary Committee of the U.S. Senate found that 93 percent of all prison wardens recommended a significant expansion of literacy and other educational programs (Elikann, 1996). Literacy and educational programs not only provide inmates with constructive activities and outlets that aid them upon release from prison, but such programs are also cost effective in decreasing a prison's reliance on guards and other forms of prisoner supervision.

The teaching of literacy to marginalized groups in U.S. society—and ex-offenders of color certainly fall into this category—cannot be successful without grounding the process in the context of the student's life (Freire, 1970; Schaafsma, 1995). Thus, we need to develop creative ways of teaching literacy both inside and outside prison that take into account the realities ex-offenders face in their quest to reenter society as productive members. These new approaches, however, are not going to be received without significant resistance in some circles: "Change to a more educative correctional experience promises everyone a tough time. Negotiating with those who have little to lose is tough and requires patience and perseverance. It also requires inmates to think and to support their demands with logic and evidence. Further, it encourages inmates to take responsibility for their actions, rather than to see the world in black and white, them and us terms. In practice, all participants in the correctional process are encouraged to explore new ways of thinking and alternative ways of responding to the attitudes and values of others" (Semmens, 1997, pp. 84–85).

Successful rehabilitation involves much more than a change in attitude by an inmate. Success is possible only when inmates believe in themselves, wish to change the course of their lives, and have the requisite competencies, in this case academic, that will allow them to compete in American society. An inability to read, write, or undertake basic math represents a very significant barrier in a society where such skills are taken for granted in jobs and social situations. When the individual with these "deficits" is also an "ex-con," the tasks associated with rehabilitation and achieving success in society become almost impossible to perform.

Experimental Gallery, Seattle, Washington

Rationale for Selection

The increased number of American youth being incarcerated in either youth detention centers or adult prisons represents a disturbing trend, as noted in chapter 2. Historically, we regarded youth who had committed a criminal offense as being able to benefit from rehabilitation, as people who could eventually become contributing members of society. This necessitated placing them in settings that facilitated the delivery of therapeutic services, education, and rehabilitation. However, thinking has slowly shifted to a more punitive perspective—partly as the result of the violence the crack epidemic wrought in cities across the United States. Recent incidents of school violence that have resulted in multiple killings or have featured perpetrators as young as 6 years of age have provided a stronger excuse for the punitive perspective. Ironically, the thrust toward more punitive measures comes at a time when youth-related crime has decreased significantly from that of the 1980s and 1990s.

The unique circumstances of serving a sentence in a total institution has increased the importance of prisoners finding creative outlets for their frustrations and means of expressing their "inner voices." This need is even greater than it is for the general population. An ability to express one's frustrations in a constructive manner is a goal all societies would like to see their citizens achieve. Prisons, too, regardless of the age or gender of the prisoners, have their share of individuals with artistic and musical abilities. Consequently, in the process of creating an atmosphere in an institution that silences rather than encourages expression, the field of corrections often overlooks an important medium to help prisoners express themselves.

Thus, the case of the Experimental Gallery in Seattle, Washington, is unique, not only because it uses the arts and humanities as vehicles for reaching prisoners, in this case youth, but also because it uses the arts as a means for getting former prisoners jobs upon their release from prison. It is rare to see a children's museum involved in the correctional field, although there is no logical reason why such institutions shouldn't be (Delgado, 2000b). Museums often are in strategic positions to address the needs of the most marginalized members of society; however, few museums, such as the one in Seattle, have taken as their mission serving those who have been incarcerated. Further, this program has benefited from a detailed and methodologically sound evaluation conducted by social work faculty from the University of Washington School of Social Work in Seattle. Thus, the unique approach utilized by the Experimental Gallery with incarcerated youth provides the reader with a wonderful example of what is possible when there is a commitment and use of creativity in program design.

Overview of Literature

The greater attention that has been paid juvenile offenders in the last two decades has resulted, unfortunately, in greater efforts to either incarcerate them or treat them as adults in the nation's courts, as addressed in earlier chapters (Anderson, 1998b; Price, 1996). Incarceration of youth, in turn, has adopted a focus on punishment rather than rehabilitation, resulting in youth inmates being subject to numerous abuses; in some cases, it has resulted in an inmate's suicide (Associated Press, 1998a; Butterfield, 2000b; Campbell, 1995; "Trouble in Virginia's Juvenile Prisons," 1999). In New York City, juvenile arrests have declined in recent years, but the number of juveniles held in jails in 1999 increased to a daily average of 360 (Sengupta, 2000). This figure is higher than it was at the peak of juvenile crime rates five years ago and almost double the 191 jailed on any given day in 1991 (Sengupta, 2000). Although it is too early to tell whether similar increases can be found in other cities across the country, there is concern about the social and economic costs. Youth, then, have been caught up in the nation's thrust toward incarcerating offenders. The consequences of this policy are in many ways even more disastrous because of the age of the inmates. In many circles, a future with a prison record is considered not much of a future.

Youth of color, particularly African American and Latino youth, as noted earlier in this book, face more severe treatment in the juvenile justice system than their white, non-Latino counterparts. Youth of color are more likely to be arrested, held in jail, and stand trial than white non-Latinos. In addition, they are more likely to be incarcerated for a longer period for violence-related crimes (whites, 193 days; African Americans, 254 days; Latinos, 305 days) and to be waived to adult courts (Butterfield, 2000c).

The boom in prison construction addressed in chapter 2 has not been restricted to adult institutions (Casa, 1999). Juvenile facilities also have shown a resurgence: "Prompted by a decade-long public outcry about juvenile crime and by federal grants for secure facilities for young offenders, states and counties are building jails for kids at a rapid clip. The construction confirms the decades-long fear of youth advocates that officials keep missing a key point in juvenile justice reform: that despite what the public thinks, not all young offenders need to be locked up prior to trial to ensure public safety" (Kresnak, 1999, p. 28).

California, a state known for setting trends in the United States, recently passed an initiative known as Proposition 21 (Gang Violence and Juvenile Crime Prevention Act of 1998), which toughens sentencing of juveniles convicted of perpetrating a crime (Nieves, 2000). It increases the power of prosecutors in deciding whether juveniles 14 or older are charged as adults; it institutes minimum and longer sentences for certain offenses; it also denies many of the rights accorded juveniles adjudicated in juvenile courts.

The cost to taxpayers for instituting these changes is astronomical: "Proposition 21 would cost more than $1 billion in prison construction costs and $300 million a year to carry out, according to the state's legislative analyst, or $1.3 billion for construction and $600 million in annual expenses, according to the National Council on Crime and Delinquency which opposes the measure" (Nieves, 2000, p. A15). Ironically, this initiative comes at a time when juvenile-related crime is down in California and throughout most of the country.

The shift toward dealing with juvenile offenders as adults, as a consequence, has created the need to either build more prisons for youthful offenders or incarcerate them along with adult offenders (Anderson, 1998b; Casa, 1999; Price, 1996). The latter response, unfortunately, has not met with public outcry regarding the long-term consequences for youth and society. The negative long-range implications for youth and society can only be imagined. Youth are housed in prisons alongside adults and either subject to abuse, sexual and physical, or exposed to the knowledge the older inmates possess concerning crime. Neither situation lends itself to rehabilitation for youth.

The preference for punishing rather than rehabilitating youthful offenders has profound long-term implications for the nation because of their young age. An "early" start in the nation's prisons will very often serve as a predictor of a "lifelong" history of incarceration, and of a life that is measured in terms of the total number of years behind bars rather than the number of years spent in freedom. Thus, any effort that specifically seeks to reorient youth on a productive path warrants closer scrutiny and attention. The economic and social costs of such efforts will no doubt have to be addressed by the nation in the no-so-distant future (Price, 1996).

It is not unusual, for example, to find that a youth involved in crime has no positive male role models in his life, an absent father being one type:

> One Mother's Day, the violent offenders wing of the juvenile prison near Tucson was packed with moms. But tomorrow—Father's Day—less than a handful of dads are expected to attend a party in the Crossroads cottage. "I didn't know what to do about Father's Day," said Terri Rahner, supervisor of Catalina's Crossroads program for violent offenders. "Fathers seem to be less in the picture, for whatever reason." Jesus, 17, is in Crossroads for aggravated robbery. He has a juvenile court file thick with refer-

rals. By law, he'll be released in October when he turns 18. He plans to live with his girlfriend, Aimee, 18, and their 7 and a half-month-old daughter, Elisa Monique. (Innes, 1996, p.1A)

The consequences of juvenile crime are complex; however, the existence of positive role models in the life of youth is widely considered to be very important.

The field of youth development has frequently drawn upon a variety of activities, such as the arts (performing and visual), humanities, and sports, to reach and engage youth (Delgado, 2000b). These activities systematically build upon youth strengths as a means of enhancing their abilities to make a successful transition from youth to adulthood. More specifically, the use of the arts and humanities as an intervention has recently received more attention, particularly in the field of youth development (Delgado, 2000b). Getting troubled youth to share feelings and concerns, in collaboration with peers, is often cited as a primary goal of youth development. Drama, for example, when combined with script development, channels creative urges and provides "acceptable" outlets for youth who are suspicious of traditional outlets such as counseling.

Creative outlets for youth who have histories of abuse and neglect and who have difficulty being taken seriously by adults are very much in order; however, they take on added importance when youth are incarcerated. If an activity facilitates youth taking on decision-making powers and responsibility, then it brings an added and much needed dimension. Prisons, after all, rarely give inmates, regardless of age or gender, an opportunity to exercise control over their surroundings.

The potential benefits to be derived from the arts have not been lost on the criminal justice field. The Department of Justice, Office of Juvenile Justice and Delinquency Prevention, in collaboration with the National Endowment for the Arts, recently announced the issuance of grants to six grantees (three for $25,000 each to support existing programs and three for $100,000 to establish programs) to support the use of the arts with juvenile offenders. One organization receiving a grant was the Experimental Gallery.

Delancey Street Foundation, San Francisco, California

Rationale for Selection

The period immediately after an inmate's release from prison can prove to be the most critical in his or her postincarceration experience, similar to the period immediately following a substance abuser's release from detoxification. The anxiety and temptations that arise soon after release can easily result in the suspension of judgment and the commission of a crime. This vulnerable period of time necessitates that former inmates have a safe and secure place to live, structure that stresses positive actions, and a plan of action for the future. Needless to say, these goals and activities are quite formidable. Stigma and lack of direction following release from prison result in a need for comprehensive services that address the "total" person rather than one aspect of his or her life.

The state of California experienced one of the nation's most precipitous increases in incarceration during the 1990s; consequently, a case study based in that state is warranted. Fortunately, the case of Delancey Street Foundation also provides the reader with an example of a program that is highly creative and comprehensive and highlights both the rewards and challenges of providing all-encompassing services to former inmates regardless of their gender, ethnicity, or race. Further, Delancey Street illustrates the importance of dedication and longevity of leadership in broadening and stabilizing an organization serving ex-offenders.

Delancey Street Foundation enjoys a national and international reputation based upon its creative approach and success in reaching former inmates in California and in other states (New York, New Mexico, and North Carolina). The organization has creatively developed a wide range of services and businesses to help rehabilitate the correctionally supervised regardless of their socioeconomic background, gender, or race/ethnicity. California, as already noted, is one of the country's leaders in the use of incarceration. Thus, a case example based there was very much in order.

Overview of Literature

Successful rehabilitation rests on a four-part strategy in prison—substance abuse treatment, education, job-related training, and recreation. The post-incarceration period for a former inmate is often fraught with challenges: "Following years of imprisonment, existing on the outside can be a bigger struggle than life behind bars. Rap sheets are an obstacle to gaining employment and accessing housing, and ex-offenders may be shunned by friends and family members. In other instances, they may rekindle relationships with people who expose them once again to drugs, alcohol and other catalysts for criminal acts" (Silverman, 1999, p. 9).

An inmate's time in prison can often be characterized as strictly surviving until release. Thus, release often finds a former inmate with the challenge of having to adapt to a world that has changed dramatically, depending on the length of sentence, from the day he or she was incarcerated. On the other hand, inmates can learn a great deal about themselves while in prison and adopt methods of survival that have applicability upon release, if they are properly counseled. One inmate's comments pertaining to the nature of skills required to succeed in the outside world sum up the importance of those skills: "People have to understand that the skills needed to survive in prison are the very skills you have to give up on the outside."

The subject of recidivism is one that is on the minds of most politicians, policymakers, correctional officials, taxpayers, and last but certainly not least, ex-offenders themselves. The vicious cycle often associated with being an "ex-con" is well understood in all human services circles (Silverman, 1999). The tremendous number of inmates living in U.S. prisons raises important issues about how they can eventually leave, become productive members of society, and not return to prison. California, for example, has thirty-three penitentiaries and approximately 160,000 inmates, over 50 percent of whom are expected to be released between 1999 and 2001:

> California is hardly unique in churning out convicts whose only honed skill seems to be the ability to victimize again. Voices now urging a better balance between punishment and programs can be heard across the country. But because California boasts the nation's largest prison population and one of the highest recidivism rates, a consensus has begun to build among prison experts and top correction officials past and present, liberal and conservative. They say that the state's focus on ever more harsh punishment—coupled with the absence of remedial programs—has served California poorly. (Arax, 1999a, p. 14)

Consequently, models that successfully help ex-inmates make the transition back to the community are very much needed, from an economic and social perspective. Models that stress ex-offenders' development of marketable skills are in particular demand (Boyd, 1997). When the models systematically eschew government funding and provide comprehensive services, there is much to be learned from them. Such an approach is rare and represents a philosophical stance that has wide appeal to both the political left and right. Rehabilitation is a difficult goal to achieve in any setting; however, it takes on added importance when addressing the ex-offender. When rehabilitation uses ex-offenders in a central role in the process, it brings a much-needed dimension. Programs that actively involve ex-offenders in rehabilitating housing, for example, not only provide participants with job-related skills but also transform a community by transforming buildings that have been abandoned into livable dwellings (Boyd, 1997).

People Animals Love, Washington, D.C.

Rationale for Selection

There is a tremendous need for creative approaches to engaging and preparing prison inmates for their eventual release back into society. Their time in prison, as already noted in this book, can often be classified as "making time" rather than "productive time." Further, being isolated from family and friends in a brutal system where degradation, rape, and other forms of violence are not uncommon renders inmates to a state of mind and existence that is "inhuman." Consequently, programs that provide direction and hope and engender feelings of caring and empathy serve a critical function in total institutions such as prisons. Programs such as these are unfortunately too rare in U.S. prisons.

When these programs also teach a skill that can result in gainful employment in the community, they have added significance for both prisons and communities alike. There is no question that the field of criminal justice must actively seek and institute creative approaches toward rehabilitation. These approaches must cover a range of types that take into account individual circumstances and goals.

The case study of People Animals Love (PAL) was selected because it provides the reader with an example of an organization that uses an "unconventional" approach to work with prisoners—namely, the use of animals. This organization is headed by a veterinarian, a helping professional, true, but not your typical one, at least from a human services perspective. Further, the program that targets prisoners is only one dimension, although a critical one, of the organization. I would argue that most services involving the correctionally supervised are not provided exclusively by a "criminal justice" organization. Thus, most social service organizations have a percentage of their clientele, or close relatives of clients, under court supervision of some kind. The effective use of animals to reach, engage, and rehabilitate inmates cannot be applied undifferentially; however, it is a viable alternative that must be seriously considered, and is thus worthy of a case study in this book. Its potential for rehabilitation has yet to be tapped to the extent that is warranted in this field of practice.

Overview of Literature

The use of animals to help the disabled has a long and distinguished history in the human services field, both in this and other countries around the world. Animals not only have helped people with disabilities by acting as their eyes and hands but also have provided valuable companionship. However, using animals in the prison system provides an important, yet often overlooked, perspective on pets. Pets in prisons can help social workers and other providers achieve multiple goals.

A number of case examples of using pets for therapeutic purposes in U.S. prisons can be traced back to the 1960s. The Birdman of Alcatraz, made famous by a book and movie of the same title, is probably the most well-known example of pet-facilitated therapy in the United States. On a more purposefully planned level, there were several pet therapy programs (PETs) in operation during the 1970s and 1980s.

In the 1970s, a social worker named David Lee initiated a PET at Oaskwood Forensic Center in Lima, Ohio, targeting inmates who had been labeled as "criminally insane." The program utilized parakeets and a fish aquarium with a goal of helping inmates cope with loneliness, depression, and hostility toward others in the prison. The result, when compared with a control group, showed that the inmates in the program displayed a considerable (50 percent) reduction in medication use and a significant decline in violence and suicide attempts (Moneymaker and Strimple, 1991). The Wild Horse Project in Cannon City, Colorado, represents yet another dimension of using animals to help inmates. The program, the result of a collaboration between the National Organization for Wild American Horses and the National Humane Association, trains inmates (class and field instruction) in all phases of horsemanship from husbandry to training to appropriate veterinary and furrier skills (Moneymaker and Strimple, 1991).

The People-Pet-Partnership Program focused on providing participants with skills in canine husbandry and behavior, obedience training, and specialized training designed to meet the needs of people with disabilities such as cerebral palsy, multiple sclerosis, and epilepsy:

> Once the long period of training is over there is a time of sorrow in seeing the animals leave to a new owner. This "tearing away" for both the trainer and dog creates considerable anxiety, but the women know that they have contributed to a very worthy cause and they have built within themselves a positive self-image, better self-control, and all the while they have learned a vocational skill that will help them find employment opportunities upon their release. Most importantly, the program has given the women a new perspective to live by, namely, to think of others who cannot help themselves, and by training dogs to help them, these women have shown their honesty, devotion, and commitment to love. (Moneymaker and Strimple, 1991, pp. 135–36)

Summit House, Greensboro, North Carolina

Rationale for Selection

The creation of alternatives to incarceration is of sufficient importance to warrant a case study in any book examining the criminal justice system and how society punishes offenders. The subject of community alternatives has not received the attention it deserves in this country because of an overreliance on incarceration as the preferred method for punishing offenders. This overreliance has been addressed throughout this book. Alternatives, however, not only save taxpayers money but are a more humane way of society issuing punishment. Further, punishment is carried out in a manner that has a higher likelihood, when compared with imprisonment, of rehabilitating an offender.

The costs associated with building and maintaining prisons are prompting a search for alternatives involving nonviolent offenders. The average cost of keeping an adult prisoner ranges from $30,000 to $75,000 per year. The costs of building and maintaining prisons increased from $7 billion in 1980 to more than $38 billion in 1996 (Casa, 1999). Increased costs, in turn, require that authorities find alternatives that meet the need to punish, increase the likelihood offenders being rehabilitated, and are cost efficient. In the case of mothers, alternatives bring the added benefit of increasing contact between offenders and their children, thereby minimizing the disruption in familial roles associated with prisons.

According to the Women in Prison Project of the National Women's Law Center (1995, p. 3–4), five basic strategies need to be implemented in order to better address the needs of women prisoners: First, expand community alternatives, intermediate sanctions, and residential treatment for women in prison, including pregnant women, and include women in discussing these alternatives. Second, offer programs in prisons and jails that are specifically targeted to women and that address the root issues that trigger criminal conduct and alcohol and drug use. Third, within the correctional system, begin to address the serious medical needs of women who are under the system's jurisdiction and provide follow-up of these women once they leave. Fourth, begin to see the needs of women in the criminal justice system broadly and make strategic collaborations with other organizations that provide services to low-income people. And fifth, provide services to pregnant and parenting women.

The Summit House case addresses the importance of mothers being with their children in a setting that allows, encourages, and enhances their parenting roles, does so in a community context, and incorporates many of the programmatic recommendations made by the Women in Prison Project. The evolution of Summit House from one house to several in cities throughout North Carolina stands as a testament to the importance of work in reunifying and keeping mothers with their children. Community alternatives become more important in an age when the country is determined to incarcerate law breakers. A case study that specifically targets community alternatives brings a much-needed dimension to this book and provides social workers with some possibilities to apply to practice in this type of setting.

Review of Literature

The incarceration of parents who have young children is not often talked about in public debate about prisons and prisoners. Debate generally centers on how a crime has affected a victim and a community. However, children of offenders constitute a dimension that must be considered in the development of policies related to corrections. The consequences for children of parental imprisonment can be lifelong, as noted in the following example: " 'It's like she wasn't a part of me. But I feel like she is a part of me,' Rock says in a voice so soft it's barely audible. It is not what you would expect to hear from a 15-year-old sporting a streetwise attitude and a bandanna wrapped around his head. Rock says that when his mother came out of prison after serving a two-year sentence, and then went back up again a few months later, it was hard to understand. And it hurt. 'We're not that close anymore,' he adds, struggling to find the words to explain how it is now. 'We were closer before she went away" ("When the Voices," 1995, p. 16). The case of Rock, unfortunately, is not atypical.

The rise in the number of women entering prisons this past decade has presented prison systems with inevitable challenges because the systems were originally established to imprison men:

> A masculine mathematics prison life: the square feet and angles of a cell, the sizes of the uniforms, the sentences measured in years and months, the days marked off by counts and lock downs. Nothing is soft or curved or feminine. Prisons are built for men, the vast majority of prisoners. But the number of women in prison in the United States has increased fivefold since 1980. Officially, male and female inmates are treated equally. But women are not men. They are less likely to have been incarcerated for violent crimes. Their physical and emotional needs are different. And they bear children. (Dowling, 1997, p. 7)

The number of women prisoners in state institutions has tripled since 1985 (Casa, 1999). Incarceration of women puts them in a place where they are vulnerable to abuse (Bill, 1998). Childhood abuse and victimization of women is widely considered to be a precursor to females engaging in criminal behavior (Bill, 1998; Smith, 1998). Yet their entering the prison system may result in further victimization at the hands of prison guards as well as other prisoners (Bill, 1998; Diaz-Cotto, 1996; Watterson, 1996). Such experiences, in turn, can further affect women upon their release back into the community and can undermine their parenting role when reunified with their children.

Fifty to 60 percent of women inmates with children have never been visited by their children since they were incarcerated (Mauer, 1999). The distance from the children's home to prison (more than one hundred miles on average) is often cited as the primary reason for lack of visits. The following description of a visit to an inmate captures the essence of the challenges in keeping families connected during the imprisonment of a parent:

> Some have driven many hours to get here. For others, who have relocated to be closer to their loved ones, it takes only minutes. But no matter what length of time, everyone knows it's first come first serve so upon arrival they scurry to get in line. It's visitor's day at the Dallas State Correctional Institution. Like all prisons, there's law and order to follow. That means, upon arrival everyone must have their identification checked by the desk clerk. Then the inmate's chart is scanned to see if the visitor's name is listed. If everything checks out the visitor is seated until the inmate is called to the visiting room. Those who come to see inmates housed in the general portion of the facility will most likely be called quickly because the process for their visits is simpler. Those coming to visit inmates in the restrictive housing units will have a much longer wait. Here, the process is tedious and the inmates are only allowed an hour visit. The average waiting period can

range from half an hour to several hours. But to family members anticipating a few brief moments with a loved one who's been locked away for years, the hours seem like mere seconds. (Roberts, 1995, p. 17)

Lack of parental contact with children during their formative years increases the likelihood that contact after prison release may be awkward and unproductive in reconstituting families. Prisons historically have not been established to address the unique needs of mothers and their children (Hairston, 1991; Harm, 1992). The Adoption and Safe Families Act of 1997, which forces states to terminate parental rights in cases where children have been in foster care for fifteen out of twenty-two months, effectively means that women who are imprisoned for longer periods lose their children (Dowdy, 1999). Community alternatives to incarceration, particularly those that pay special attention to parenting roles, are widely considered to be the way to allow mothers to serve their sentence in a way that minimizes the disruption, or prevents the destruction, of the mothering role; such alternatives increase the likelihood that women offenders who are mothers do not lose their rights as parents because of the length of a prison sentence (Thompson and Harm, 1995).

As already noted, most female prisoners are mothers, too. The majority of female prisoners, in turn, are imprisoned for nonviolent crimes, making alternatives to prison a more suitable and cost-effective option when compared to the case of men (Belenko and Peugh, 1998; Huie, 1992; Immergut, 1997; Johnson, Selber, and Lauderdale, 1998). In 1998, more than 2,000 women arrested were pregnant and an estimated 200,000 children had mothers in jail or prison (Casa, 1999). Women are typically imprisoned for larceny, petty theft, forgery, prostitution, and drug abuse. These offenses, although punishable by imprisonment, are generally not considered as constituting major threats to society, making community alternatives for women economically and socially feasible.

The social and economic costs of child abuse resulting from parental substance abuse are staggering, as noted in chapter 4. The social costs of broken families, children witnessing parents abusing drugs, placement in foster homes, babies being born with physical and cognitive damage because of mothers using drugs during pregnancy, and imprisonment affect all sectors of a community and nation. According to one estimate, 70 to 90 percent of all child welfare spending in the United States can be traced to substance-abusing parents (CASA, 1999). When parents, particularly mothers who abuse drugs, are imprisoned and not provided with treatment, parenting skills training, and opportunities to reestablish their parenting roles, it limits their potential contribution to their families, communities, and society.

Many people believe that prisons are probably the best place to put offenders who abuse drugs. They are under the mistaken impression that such settings are an effective way of keeping drug abusers away from drugs and that community alternatives, in turn, make it too easy for substance-abusing offenders to obtain drugs. However, just because a prisoner is behind bars does not mean he or she cannot continue to have access to drugs: "Resourceful inmates can maintain their addictions with the help of friends, relatives, and corrupt prison employees. And long-term, intensive treatment, which experts say could turn around their lives, is scarce; costly rehabilitation programs are unpopular with taxpayers" (Purdy, 1995a, p. 1). Ironically, prison guards may be more concerned about weapons than drugs (Purdy, 1995b).

The concept of alternatives to prisons is not new in this or other countries (Peters, 1998; Zimring and Hawkins, 1991). Alternatives to incarceration provide sentencing authorities with multiple options concerning the nature of the punishment for an offender, in addition to saving taxpayers money when compared with the costs of imprisonment: "In the last decade, the overburdened criminal justice system has slowly begun to realize that incarceration does not eliminate the need for effective rehabilitation. While incarceration serves to relieve public concerns about safety, the fiscal burdens of incarceration demand that state officials seek other less costly and more effective preventive responses" (Johnson, Selber, and Lauderdale, 1998, p. 612). One estimate comparing the costs of prison and treatment programs for women offenders who abuse drugs notes that women in prison cost taxpayers about $30,000 per inmate per year compared with $17,000 to $20,000 for a residential treatment program, or $2,700 to $3,600 for treatment on an outpatient basis (Immergut, 1997).

The three primary goals of imprisonment are to punish, rehabilitate, and prepare the ex-offender for reentry into society. Rehabilitation and reentry into society, with some exceptions, are greatly facilitated when the offender is not incarcerated. The community context best replicates the experience ex-offenders will encounter upon release from prison. The freedom associated with living in a community is more often than not listed as the biggest fear ex-offenders face upon release from prison. Thus, any effort that can minimize the fears associated with living on the "outside" will go a long way toward increasing the likelihood of success in the reentry phase.

Community alternatives to incarceration are generally considered for individuals convicted of nonviolent offenses (Elikann, 1996). Of the various types of community alternative sentences, the following three are the most frequently used: (1) attenuated probation (detention at home is one form); (2) probation (suspended sentences to conditional release); and (3) alternatives to custodial sentences (community service is an example) (De La Cuesta Arzameni, 1998; Johansson, 1998; Peters, 1998; Zimring and Hawkins, 1991). Alternative-to-prison programs, contrary to common opinion, are invariably considered to be a tough alternative to prison time for offenders: "These programs can be even more rigorous than incarceration and can last far longer. Offenders who don't complete their sentences go directly to jail. One participant said, 'Program time is hard time. Jail is easy time.' Some defendants turn down the opportunity for an alternative sentence and choose less-rigorous cell time" (Elikann, 1996, p. 13).

One estimate by the state of Michigan found that the state was able to avoid building up to six new prisons by using electronic bracelets (Elikann, 1996).

The criminal justice system rarely takes into account whether an offender has children (Hostetter and Jinnah, 1993; Jacobs, 1997). The system's focus is on punishing the offender, with security being the primary goal and not family preservation: "[Women inmates] tell of a violent and dehumanizing society that condemns successive generations of mothers and their daughters to the 'concrete womb'—a place where women are treated like little children, are worried about their real children and the people they love, but have very little power to do anything about their lives. Prison officials demonstrate that if you are in prison you forfeit your right to be loved, to be treated with respect, or to simply be yourself ("In the Criminal Injustice System," 1996, p. 19). A rush to punish results in a disruption of the family and the community in which they live.

This almost singular focus on punishment and security severely limits the nature and extent of contact prisoners have with their children and family (Hostetter and Jinnah, 1993). Children of offenders are effectively "punished" through separation from their parents. In addition, children may develop a contempt for the law that may lead them into extralegal activities: "Children who see a parent arrested and handcuffed, and who are frisked by guards during a prison visit, become contemptuous toward law enforcement. More troublesome, many children with a father behind bars make a hero out of him" (Butterfield, 1999a, p. A18). Mothers who are imprisoned, however, are rarely made heroes by their children and are very often viewed shamefully by them. Women offenders who are pregnant bring with them particular challenges to the corrections field. Their condition necessitates that prisons make necessary accommodation, often on a very limited basis and for a limited time. Once they are born, infants are separated from their mothers.

It is estimated that of 1.8 million inmates imprisoned in the United States, approximately 40 percent have a parent, brother, or sister in jail or prison, too (Butterfield, 1999a). Prison, in some families and communities, may be viewed as a rite of passage rather than carrying a stigma (Casa, 1999; Palmer, 1999). As a result, it is not unusual to hear about whole families being in prison concurrently. In one case at Allegheny County Jail, Pittsburgh, a father, mother, four sons, and two daughters were all imprisoned for different crimes. Another case in California found a daughter, her mother, and her grandmother all serving sentences in one prison for separate crimes (Butterfield, 1999a).

Community-based alternatives to prisons are clearly not for every offender and circumstance, or community, for that matter. Yet the social and economic benefits of this form of punishment must not be lost in the hysteria that currently influences public policy in this arena. Community alternatives, as already noted, are a form of punishment, and one that very often is not preferred by the offender because of the high expectations associated with this form of punishment.

The Center for Substance Abuse Treatment (CAST) identified a series of programmatic components that are essential for meeting the needs of pregnant and drug-dependent women: programs must be multidisciplinary, multifaceted, and comprehensive (Smith, 1998). In addition, they must establish collaborative relationships with a wide range of social service agencies so that women offenders and their children can receive needed care and services. CAST notes further: "We must be in the forefront of advocating for policy priorities and services that increase women's chances of being able to support themselves and keep their families intact. These services include alcohol and drug treatment, housing, educational and vocational training, and access to comprehensive preventive and chronic medical care" (Smith, 1998, p. 3).

Although there are an increasing number of in-prison programs that allow mothers and children to be reunited for an extended period of time (Dowdy, 1999; Immergut, 1997), community alternatives seem to offer the most flexibility and least stigmatizing context in which to unite parents, most likely mothers, and their children. If the need to provide substance abuse treatment is a key element in an offender's rehabilitation, then community alternatives take on added appeal. These settings facilitate substance abuse treatment within a context of preparing the offender for both a drug-free and prison-free life in the community.

Moving Ahead Program, St. Francis House, Boston, Massachusetts

Rationale for Selection

The plight of the homeless in the United States is well understood in most sectors of society. Homelessness, as we know it today, is a relatively recent social problem. When I grew up in the 1950s and 1960s, only the "skid row bums" were homeless. Those individuals, because of their "drinking problems," no longer had homes to go to. However, the 1980s witnessed an unprecedented number of people become homeless, not because of alcohol or other drug-related problems, but because of a lack of affordable housing, inadequate discharge planning from mental institutions, and changes in the nation's policies regarding public housing. These and other factors all contributed to creating a population group that very often represented entire families, including children.

A case study of a program or organization that targets the homeless, as a result, affords a perspective that should be present in any book targeting the correctionally supervised. The Moving Ahead Program (MAP) of St. Francis House, Boston, was selected for a variety of reasons. First, a large number of former prisoners patronize both the program and the organization. It should come as no surprise to anyone who has worked with the homeless that a high percentage of them, particularly single men, have been institutionalized in a prison or some form of mental health hospital or shelter. Consequently, these individuals bear the double stigma of being ex-convicts or ex-mental patients and homeless. If the homeless person is a women and she is a former prisoner, then the stigma is even greater.

Second, I had the privilege of working with St. Francis House during a sabbatical and got to know the organization and the staff well. This knowledge of the organization, staff, and guests served to ground me in how MAP's mission is operationalized on a daily basis and how a capacity enhancement perspective permeates service delivery, hiring of staff, and program structure. St. Francis House is not the only shelter of its type in the United States. Thus, reaching out to ex-offenders can be done through shelters because of the high percentage of guests with criminal records and correctional experiences.

Overview of Literature

The homeless issue, and the question of who "deserves" shelter and services and who doesn't, is a subject of much debate in some of the nation's cities, particularly New York (Bernstein, 1999b). The importance of developing a greater understanding of who is homeless, their circumstances, and needs is apparent. Services must target specific groups in order to better serve them.

It is estimated that anywhere from seven hundred thousand to two million people are homeless in this country (Kilborn, 1999). The majority of homeless people are of color, with the breakdown as follows—41 percent are white non-Latino; 40 percent are African American; 11 percent are Latino; and 9 percent other ("Homeless in America," 1999).

Sometimes the homeless get sentenced to prison because of their status of being homeless, and sometimes harsh "three strikes" prison sentences are meted out, as in the following case:

> More than words, it is the numbers that tell the story, yet behind every statistic is a story waiting to be told. One is about Gregory Taylor, a homeless man arrested in the wee hours of the morning after security guards spotted him trying to pry open the metal screen over the kitchen door at St. Joseph's Church in Los Angeles. At Taylor's trial, Fr. Allan McCoy, the parish priest, testified that he had often given Taylor food and let him sleep at the church occasionally. But Taylor was convicted of burglary, and because he had two prior "strikes" against him, he was sentenced to 25 years to life in prison. The harsh punishment was handed down despite a plea by McCoy, technically the "crime victim," against imposing a three-strikes sentence. Lawyers for Taylor appealed, saying the defendant may have honestly believed he was entitled to the food because priests had regularly given him food and shelter in the past, but the 2nd District Court of Appeals in April denied the appeal in a 2 to 1 vote. (Casa, 1999, p. 15)

The literature on the homeless in the United States has expanded over the last fifteen years as the problem has gained national scope. Interestingly, none of the leading books on the subject of incarceration have mentioned the subject of homelessness (Best, 1999; Donziger, 1996; Elikann, 1996; Mauer, 1999; Parenti, 1999; Zimring and Hawkins, 1991). Yet there are probably very few shelters in this country where former inmates do not constitute a major, ever-increasing sector of the guests patronizing the program. Estimates put the percentage of homeless people who are abusing alcohol or drugs at between 30 to 35 percent; 25 percent of the homeless are single adults suffering from mental illness—these two conditions, however, may not be mutually exclusive (Kilborn, 1999). According to national estimates, families with children make up 40 percent of the homeless, and the remaining 60 percent are single people (Da Costa Nunez, 1998; Kilborn, 1999; "Homeless in America," 1999). An increasing number of children are finding themselves homeless (Hagan and McCarthy, 1998).

All major U.S. cities have experienced an increase in the number of homeless, some (those with very high rents and high demand for housing) more so than others ("Homeless in America," 1999). States' increased emphasis on deinstitutionalizing former mental patients combined with an increased number of inmates being released from prison, many with substance-abusing backgrounds, has severely strained existing programs that have historically served the homeless. These programs, in turn, have had to expand services related to legal rights, as one consequence of efforts to protect the legal rights of program participants. The expansion of services to reach former prisoners, however, is not restricted to men. The increase in women being incarcerated has resulted in larger numbers of ex-offenders who are homeless and female.

We must not think of the homeless as unidimensional—namely, people in need of housing. Although some of them would clearly need only housing, few, unfortunately, would fall into that category. Substance abuse is prevalent among the homeless : "A number of studies have shown that homeless people not only lack the support systems and resources they need to obtain food, health care, and shelter . . . but they also have high rates of drug and alcohol abuse, mental disorders, and infectious diseases. . . . Although any enhancement in substance abuse treatment and prevention services for the homeless is likely to be beneficial, efficient targeting of resources requires an understanding of which subgroups are at greatest risk of having these and related problems" (Lambert and Caces, 1995, p. 455).

Ex-offenders who have substance-abusing backgrounds and are homeless represent such a subgroup. A 1991 study of homeless and transient people in Washington, D.C., found, for example, that those who had been incarcerated in correctional institutions that past year were more likely to have used drugs (marijuana and cocaine) than those who had not been incarcerated (Lambert and Caces, 1995).

Women's Prison Association, New York City

Rationale for Selection

The U.S. trend toward incarcerating more and more men and women has not taken place without its share of critics and without a social, economic, and political toll. Some of the most forceful and influential critics have been organizations established specifically to advocate for the rights of prisoners. These organizations have advocated, sponsored conferences, undertaken studies, and released policy papers highlighting the consequences of an increased use of incarceration for individuals, families, communities, and the nation. Some have also taken on the mission of delivering a wide range of social services to former offenders (Morton, 1995). Many such organizations have specifically established main offices in Washington, D.C., and New York City to facilitate lobbying efforts on behalf of prisoners.

Although a case study on such organizations would not normally "fit" in a chapter focused on programmatic efforts at delivery services, such a case would nevertheless add immensely to examples of capacity enhancement and the correctionally supervised. Prison rights and reform organizations take a fundamental position toward inmates that can best be classified as empowering, rights-driven, and capacity enhancing. The case of the Women's Prison Association was selected because of the historical role it has played in addressing the rights and needs of women imprisoned in this country, and its continued focus on bringing national attention to their plight in the correctional system. The organization is well over 150 years old and holds a prominent place in the struggle to better the life of women offenders in this country.

Overview of Literature

Although women have been incarcerated at record rates this past decade, women and prisons historically have not been foreign to each other. Still the general public and the criminal justice system equate incarceration with males (Valentine, 1998). Public debate on incarceration, as a result, needs to shift to take into account gender as a key factor in any form of service delivery. The same applies to those who undertake research in this arena, communication research being one example: "While we are waiting or working for . . . a transformative model, we women in communication can volunteer, teach, and do research with and for the women in our communities whose minds and bodies are locked up. Women in communication can investigate conditions for women and girls in jails and prisons and then can, through their efforts, change the revenge model so women have the skills and knowledge necessary to contribute to themselves, their family, and their communities" (Valentine, 1998, p. 244).

Women offenders differ from their male counterparts in a variety of ways (Conly, 1999; Fogel and Martin, 1992; Garcia, in press; Gilbert, 1999; Jordon, Schlenger, Fairbank, and Caddell, 1996; Sametz, 1980; Zaitzow, 1999):

1. In regard to drug use and drug-related crime, women have a higher likelihood of having used drugs and of having committed crimes to support their addiction.
2. Because of pregnancies and a higher rate of HIV infection, women have unique health care needs.
3. Women are more likely to have experienced physical and sexual abuse sometime prior to incarceration.
4. Women are more likely to be a parent and caretaker up until their incarceration.
5. Women are less likely to have been sentenced in the past, and those with prior records are more likely to have been convicted of a nonviolent offense.
6. Women are more likely to have committed nonviolent crimes.
7. Women who are convicted of committing a violent offense are more likely (twice as likely) to have committed a murder.

These differences require that a woman offender's needs be addressed with a keen understanding of how services must take gender into account. This perspective, unfortunately, necessitates major changes in the correctional system, changes that will undoubtedly encounter resistance because of the focus of criminal justice on punishment and not rehabilitation.

The multifaceted needs female offenders present society very often are ignored or misunderstood because of our stereotypes of female offenders: "Women in prison aren't who people think they are. When the public becomes aware of the real faces and stories of incarcerated women, they begin to develop an approach to public policy that addresses a broader range of issues. That's the only way we'll ever get decent criminal justice or social justice legislation" (Jacobs, 1997, p. 45). Thus, our challenge is to put faces and stories before the general public in the hopes of changing policies and obtaining the necessary resources to help women ex-offenders reenter society. Human services providers, in turn, will need to rethink how services targeting offenders can be gender biased and create new models of service delivery that specifically address the unique issues and needs female ex-offenders face (Austin, Bloom, and Donahue, 1992).

The importance of rehabilitating inmates, male and female, as noted throughout this book, has either played second fiddle to security or simply disappeared. Monies that historically had been targeted to rehabilitation have slowly been transferred to creating and maintaining more prison cells (Casa, 1999). Moreover, increases in state taxes to cover both the costs of building and maintaining more prisons are a likely prospect. Asking for additional tax dollars to cover the costs of rehabilitation, however, faces an unlikely future. The nation's prisons are becoming increasingly of color—both male and female populations—and this diminishes the public's desire to invest money in prevention, treatment, and rehabilitation (Smith, 1998). The consequences for the United States in the twenty-first century can hardly be imagined. When inmates are HIV-positive or have AIDS, the need to provide quality health care during and after incarceration adds even more costs. It is estimated that only 10 percent of state and federal prisons and 5 percent of city and county jails offer comprehensive HIV programs for inmates (Altman, 1999).

Bliss Unlimited, Glendale, California

Rationale for Selection

Numerous advocates and scholars have argued that the nation needs strategies for the prevention of crime and drug abuse. What better place to institute such strategies than with youth? The youth/community development field has many examples of strategies that are both creative and nonstigmatizing in their approach to youth at risk for drug and criminal careers. This case example differs from the other nine case studies in that it targets a population group before it enters the criminal justice system. Bliss Unlimited, a subdivision of We Care for Youth, approaches prevention by seeking to involve and collaborate with sectors of the community that we, in social work, rarely think of approaching—namely, the business sector and the development of businesses run by youth.

Overview of Literature

Bliss Unlimited was developed specifically to give youth alternatives to joining gangs in Glendale, California. Consequently, this literature overview will focus on gangs, youth development, and the business sector's potential to play an influential role in preventing youth from joining gangs. According to recent estimates by the U.S. Department of Justice, there are more than 4,800 gangs and 250,000 gang members in the United States (Bureau of Justice Assistance, 1998). Successfully addressing gangs at the community level requires the creation of interventions that are based on local issues and circumstances: "The diversity in gang types and in causes of gang formation and membership involves a broad range of social, political, family, educational, health, and other community factors. Such diversity suggests that prevention, intervention, and suppression activities should be designed to accommodate individual communities' unique characteristics, needs, gang population, and specific gang-related harm. No universal strategy works to address all gang problems" (Bureau of Justice Assistance, 1998, p. 111).

Although the subject of how best to prevent youth from joining gangs is not without controversy or a dearth of approaches, there is a common agreement that youth who join gangs often have few perceived positive alternatives (Decker and Van Winkle, 1996; Phillips, 1999; Sheldon, Tracy, and Brown, 1997). Generally speaking, these youth have few recreational outlets, limited access to jobs with a future, and limited formal academic skills. Gangs have been viewed from a variety of perspectives, including as a business entity (Decker and Van Winkle, 1996; Sheldon, Tracy, and Brown, 1997). These factors, when combined with the need to involve a broad sector of the community, essentially provide social work and other human services practitioners with a sense of direction in the creation of interventions. The economic future of youth at risk for joining gangs or following a path of crime is often perceived as limited in scope and possibility, with youth of color increasingly being dislocated from the economy—both male and female (De Leon, 1996; Leadbeater and Way, 1996; McLoyd and Hernandez Jozefowiez, 1996; Willis, 1998). There are many scholars who would argue that "vocational" identity is a critical component of overall identity (De Leon, 1996). After all, one of the principal tasks of adolescence is selecting and preparing for an eventual career.

The capacity to learn business skills (Padilla, 1993) and generate income can be found among gang members: "One of the most striking factors I observed was how much the entrepreneurial spirit, which most Americans believe is the core of their productive culture, was a driving force in the worldview and behavior of gang members. If entrepreneurial spirit denotes the desire to organize and manage business interests toward some end that results in the accumulation of capital, broadly defined, nearly all the gang members that I studied possessed, in varying degrees, . . . [attributes] either entrepreneurial in character or that reinforce entrepreneurial behavior" (Jankowski, 1991, p. 101). Jankowski (1991) identified five key attributes that reinforce an entrepreneurial attitude or behavior among gang members: (1) competitiveness, (2) the desire and drive to accumulate money and material possessions, (3) status-seeking, (4) the ability to plan, and (5) the ability to take risks. These attributes are clearly highly desirable in business, yet they are viewed as undesirable by society when applied to gang members.

Preventing youth from joining gangs cannot be achieved by any one organizational entity (Chaiken, 1998); it requires a broad-based community effort that stresses participation from all significant sectors, including the business sector. The community's business sector has the potential to help youth develop both their employment skills and their academic skills. The economic implications of youth who are working go far beyond that of the individual who is employed. The generation of funds helps youth's families and their community through an increased purchasing power that has a multiplier effect on local commerce.

The provision of a viable alternative to gangs rests very much on youth development principles. The youth development field has grown tremendously in the past decade in terms of programming, funding, research, and scholarship (Delgado, 2000b; Lakes, 1996). The National

Collaboration for Youth defines positive youth development as "a process which prepares young people to meet the challenges of adolescence and adulthood through a coordinated, progressive series of activities and experiences which help them to become socially, morally, emotionally, physically, and cognitively competent. Positive youth development addresses the broader developmental needs of youth, in contrast to deficit-based models which focus solely on youth problems" (1998, p. 7). Youth development, as a result, can be achieved using a variety of approaches, including the initiation of entrepreneurial projects that stress acquisition of skills that can be directly applied to business, but that can also be transferred to other areas.

The fields of youth development and community development have converged in some sectors by stressing the interrelation between youth and their community (Armistead and Wexler, 1998; Delgado, 2000b). Youth cannot develop without a concomitant development of their community. The field of youth development has also expanded into new and exciting domains not historically a part of the field. Expansion into business is one example. It is not only possible but also highly desirable to enhance youth skills and to do so in an entrepreneurial context in which youth acquire knowledge and learn skills that will benefit them as they seek employment or pursue a career (Partee, 1996).

According to the American Youth Policy Forum (1995) two fundamental premises serve as a foundation for youth development in this country and have direct relevance to gang prevention:

(1) Youth development is an ongoing process in which young people are engaged and invested. Throughout this process, young people seek ways to meet their basic physical and social needs and to build competencies and connections they need for survival and success. All youth are engaged in the process of development. . . . (2) The acquisition of a broad range of competencies and the demonstration of connections to self, others, and the larger community mark youth development. Confidence, compassion, commitment and character are terms commonly used to express the attitudes and behaviors that determine whether and how learned competencies will be used. (p. 1)

Thus, it is possible to examine gang membership from a variety of perspectives that stress the importance of youth playing an active and meaningful role in their own education while concomitantly earning a living and possibly starting a career. Creating a context that promotes youth development and community development necessitates that a partnership transpire between all significant sectors in a community. This grounding in the community, in turn, maximizes the benefits derived by participants.

Program for Female Offenders, Pittsburgh, Pennsylvania

Rationale for Selection

Advocates and scholars alike have identified the importance of women prisoners maintaining contact and relationships with their children. The reunification of mothers with their children often is considered the primary factor in helping ex-offenders maintain a crime-free lifestyle. Barriers to the process are considerable, as noted in the Summit House case study and in the literature reviewed throughout this book. The importance of the subject, as a result, justifies a second case study focusing on a different part of the country (Pittsburgh) and on a different model from that covered in the Summit House case study.

The Program for Female Offenders, a nonprofit organization located primarily in Pittsburgh and Harrisburg, Pennsylvania, was selected for this book based on several considerations. First, given its focus on female offenders in their roles as mothers and their capacity to raise their children, it is an excellent example of a capacity enhancement agent. Second, it is widely recognized as an exemplary model of addressing the needs of female offenders who are mothers and wish to play an active and meaningful role in raising their children. Professor Flynn of the Northeastern Criminal Justice Program at Northeastern University notes: "I think comprehensive programming for women like that offered by the Program for Female Offenders needs to be welcomed because, essentially, what we have is a criminal justice program that concentrates on males only. . . . [The residential and parenting skills component makes up] a valuable program that provides important services" (Harris and Clines, 1997, p. 54).

In addition, this case illustrates an empowerment perspective that takes into account how women of color historically have been disempowered and oppressed. The agency setting shows how families can exist and thrive—as opposed to a harsh prison environment that serves not only to dehumanize but also to separate families. Community alternatives to incarceration are both socially and economically effective: "Incarceration in traditional facilities is expensive, costing up to $28,000 per inmate per year . . . [while the Program for Female Offenders] manages to treat the 650 women who come through [its] doors every year for less than $15,000 each" (Harris and Clines, 1997, p. 54). Effectiveness ultimately must be measured by recidivism rates. While the national recidivism rate for women can be as high as 71 percent, the Program for Female Offenders' recidivism rate is 15 percent. Finally, this agency is worthy of a case study because it addresses those who are helped the least in the criminal justice system. Women are increasingly being imprisoned and are not considered capable mothers. Resources, in turn, are not devoted to helping them carry out their maternal roles. The criminal justice system originally was established to meet the needs of men, not women—least of all, women of color. The Program for Female Offenders, as shall be addressed in further detail, was founded on the notion of helping this group because the current criminal justice system has failed to do so in a manner that is affirming and capacity enhancing.

Overview of Literature

Alternatives to prison should not be considered alternatives to punishment, as they are widely perceived. Wood and Grasmick (2000), in their Oklahoma study ranking the severity of various alternative sanctions compared with prison, found that inmates do not think of prison alternatives as more desirable and easy. They found that the uncertainty of completing the requirements of a community alternative combined with fears about how program officials and staff may carry out their responsibilities served to discourage participation. However, they also found that inmates with children were more likely to consider participating in community alternatives to prison when compared with childless inmates. It is common to hear that "when a man goes to prison, he loses his freedom, but when a woman goes to prison, she loses her children."

Women offenders, as already noted in several other case studies and other sections of this book, face incredible challenges in achieving rehabilitation and making successful reentries into the community (Bill, 1998; Jacobs, 1997). Women, when compared with their male counterparts, often have extensive histories of being abused, both in their childhood and in their adult relationships. In addition, they often face the dual challenge of raising their children and meeting all the demands associated with addiction to drugs. Their self-image, not surprisingly, suffers as a result of years of abuse and neglect. Consequently, any successful effort at helping them succeed upon release from correctional supervision, be it from prison or a community alternative to prison, requires a systematic and comprehensive approach to service delivery.

The professional literature is explicit in identifying the kinds of services and settings that are most conducive to turning women's lives around. Community alternatives to incarceration for women who are mothers must be comprehensive in nature to take into account the special needs (medical, social, financial, psychological) women present to the criminal justice system: (1) a history of having other incarcerated family members—there is a high likelihood that a sibling or other significant family member has been imprisoned; (2) a history of sexual or physical abuse; (3) a history of under- or unemployment; (4) being a custodial parent at the time of arrest or sentencing; (5) parents or close relative having custody of children while parent is in the criminal justice system; (6) pregnancy—almost 25 percent of women are either pregnant or postpartum upon entering prison; and (7) medical problems—a host of medical needs that can include drug abuse, pregnancy, HIV/AIDS, sexually transmitted diseases, and tuberculosis (Austin, Bloom, and Donahue, 1992; Bill, 1998; Diaz-Cotto, 1996; Engle, 1999; Martin, 1997; Sheridan, 1996; Smith, 1998;

Watterson, 1996). It is estimated that approximately 33 percent of women leaving prisons and jails are homeless (Engle, 1999).

Comprehensive service provision also must include advocacy. The advocacy issues and needs of women in the correctional system have increased as the result of more punitive legal sanctions against them, along with a lack of viable treatment for substance abuse and limited community alternatives to incarceration (Jacobs, 1997; Kelly and Empson, 1999). Being placed in a community alternative to prison does not end the need for advocacy. Advocacy in community alternative programs may entail a wide range of responses from writing letters to authorities of various types to representing the interests of the client in getting her children back to empowerment. Advocacy also can involve undertaking public awareness campaigns publicizing the unique needs and issues of female ex-offenders. The role of the advocate is not exclusively one to be carried out by paid program staff. Volunteers, as well, can assume roles as advocates. The criminal justice system historically has understood the importance of involving volunteers in service delivery, including carrying out advocacy roles (Connelly, 2000).

References

ACE Program. (1998). *Breaking the walls of silence: AIDS and women in a New York state maximum-security prison*. Woodstock and New York: Overlook Press.

Adam, B. D. and Sears, A. (1996). *Experiencing HIV: Personal, family, and work relationships*. New York: Columbia University Press.

AIDS in Prison Project. (1996). *Facts sheet—national, New York state, New York City*. New York: Author.

Albanese, J. S. (1999). *Criminal justice*. Boston: Allyn and Bacon.

Allen-Meares, P. and Lane, B. A. (1990). Social work practice: Integrating qualitative and quantitative data collection techniques. *Social Work, 35,* 452–58.

Altman, L. K. (1999, September 1). Much more AIDS in prisons than in general population. *New York Times,* p. A14.

Ambrosio, T. and Schiraldi, V. (1997). *Trends in state spending, 1987–1995, executive summary—February 1997*. Washington, DC: Justice Policy Institute.

American News Service. (1998, November 4). Prison program uses reading to rehabilitate. *Times Union* (Albany, NY), p. 8.

American Youth Policy Forum. (1995). *Contract with America's youth: Toward a national youth development agenda*. Washington, DC: Author.

Amnesty International. (1999). *Not part of my sentence: Violations of human rights of women in custody*. Washington, DC: Author.

Anderson, D. C. (1998a). *Sensible justice: Alternatives to prison*. New York: New Press.

———. (1998b, May 1). When should kids go to jail? *American Prospect,* pp. 72–78.

Aoki, N. (1999, June 28). State prison to be used solely for inmates who need assisted-living care. *Virginian-Pilot and Ledger Star* (Norfolk, Va.), pp. 13–14.

Arax, M. (1999a, June 1). A return to the goal of reforming inmates. *Los Angeles Times,* p. 14.

———. (1999b, June 1). Inmates use "gassing" to strike back at the system. *Los Angeles Times,* p. 12.

Archwamety, T. and Katsiyannis, A. (1998). Factors related to recidivism among delinquent females at a state correctional facility. *Journal of Child and Family Studies, 7,* 59–67.

Armistead, P. J. and Wexler, M. B. (1998). Community development and youth development. *New Designs for Youth Development, 14,* 27–33.

Associated Press. (1997, June 26). U.N. estimates drug business equal to 8 percent of world trade.

———. (1998a, June 29). Abuse of teen inmates common in Louisiana prison. *Pantagraph* (Bloomington, LA), p. 3.

———. (1998b, November 29). Women's prison helps inmates become better mothers. *Arizona Daily Star,* p. 10.

Austin, J., Bloom, B., and Donahue, T. (1992). *Female offenders in the community: An analysis of innovative strategies and programs.* San Francisco: National Council on Crime and Delinquency.

Average stay down slightly on death row. (1999, December 13). *New York Times,* p. A18.

Baird, I. C. (1997). Imprisoned bodies—free minds: Incarcerated women and liberatory learning. In *AERC Proceedings of the 1997 Conference* (pp. 1–6). Lanham, MD: Correctional Education Association.

Barstow, D. (2000, April 1). Antidrug tactics exact price on a neighborhood, many say. *New York Times,* pp. A1, A12.

Bartollas, C. and Miller, S. J. (1994). *Juvenile justice in America,* (2nd ed.). Upper Saddle River, NJ: Prentice Hall.

Bates, E. (1998, January 5). Prisons for profit. *The Nation,* pp. 11–18.

Batiuk, M. E. (1997). Liberal education and recidivism: New insights. In C. R. Eggleston (Ed.), *Yearbook of correctional education, 1995–97* (pp. 103–18). Lanham, MD: Correctional Education Association.

Beck, A. J. and Shipley, B. (1989). *Recidivism of prisoners released in 1983.* Washington, DC: U.S. Department of Justice, Bureau of Justice Statistics.

Beckerman, A. (1998). Charting a course: Meeting the challenge of permanency planning for children with incarcerated mothers. *Child Welfare, 77,* 513–29.

Belenko, S. and Peugh, J. (1998). Fighting crime by treating substance abuse. *Issues in Science and Technology, 15,* 53–61.

Benjamin, D. K. and Miller, R. L. (1991). *Undoing drugs: Beyond legalization.* New York: Basic Books.

Bernstein, N. (1999a, September 13). Back on the streets without a safety net. *New York Times,* p. A17.

———. (1999b, December 5). Seeking to label the homeless, with compassion or contempt. *New York Times* [New York Report], pp. 41, 44.

Best, J. (1999). *Random violence: How we talk about new crimes and new victims.* Berkeley: University of California Press.

Bethesda Mission. (1999). *Report on homelessness.* Harrisburg, PA: Author.

Bewley-Taylor, D. R. (1999). *The United States and international drug control, 1909–1997.* New York: Printer Press.

Bill, L. (1998). The victimization . . . and . . . revictimization of female offenders. *Corrections Today, 60,* 106–15.

Bilt, J. V., Raynovich, J., and Shaffer, H. J. (1999). *MAP evaluation*. Boston: Harvard Medical School, Division on Addictions.

Binkley-Jackson, D., Carter, V. L., and Rolison, G. L. (1993). African-American women in prison. In B. R. Fletcher, L. D. Shaver, and D. B. Moon (Eds.), *Women prisoners: A forgotten population* (pp. 65–74). Westport, CT: Praeger.

Bliss Unlimited. (1998). Bliss Unlimited. *Maxi*, p. M6.

———. (1999). *Executive summary*. Glendale, CA: Author.

Block, K. J. and Potthast, M. J. (1998). Girl scouts beyond bars: Facilitating parent-child contact in correctional settings. *Child Welfare, 77*, 561–78.

Bloom, B. (1995). Public policy and the children of incarcerated parents. In K. Gabel and D. Johnston (Eds.), *Children of incarcerated parents* (pp. 271–84). New York: Lexington Books.

Bloom, B. and Steinhardt, D. (1993). *Why punish the children? A reappraisal of 368 children of incarcerated women*. Indianapolis: National Council on Crime and Delinquency.

Blumenson, E. and Wilson, E. (1998). Policing for profit: The drug war's hidden economic agenda. *University of Chicago Law Review, 65*, 35–114.

Blumstein, A. (1995). Making rationality relevant. *Criminology, 31*, 1–16.

Bok, M. and Morales, J. (1997). The impact and implications of HIV on children and adolescents: Social justice and social change. *Journal of HIV/AIDS Prevention and Education for Adolescents, 1*, 9–34.

Boston Rescue Mission. (1997). *Who is homeless?* Boston: Author.

Boudin, K., et al. (1999). ACE: A peer education and counseling program meets the needs of incarcerated women with HIV/AIDS issues. *Journal of the Association of Nurses in AIDS Care, 10*, 90–100.

Boyd, H. (1997, March 15). Program to teach ex-prisoners how to fix buildings to live in. *New York Amsterdam News*, p. 9.

Bradsher, K. (1999, November 17). Michigan boy who killed at 11 is convicted of murder as adult. *New York Times*, pp. A1, A19.

———. (2000, January 14). Boy who killed gets 7 years; judge says law is too harsh. *New York Times*, pp. A1, A21.

Bratt, L. (1998). Rehab through reading. *HOPE, 12*, 12–13.

Broder, D. S. (1999, August 30). Real concerns about drugs. *Boston Globe*, p. A19.

Brooke, J. (1999, June 13). In "super max," terms of endurance. *New York Times*, p. 30.

Browne, M. W. (1999, September 17). Town backs prison over untarnished sky. *New York Times*, p. A20.

Brownell, P. (1998). Female offenders in the criminal justice system: Policy and program development. In A. R. Roberts (Ed.), Social work in juvenile and criminal justice settings (2nd. ed., pp. 325–49). Springfield, IL: Charles C Thomas.

Bruni, F. (1999, February 21). Crimes of the war on crime—behind police brutality: public assent. *New York Times* (Week in Review), pp. 1, 6.

Burawoy, M. (1991). The extended case method. In M. Burawoy et al. (Eds.), *Ethnography unbound: Power and resistance in the modern metropolis* (pp. 271–87). Berkeley: University of California Press.

Bureau of Justice Assistance. (1997). *Urban street gang enforcement* (NCJ 161845). Washington, DC: U.S. Government Printing Office.

———. (1998). *Addressing community gang problems: A practical guide* (NCJ 164273). Washington, DC: U.S. Government Printing Office.

Bureau of Justice Statistics. (1988). *Report to the nation on crime and justice.* Washington, DC: U.S. Government Printing Office.

———. (1993). *Sentencing in the federal courts: Does race matter? The transition to sentencing guidelines, 1986–90* (BJS Publication No. NCJ 145328). Washington, DC: U.S. Government Printing Office.

———. (1994). *Young black male victims* (BJS Publication No. NCJ 147004). Washington, DC: U.S. Government Printing Office.

———. (1996). *Sourcebook of criminal justice statistics.* Washington, DC: U.S. Government Printing Office.

———. (1997a). *Prisoners in 1996* (BJS Publication No. NCJ 164619). Washington, DC: U.S. Government Printing Office.

———. (1997b). *Sourcebook of criminal justice statistics, 1997.* Washington, DC: U.S. Government Printing Office.

———. (1998a). *A profile of female offenders.* Washington, DC: U.S. Government Printing Office.

———. (1998b). *Criminal offender statistics, 1996.* Washington, DC: U.S. Government Printing Office.

———. (1998c). *Bureau of Justice Statistics, fiscal year 1998: At a glance* (BJS Publication No. NCJ 169285). Washington, DC: U.S. Government Printing Office.

———. (1998d). *Capital punishment 1997* (BJS Publication No. NCJ 172881). Washington, DC: U.S. Government Printing Office.

———. (1998e). *Alcohol and crime* (BJS Publication No. NCJ 168632). Washington, DC: U.S. Government Printing Office.

———. (1998f). *Homicide trends in the U.S.: Age, gender and race.* Washington, DC: U.S. Government Printing Office.

———. (1999a). *Correctional populations in the United States* (BJS Publication No. NCJ 170013). Washington, DC: U.S. Government Printing Office.

———. (1999b). *Truth in sentencing in state prisons* (BJS Publication No. 170032). Washington, DC: U.S. Government Printing Office.

———. (1999c). *Prisoners in 1998* (BJS Publication No. NCJ 175687). Washington, DC: U.S. Government Printing Office.

———. (1999d). *State prison expenditures, 1996* (BJS Publication No. NCJ 172211). Washington, DC: U.S. Government Printing Office.

———. (1999e). *Probation and parole in the United States, 1998* (BJS Publication No. NCJ 178234). Washington, DC: U.S. Government Printing Office.

———. (1999f). *Time served in prison by federal offenders, 1986–97* (BJS Publication No. NCJ 171682). Washington, DC: U.S. Government Printing Office.

———. (1999g). *DWI offenders under correctional supervision* (BJS Publication No. NCJ 172212). Washington, DC: U.S. Government Printing Office.

———. (1999h). *Prison and jail inmates at midyear 1998* (BJS Publication No. NCJ 173414). Washington, DC: U.S. Government Printing Office.

———. (1999i). *Substance abuse and treatment, state and federal prisoners, 1997* (BJS Publication No. NCJ 172871). Washington, DC: U.S. Government Printing Office.

Burke, E. M. (1978). *A participatory approach to urban planning*. New York: Human Sciences Press.

Busway, S. D. (1998). The impact of an arrest on the job stability of young white American men. *Journal of Research in Crime and Delinquency, 35*, 454–79.

Butterfield, F. (1995). *All God's children: The Bosket family and the American tradition of violence*. New York: Avon Books.

———. (1997, September 28). Crime keeps on falling, but prisons keep on filling. *New York Times*, pp. 41, 44.

———. (1998, December 28). Decline of violent crime is linked to crack market. *New York Times*, p. A16.

———. (1999a, April 7). As inmate population grows, so does a focus on children. *New York Times*, pp. A1, A18.

———. (1999b, May 17). Crime fell 7 percent in '98, continuing a 7-year trend. *New York Times*, p. A12.

———. (1999c, July 12). Prisons brim with mentally ill, study finds. *New York Times*, p. A10.

———. (1999d, September 8). Police chiefs shift strategy, mounting a war of weapons. *New York Times*, pp. A1, A13.

———. (2000a, March 4). Cities reduce crime and conflict without New York–style hardball. *New York Times*, pp. A1, B17.

———. (2000b, March 16). Privately run juvenile prison in Louisiana is attacked for abuse of 6 inmates. *New York Times*, p. A14.

———. (2000c, April 26). Racial disparities seen as pervasive in juvenile justice: A snowballing effect. *New York Times*, pp. A1, A18.

Byrne, J., Lurigio, A., and Petersilia, J. (1992). *Smart sentencing: The emergence of intermediate sanctions*. Newbury Park, CA: Sage.

Camero, A. (1999, August 27). Personal correspondence.

Campbell, B. (1995, July 20). Paying the price of life inside: More and more young offenders are unable to handle being behind bars and turn to suicide as their only recourse. *Weekly Journal*, p. 2.

Carbone, D. J. (1996). Under lock and key: Living with HIV/AIDS in youth lockups. *Body Positive, 9*, 1–4.

CASA [National Center on Addiction and Substance Abuse]. (1996). *Substance abuse and urban America: Its impact on an American city, New York*. New York: Author.

———. (1998). *Behind bars: Substance abuse and America's prison population*. New York: Columbia University.

———. (1999). *No safe haven: Children of substance-abusing parents*. New York: Columbia University.

Casa, K. (1999). Prisons: The new growth industry. *National Catholic Reporter, 35*, 15.

Castle, M. N. (1991). *Alternative sentencing: Selling it to the public*. Washington, DC: National Institute of Justice.

Caulkins, J. P., Rydell, C. P., Schwabe, W. and Chies, J. R. (1997). *Mandatory minimum drug sentences: Throwing away the key or the taxpayers' money?* Santa Monica, CA: Rand Corporation.

Cavise, L. L. (1998). Prisons for profit. *The UNESCO Courier, 51*, 20–22.

Census of State and Federal Correctional Facilities, 1995. (1996). Washington, DC: Bureau of Justice Statistics.

Chaiken, M. R. (1998). *Kids, cops, and communities.* Rockville, MD: NCJRS.

Chambliss, W. J. (1999). *Power, politics, and crime.* Boulder, CO: Westview Press.

Chandler, S. M. and Kassebaum, G. (1994). Drug-alcohol dependence of women prisoners in Hawaii. *Affilia, 9,* 157–170.

Chapple, K. V., Cox, E. P., and MacDonald-Furches, J. (1997a, September/October). Summit House: Alternative to prison for mothers, better future for kids. *Community Corrections Report,* pp. 85–88.

———. (1997b). Summit House: A program to keep families together while changing women's and children's lives. In C. Blinn (Ed.), *Maternal ties: A selection of programs for female offenders* (pp. 99–112). Lanham, MD: American Correctional Association.

Chasnoff, I. J., Landress, H. J., and Barret, M. E. (1990). The prevalence of illicit-drug or alcohol use during pregnancy and discrepancies in mandatory reporting in Pinellas County, Florida. *New England Journal of Medicine, 322,* 1202–6.

Chevigny, B. G. (Ed.). (1999). *Doing time: 25 years of prison writing.* New York: Arcade.

Christianson, S. (1998). *With liberty for some: 500 years of imprisonment in America.* Boston: Northeastern University Press.

Cleaver, E. (1968). *Soul on ice.* New York: McGraw-Hill.

Cloud, J. (1999, February). A get-tough policy that failed. *Time Magazine,* pp. 12–13.

Collier's Year Book: International year book covering the year 1997. (1998). New York: Collier.

Collier's Year Book: International year book covering the year 1998. (1999). New York: Collier.

Conly, C. (1999). *The Women's Prison Association: Supporting women offenders and their families.* National Institute of Justice. Washington, DC: U.S. Government Printing Office.

Connelly, M. (2000, January 18). *Mentors and tutors: An overview of two volunteer programs in Oklahoma corrections* [On-line]. Available: http://www.doc.state.ok .us/DOCS/OCJRC95/9507b.htm.

Cunningham, G. (1998). Social work and criminal justice: Historical dimensions in practice. In A. R. Roberts (Ed.), *Social work in juvenile and criminal justice settings* (2nd. ed., pp. 295–303). Springfield, IL: Charles C Thomas.

Currie, E. (1998). *Crime and punishment in America.* New York: Henry Holt and Co.

Curtis, L. A. (1992, August). *Youth investment and community reconstruction: Street lessons on drugs and crime for the nineties.* Paper presented to the American Sociological Association, Chicago.

Curtis, R., Freidman, S. R., Neiagus, J. B., Goldstein, M., and Ildefonso, G. (1994). *Street-level drug markets: Network structure and HIV risk.* New York: National Development and Research Institutes.

Da Costa Nunez, R. (1998). Homeless families today: Our challenge tomorrow—a regional perspective. *Journal of Children and Poverty, 4,* 71–83.

Davis, N. J. (1999). *Youth crisis: Growing up in the high-risk society.* Westport, CT: Praeger.

Decker, S. H. and Van Winkle, B. (1996). *Life in the gang: Family, friends, and violence.* New York: Cambridge University Press.

De La Cuesta Arzameni, J. L. (1998). Alternatives to jail. *UNESCO Courier, 51,* 10–12.

Delancey Street Foundation. (1999a). *Program database.* San Francisco: Author.

———. (1999b). *Learning new skills.* San Francisco: Author.

De Leon, B. (1996). Career development of Hispanic adolescent girls. In B. J. R. Leadbeater and N. Way (Eds.), *Urban girls: Resisting stereotypes, creating identities* (pp. 380–98). New York: New York University Press.

Delgado, M. (1996). Puerto Rican food establishments as social service organizations: Results of an asset assessment. *Journal of Community Practice, 3,* 55–77.

———. (1999). *Social work practice in nontraditional urban settings.* New York: Oxford University Press.

———. (2000a). *Community social work practice within an urban context: The potential of a capacity enhancement perspective.* New York: Oxford University.

———. (2000b). *New arenas for community social work practice with urban youth: The use of the arts, humanities, and sports.* New York: Columbia University Press.

———. (in press). *Death at an early age and the urban scene: The case for memorial murals and community healing.* Westport, CT: Praeger.

Delgado, M. and Barton, K. (1998). Murals in Latin communities: Social indicators of community strengths. *Social Work, 43,* 346–56.

Department of the Treasury and Department of Justice. (1999). *Gun crime in the age group 18–20.* Washington, DC: U.S. Government Printing Office.

Diaz-Cotto, J. (1996). *Gender, ethnicity, and the state: Latina and Latino prison politics.* Albany: State University of New York Press.

DiMascio, W. M. (1995). *Seeking justice: Crime and punishment in America.* New York: Edna McConnell Clark Foundation.

Doan, B. (1997). Death penalty policy, statistics, and public opinion. *Focus, 12,* 1–2.

Donnelly, J. (2000a, February 21). Rhetoric, budget priorities are uneven match. *Boston Globe,* p. A9.

———. (2000b, March 22). Drug deaths reach a peak as prices fall. *Boston Globe,* pp. A1, A23.

Donnelly, J. and Chacon, R. (2000, February 21). A deadly grip: Treatment advocates are at odds with proponents of force. *Boston Globe,* pp. A1, A8–A9.

Donziger, S. R. (Ed.). (1996). *The real war on crime: The report of the national criminal justice commission.* New York: HarperCollins.

Dowdy, Z. R. (1999, August 10). US MA: The families left behind. *Boston Globe,* p. 24.

Dowling, C. G. (1997, October). Part 1: Women behind bars. *Life Magazine, 20,* 77–80.

Dowling, C. G. and Nyary, S. (1997, October 1). Part 2: When mom can't come home. *Life Magazine, 20,* 84, 87–90.

Drucker, E. (1998). Drug prohibition and public health. *Public Health Reports, 114,* 709–27.

Drug war is failing. (1998, November 25). *San Jose Mercury* [editorial], p. 15, sec. 1.

Duguid, S. (1997). The transition from prisoner to citizen: Education and recidivism.

In C. R. Eggleston (Ed.), *Yearbook of correctional education, 1995–1997. Correctional education: The transformational imperative* (pp. 35–55). Lanham, MD: Correctional Education Association.

Dyer, J. (2000). *The perpetual prisoner machine: How America profits from crime.* Boulder, CO: Westview Press.

Education Development Center. (1999). *The Moving Ahead Program curriculum.* Newton, MA: Author.

Egan, T. (1999a, March 7). Less crime, more criminals. *New York Times* [Week in Review], pp. 1, 16.

———. (1999b, September 19). A drug ran its course, then hid with its users. *New York Times,* pp. 1, 33.

———. (1999c, February 28). War on crack retreats, still taking prisoners. *New York Times,* pp. 1, 22–23.

Eisenberg, M. (1991). *Five-year outcome study: Factors associated with recidivism.* Austin: Texas Department of Criminal Justice.

Elikann, P. T. (1996). *The tough-on-crime myth.* New York: Insight Books.

———. (1999). *Superpredators: The demonization of our children by the law.* New York: Insight Books.

Elser, C. (1998, August 9). Aging behind bars: Lengthy jail terms have left Pa. with costly problem of caring for elderly inmates. *Allentown Morning Call,* pp. 18–19.

Engle, L. (1999). The rocky road home: Making the transition from prison to the community. *Body Positive, 12,* pp. 1–7.

Eno, C. (1998, January 21). Shelters crowded by ex-cons. *Daily Free Press* (Boston University), p. 1.

Experimental Gallery. (1997). We are your future too. Seattle, WA: Children's Museum of Seattle.

———. (1998). *A Changed World: Evaluation of the third year.* Seattle, WA: Experimental Gallery, Children's Museum of Seattle.

Feld, B. C. (1998). *Bad kids: Race and the transformation of the juvenile court.* New York: Oxford University Press.

Fessenden, D. and Rohde, D. (1999, August 23). Dismissed by prosecutors before reaching court, flawed arrests in New York City. *New York Times,* p. A15.

Feucht, T. E. and Keyser, A. (1999, October). Prisons can reduce drug use. *National Institute of Justice Journal,* pp. 10–15.

Finder, A. (1999, June 6). Jailed until found not guilty. *New York Times,* p. 33.

Fishman, S. H. and Alissi, A. S. (1997). Strengthening families as natural support systems for offenders. In A. R. Roberts (Ed.), *Social work in juvenile and criminal justice settings* (2nd. ed., pp. 375–85). Springfield, IL: Charles C Thomas.

Fitzgerald, E. F., D'Atri, D. A., Kasl, S. V., and Ostfeld, A. M. (1984). Health problems in a cohort of male prisoners at intake and during incarceration. *Journal of Prison and Jail Health, 4,* 61–76.

Flynn, K. (1999a, October 2). How to sue the police and win: Lawyers share trade secrets of a growth industry. *New York Times,* p. A11.

———. (1999b, November 5). Rebound in city murder rate puzzling New York officials. *New York Times,* p. A1, A29.

Fogel, C. I. and Martin, S. (1992). The mental health of incarcerated women. *Western Journal of Nursing Research, 14,* 30–47.

Ford, R. (1998, May 24). Razor's edge. *Boston Globe Magazine, 12,* 22–28.

Forero, J. (1999, December 12). Have you the right to remain silent? *New York Times* [Week in Review], p. WK3.

Forty-three women sit on death row in U.S. prisons; twelve are black. (1998, March). *Jet Magazine,* pp. 46–48.

Fox, J. (1995, May 19). Commendable kids. *Glendale News-Press,* p. 12.

———. (1998, December 1–6). Peace and love for sale. *Los Angeles Times* (Glendale/Foothills), p. 40.

Free, M. D., Jr. (1998). The impact of federal sentencing reforms on African Americans. *Journal of Black Studies, 28,* 268–86.

Freire, P. (1970). *Pedagogy of the oppressed.* New York: Seabury.

Friedman, M. (1998). There's no justice in the war on drugs. In J. A. Schaler (Ed.), *Drugs: Should we legalize, decriminalize, or deregulate?* (pp. 209–11). Amherst, NY: Prometheus Books.

Fritsch, J. (2000, March 5). Squads that tripped up walking the bad walk. *New York Times* [Week in Review], p. 6.

Gainous, F. J. (1992). *Alabama: Correctional education research.* Unpublished manuscript.

Galper, J. H. (1975). *The politics of social services.* Englewood Cliffs, NJ: Prentice Hall.

Garbarino, J. (1983). Social support networks: Rx for the helping professions. In J. K. Whittaker and J. Garbarino (Eds.), *Social support networks: Informal helping in the human services* (pp. 3–28). New York: Alpine.

Garcia, B. (in press). Health concerns of incarcerated Latinas: Special issues and practice implications. *Journal of Health and Social Policy.*

Garr, R. (1995). *Reinvesting in America.* Reading, MA: Addison-Wesley.

Gehring, T. (1997). Social maturation and the field of correctional education. In C. Eggleston (Ed.), *Yearbook of correctional education 1995–1997. Correctional education: The transformational imperative* (pp. 13–22). Lanham, MD: Correctional Education Association.

Gelman, S. R. and Pollack, D. (1997). Correctional policies: Evolving trends. In A. R. Roberts (Ed.), *Social work in juvenile and criminal justice settings* (2nd. ed., pp. 57–76). Springfield, IL: Charles C Thomas.

Gendreau, P. (1994). *What works in community corrections: Promising approaches to reduce criminal behavior.* Presentation at IARCA Research Conference, Seattle, Washington.

———. (1996). Offender rehabilitation: What we know and what needs to be done. *Criminal Justice and Behavior, 23,* 144–61.

General Accounting Office. (1998). *Law enforcement: Information on drug-related police corruption.* Washington, DC: U.S. Government Printing Office.

———. (1999). *Drug control: Narcotics threat from Colombia continues to grow.* Washington, DC: U.S. Government Printing Office.

Genty, P. M. (1998). Permanency planning in the context of parental incarceration: Legal issues and recommendations. *Child Welfare, 77,* 543–59.

Gibbs, J. Y. (1988). Young, black, and male in America: An endangered species. Dover, MA: Auburn House.

Gibelman, M. and Schervish, P. H. (1997). *Who we are: A second look.* Washington, DC: NASW Press.

Gilbert, E. (1999). Crime, sex, and justice: African American women. In S. Cook and S. Davies (Eds.), *Harsh punishment: International experiences of women's imprisonment* (pp. 230–49). Boston: Northeastern University Press.

Gilgun, J. F. (1994). A case for case studies in social work research. *Social Work, 39,* 371–80.

Gilliard, D. and Beck, A. (1998). *Prisoners in 1997.* Washington, DC: Bureau of Justice Statistics.

Girshick, L. B. (1996). *Soledad women: Wives of prisoners speak out.* Westport, CT: Praeger.

Golden, T. (1999, November 26). U.S. brushed aside Mexican role, former drug chief says. *New York Times,* p. A12.

Gorov, L. (1999, October 2). Los Angeles police keep eyes on their own. *Boston Globe,* p. A3.

Green, F. (1998, September). Prisons—media coverage; reporters and reporting—technique. *The Quill,* p. 16.

Griffin-Wiesner, J. and Hong, K. (1998–1999, Winter). A closer look at the asset categories. Part 3. *Assets,* p. 5.

Gross, J. (1989, March 1). Ex-convicts are serving blintzes instead of time. *New York Times,* p. A32.

Grossfield, S. (1999a, November 29). Kids who kill: Juveniles and the death penalty. *Boston Globe,* pp. A1, A12.

———. (1999b, November 30). Voices of 6 who await their fate. *Boston Globe,* pp. A1, A16.

Gutierrez, L. and Lewis, E. A. (1999). *Empowering women of color.* New York: Columbia University Press.

Haberman, C. (2000, January 9). Attica: Exorcising the demons, redeeming the deaths. *New York Times* [Week in Review], p. 3.

Hagan, J. and McCarthy, B. (1998). *Means streets: Youth crime and homelessness.* New York: Cambridge University Press.

Hairston, C. F. (1991). Mothers in jail: Parent-child separation and jail visitation. *Affilia, 7,* 90–108.

———. (1998a). The forgotten parent: Understanding the forces that influence incarcerated fathers' relationship with their children. *Child Welfare, 77,* 617–39.

———. (1998b). Foreword to the second edition. In A. R. Roberts (Ed.), *Social work in juvenile and criminal justice settings* (2nd ed., pp. ix–xi). Springfield, IL: Charles C Thomas.

Halstead, S. (1997). Growing up—getting out—staying real: A search for indicators of social maturity. In C. Eggleston (Ed.), *Yearbook of correctional education, 1995–1997. Correctional education: The transformational imperative* (pp. 23–34). Lanham, MD: Correctional Education Association.

Haney, C. and Zimbardo, P. (1998). The past and future of U.S. prison policy: Twenty-five years after the Stanford prison experiment. *American Psychologist, 53,* 1–18.

Hardcastle, D. A, Wenocur, S., and Powers, P. R. (1998). *Community practice: Theories and skills for social workers.* New York: Oxford University Press.

Harer, M. D. (1994). *Recidivism among federal prison releases in 1987: A preliminary report.* Washington, DC: Department of Justice, Bureau of Justice Statistics.

Harlow, C. W. (1991). *Drugs and jail inmates, 1989.* Washington, DC: Bureau of Justice Statistics Special Report.

Harm, N. J. (1992). Social policy on women prisoners: A historical analysis. *Affilia, 6,* 9–27.

Harris, J. (1995). Foreword. In K. Gabel and D. Johnston (Eds.), *Children of incarcerated parents* (pp. vii–viii). New York: Lexington Books.

Harris, M. and Clines, F. X. (1997). When mothers do time. *Hope, 10,* 52–59.

Heath, D. B. (1998). The war on drugs as a metaphor in American culture. In J. A. Schaler (Ed.), *Drugs: Should we legalize, decriminalize, or deregulate?* (pp. 135–54). Amherst, NY: Prometheus Books.

Heilbroner, D. (1994, December 11). The law goes on a treasure hunt. *New York Times,* p. 70.

Helms, A. D. (1995, July 21). Sentenced to a second chance. *Charlotte Observer,* pp. 1E–2E.

Holloway, J. and Moke, P. (1986). *Post secondary correctional education: An evaluation of parolee performance.* Wilmington, OH: Wilmington College.

Holmes, K. A. (1996). Headed for the future: Families in the twenty-first century. In P. R. Raffoul and C. A. McNeece (Eds.), *Future issues for social work practice* (pp. 172–79). Boston: Allyn and Bacon.

Homeless in America: A statistical profile. (1999, December 12). *New York Times,* p. WK3

Horatio Alger Association. (1998–1999). *The state of our nation's youth.* Alexandria, VA: Author.

Hostetter, E. C. and Jinnah, D. T. (1993). *Research summary: Families of adult prisoners.* Washington, DC: Prison Fellowship Ministries.

Huffaker, D. (1999a, May 6). Teens to seek end to violence. *Glendale Daily News,* p. 3.

———. (1999b, May 9). School puts on youth conference. *Glendale Daily News,* p. 22.

Huie, V. A. (1992, April). Mom's in prison: Where are the kids? *The Progressive, 56,* pp. 22–23.

Hunt, G., Riegel, S., Morales, T., and Waldorf, D. (1992). Changes in prison culture: Prison gangs and the case of the "Pepsi generation." *Social Relations, 40,* 398–409.

Iglehart, A. P. and Becerra, R. M. (1995). *Social services and the ethnic community.* Boston: Allyn and Bacon.

Immergut, D. J. (1997). Imagined families: Women behind bars. *Tikkun, 12,* 29.

Inciardi, J., Pottieger, D., and Lockwood, A. (1993). *Women and crack cocaine.* New York: Macmillan.

Ingram-Fogel, C. (1991). Health problems and needs of incarcerated women. *Journal of Prison and Jail Health, 10,* 43–57.

———. (1993). Hard time: The stressful nature of incarceration for women. *Journal of Prison and Jail Health, 12,* 10–19.

Innes, S. (1996, June 15). At juvie prison, Father's Day is a sad reminder many of these teens didn't have a male role model. And many of them already are fathers. *Tucson Citizen*, p. 1A.

In the criminal injustice system. (1996). *Women's Review of Books, 14,* 19–20.

Irwin, J., Schiraldi, V., and Ziedenberg, J. (1999). *America's one million nonviolent prisoners.* Washington, DC: Justice Policy Institute.

Jacobs, A. (1997). More than halfway. *Women's Review of Books, 14,* 44–45.

Jankowski, M. S. (1991). *Islands in the street: Gangs and American union society.* Berkeley: University of California Press.

Janofsky, M. (1998). Some midsize cities miss trend as drug deals and killings soar. *New York Times,* pp. A1, A16.

———. (1999, August 22). A governor who once dabbled in drugs says war on them is misguided. *New York Times,* pp. 16.

Johansson, L. (1998). Invisible chains: Sweden's electronic tagging project. *UNESCO Courier, 51,* 13–14.

Johnson, D. (2000, February 1). Illinois, citing faulty verdicts, bars execution. *New York Times,* p. A1, A16.

Johnson, E. (1996). The paradox of Japanese women's rising imprisonment rate. *Journal of Offender Rehabilitation, 24,* 61–87.

Johnson, H. W. (1998). Rural and urban criminal justice. In A. R. Roberts (Ed.), *Social work in juvenile and criminal justice settings* (2nd ed., pp.77–101). Springfield, IL: Charles C Thomas.

Johnson, T., Selber, K., and Lauderdale, M. (1998). Developing quality services for offenders and families: An innovative partnership. *Child Welfare, 77,* 595–615.

Johnston, D. (1995a). The care and placement of prisoners' children. In K. Gabel and D. Johnston (Eds.), *Children of incarcerated parents* (pp. 103–23). New York: Lexington Books.

———. (1995b). Parent-child visitation in the jail or prison. In K. Gabel and D. Johnston (Eds.), *Children of incarcerated parents* (pp. 135–43). New York: Lexington Books.

———. (1999, August 29). It may not feel true, but gunshot deaths are down. *New York Times* [Week in Review], p. 5.

Jordon, B. K., Schlenger, W. E., Fairbank, J. A., and Caddell, J. M. (1996). Prevalence of psychiatric disorders among incarcerated women. Archives of 390. *General Psychiatry, 53,* 513–19.

Kahn, R. (1999, January 22). Many from state facilities fill shelters, study finds. *Boston Globe,* p. E17.

Kaplan, E. (1998, November). Organizing inside. *POZ,* p. 1–10.

Kassebaum, P. A. (1999). *Substance abuse treatment for women offenders* (Technical Assistance Publication Series 23). Rockville, MD: U.S. Department of Health and Human Services.

Katz, P. C. (1998). Supporting families and children of mothers in jail: An integrated child welfare and criminal justice strategy. *Child Welfare, 77,* 495–511.

Kellogg Foundation. (1996). *Safe passages through adolescence: Communities protecting the heath and hopes of youth.* Battle Creek, MI.: Author.

Kelly, K. and Empson, G. (1999). *Advocating for women in the criminal justice and addiction treatment systems* (Advocacy Paper No. 13). Washington, DC: American Counseling Association.

Kilborn, P. T. (1999, December 5). Gimme shelter: Same song, new tune. *New York Times* [Week in Review], p. 5.

Kraska, P. and Kappeler, V. (1997). Militarizing American police: The rise and normalization of paramilitary units. *Social Problems, 44,* 14–29.

Kresnak, J. (1998). Sweating it out in Uncle Sam's bug house. *Youth Today, 7,* 1, 48–50.

———. (1999). Modern youth jails grow as youth advocates try to thin the crowd. *Youth Today, 8,* 28–29.

Kreuger, L. W. (1997). The end of social work. *Journal of Social Work Education, 33,* 19–27.

Kupers, T. (1999). *Prison madness.* San Francisco: Jossey-Bass.

Lakes, R. D. (1996). *Youth development and critical education.* Albany: State University of New York Press.

Lambert, E. Y. and Caces, M. F. (1995). Correlates of drug abuse among homeless and transient people in the Washington, DC, metropolitan area in 1991. *Public Health Reports, 110,* 455–54

Larivee, J. J. (1999, December 4). Helping prisoners after their release. *Boston Globe,* p. A19.

Latour, F. (1999, October 29). FBI probing abuse of inmates. *Boston Globe,* p. B8.

Leadbeater, B. J. R. and Way, N. (1996). Career development. In B. J. R. Leadbeater and N. Way (Eds.), *Urban girls: Resisting stereotypes, creating identities* (pp. 353–54). New York: New York University Press.

Lee, J. A. B. (1994). *The empowerment approach to social work practice.* New York: Columbia University Press.

Leigh, J. W. (1998). *Communicating cultural differences.* Needham Heights, MA: Allyn and Bacon.

Leonhardt, D. (2000, March 19). As prison labor grows, so does the debate. *New York Times,* pp. 1, 22.

Levy, D. (1997). Viewpoint—alternative to jail: Hope for incarcerated PWAs. *Body Positive, 11,* 14–15.

Lewin, T. (2000, February 3). Racial discrepancy found in trying of youth. *New York Times,* p. A14.

Lewis, D. E. (1999, September 26). The rise of prison inc. *Boston Globe,* pp. G1, G4.

Lichtblau, E. (1999, December 6). "Deep trouble" seen amid plenty. *Boston Globe,* p. A7.

Light, K. and Donovan, S. (1997). *Texas death row.* Biloxi: University of Mississippi Press.

Lightner, D. L. (Ed.). (1999). *Asylum, prison, and poorhouse: The writings and reform work of Dorothea Dix in Illinois.* Carbondale: Southern Illinois University Press.

Lille-Blanton, M. (1998). *Studies show treatment is effective, but benefits may be overstated* (GAO/T-HEHS-98-185). Washington, DC: U.S. Government Printing Office.

Lipton, D. (1995). *The effectiveness of treatment for drug abusers under criminal justice supervision* (U.S. Department of Justice Publication No. NCJ 157642). Washington, DC: U.S. Government Printing Office.

Long, L. D. and Ankrah, E. M. (Eds.). (1997). *Women's experiences with HIV/AIDS: An international experience*. New York: Columbia University Press.

Longres, J. F. (1996). Radical social work: Is there a future. In P. R. Raffoul and C. A. McNeece (Eds.), *Future issues for social work practice* (pp. 229–39). Boston: Allyn and Bacon.

Loury, G. (1996, January 1). The impossible dilemma between black crime and judicial racism. *New Republic*, pp. 21–25.

Lovinger, C. (1999, August 22). Death row's living alumni. *New York Times* [Week in Review], pp. 1, 4.

Lynch, R. S. and Mitchell, J. (1995). Justice system advocacy: A must for NASW and the social work community. *Social Work, 40*, 9–12.

MacDougall, D. S. (1998, April). HIV/AIDS behind bars. *Journal of the International Association of Physicians in AIDS Care*, pp. 20–35.

MacLeod, C. (1999). Rehabilitation. *The Cell Door, 1*, 12–13.

MADD [Mothers Against Drunk Driving]. (1999, July 12). *Justice department and MADD announce expanded battle against underage drinking in America*. Irving, TX: Author.

Maguire, K. and Pastrone, A. L. (Eds.). (1997). *Sourcebook of criminal justice statistics, 1996*. Washington, DC: U.S. Government Printing Office.

Malcom X and Haley, A. (1951). *The autobiography of Malcom X*. New York: Random House.

Maldonado, M. (1999). State of emergency: HIV/AIDS among African Americans. *Body Positive, 12*, pp. 1–8.

Males, M. A. (1999). *Framing youth: 10 myths about the next generation*. Monroe, ME: Common Courage Press.

Margolin, L. (1997). *Under the cover of kindness: The invention of social work*. Charlottesville: University Press of Virginia.

Martin, M. (1997). Connected mothers: A follow-up study of incarcerated women and their children. *Women and Criminal Justice, 8*, 1–23.

Martinez-Brawley, E. E. (1990). *Perspectives on the small community: Humanistic views for the practitioner*. Washington, DC: NASW Press.

MATCH/PATCH. (1999). *Program description*. San Antonio, TX: Author.

Matthews, R. (1999). *Doing time: An introduction to the sociology of imprisonment*. London: Macmillan.

Mauer, M. (1999). *Race to incarcerate: The sentencing project*. New York: New Press.

Mauer, M., Potler, C. and Wolf, R. (1998). *Gender and justice: Women, drugs and sentencing policy*. Washington, D.C.: The Sentencing Project

Maull, F. W. (1998). Issues in prison hospice: Toward a model for the delivery of hospice care in a correctional setting. *Hospice Journal, 12*, 57–82.

May, T. and Vass, A. A. (Eds.). (1996). *Working with offenders: Issues, contexts, and outcomes*. Thousand Oaks, CA: Sage.

McKnight, J. L. and Kretzmann, J. (1990). *Mapping community capacity*. Evanston, IL: Center for Urban Affairs and Policy Research, Northwestern University.

McLoyd, V. C. and Hernandez Jozefowiez, D. M. (1996). Sizing up the future: Predictors of African American females' expectancies about their economic fortunes and family life courses. In B. J. R. Leadbeater and N. Way (Eds.), *Urban girls: Resisting stereotypes, creating identities* (pp. 355–79). New York: New York University Press.

McNeece, C. A. (1997). Juvenile justice policy: Current trends and twenty-first century issues. In A. R. Roberts (Ed.), *Social work in juvenile and criminal justice settings* (2nd. ed., pp. 34–56). Springfield, IL: Charles C Thomas.

McPherson, R. B. and Santos, M. G. (1997). Transcending the wall: The professor as mentor and the prisoner as student. In C. R. Eggleston (Ed.), *Yearbook of correctional education, 1995–1997* (pp. 119–34). Lanham, MD: Correctional Education Association.

McQuaide, S. and Ehrenreich, J. H. (1998). Women in prison: Approaches to understanding the lives of a forgotten population. *Affilia: Journal of Women and Social Work, 13,* 233–46.

Meierhoefer, B. S. (1992). *The general effect of mandatory minimum prison terms: A longitudinal study of federal sentences imposed.* Washington, DC: Federal Justice Center.

Mieckowki, T. (1990). Crack distribution in Detroit. *Contemporary Drug Problems, 17,* 9–30.

Miller, J. G. (1992). *Hobbling a generation: Young African-American males in the criminal justice system of America's cities: Baltimore, Maryland.* Alexandria, VA: National Center on Institutions and Alternatives.

Minkler, M. and Roe, M. (1993). *Grandmothers as caregivers: Raising children of the crack cocaine epidemic.* Thousand Oaks, CA: Sage Publications.

Molotsky, I. (1999, June 14). U.S. cites drop in arrests for drunken driving. *New York Times,* p. A14.

Moneymaker, J. M. and Strimple, E. O. (1991). Animals and inmates: A sharing companionship behind bars. *Journal of Offender Rehabilitation, 16,* 133–52.

Moon, D. G., Thompson, R. J., and Bennett, R. (1993). Patterns of substance use among women in prison. In B. R. Fletcher, L. D. Shaver, and D. C. Moon (Eds.), *Women prisoners: A forgotten population* (pp. 45–54). Westport, CT: Praeger.

Moore, J., Garcia, R., Garcia, C., Cerda, L., and Valencia, F. (1978). *Homeboys: Gangs, drugs, and prison in the barrios of Los Angeles.* Philadelphia: Temple University Press.

Moore, M. H. (1999). Security and community development. In R. F. Ferguson and W. T. Dickens (Eds.), *Urban problems and community development* (pp. 293–337). Washington, DC: Brookings Institution Press.

Moreno, C. M., Garrido, V. and Esteban, C. (1997). Developing prosocial thinking in offenders. In C. R. Eggleston (Ed.), *Yearbook of correctional education, 1995–1997* (pp. 57–71). Lanham, MD: Correctional Education Association.

Morton, J. B. (1995). The "agency of women"—women and ACA (American Correctional Association). *Corrections Today, 57,* 74–84.

Moses, M. (1995). Girl scouts beyond bars: A synergistic solution for children of incarcerated parents. *Corrections Today, 57,* 124–29.

M. S. Eisenhower Foundation. (1999). *To establish justice, to insure domestic tranquility: A thirty-year update of the National Commission on the Causes and Prevention of Violence.* Washington, DC: Author.

Munger, M. (1997, Summer). The drug threat: Getting priorities straight. *Parameters,* pp. 1–3.

Murdock, S. H. and Michael, M. (1996). Future demographic change: The demand for social welfare services in the twenty-first century. In P. R. Raffoul and C. A. McNeece (Eds.), *Future issues for social work practice* (pp. 3–18). Boston: Allyn and Bacon.

Murray, F. L. (1998, June 16). Court requires prisons to obey disabilities law. *Washington Times*, p. 5.

National Coalition of Hispanic Health and Human Service Organizations. (1998). *HIV/AIDS: The impact on minorities*. Washington, DC: Author.

National Collaboration for Youth. (1998). *Positions for youth: Public policy statements of the National Collaboration for Youth, 1998*. Washington, DC: Author.

National Prison Project. (1996). *Sexual abuse of women prisoners*. Washington, DC: American Civil Liberties Union.

National Rifle Association. (1997). *Crimestrike, stopping the fraud: Truth in sentencing*. Washington, DC: Author.

National Women's Law Center. (1995). *Women in Prison*. Washington, DC: Author.

Neuspiel, D. R. (1996). Racism and perinatal addiction. *Ethnicity and Disease, 6*, 47–55.

News from death row. (1990, June). *The Progressive*, p. 12.

New York Department of Correctional Services. (1986). *Hispanic inmate needs task force final report*. Albany, NY: Author.

Nieves, E. (2000, March 6). California proposal toughens penalties for young criminals. *New York Times*, pp. A1, A15.

Norman, J. A. (1995). Children of prisoners in foster care. In K. Gabel and D. Johnston (Eds.), *Children of incarcerated parents* (pp. 124–34). New York: Lexington Books.

November Coalition. (1999). *More about the November Coalition*. Colville, WA: Author.

Office of Juvenile Justice and Delinquency Prevention. (1996). *Juvenile offenders and victims: 1996 update on violence*. Washington, DC: Author.

Office of the Press Secretary. (1999, June 9). *Fairness in law enforcement: Collection of data*. Washington, DC: White House.

Officials ban gun shows on Los Angeles county sites. (1999, September 12). *New York Times*, p. 19.

Ogawa, B. K. (1999). *Color of justice: Culturally sensitive treatment of minority victims* (2nd ed.). Boston: Allyn and Bacon.

O'Leary, K. (1999, December 3). Flying ace: Francine Rodriguez reaches for the sky [On-line]. Available: http://www.aids memorial.com/poz/profiles/11_98rrodri-guez.html

ONDCP [Office of National Drug Control Policy]. (1998). *Drug treatment in the criminal justice system, August 1998*. Washington, DC: Author.

———. (1999). *National drug control strategy, 1999*. Washington, DC: Author.

O'Shea, K. A. (1993). Women on death row. In B. R. Fletcher, L. D. Shaver, and D. C. Moon (Eds.), *Women prisoners: A forgotten population* (pp. 75–89). Westport, CT: Praeger.

Osterman, P. (1995). Apprenticeship programs for the American youth market. In S. Halpern et al. (Eds.), *Contract with America's youth: Toward a youth development agenda* (pp. 48–59). Washington, DC: American Youth Policy Forum.

Padilla, F. M. (1993). *The gang as an American enterprise*. New Brunswick, NJ: Rutgers University Press.

Palmer, L. D. (1999, March 2). Number of blacks in prison nears 1 million. "We're incarcerating an entire generation of people." *Seattle Post-Intelligencer*, p. 32.

Parenti, C. (1996, July). Life in prison: Pay now, pay later, states impose prison peonage. *The Progressive, 60,* 26–29.

———. (1999). *Lockdown America: Police and prisons in the age of crisis*. New York: Verso.

Partee, G. (1996). *Youth work, youth development, and the transition from schooling to employment in England*. Washington, DC: American Youth Policy Forum.

Patton, M. Q. (1987). *How to use qualitative methods in evaluation*. Newbury Park, CA: Sage.

Paul, W. G. (1999). *America on the threshold of setting shameful record*. Washington, DC: American Bar Association Juvenile Justice Center.

Pear, R. (1999, June 6). As welfare rolls shrink, cities shoulder bigger load. *New York Times*, p. 22.

Pennington, H. (1995). Learning and doing: A new vision. In S. Halpern et al. (Eds.), *Contract with America's youth: Toward a youth development agenda* (pp. 33–34). Washington, DC: American Youth Policy Forum.

Peters, T. (1998). From revenge to reparation. *UNESCO Courier, 51,* 15–19.

Phillips, S. A. (1999). *Wallbangin': Graffiti and gangs in L.A.* Chicago: University of Chicago Press.

Phillis, S. and Bloom, B. (1998). In whose best interest? The impact of changing public policy on relatives caring for children with incarcerated parents. *Child Welfare, 77,* 531–41.

Poole, D. (1997). Building community capacity to promote social and public health: Challenges for universities. *Heath and Social Work, 22,* 163–70.

Pozatek, E. (1994). The problem of certainty: Clinical social work in the postmodern era. *Social Work, 39,* 396–403.

Price, H. (1996, April 3). The taxpayer's stake in youth crime prevention. *Washington Informer*, p. 12.

Priestley, P., McGuire, J., Flegg, D., Hemseley, V., Welham, D., and Barnitt, R. (1992). *Social skills in prison and the community: Problem solving for offenders*. London: Routledge and Kegan Paul.

Program for Female Offenders. (1998–1999). *The program year end report*. Pittsburgh: Author.

———. (n.d.-a). *Dedicated to rebuilding lives brochure*. Pittsburgh: Author.

———. (n.d.-b). *The Program News* [newsletter]. Pittsburgh: Author.

———. (n.d.-c). *Woodside Family Center guidebook*. Pittsburgh: Author.

Pugh, T. (1998, September 14). Safety and privacy concerns class as HIV spreads in prisons. *Philadelphia Inquirer*, p. 16.

Purdum, T. S. (1999, September 18). Former Los Angeles officer sets off corruption scandal. *New York Times*, p. A7.

Purdy, M. (1995a, July 2). Bars don't stop flow of drugs into the prison. *New York Times*, p. 1, 28–29.

———. (1995b). At Rikers, guards watch for weapons but shrug at drugs. *New York Times*, p. 28.

Ranalli, R. (1999, September 26). Crack sentence debate reopened: Proof whites, blacks treated equally asked. *Boston Globe*, pp. B1, B4.

Reeser, L. (1996). The future of professionalism and activism in social work. In P. Raffoul and C. A. McNeece (Eds.), *Future issues for social work practice* (pp. 240–53). Boston: Allyn and Bacon.

Reibstein, L. (1997, August 25). Lessons from the big house. *Newsweek*, p. 64.

Rigert, J. (1997a, December 14). Drug sentences often stacked against women. *Minneapolis–St. Paul Star Tribune*, pp. 10–12.

———. (1997b, December 15). The problem with life without mom. *Minneapolis–St. Paul Star Tribune*, pp. 22–24.

Rimer, S. (2000, March 1). Questions of death row justice for poor people in Alabama. *New York Times*, pp. A1, A16

Rivero, E. (1997, December 8). Minding their own business: At-risk teens shine by setting up own shop at Glendale Galleria. *Glendale Daily News*, pp. 1, 3.

Roberts, A. (Ed.). (1998). *Social work in juvenile and criminal justice settings* (2nd ed.). Springfield, IL: Charles C Thomas.

Roberts, A. R. and Brownell, P. (1999). A century of forensic social work: Bridging the past to the present. *Social Work, 44,* 359–69.

Roberts, P. (1995, September 29). Outside the prison walls: The families left behind. *Philadelphia Tribune*, p. 17.

Robertson, T. (1997, December 16). Minnesota judge offers woman second chance. *Minneapolis–St. Paul Star Tribune*, pp. 16–17.

Robinson-Jacobs, K. (1999, May 9). Teens gather to give peace a chance. *Los Angeles Times*, pp. B1, B5.

Rodarmor, W. (1990, December). A conversation with Mimi Silbert. *California Monthly*, pp. 16–20.

Rohde, D. (2000, January 16). Men in wheelchairs scarred by crack war. *New York Times* [New York Report], pp. 23, 24.

Rook, A. (1998). At-risk youth art programs come up tall. *Youth Today, 7,* 14–17.

Rook, A. and Alexander, B. (1999). Senate passes juvenile crime bill, and it's loaded. *Youth Today, 8,* 37–38.

Rosenthal, M. S. (1998). *Treatment and criminal justice. Consensus meeting on drug treatment in the criminal justice system, March 23–25, 1998.* Washington, DC: Office of National Drug Control Policy.

Rossi, P. H. and Berk, R. A. (1997). *Just punishments: Federal guidelines and public views compared.* Hawthorne, NY: Aldine de Gruyter.

Rothman, J. (1974). *Planning and organizing for social change.* New York: Columbia University Press.

Rydell, C. P. and Everingham, S. S. (1994). *Controlling cocaine* (Prepared for the Office of National Drug Control Policy and the United States Army). Santa Monica, CA: Rand Corporation.

Saleebey, D. S. (Ed.). (1992). *The strengths perspective in social work practice.* New York: Longman.

Sales, G. (1976). *John Maher of Delancey Street.* New York: Norton.

Sametz, L. (1980). Children of incarcerated women. *Social Work, 25,* 298–303.

Sasson, T. (1995). *Crime talk: How citizens construct a social problem.* Hawthorne, NY: Aldine de Gruyter.

Scales, P. C. and Leffert, N. (1999). *Developmental assets: A synthesis of the scientific research on adolescent development.* Minneapolis: Search Institute.

Schaafsma, D. (1995). *Eating on the street: Teaching literacy in a multicultural society.* Pittsburgh: University of Pittsburgh Press.

Schichor, D. (1995). *Punishment for profit: Private prisons/public concerns.* Thousand Oaks, CA: Sage.

Schittroth, L. (Ed.). (1991). *Statistical record of women worldwide.* Detroit: Gale Research.

Schlosser, E. (1998, December). The prison-industrial complex. *Atlantic Monthly,* pp. 51–77.

Schmid, R. E. (1999, August 23). Parole, probation numbers top 4 million. *Boston Globe,* p. A8.

Schneider, A. and Flaherty, M. P. (1991, August 11). Presumed guilty: The law's victims in the war on drugs. *Pittsburgh Press,* p. 11.

Sells, S. P., Smith, T. E., and Newfield, N. (1997). Teaching ethnographic research methods in social work: A model course. *Journal of Social Work Education, 33,* 167–84.

Semmens, B. (1997). Correctional education for democratic citizenship. In C. Eggleston (Ed.), *Yearbook of correctional education, 1995–1997. Correctional education: The transformational imperative* (pp. 73–87). Lanham, MD: Correctional Education Association.

Sengupta, S. (2000a, April 16). Detention of juveniles is increasing. *New York Times,* pp. 29, 30.

———. (2000b, November 3). Felony costs voting rights for a lifetime in 9 states. *New York Times,* p. A18.

The Sentencing Project. (1998a). *Factsheet: Prisons and prisoners.* Washington, D.C.: Author.

The Sentencing Project. (1998b). *Proposed changes in crack/cocaine sentencing laws would increase number of minorities in prison, have little impact on drug abuse.* Washington, D.C.: Author.

Seymour, C. (1998). Children with parents in prison: Child welfare policy, program, and practice issues. *Child Welfare, 77,* 469–93.

Sharpe, K. and Bertram, E. (1997, February 23). Drug war inflates the price of hypocrisy. *Boston Globe,* p. E2.

Sheley, J. F. and Wright, J. D. (1995). *In the line of fire: Youth, guns, and violence in urban America.* New York: Aldine de Gruyter.

Sheldon, R. G., Tracy, S. K., and Brown, W. B. (1997). *Youth gangs in American society.* Belmont, CA: Wadsworth.

Sheridan, M. J. (1996). Comparison of the life experiences and personal functioning of men and women in prison. *Families in Society: Journal of Contemporary Human Services, 77,* 423–34.

Shilling, R., El-Bassel, N., Ivanoff, A., Gilbert, L., Su, K., and Safyer, S. M. (1994). Sexual risk behavior of incarcerated, drug-using women, 1992. *Public Health Reports, 109,* 539–47.

Shilstone, R. (1998). A friend indeed: The Prison Pet Partnership Program. *Orion, 17,* 52–57.

Shine, C. and Mauer, M. (1993). *Does punishment fit the crime? Drug users and drunk drivers, questions of race and class.* Washington, DC: Sentencing Project.

Sickmund, M., Stahl, A. L., Finnegan, T. A., Snyder, H. N., Poole, R. S., and Butts, J. A. (1998). *Juvenile court statistics, 1995.* Washington, DC: Department of Justice, Office of Juvenile Justice and Delinquency Prevention.

Siegel, G. (1997). A research study to determine the effect of literacy and general education development programs on adult offenders on probation. In C. R. Eggleston (Ed.), *Yearbook of correctional education, 1995–1997* (pp. 89–102). Lanham, MD: Correctional Education Association.

Silverman, S. (1999, October 31). Former inmates rebuild their lives. *Pantagraph* (Bloomington, IL), p. 9.

Simon, B. L. (1994). *The empowerment tradition in American social work.* New York: Columbia University Press.

Singer, M. I., Bussey, J., Song, L. Y., and Lunghofer, L. (1995). The psychosocial issues of women serving time in jail. *Social Work, 40,* 103–13.

Singer, S. I. (1996). *Recriminalizing delinquency: Violent crime and juvenile justice reform.* New York: Cambridge University Press.

Sisson, P. L. (1979). *The Hispanic experience of criminal justice.* New York: Fordham University Hispanic Research Center.

Smith, B. V. (1998). *Special needs of women in the criminal justice system.* Rockville, MD: Center for Substance Abuse Treatment.

Smith, T. J. and Jucovy, K. (1996). *Americorps in the field: Implementation of the National and Community Trust Act in nine states.* Washington, DC: American Youth Policy Program.

Solomon, B. B. (1976). *Black empowerment: Social work in oppressed communities.* New York: Columbia University Press.

Specht, H. and Courtney, M. E. (1994). *Unfaithful angels: How social work abandoned its mission.* New York: Free Press.

Spradley, J. P. (1979). *The enthnographic interview.* New York: Holt, Rinehart and Winston.

Stake, R. E. (1995). *The art of case study research.* Thousand Oaks, CA: Sage.

Staples, B. (1999, May 10). Why some get busted—and some go free. *New York Times* [editorial], p. A34.

Staples, L. (Ed.). (1984). *Roots to power: A manual for grassroots organizing.* New York: Praeger Press.

Stein, R. (1996, March 1). Mimi Silbert stays tough for Delancey. *San Francisco Chronicle,* pp. 11–12.

Steinberg, J. (1999, January 3). The coming crime wave is washed up. *New York Times,* p. 4.

Steinman, J. (1997, December 28). Minding the store. *Los Angeles Times,* p. B6.

Steurer, S. J. (1991). Inmates helping inmates: Maryland's peer tutoring reading academies. In S. Duguid (Ed.), *Yearbook of correctional education, 1991* (pp. 133–39). Laurel, MD: Correctional Education Association.

St. Francis House. (1998). *Mission statement.* Boston: Author, pp. 1–2.

Stodghill II, R. (1999, February 1). Unequal justice: Why women fare worse. *Time Magazine,* pp. 19–20.

Stodghill, R. and Anderson, I. (1999). Unequal justice: Why women fare worse. *Law,* *153,* 1–2.

Streib, V. L. (1999). The juvenile death penalty today: Death sentences and executions for juvenile crimes, January 1973–June 1999 [On-line]. Available: http://www.law.onu.edu/faculty/streib/juvdeath.htm

Strimple, E. O. (1995). *How it all began—the historical perspective.* Paper presented at the Seventh International Conference on Human-Animal Interactions, Geneva, Switzerland.

———. (1998). *Animals as teachers: From prisons to "kids-at-risk."* Paper presented at the Fourth International Congress on the Benefits of Companion Animals, Barcelona, Spain.

Sullivan, J. (1999, November 30). Albany makes top dollar from collect calls by prison inmates. *New York Times,* p. A20.

———. (2000, January 30). States and cities removing prisons from courts' grip. *New York Times,* pp. 1, 26.

Sum, A., Mangum, S., De Jesus, E., Walker, G., Gruber, D., Pines, M., and Pring, W. (Eds.). (1997). *A generation of challenges: Pathways to success for urban youth.* Baltimore: Johns Hopkins University Institute for Policy Studies.

Summit House. (1998). *Annual report, 1997–1998.* Charlotte, NC: Author.

Sweet, L. J. (1999, September 29). Inmates give a little back to community by training guide dogs. *Boston Herald,* p. 21.

Synder, H. N. and Sickmund, M. (1995). *Juvenile offenders and victims: A focus on violence—statistics summary.* Washington, DC: Office of Juvenile Justice and Delinquency Prevention.

Tanaka, R. (1998, April 6). Search for peace. *Glendale News-Press,* p. A3.

———. (1999, May 8–9). Peace is the word. *Glendale Daily News,* p. 12.

Tarcy, B. (1999, June 27). Program gives officials, inmates a little breathing room. *The Boston Globe,* 1.

Taxman, F. S. (1998). *Reducing recidivism through a seamless system of care: Components of effective treatment, supervision, and transition services in the community.* Washington, DC: Office of National Drug Control Policy.

Taylor, C. S. (1996, January). *Growing up behind bars: Confinement, youth development, and crime.* Paper presented at a conference organized by the Vera Institute of Justice, New York.

Tenneson, M. (1999). Editorial. *The Cell Door,* 1, 8–9.

Terrell, N. E. (1998). A means for re-integrating African Americans convicted of nonviolent crimes. *Journal of Offender Rehabilitation, 27,* 25–35.

Thomas, P. (1997, January 30). Study suggests black male prison rate impinges on political process. *Washington Post,* A3.

Thompson, C. W. (1997, August 26). Young blacks entangled in legal system. *Washington Post,* p. B01.

Thompson, P. J. and Harm, N. J. (1995). Parent education for mothers in prison. *Psychiatric Nursing, 21,* 552–55.

Tonry, M. (1995). *Malign neglect—race, crime, and punishment in America.* New York: Oxford University Press.

Towney, R. D. (1981). The incarceration of black men. In L. E. Gary (Ed.), *Black men* (pp. 229–56). Beverly Hills, CA: Sage.

Trattner, W. (1994). *From poor law to welfare state: A history of social welfare in America.* New York: Free Press.

Treatment, not jail, for addicts over arrest. (1998, November 23). *Chicago Tribune* [editorial], p. 25.

Trolander, J. A. (1988). *Professionalism and social change: From the settlement house movement to neighborhood centers.* New York: Columbia University Press.

Trouble in Virginia's juvenile prisons. (1999, October 15). *Roanoke Times and World News,* p. 13.

Twaddle, A. C. (1976). Utilization of medical services by a captive population: An analysis of sick call in a state prison. *Journal of Health and Social Behavior, 17,* 236–48.

U.S. Department of Justice. (1993). *Survey of state prison inmates, 1991* (Report No. NCJ-136949). Washington, DC: Bureau of Justice Statistics.

———. (1994). *An analysis of non-violent drug offenders with minimal criminal histories.* Washington, DC: U.S. Government Printing Office.

U.S. General Accounting Office. (1995). *Juveniles processed in criminal courts and case dispositions* (GAO/GGD-95-170). Washington, DC: U.S. Government Printing Office.

U.S. Sentencing Commission. (1995). *Special report to Congress: Cocaine and federal sentencing policy.* Washington, DC: U.S. Government Printing Office.

Valentine, K. B. (1998). "If the guards only knew": Communication education for women in prison. *Women's Studies in Communication, 21,* 238–43.

Vass, A. A. (1996a). Crime, probation, and social work with offenders. In A. A. Vass (Ed.), *Social work competencies: Core knowledge, values, and skills* (pp. 132–89). Thousand Oaks, CA: Sage.

———. (1996b). Competence in social work and probation practice. In A. A. Vass (Ed.), *Social work competencies: Core knowledge, values, and skills* (pp. 190–219). Thousand Oaks, CA: Sage.

Verhovek, S. H. (1999, September 12). The face of guns: Who owns them and why. *New York Times* [Week in Review Section], p. 5.

Viadro, C. I. and Earp, J. A. (1991). AIDS education and incarcerated women: A neglected opportunity. *Women and Health, 17,* 105–17.

Vigil, J. D. (1989). *An emerging barrio underclass: Irregular lifestyle among former Chicano gang members* (Working Paper No.7, New Directions for Latino Public Policy Research). Austin, TX: Center for Mexican American Studies.

Violent Crime Control and Law Enforcement Act of 1994, Pub. L. No. 103-322, 108 Stat. 1996 (1994).

Violent crime falls 7 percent, to lowest level in decades. (1999, July 19). *New York Times,* p. A10.

Walker, A. (1998, January 18). Shelter tally cites record crowding; more ex-convicts, young adults. *Boston Globe,* p. B1.

Warner, S. (1999). *Art programs for incarcerated youth: Four studies with national and international comparative material and implications.* Unpublished manuscript, Antioch University Graduate Programs in Education, Seattle, WA.

Watterson, K. (1996). *Women in prison: Inside the concrete womb.* Boston: Northeastern University Press.

Weick, A., Rapp, C., Sullivan, W. P., and Kisthardt, W. (1989). A strengths perspective for social work practice. *Social Work, 34,* 350–54.

Weinman, M. L. and Smith, P. B. (1996). Teen pregnancy in the twenty-first century. In. P. R. Raffoul and C. A. McNeece (Eds.), *Future issues in social work practice* (pp. 180–87). Boston: Allyn and Bacon.

Weissman, M. and Larue, C. M. (1998). Earning trust from youths with none to spare. *Child Welfare, 77,* 579–94.

Wellons, K. W. (1996). Aspects of aging in the twenty-first century: Opposing viewpoints. In P. R. Raffoul and C. A. McNeece (Eds.), *Future issues in social work practice* (pp. 117–24). Boston: Allyn and Bacon.

When the voices of children are heard. (1995). *City Limits, 20,* 16.

Where prison plans cast a pall unto the heavens. (1999, June 28). *New York Times,* p. A13.

Whittemore, H. (1992, March 15). Hitting bottom can be the beginning. *Parade,* pp. 4–6.

Wilentz, A. (1996, October 20). Mimi's mission: Delancey Street's great adventure. *San Francisco Examiner,* pp. 1–10.

Willing, R. (1997, September 18). Tracking teen crime. *USA Today,* pp. 1–2.

Willis, S. (1998). Teens at work: Negotiating the jobless future. In J. Austin and M. N. Willard (Eds.), *Generations of youth: Youth cultures and history in twentieth-century America* (pp. 347–57). New York: New York University Press.

Wilson, J. (2000). Crying for justice: When victims in grief meet offenders in shame, profound new healings take place. *HOPE, 21,* 52–57, 71.

Wilson, J. S. and Leisure, R. (1991). Cruel and unusual punishment: The health care of women in prison. *Nurse Practitioner, 16,* 32–34, 36, 38–39.

Wilson, M. K., Quinn, P., Beville, B. A., and Anderson, S. C. (1998). Reducing recidivism for women inmates: The search for alternatives. *Journal of Offender Rehabilitation, 27,* 61–76.

Wilson, W. J. (1996). *When work disappears.* New York: Knopf.

Winerip, M. (1999, May 23). Bedlam on the streets: Increasingly, the mentally ill have nowhere to go. That's their problem—and ours. *New York Times Magazine,* pp. 42–49, 56, 65–66, 70.

Women prisoners with HIV speak out. (1994, Summer). *Women Alive,* pp. 1–5.

Wood, P. B. and Grasmick, H. G. (2000, January 18). Inmates rank the severity of ten alternative sanctions compared to prison [On-line]. Available: http://www.state.ok.us/DOCS/OCJRC/OCJRC95/95725j.htm.

Wormer, K. V. and Roberts, A. R. (1999). *Teaching forensic social work: Course outlines on criminal and juvenile justice and victimology.* Alexandria, VA.: Council on Social Work Education.

Wren, C. S. (1996, December 15). Why seizing drugs barely dents supply. *New York Times* [Week in Review], p. 4.

———. (1999, December 9). Nation's top drug official proposes shift in policy. *New York Times,* p. A20.

Yardley, J. (2000, January 9). A role model for executions. *New York Times* [Week in Review], p. 5.

Yin, R. K. (1994). *Case study research: Design and methods.* Thousand Oaks, CA: Sage.

Yost, P. (1999, June 14). US report says more motorists paying price for drunken driving. *Boston Globe*, p. A7.

Young, D. S. (1999). Ethnicity and health service use in a women's prison. *Journal of Multicultural Social Work, 7*, 69–93.

Youniss, J. and Yates, M. (1998). *Community service and social responsibility in youth.* Chicago: University of Chicago Press.

Zaitzow, B. H. (1999). Women prisoners and HIV/AIDS. *Journal of the Association of Nurses in AIDS Care, 10*, 78–92.

Zimring, F. E. (1998). *American youth violence.* New York: Oxford University Press.

Zimring, F. E. and Hawkins, G. (1991). *The scale of imprisonment.* Chicago: University of Chicago Press.

Subject Index

Adoption and Safe Families Act of 1997, 240

African-Americans, 4, 8, 19, 20, 25, 26, 27, 28, 29, 32, 33, 34, 39, 43, 48, 52, 58, 73, 150, 164, 172, 185, 223, 231, 244

AIDS: adolescents, 223–24; barriers, 67, 180, 222, 224; deaths in prison, 29, 125, 223; diagnosis, 181; drug-related, 129, 223; education, 132, 192, 193, 194, 222, 225; fears, 129; general factors, 129, 130, 132, 136, 177, 178, 223, 225, 252; health needs, 130, 131, 180, 224, 225; HIV, 67, 129, 130, 132, 178, 179, 180, 181, 194, 222, 225, 248, 252; New York state prisons, 129, 222; in prisons, 25, 129, 214, 222, 224, 245, 248; social work, 136; statistics, 223, 224; stigma, 222, 224, 225; testing, 67, 131; treatment, 222, 225; women, 129, 178, 181, 214, 223, 224; youth, 223–24

AIDS Counseling Education (ACE), 128–37, 222–25: capacity enhancement methods, 131–33; collaborations, 131; confidentiality, 132; context setting, 128–30; health concerns, 130, 222; history of, 130; individual story highlighted, 133–35; lessons for social work, 135–37; New York state prisons, 129; overview of relevant literature, 222–25; principles, 130–31; rationale for case selection, 221–22; social work, 131; training workshops, 132

AIDS in Prison Project, 129

Alabama, 21, 33, 228

Allegheny County Jail, Pittsburgh, 242

Allegheny County Treatment Center (ACTC), 199

American Bar Association, 33, 35

American Civil Liberties Union (ACLU), 67

American Civil War, 22

American Convention on Human Rights, 35

American Express Corporation, 187

American Society of Criminology, 33

American Youth Policy Forum, 250

Amnesty International, 27

Animals: attachments, 159, 237; Bird Man of Alcatraz, 236; birds, 158, 161; careers, 237; cats, 158; cows, 158; disabilities, 236; dogs, 150, 160, 237; ducks, 158; empathy, 103, 160; employment potential, 236–37; fish, 236; goats, 158; grooming, 100, 160; history in prison use, 236; horses, 236; husbandry, 237; parakeets, 236; pigs, 158; rabbits, 158; therapeutic value, 159–60, 161, 236;

Name Index

DATE DUE
